pentawards

THE PACKAGE DESIGN BOOK

TASCHEN
Bibliotheca Universalis

diamond

22

beverages

48

food

230

FOREWORD
by Jean Jacques & Brigitte Evrard

6

INTRODUCTION
by Gérard Caron

10

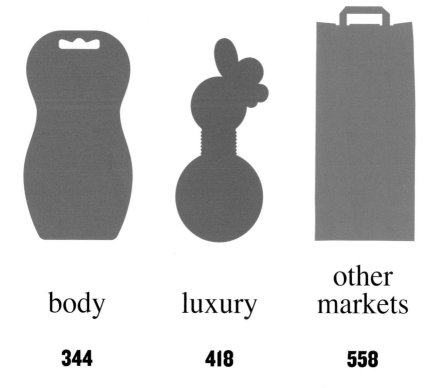

body

344

luxury

418

other
markets

558

THE JURY
654

INDEX
662

FOREWORD

Jean Jacques & Brigitte Evrard
Founders of Pentawards

In only a decade, the Pentawards have come to set the international benchmark for packaging design. Such success is not only because of competition itself, but also the sheer quality of the creations competing in this annual event.

Half the members of the multinational Pentawards jury are well-known names in packaging design, while the rest are marketing specialists representing major brands: Danone Waters (France), Suntory (Japan), Bic (USA), Procter & Gamble (Europe), Jahwa (China), Henkel Dial (USA), Aekyung (South Korea). Each year, more than 1,500 entries from all four corners of the Earth are assessed for creativity, innovation and marketing relevance. The most outstanding receive Bronze, Silver, Gold or Platinum Pentawards. The single entry that most impresses the judges and gets the most votes receives the prestigious Diamond Pentaward.

This book brings together a selection of 538 of the most representative packaging design of the last decade. It showcases the very best in present-day worldwide packaging design, while serving as a benchmark and source of inspiration for everyone who is passionate about packaging—people such as students, manufacturers, designers, packaging engineers, brand managers or consumers.

Apart from awarding prizes, Pentawards aims to promote packaging design to commerce and industry, the press, financial and political authorities, and the general public around the world.

We hope you will enjoy looking through this reference book and that it will give you a completely new take on products you buy every day, enabling you to see them from a completely different angle—the angle of creativity, quality, and innovation, which are the driving forces behind our modern civilisation.

Bon voyage to the world of packaging!

VORWORT

In nur einem Jahrzehnt sind die Pentawards zum internationalen Maßstab für das Verpackungsdesign geworden. Ein solcher Erfolg wurzelt nicht nur im Wettbewerb und der Konkurrenz selbst, sondern rein auch in der Qualität der Kreationen, die bei diesem jährlichen Event gegeneinander antreten.

Eine Hälfte der multinationalen Pentawards-Jury sind wohlbekannte Namen aus dem Verpackungsdesign, und die andere gehört als Marketing-Spezialisten zu großen Marken: Danone Waters (Frankreich), Suntory (Japan), Bic (USA), Procter & Gamble (Europa), Jahwa (China), Henkel Dial (USA), Aekyung (Südkorea). Jedes Jahr werden über eintausend Werke aus allen Gegenden der Welt eingereicht und dann auf Kreativität, Innovation und Marketingrelevanz geprüft. Die Preisträger erhalten ihre Pentawards in Bronze, Silber, Gold oder Platin. Jenem Einzelwerk, von dem die Juroren am stärksten beeindruckt sind und das die meisten Stimmen auf sich vereinen kann, wird der prestigeträchtige Pentaward Diamond verliehen.

Dieses Buch vereint eine Auswahl der 538 bemerkenswertesten Preisträger des letzten Jahrzehnts. Es zeigt das Beste vom Besten des heutigen weltweiten Verpackungsdesigns und dient als Maßstab und Inspirationsquelle für alle, die sich leidenschaftlich für Verpackung interessieren: Studierende, Hersteller, Designer, Verpackungsingenieure, Markenmanager oder Verbraucher.

Über die Preisverleihung hinaus haben die Pentawards zum Ziel, das Verpackungsdesign in einer Welt von Kommerz und Industrie, Presse, finanziellen und politischen Behörden sowie der allgemeinen Öffentlichkeit überall in der Welt zu bewerben und zu fördern.

Wir hoffen, dass Sie viel Freude beim Durchsehen dieses Referenzwerks haben und so einen völlig neuen Blick auf die Produkte gewinnen, die Sie alltäglich kaufen. Die können Sie nun wohl unter einem ganz anderen Aspekt betrachten: aus der Perspektive von Kreativität, Qualität und Innovation – jenen Antriebskräften hinter unserer modernen Zivilisation.

Bon Voyage in die Welt der Verpackung!

PRÉFACE

En quelques années seulement, les Pentawards sont devenus la référence mondiale parmi les professionnels du design de packaging. Ce succès n'est pas seulement dû à la compétition elle-même : il se doit aussi à la qualité remarquable des créations qui y sont présentées chaque année.

Le jury international des Pentawards est composé pour moitié de noms réputés du design de packaging et, d'autre part, de responsables marketing de grandes marques : Danone Waters (France), Suntory (Japon), Bic (États-Unis), Procter & Gamble (Europe), Jahwa (Chine), Henkel Dial (États-Unis), Aekyung (Corée du Sud). Chaque année, plus de 1 500 emballages provenant des quatre coins du monde sont jugés pour leur créativité, leur innovation, leur pertinence marketing, et les plus remarquables sont récompensés de Bronze, Silver, Gold et Platinum Pentawards. L'emballage qui a su séduire l'ensemble du jury et qui a remporté le plus de suffrages reçoit l'unique et prestigieux Diamond Pentaward.

Ce livre regroupe une sélection de 538 créations des plus représentatives de la dernière décennie. Il s'agit donc de ce qui se fait aujourd'hui de mieux dans le monde dans le domaine du design de packaging une référence et source d'inspiration pour tous les passionnés d'emballages, étudiants, designers, fabricants, ingénieurs, responsables de marques, consommateurs ...

Outre la remise de récompenses, Pentawards a pour mission la promotion partout dans le monde du design de packaging auprès des sociétés, de la presse, des autorités économiques et politiques et du grand public en général.

Nous vous souhaitons beaucoup de plaisir à parcourir ce livre référence et espérons qu'il vous fera découvrir les produits que vous achetez quotidiennement sous un autre angle : celui de la créativité, de la qualité et de l'innovation, qui sont les moteurs de notre civilisation.

Bon voyage au pays des emballages !

THE SECRETS OF PENTAWARDS

Gérard Caron
Founder of Carré Noir
Chair of the Pentawards jury between 2007 and 2016

The marketing director of a large group in the food-processing industry once told me that every year he and his team make a close analysis of Pentaward winners. "My product managers and I study them carefully. We stop and look at the most innovative and discuss whether such and such a product or such and such a packaging might have a chance of success in our market."

Brigitte and Jean Jacques Evrard, founders of these international awards, probably hold one of the keys to the staggering success of the Pentawards. Not only does the event promote packaging design, a sphere of creativity often overshadowed by those sectors that attract more media coverage (such as fashion and interior design), but it has also become a useful means of analysis and forecasting.

What can we learn about creativity from the wide selection of Pentawards winning designs in this book? Which major trends happen simultaneously to cross the minds of designers in fifty-odd countries? What kind of customer expectations do they reflect?

In an attempt to answer these questions, I have focused not just on the prizewinners but also on all the thousand competitors, classifying all the creations from around the globe according to their most striking characteristic. Having completed this task, I found ten revealing key trends in worldwide design. Some of these have been around for a long time, while others appear in specific market sectors but with a local twist.

1 — Single idea packaging
This is the kind of packaging designed to communicate one single idea. These forms of packaging, also known as "one-shot" packaging, aim to communicate product content with no attempt to develop complex ideas or provide additional information. This form of packaging is a favorite with marketing executives who want to say everything in one go.

2 — The return of the drawing
To tell the truth, packaging design has never really stopped using drawings but they have to an extent been rejected in favor of photographs. Today, the drawing seems to have returned to its legitimate place without challenging the supremacy of the photographic reproduction. It is an ideal means of using humour or caricature, or can simply be employed as decoration, or to create a certain ambience.

3 — Packaging can be "tuned"

These days anyone can tune their car and fit it out with additional accessories to match their own taste, so making the car more "personal". Of course, when it comes to packaging, tuning is a little more subtle. For example, we might find a key stuck on to a bottle, some string arranged to create a banana shape, and even a shoe-shop carrier bag made from real shoelaces. Anything goes if it gets the product noticed!

4 — Newspaper style

They say print media is dying. Packaging is ready to take up the baton. We now see so much packaging with newspaper-like mastheads and acres of print and little or nothing in the way of visuals. Consumers at the register are more and more eager for information about the products they buy and this is a good way of speaking straight to the customer. After all, aren't we forever being told that packaging is a medium in itself?

5 — Focusing on the human story

The earliest eco-friendly and biodegradable packaging was basic, somewhat sad, and even a little crude, with colours to match the earth and sky. As time went on, this kind of packaging began to toe the line and became as appealing and colorful as the rest. Consumers had realized what was meant by bio packaging. We still have some way to go with fair trade, where we have to justify, explain and demonstrate why it is a good thing to pay a bit more for a packet of coffee to benefit a small community of producers in Guatemala. That explains the number of visuals showing real people and descriptions of the type of products originating from around the world, from Taiwan to Canada by way of the Netherlands. The day will come when committed consumers will no longer need all these justifications; they will still appear on the Internet, but will be less conspicuous on packaging.

6 — Looks come first

Design can do a lot to promote aesthetic values. Beautiful design can brighten all our lives and some packaging is designed to do no more than this. Maybe the product is well known and the market is saturated. Maybe consumers can't tell one product from another. This is where appearance is the best means of attracting consumers and encouraging them to buy. There are some fine examples of this in this book, especially in the world of wine.

7 — Signs that say "stop and look"

The whole purpose of packaging is to get the consumer to stop and look. It's what our craft is all about and is the designer's main objective. So, for example, we have logos with double meanings, graphics worthy of a road sign, and striped packaging. You can't miss them!

8 — The brand and only the brand

What more can you say when you are a world-famous, well-loved brand? Maybe "Here I am. Yes, it's me. Don't forget me!" No need for persuasion, no need to proclaim the product's advantages—there aren't any! Reputation is the best selling point. So someone must start building one...

9 — A tale to tell

There are a number of examples in the most recent crop of Pentaward candidates that tell a little story in words or pictures. Some resemble a page from a magazine with photos, drawings and text. Everyone knows about reading breakfast cereal packets, but the trend seems to be growing. Maybe it's a by-product of using the Internet, which encourages dialog between brand and consumer?

10 — Trompe-l'œil packaging

This is the most puzzling section of the book and probably the most innovative. It features packaging that bears no resemblance whatever to what it really is! The complete opposite of what they teach at schools of design, namely that the packaging is an extension of the product and should tell the consumer something about it, etc. Here we have a cigarette packet that looks like an audio-cassette, taken from a carton that resembles a tuner. And baby socks packed in what looks like a bento box from a sushi bar! Very funny and absolutely accurate in a world of products where habit kill people's curiosity about brand names.

These are some of the main features of this new and extraordinarily accomplished edition. As I said before, packaging design is the most creative of all forms of design. It is the one that comes closest to people's lives and the most surprising of all of them.

DIE GEHEIMNISSE DER PENTAWARDS

Der Marketingleiter einer großen Gruppe in der Lebensmittelbranche berichtete mir kürzlich, dass er jedes Jahr zusammen mit seinem Team die Pentawards-Gewinner genau unter die Lupe nimmt. „Meine Produktmanager und ich studieren sie sehr sorgfältig. Wir nehmen uns viel Zeit, um die innovativsten Beispiele anzusehen und zu diskutieren, ob dieses oder jenes Produkt bzw. diese oder jene Verpackung auf unserem Markt Erfolgschancen hätte."

Brigitte und Jean Jacques Evrard, die Begründer der internationalen Auszeichnung „Pentawards", halten wahrscheinlich einen der Schlüssel für ihren atemberaubenden Erfolg in Händen. Dieses Event wirbt nicht nur für das Design von Verpackungen (diese Sphäre der Kreativität wird oft von Bereichen wie Mode, Innenarchitektur oder Möbel überschattet, denen ein größeres Medienecho sicher ist), sondern wurde überdies zu einem sehr praktischen Instrument für Analyse und Prognose.

Was können wir von dieser umfassenden Auslese an Pentawards-Gewinnern über Kreativität lernen? Welche großen Trends geschehen simultan und tauchen unabhängig im Geiste der Designer aus über 50 Ländern auf? Welche Art von Kundenerwartung spiegeln sie wider?

Bei meinem Versuch, diese Fragen zu beantworten, habe ich mich nicht nur auf Preisträger konzentriert, sondern auch auf die Tausenden anderen Mitbewerber. Ich habe alle Kreationen rund um den Globus entsprechend ihrer auffälligsten Kennzeichen klassifiziert. Am Ende kristallisierten sich für mich zehn aussagekräftige Schlüsseltrends im weltweiten Design heraus. Manche Entwicklungen gibt es schon länger, andere treten in speziellen Marktsektoren auf und zeigen eine besondere lokale Prägung.

1 — Verpackung mit einer einzigen Idee
Dies ist die Art Verpackung, deren Gestaltung eine einzige Idee oder ein Konzept vermitteln soll. Auch bekannt als „One Shot Packaging", zielt sie darauf ab, den Produktinhalt zu kommunizieren, ohne dabei komplexe Ideen zu entwickeln oder zusätzliche Informationen anzubieten. Dies ist der Favorit bei Marketingleitern, die in einem Rutsch alle Aussagen über ihr Produkt vermitteln wollen.

2 — Die Rückkehr der Zeichnung
Ehrlich gesagt, hat man beim Verpackungsdesign nie aufgehört, mit Zeichnungen und

Grafiken zu arbeiten, aber sie sind in gewisser Weise zugunsten von Fotos ins Hintertreffen geraten. Heute scheinen Zeichnungen auf ihren legitimen Platz zurückzukehren, ohne die Überlegenheit der fotografischen Reproduktion herausfordern oder infrage stellen zu wollen. Zeichnungen sind ein ideales Mittel für Humor oder Karikaturen, können auch gut dekorativ eingesetzt werden oder um bestimmte Stimmungen zu vermitteln.

3 – Verpackung kann „getunt" werden

Heutzutage tunen alle ihre Autos und statten sie nach ihrem Geschmack mit zusätzlichen Accessoires aus, um sie „persönlicher" zu gestalten. Wenn es um Verpackungen geht, wird ein Tuning natürlich subtiler. Da finden wir beispielsweise einen Schlüssel an einer Flasche angebracht, mit einer Schnur wird eine Bananenform geschaffen, und Tragetaschen aus einem Schuhladen können sogar aus echten Schnürsenkeln bestehen. Anything goes – wenn das Produkt bloß wahrgenommen wird!

4 – Zeitungsstil

Überall sagt man, Druckmedien seien im Aussterben begriffen. Hier steht die Verpackung in den Startlöchern, um den Staffelstab zu übernehmen. Wir finden heutzutage viele Verpackungen mit zeitungsähnlichen Aufmachern und regelrechten Bleiwüsten, aber wenig oder gar nichts in Richtung optischem Blickfang. Die Konsumenten vor den Regalen gieren nach immer mehr Informationen über die Produkte, und dies ist ein guter Weg für direkte Kundenansprache. Immerhin werden wir ständig darauf aufmerksam gemacht, dass die Verpackung selbst schon ein Medium ist.

5 – Konzentration auf den Faktor Mensch

Die ersten umweltfreundlichen und biologisch abbaubaren Verpackungen waren schlicht, irgendwie auch traurig, ein wenig grob und mit zu Himmel und Erde passenden Farben gestaltet. Im Laufe der Zeit haben sich solche Verpackungen immer mehr angepasst, und sie wurden so ansprechend und farbenfroh wie alle anderen. Die Verbraucher hatten kapiert, was mit Bioverpackung gemeint war. Mit Blick auf den fairen Handel gibt es für uns noch einiges zu tun: Wir müssen begründen, erklären und zeigen, warum es eine gute Sache ist, etwas mehr für ein Paket Kaffee zu bezahlen, um eine kleine Herstellergemeinschaft in Guatemala zu unterstützen. Das erklärt die zahlreichen Bilder auf den Packungen, die reale Menschen zeigen und die Produkte beschreiben, die über die Niederlande aus der ganzen

Welt von Taiwan bis Kanada zu uns kommen. Der Tag wird kommen, an dem all diese Rechtfertigungen für engagierte Verbraucher nicht mehr nötig sind. Im Internet wird es das weiterhin geben, aber auf Verpackungen weniger ins Auge fallen.

6 – Aussehen steht im Vordergrund

Design kann eine Menge dafür tun, ästhetische Werte zu vermitteln. Ein schönes Design erhellt unser aller Leben, und manche Verpackung dient in ihrer Gestaltung allein diesem Zweck. Vielleicht ist das Produkt wohlbekannt und der Markt gesättigt. Vielleicht können Verbraucher die Produkte nicht mehr voneinander unterscheiden. Hier wird Aussehen das beste Mittel, um Verbraucher anzusprechen und sie zum Kaufen zu ermutigen. Es gibt ein paar sehr schöne Beispiele dafür in diesem Buch, vor allem aus der Welt der Weine.

7 – Zeichen, die sagen: „Halt, schau mich an!"

Hauptabsicht von Verpackungen ist es eigentlich, den Verbraucher auszubremsen, damit er sich etwas genauer ansieht. Darum geht es in unserer Branche, und das ist Hauptziel des Designers. Also haben wir z. B. Logos mit hintergründigen Bedeutungen, Grafiken so nachdrücklich wie ein Verkehrsschild und Packungen mit Streifen. Das kann man einfach nicht übersehen!

8 – Einzig und allein die Marke

Was bleibt einem noch zu sagen, wenn man bereits eine weltberühmte und beliebte Marke ist? Vielleicht noch etwas wie „Hier bin ich. Genau, ich bin's! Vergessen Sie mich nicht!" Nicht mehr nötig, sich fürs Überzeugen anzustrengen oder die Vorteile des Produkts zu proklamieren ... alles bekannt! Der eigene Ruf wird zum besten Verkaufsargument. Also sollte man anfangen, so etwas aufzubauen...

9 – Eine Geschichte wird erzählt

In dieser neuesten Auslese der Pentawards-Kandidaten gibt es zahlreiche Beispiele, die mit Worten oder Bildern kleine Geschichten erzählen. Manche erinnern mit ihren Fotos, Zeichnungen und Texten an Magazinseiten. Alle wissen, dass die Packung des Frühstücksmüslis gelesen wird, doch dieser Trend scheint weiter zuzunehmen. Vielleicht gar ein Nebenprodukt der Internetnutzung, das zum Dialog zwischen Marke und Konsument ermutigt?

10 — Trompe-l'Œil-Verpackungen

Dieser Teil des Buches ist besonders verblüffend und wahrscheinlich auch der innovativste. Hier werden Verpackungen vorgestellt, die in keinster Weise darauf schließen lassen, was sich darin verbirgt! Sie sind das komplette Gegenteil dessen, was an Designschulen gelehrt wird, dass nämlich Verpackung eine Erweiterung des Produkts ist und dem Konsumenten etwas darüber verraten soll etc. Hier gibt es Zigarettenpackungen, die wie Audiokassetten aussehen und aus einem Karton kommen, der an einen Tuner erinnert. Und Babysocken verpackt in etwas, das wie die Bentobox aus einer Sushi-Bar aussieht. Sehr lustig und absolut treffend in einer Welt von Produkten, in der die menschliche Neugier von Gewohnheiten völlig abgetötet worden ist.

Dies sind einige der wichtigsten Merkmale dieser neuen und außergewöhnlich zusammengestellten Edition. Wie schon gesagt, ist Verpackungsdesign die kreativste Form des Designs überhaupt. Sie kommt dem Alltag der Menschen am nächsten und birgt von allen die meisten Überraschungen.

LES SECRETS DES PENTAWARDS

Le directeur du marketing d'un grand groupe du secteur alimentaire m'a récemment dit que chaque année, lui et son équipe procèdent à une analyse détaillée des lauréats des Pentawards. « Mes chefs de produit et moi les étudions avec beaucoup d'intérêt. Nous examinons les plus novateurs et nous essayons de déterminer si tel ou tel produit ou tel ou tel emballage pourrait avoir une chance sur notre marché. »

Brigitte et Jean Jacques Evrard, les fondateurs de ces récompenses internationales, détiennent probablement l'une des clés du succès stupéfiant des Pentawards. Cet événement non seulement promeut le design de packaging, une sphère créative souvent éclipsée par les secteurs qui attirent davantage l'attention des médias, comme la mode ou la décoration intérieure mais est également devenu un instrument très utile pour analyser et prévoir les tendances.

Que pouvons-nous apprendre sur la créativité au vu du dernier millésime lauréats Pentawards ? Quelles grandes tendances ont émergé simultanément, comme par magie, dans les esprits de créatifs de plus de cinquante pays ? Reflètent-elles des attentes particulières de la part des clients ?

Pour tenter de répondre à ces questions, j'ai étudié non seulement les lauréats, mais aussi le millier de concurrents. J'ai classé les créations de tous les pays en fonction de leur caractéristique la plus frappante. Cette tâche m'a permis d'identifier dix grandes tendances révélatrices dans le design mondial. Certaines sont loin d'être nouvelles, d'autres se trouvent sur un marché spécifique, mais avec une touche locale.

1 — L'emballage centré sur une idée unique
C'est le type d'emballage qui est conçu pour communiquer une seule idée. Aussi appelés emballages « one-shot », ils visent à communiquer le contenu du produit sans essayer de développer des idées complexes ou de fournir plus d' informations. Ce genre d'emballage est très apprécié des responsables marketing qui veulent tout dire en une seule offre.

2 — Le retour du dessin
À dire vrai, le dessin n'a jamais vraiment disparu des emballages, mais il a été remplacé dans une certaine mesure par la photographie. Aujourd'hui, le dessin semble avoir retrouvé sa place légitime sans pour autant menacer la suprématie de la reproduction photographique.

C'est un véhicule idéal pour l'humour ou la caricature, mais aussi pour décorer ou pour créer une certaine atmosphère.

3 — L'emballage peut être « tuné »

Aujourd'hui, n'importe qui peut tuner sa voiture et l'équiper d'accessoires qui correspondent à ses goûts pour la personnaliser. Pour les emballages, le tuning est évidemment un peu plus subtil. Ce sera par exemple une clé collée sur une bouteille, une ficelle disposée de façon à imiter la forme d'une banane, ou le sac d'une boutique de chaussures dont les anses sont de vrais lacets. Tout est envisageable, du moment que le produit se fait remarquer !

4 — Le style journal

Il paraît que la presse écrite se meurt. L'emballage est prêt à prendre la relève. Aujourd'hui, des quantités d'emballages arborent des titres de journaux et des caractères d'imprimerie sans illustration ou presque. Sur le lieu de vente, les consommateurs sont de plus en plus en demande d'informations sur les produits qu'ils achètent, et ce type d'emballage est un bon moyen de s'adresser directement à eux. Après tout, n'entend-on pas dire sans relâche que l'emballage est un support de communication en soi ?

5 — L'histoire humaine au centre

Les premiers emballages écologiques et biodégradables étaient basiques, plutôt tristes et même un peu rudimentaires, avec des couleurs rappelant la terre et le ciel. Au fil du temps, ce type d'emballage a commencé à rattraper son retard, et est devenu aussi attrayant et coloré que les emballages traditionnels. Les consommateurs ont compris ce que l'emballage bio signifie réellement. Il y a encore du chemin à faire dans le secteur du commerce équitable, où il faut justifier, expliquer et démontrer pourquoi cela vaut la peine de payer le paquet de café un peu plus cher pour aider une petite communauté de producteurs au Guatemala. D'où le nombre de visuels montrant des personnes réelles et de descriptions de produits issus des quatre coins du monde, de Taïwan au Canada, en passant par les Pays-Bas. Le jour viendra où les consommateurs engagés n'auront plus besoin de toutes ces justifications. Elles seront toujours disponibles sur Internet, mais prendront moins de place sur l'emballage.

6 — L'esthétique avant tout

Le design peut faire beaucoup pour promouvoir les valeurs esthétiques. Un beau design peut égayer nos vies, et certains emballages ne sont conçus que dans cet unique but. Le produit peut être connu, mais sur un marché saturé, et les consommateurs peuvent ne pas faire la différence entre ce produit et un autre. C'est dans ce genre de cas que l'apparence est le meilleur moyen d'attirer les consommateurs et de les encourager à acheter. Ce livre en présente d'excellents exemples, particulièrement dans le monde du vin.

7 — Des créations qui disent «arrêtez-vous et regardez»

La mission de l'emballage est de faire en sorte que le consommateur s'arrête pour regarder. C'est toute la raison d'être de notre métier, et c'est le principal objectif du designer. C'est ainsi que l'on rencontre par exemple des logos à double signification, des graphismes dignes de panneaux indicateurs et des emballages à rayures. Impossible de les manquer !

8 — La marque et seulement la marque

Lorsqu'on est une marque connue et aimée dans le monde entier, qu'y a-t-il de plus à dire ? Peut-être « Je suis là, oui, c'est moi, ne m'oubliez pas ! » Nul besoin de convaincre ou de clamer les avantages du produit, il n'y en a pas ! La renommée est le meilleur argument de vente. Alors il faut commencer à en bâtir une …

9 — Une histoire à raconter

Dans la dernière moisson de candidats aux Pentawards, de nombreux exemples racontent une petite histoire à l'aide de mots ou d'images. Certains ressemblent à une page de magazine, avec des photos, des dessins et du texte. Tout le monde a déjà lu un paquet de céréales au petit-déjeuner, mais la tendance semble prendre de l'ampleur. Peut-être est-ce un effet secondaire d'Internet, qui encourage le dialogue entre la marque et le consommateur ?

10 — L'emballage en trompe-l'œil

C'est la section la plus surprenante du livre, et probablement la plus riche en innovation. Il présente des emballages qui ne ressemblent en rien à ce qu'ils sont vraiment ! Soit tout le contraire de ce qui est enseigné dans les écoles de design, à savoir que l'emballage est une extension du produit, dont il doit parler au consommateur, etc. Comme un paquet de cigarettes qui ressemble à une cassette audio, et que l'on extrait d'une cartoucheévoquant un tuner. Ou des chaussettes pour bébé emballées dans ce qui ressemble à une boîte bento de restaurant japonais ! Très drôle et absolument parfait dans un monde de produits où les habitudes ont réduit au néant la curiosité des gens pour les noms de marque.

Voici donc un aperçu de ce que vous trouverez dans cette nouvelle édition extraordinairement réussie. Comme je l'ai déjà dit, le design de packaging est la forme de design la plus créative de toutes. C'est celle qui se rapproche le plus de la vie des gens, et c'est aussi la plus surprenante. Et la toute dernière édition des Pentawards est là pour me donner raison.

diamond

Best of the show

PENTAWARD'S DIAMOND

A very simple idea

An international jury made up of packaging design specialists and marketing chiefs from some of the most prestigious worldwide brands represents, by its very nature, the foremost cultures of the industrialized world. In this way, eleven nationalities and hence eleven cultures are brought together on the Pentawards jury.

Of course, the deep cultural roots of the Japanese are very different from those of the French, the Swedes, or the Koreans. The same can be said of the cultural differences between citizens of the UK and the USA.

While their marketing processes, production techniques, and distribution systems comply with international norms, it is culture, in its literal sense, which forms the characters of different societies. Similarly, it is culture that gives each of us our own particular way of looking at things, based on our education and the cultural milieu in which we move.

Every year, the amalgam of nationalities and cultures that is the Pentawards jury reaches a unanimous decision on which packaging designs will have truly universal appeal. It is ten years since the first Diamond Pentaward was presented to a packaging design that stood out for its simplicity and for the original idea that inspired the designer.

This kind of simplicity is shared by all the competing designs. Each one is inspired by a mixture of humanity's many cultures and each becomes a classic from the moment it is first conceived. Yet only one among them is judged to be the most outstanding.

The Pentawards always reach the same conclusion. In the words of Mies van der Rohe: Less is more.

Eine ganz einfache Idee

Eine internationale Jury aus Spezialisten für Verpackungsdesign und die Marketingchefs einiger der weltweit prestigeträchtigsten Marken repräsentiert seiner Natur nach die führenden Kulturen der industrialisierten Welt. Elf Nationalitäten und somit auch elf Kulturen kommen in der Pentawards-Jury zusammen.

Natürlich unterscheiden sich die tiefen kulturellen Wurzeln eines Japaners von denen eines Franzosen, Schweden oder Koreaners. Das Gleiche lässt sich über die kulturellen Differenzen zwischen Bürgern aus England und den USA sagen.

Während die Marketingprozesse, Produktionstechniken und Distributionssysteme internationalen Normen entsprechen, ist es in ihrem ursprünglichen Sinne die Kultur, die den Charakter unterschiedlicher Gesellschaften formt. Entsprechend prägt Kultur, wie wir Dinge betrachten. Das beruht auf unserer Bildung und dem kulturellen Milieu, in dem wir uns bewegen.

Jedes Jahr gelangt die Pentawards-Jury als Amalgam aus Nationalitäten und Kulturen zu einer einstimmigen Entscheidung darüber, welchen Verpackungen eine wirklich universelle Anziehungskraft eigen ist. Vor zehn Jahre wurde der erste Diamond Pentaward für ein Verpackungsdesign präsentiert, das wegen seiner Einfachheit und der originellen Idee, die die Designer inspiriert haben, besticht.

Diese Art Einfachheit ist allen konkurrierenden Designs gemeinsam. Jedes Design lässt sich von einer Melange der vielen Kulturen der Menschheit inspirieren, und jedes wird in dem Moment zum Klassiker, in dem es zuerst erdacht wurde. Doch nur einer unter ihnen wird als würdig erachtet, besonders hervorragend zu sein.

Die Pentawards gelangen stets zur gleichen Schlussfolgerung. Mit den Worten von Mies van der Rohe: Weniger ist mehr.

Une idée toute simple

Un jury international composé de spécialistes en design de packaging et de responsables marketing de grandes marques mondiales est, par essence, la représentation des principales cultures du monde industrialisé. Le jury Pentawards regroupe onze nationalités, et donc onze cultures.

Bien sûr, les racines culturelles d'un Japonais seront bien différentes de celles d'un Français, d'un Suédois ou d'un Coréen. Idem entre un Anglais et un Américain.

Si les processus marketing, les techniques de production et les systèmes de commercialisation des produits répondent à des normes internationales, la culture au sens propre, celle qui caractérise les différentes civilisations, donne aussi à chaque individu un regard personnel, fruit de son éducation et de son milieu culturel.

Chaque année, le jury des Pentawards, toutes cultures et nationalités confondues, s'accorde à désigner unanimement certains emballages comme possédant des qualités universelles. Il y a 10 ans était décerné le premier Diamond Pentaward à un emballage caractérisé par sa simplicité, par l'idée unique qui a guidé le designer dans sa conception.

Cette simplicité est universelle. Ces emballages sont universels, fruits de toutes les cultures de l'humanité mélangées, des classiques dès leur naissance. Et parmi ceux-là, un seul est choisi comme étant le plus marquant.

On arrive toujours à la même conclusion : « Less is more » (Mies van der Rohe).

SWINCKELS' SINDS 1680

Design: Olof ten Hoorn,
Andrea Gadesmann, Raul Rodriguez
Company: Design Bridge Amsterdam
Country: Netherlands

DIAMOND PENTAWARD 2007

Swinckels' is a fresh, unpasteurized premium-concept pilsener beer which is kept cool from the moment it is produced and has a shorter shelf life than conventional beers. The bottle neck's signature flat panel feature is not just tactile and memorable, it carries the label which doubles as a breakable seal for the cap, emphasizing the product's quality and freshness. The Swinckel family has seven generations of credibility in the brewing industry. The heritage claim, Sinds 1680, is magnified through the beer itself.

Swinckels' ist ein frisches, unpasteurisiertes Premiumbier, das vom Moment seiner Produktion an gekühlt wird und damit eine kürzere Haltbarkeit als konventionelle Biere hat. Besonderes Merkmal ist der abgeflachte, angenehm in der Hand liegende Flaschenhals, an dem auch das Etikett angebracht ist. Dieses dient zugleich als Frischesiegel und hebt die Qualität des Bieres hervor. Die Swinckel-Familie ist seit sieben Generationen eine Institution in der Brauereibranche. Das geprägte Wappen mit dem Schriftzug „Sinds 1680" wird durch die Flüssigkeit optisch vergrößert.

Swinckels' est une bière pils non pasteurisée de première qualité, gardée fraîche après sa production et dont le temps de conservation est inférieur à la moyenne. La surface plane du goulot est agréable au toucher et accueille une étiquette-sceau pour souligner la qualité et la fraîcheur du produit. La crédibilité de la famille Swinckel dans l'industrie brassicole remonte à sept générations. Cet héritage, Sinds 1680, est affirmé par la propre bière.

PIPER HEIDSIECK VIKTOR & ROLF

Design: Viktor & Rolf, Betc Design
Company: Sleever International
Country: France

DIAMOND PENTAWARD 2008

How to create something new with a timeless product? The answer from Dutch fashion designers **Viktor & Rolf** for **Piper Heidsieck** was to reverse the directions. Still keeping the main classic graphic features (bottle, cork, ice bucket, glass, and labels) vital to the champagne market, the idea was that, if champagne could turn one's head, it was only necessary to reverse all these visual elements to amplify this impression, and especially to differentiate the brand from its competitors by recreating the packaging. The bottles of Piper Heidsieck Rosé Sauvage signed by Viktor & Rolf were launched on the market in October 2007 in several duty-free shops and in exclusive bars and wine bars. The glass bottles are covered by a sleeve produced by Sleever International.

Wie kann man mit einem zeitlosen Produkt etwas ganz Neues schaffen? Die Antwort der niederländischen Modedesigner **Viktor & Rolf** für **Piper Heidsieck** lautete, die Richtung zu wechseln. Hier werden die für den Champagnermarkt wichtigen klassischen grafischen Merkmale (Flasche, Korken, Eiskühler, Glas und Etikett) bedient. Gleichzeitig wird aber mit der Idee gespielt, dass Champagner einem den Kopf verdreht. Alles, was man tun muss, um diesen Eindruck zu verstärken, ist, diese visuellen Elemente umzukehren. Dadurch, dass die Verpackung neu geschaffen wurde, hob sich die Marke vor allem auch von ihren Konkurrenten ab. Die von Viktor & Rolf signierten Piper-Heidsieck-Rosé-Sauvage-Flaschen wurden im Oktober 2007 auf dem Markt eingeführt und zwar in verschiedenen Duty-Free-Shops sowie in exklusiven Bars und Weinläden. Die Glasflaschen werden von einer von Sleever International produzierten Hülle bedeckt.

Comment innover avec un produit intemporel? La réponse des créateurs de mode néerlandais **Viktor & Rolf** pour **Piper Heidsieck** a été d'inverser les réalités. Tout en gardant les éléments graphiques classiques (bouteille, bouchon, seau à glace, verre et étiquettes) essentiels sur le marché du champagne, l'idée était que, si le champagne peut vous faire tourner la tête, il suffisait de renverser tous ces éléments visuels pour amplifier cette impression, et plus particulièrement pour différencier la marque de ses concurrents en réinventant le packaging. Les bouteilles de Piper Heidsieck Rosé Sauvage signées Viktor & Rolf ont été lancées sur le marché en octobre 2007 dans plusieurs boutiques duty-free et dans des bars et bars à vins exclusifs. Les bouteilles en verre sont recouvertes d'un manchon fabriqué par Sleever International.

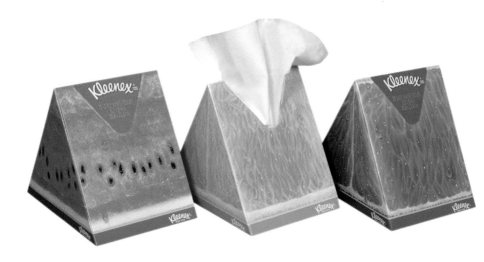

Einige der besten kreativen Ideen sind gleichzeitig auch die einfachsten. Heutzutage ist in hygienischer und praktischer Hinsicht kaum etwas banaler als Papiertücher. **Kleenex** hat sich in diesem Bereich zum unangefochtenen Marktführer entwickelt, aber bisher waren die dazugehörigen Kartons bestenfalls dekorativ. In diesem Fall bekamen die für Kleenex tätigen Designer den Auftrag, einen Karton als „Limited Edition" zu gestalten, mit dem der Sommer gefeiert werden und der die Verbraucher begeistern sollte. Kleenex (Kimberly-Clark Corporation) hat die Regeln gesprengt, um in perfekter Harmonie eine ganz neue Kombination aus Struktur und Grafiken anzubieten, und taufte das Ganze „A Slice of Summer" (Eine Scheibe Sommer). Eine dreieckige Schachtel wurde so gestaltet, dass sie wie das saftige Stück einer Wassermelone, einer Orange oder einer Zitrone erscheint – so verführerisch, dass man reinbeißen möchte.

Les grandes idées créatives sont parfois aussi les plus simples. Aujourd'hui, peu de produits sont aussi courants (hygiéniques et pratiques) que les mouchoirs en papier. **Kleenex** s'est imposé en tant que leader incontesté dans ce secteur, et jusqu'à présent leurs boîtes étaient tout au plus décoratives. Dans ce cas, les designers de la marque ont été chargés de créer une boîte en édition limitée pour fêter l'été et réjouir les consommateurs. Et Kleenex (Kimberly-Clark Corporation) a pris des libertés pour proposer un design frais où structure et graphisme sont en parfaite harmonie, baptisée « une tranche d'été ». C'est une boîte triangulaire déguisée en tranche de fruit juteux, pastèque, orange ou citron, suffisamment appétissante pour mettre l'eau à la bouche.

KLEENEX
SLICE OF SUMMER

Creative Director: Christine Mau
Senior Designer: Jennifer Brock
Brand Design Manager: Jane Kelly
Illustration: Hiroko Sanders
Company: Kimberly-Clark
Country: USA

DIAMOND PENTAWARD 2009

Some of the greatest creative ideas are also the simplest. There are few things more banal (hygienic and practical) nowadays than paper tissues. **Kleenex** has emerged as the uncontested leader in this field, and up to now their boxes too were at most decorative. In this case, the designers working for Kleenex were asked to create a limited-edition carton that would celebrate the summer season and drive consumer delight. And Kleenex (Kimberly-Clark Corporation) has broken the rules to offer a fresh combination of structure and graphics in perfect harmony, christened a "slice of summer." A triangular box illustrated to appear like a section of different juicy fruits, watermelon, orange or lemon, that look enticing enough to eat.

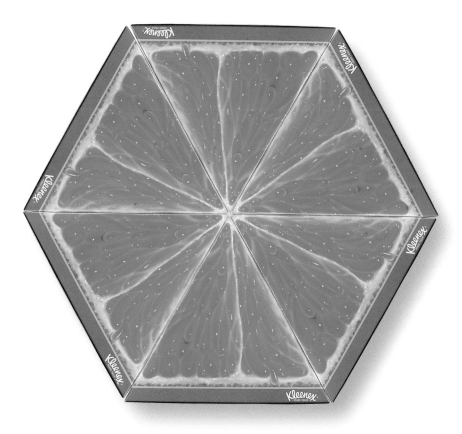

HOYU 3210

Creative Director: Tomohiro Sakurai (ADK)
Art Director: Mutsumi Ajichi (ADK), Kunikazu Hoshiba (Katachi)
Designer: Murakami Takashi, Hiro Kinoshita (Katachi), Yasuhiro Nagae (Iro)
Company: ADK
Country: Japan
DIAMOND PENTAWARD 2010

Hoyu is a well-established brand in the Japanese professional hair-colour products market, but a newcomer in professional hair-styling products. The brief was to introduce **Hoyu** professional styling products into the very competitive, top-class hair salons, and establish a presence, using a very bold and memorable approach. The concept for this brand is "countdown". As the hairdresser is about to finish the customer's hair, the customer's anticipation reaches a high point. The product is then used to conclude this "countdown" to the finish.

Hoyu ist auf dem japanischen Markt eine gut eingeführte Marke für professionelle Haarfärbeprodukte, aber ein Newcomer bei den Profi-Hairstyling-Produkten. Das Briefing lautete, die Profi-Styling-Produkte von **Hoyu** in den heiß umkämpften Topclass-Friseursalons zu etablieren. Auf sehr mutige und prägnante Weise sollte dort die Präsenz des Produkts verankert werden. Diese Marke greift das Konzept „Countdown" auf: Wenn der Coiffeur sich daran macht, den Haaren der Kundin den letzten Schliff zu verleihen, erreichen ihre Erwartungen den Höhepunkt. Das Produkt wird nun eingesetzt, um diesen „Countdown" bis zur Vollendung abzuschließen.

Hoyu est une marque reconnue sur le marché japonais des produits de coloration professionnels, mais c'est une nouvelle venue dans le domaine des produits de coiffage. La mission était d'introduire les produits de coiffage professionnel de **Hoyu** dans les salons haut de gamme, où la concurrence fait rage, et de leur y assurer une présence grâce à une démarche audacieuse et mémorable. Le concept de cette marque est le « compte à rebours ». Lorsque le coiffeur est sur le point de terminer le coiffage, l'impatience du client atteint son paroxysme. Le produit permet de mettre un point final à ce « compte à rebours ».

Ramlösa is a table-water from an accredited natural mineral source in Sweden and has been a widely recognised brand in the country since the well was discovered in 1707. Being sold in exclusive restaurants, venues and night-clubs a premium packaging was needed to distinguish it from the standard PET bottle sold in stores. The new premium bottle in PET, a plastic not associated with exclusivity by the target group, gained plaudits for its aesthetics as well as the environmentally positive effects compared with glass. Form and shape were modeled on old crystal glasses, the creative work being made harder because carbonated water makes plastic materials expand.

Ramlösa ist ein Tafelwasser aus einer zertifizierten schwedischen Quelle, 1707 entdeckt. Die Marke ist seither landesweit bekannt. Weil sie nun auch in exklusiven Restaurants, Tagungsorten und Nightclubs angeboten wird, war eine Premium-Verpackung nötig, um sich von der PET-Standardflasche im Einzelhandel abzuheben. Die neue Premium-Flasche aus PET (einem Kunststoff, den die Zielgruppe nicht mit Exklusivität verbindet) erhielt für ihre Ästhetik ebenso Beifall wie für die ähnlich dem Glas positiven Umwelteffekte. Form und Prägung wurden von alten Kristallgläsern abmodelliert. Die kreative Ausarbeitung wurde dadurch erschwert, dass sich Kunststoffe durch die Kohlensäure im Wasser ausdehnen.

Ramlösa est une eau de table qui provient d'une source minérale naturelle certifiée en Suède. C'est une marque très connue dans ce pays depuis que la source a été découverte en 1707. Étant vendue dans des restaurants, boîtes de nuit et autres lieux exclusifs, il lui fallait une bouteille de qualité supérieure pour la distinguer des bouteilles standard en PET en vente dans les magasins. Cette nouvelle bouteille haut de gamme en PET, un plastique que la cible de marché n'associe pas à l'exclusivité, a été applaudie pour son esthétique et ses effets positifs sur l'environnement par rapport au verre. Sa forme a été modelée sur des verres en cristal anciens. Le travail créatif a été compliqué par le fait que l'eau gazéifiée suppose une dilatation du plastique.

RAMLÖSA

Client Service Direction: Lotta Onajin
Creative Direction: Isabelle Dahlborg Lidström
Industrial Design: Åsa Johnsson, Sofia Berg (No Picnic)
Graphic Design: Björn Studt, Jonas Torvestig
Account Management: Pia Lundström
Company: Nine
Country: Sweden

DIAMOND PENTAWARD 2011
ESKO PRIZE

DIET COKE CROP PACKAGING

Creative Direction: David Turner, Bruce Duckworth, Sarah Moffat
Design: Rebecca Williams, Josh Michels
Design Direction: Pio Schunker, Hazel Van Buren (The Coca-Cola Company)
Company: Turner Duckworth, London & San Francisco
Country: UK

DIAMOND PENTAWARD 2012
ESKO PRIZE

With the nationwide release of new **Diet Coke** packaging a fresh look was created for the fall season in the US. As the country's number-2 sparkling beverage brand, Diet Coke was already well known to consumers, and the Coca-Cola Company North America set the challenge of extending that confidence in the brand to packaging. The resulting design delivered a bold perspective by focusing on the union of the "D" and "K" as the key recognisable elements of the logo. The unique crop of the main logo is at the centre of a visual identity, which appears in the brand name and in advertising for the drink.

Mit dieser Version einer neuen **Diet Coke**-Verpackung wurde ein frischer neuer Look für die Herbstsaison in den USA geschaffen. Den Verbrauchern war Diet Coke als Nummer zwei der prickelnden Getränkemarken bereits wohlbekannt, und Coca-Cola North America stellte sich der Herausforderung, dieses Vertrauen in die Marke auch auf die Verpackung auszuweiten. Das Design zeugt von einer mutigen Perspektive: Es konzentriert sich auf die Zusammenführung von „D" und „K" als Elemente des Logos mit zentralem Wiedererkennungswert. Der unverwechselbare Anschnitt des Hauptlogos steht im Zentrum der visuellen Identität, die sowohl am Point of Sale als auch in der Werbung für dieses Getränk besticht.

Un look novateur a été conçu pour la mise sur le marché américain d'un nouvel emballage de **Diet Coke** à l'automne. En tant que marque numéro 2 de boisson gazeuse dans le pays, Diet Coke était déjà bien connue des consommateurs, et la Coca-Cola Company d'Amérique du Nord a décidé de traduire sur l'emballage cette confiance dans la marque. Le graphisme qui en résulte offre une perspective audacieuse en faisant du « D » et du « K » les éléments clés du logo. Le cadrage original du logo principal est au cœur de l'identité visuelle, qui apparaît sur le point de vente et dans les publicités.

ABSOLUT VODKA
ABSOLUT UNIQUE

Creative Direction: John Lagerqvist, Marten Knutsson
Account Direction: Cecilia Steenberg Forsberg
Art Direction: Fredrik Lindquist
Copywriting: Tove Norstrom
Account Management: Anna Andrén
Final Art: Andy Chong, Anna Jarl
Client: The Absolut Company, Jonas Thalin,
Mattias Westphal, Louise Arén,
Anna Bergfeldt, Erik Naf
Company: Family Business
Country: Sweden

**DIAMOND PENTAWARD 2013
ESKO PRIZE**

For years **Absolut Vodka** has led the way with innovation in vodka packaging, with limited-edition series such as Absolut Disco, Absolut Rock and Absolut Illusion. For 2012, it was time to redefine the limited edition itself. The idea was to make four million unique bottles, so that each and every one became a limited edition on its own. This meant the production line had to be completely rebuilt, and every possible aspect of glass decoration be reemploy in a new way. Nearly every bottle sold out before the campaign period was over, without any discount, which in general is a must when retailing during the busy end-of-year season.

Schon seit Jahren führt **Absolut Vodka** bei der innovativen Verpackung von Wodkaflaschen und brachte in Sonderauflagen Absolut Disco, Absolut Rock und Absolut Illusion heraus. 2012 war die Zeit gekommen, die Limited Edition selbst neu zu definieren. Die Idee war, vier Millionen Flaschen als Unikate herzustellen, sodass jede eine eigene Limited Edition darstellte. Das bedeutete, die Fertigungsstraße vollständig neu zu organisieren, damit alles, was bei der Glasverzierung möglich ist, auf neuartige Weise eingesetzt werden konnte. Noch vor Ablauf der Kampagne war praktisch jede Flasche verkauft, und das ohne Rabatte, was bei Angeboten in der Hauptsaison Ende des Jahres ansonsten unverzichtbar ist.

Pendant des années, **Absolut Vodka** a été le pionnier des emballages innovants de vodka, avec des éditions limitées comme Absolut Disco, Absolut Rock et Absolut Illusion. En 2012, la révision du concept même d'édition limitée s'est imposée : l'idée était de fabriquer quatre millions de bouteilles, chacune unique en son genre. La ligne de production a donc dû être entièrement repensée et chaque touche décorative réutilisée différemment. Quasiment toutes les bouteilles se sont vendues avant la fin de la campagne sans appliquer de réductions, tout un luxe au moment des fêtes de fin d'année.

EVIAN
PURE DROP

Design: Frédéric Brasse, Grand Angle Design
Company: Evian (Danone Group)
Country: France

DIAMOND PENTAWARD 2014
ESKO PRIZE

From the outset, **Evian Drop** was conceived as a project putting consumers' needs at its heart and to locate the bottles in outlets where they wouldn't typically be found. The new design emphasizes purity and presents a bottle which can be drunk in one go, like a glass of water, and which has no cap but a lid, no label but a sticker on the top. By retailing the bottles in places like premium non-food stores, hairdressers and pharmacies, and most radically from mobile units selling them in heavy traffic in Paris, this changes the rules of the game: water now comes to the consumer, instead of them having to go and look for it in a shop.

Von Anfang an konzipiert sich **Evian Drop** als Produkt, das den Bedarf der Verbraucher ins Zentrum stellt und Flaschen dort anbietet, wo man sie normalerweise nicht vermutete. Das neue Design betont Reinheit und präsentiert eine Flasche, die auf einmal weggetrunken werden kann wie ein Glas Wasser. Sie ist nicht mit Kronkorken, sondern Folie verschlossen und weist kein Etikett, sondern einen Aufkleber oben auf. Durch den Verkauf der Flaschen z.B. in Premium-Nonfood-Läden, Friseurgeschäften und Apotheken und am radikalsten durch mobile Units im dichten Pariser Straßenverkehr änderte Evian die Spielregeln: Der Kunde braucht sich keinen Laden mehr zu suchen, sondern lässt das Wasser zu sich kommen.

Le projet **Evian Drop** a d'emblée été pensé pour cibler les besoins des consommateurs et distribuer les bouteilles via un réseau atypique. Le nouveau design rime avec pureté et la bouteille peut être bue d'un trait, comme un verre d'eau. Le bouchon a été remplacé par un opercule qui fait office d'étiquette. La vente des bouteilles dans des magasins non alimentaires haut de gamme, des salons de coiffure et des pharmacies, et même à des stands mobiles au milieu des embouteillages parisiens, change radicalement les règles du jeu : l'eau vient au consommateur, au lieu que ce dernier doive chercher où se la procurer.

Kiss Pop ist eine neue Kollektion Lippenstifte und Make-up aus der Beauty Line von **Marc Jacobs** mit Kiss Pop Lip Color Sticks, Twinkle Pop Stick Eyeshadows und Smart Wand Tinted Face Sticks. Die kraftvollen Farben und die Form von Stiften, mit denen man das Make-up direkt aufträgt, erinnert an Wachsmalkreide oder Malstifte von Künstlern. So präsentiert das Design eine neue und spielerische Weise, sich zu schminken.

Kiss Pop est une nouvelle collection de rouges à lèvres et de maquillage de la gamme beauté **Marc Jacobs**, avec les sticks de fard à lèvres Kiss Pop, les sticks de fard à paupières Twinkle Pop et les sticks de fond de teint Smart Wand. La palette vive et la présentation sous forme de crayons rappelle immédiatement les accessoires d'un artiste, et le concept offre une façon nouvelle et ludique de donner de la couleur au visage.

MARC JACOBS BEAUTY LINE

Creative Direction: Sam O'Donahue
Company: Established
Country: USA
Category: Best of show
DIAMOND PENTAWARD 2015
ESKO PRIZE

Kiss Pop is a new collection of lipsticks and make-up in the **Marc Jacobs** beauty line, which features Kiss Pop Lip Color Sticks, Twinkle Pop Stick Eyeshadows, and Smart Wand Tinted Face Sticks. The use of a palette of bold colors and pencil-shaped implements for applying them immediately calls to mind an artist's crayons or pastel, so that the design presents a novel and playful way to add color to the face.

Im Laufe der Zeit häuften sich auf der Packung der **Domino's**-Pizzas immer mehr allgemeine Infos an. Für Verbraucher waren sie bedeutungslos, überdies spielte das Markenzeichen nur noch eine Nebenrolle. Durch die Neugestaltung der Lieferkartons in Großbritannien sollte der Artikel wieder maßgeblich werden. Und dafür sollte ein mutiger, schlichter Ansatz dienen: Durch Abspecken all der Beschriftungen auf den Kartons konzentriert man sich wieder auf das auffällig zweifarbige Logo der Marke. Weil 96 Prozent der Domino's-Pizzas paarweise verkauft werden, griff man den Combo-Deal der Marke als Basis für das neue Design auf. Dazu ist der eine Karton rot und der andere blau. Als Ergebnis lud man offen zum Teilen und Spielen ein und vermittelte den Slogan: Bestell nicht Pizza, bestell Domino's.

Avec le temps, une surcharge d'informations génériques avait envahi les emballages à pizza de **Domino's** qui avaient perdu tout impact sur les consommateurs : la marque avait été reléguée à un plan secondaire. Le relookage de ses boîtes de livraison pour le Royaume-Uni devait lui permettre de retrouver son statut, et ce grâce à une démarche simple et radicale se concentrant sur le logo bicolore de la marque. Comme 96 pour cent des pizzas Domino's sont vendues par paires, c'est le duo de pizzas qui a servi de base pour le nouveau concept, avec une boîte rouge et une bleue. Le résultat est une invitation au partage et au jeu qui dit « ne commandez pas une pizza, commandez Domino's ».

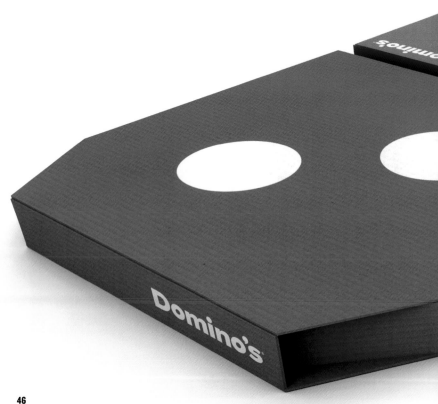

Over the years, **Domino's** pizza packaging had become overloaded with generic information that had lost impact with consumers, while the brand mark had become relegated to a small endorsement. Redesigning its delivery boxes in the UK would enable it to become the definitive article again, and this meant taking a bold and simple approach to replace the clutter on the boxes and focus instead only on the brand's distinctive two-color logo. Since 96 percent of all Domino's pizzas are sold in pairs, the brand's pizza combo deal was used as the basis for the new design, with one red box and one blue. The result was an open invitation for sharing and play that said don't order a pizza, order Domino's.

DOMINO'S

Creative Direction: Sean Thomas
Design Direction: Brett Stabler
Design: Luke Thompson
Strategy Direction: Lee Rolston
Account Direction: Leonie Payne
Visualization: Rory McNicol
Realization: Darren Beer
Production Direction: Christie Nelson
Global Marketing Direction: Matt Parkes
Marketing Management: Amy Maw
Company: Jones Knowles Ritchie
Country: UK
Category: Best of show 2016
DIAMOND PENTAWARD 2016
ESKO PRIZE

Milk*

*pinot noir

A milk bottle?
Yes, we know that you have
never received this kind of gift.
That's why we've packed our
finest Pinot Noir in this
bottle of milk.
Enjoy it!

ampro design

Best of the category
Water
Soft drinks, juices
Coffee, tea
Functional beverages/drinks
Beer
Ciders, low-alcohol drinks
Wines

beverages

Wine as bag-in-box
Spirits
Limited editions, limited series, event creations, collectors' items
Distributors'/Retailers' own brands, private labels
Casks, cases, gift boxes, ice buckets
Self-promotion
Packaging concept

ABSOLUT VODKA
ABSOLUT ORIGINALITY

Creative Direction: Magnus Skogsberg Tear (Happytear)
Account Direction: Joakim Pettersson (Happytear)
Production Management: Susan Norrgards (Happytear)
Art Direction: Ola Johansson (Destrito)
Photography: Magnus Torsne (Hall & Lundgren)
Retouch: Andreas Lindstrom (Bildinstitutet)
Client: Elin Berg (The Absolut Company)
Company: Happytear
Country: Sweden
Category: Best of the category

PLATINUM PENTAWARD 2014

Through inventive engineering, a drop of blue
cobalt may be added to molten glass at an exact
moment during bottle production, resulting in
beautiful blue streaks, each different from one
another. Four million such bottles were produced
for **Absolut Vodka**, elegantly drawing attention
to the brand and at the same time representing
its spirit of originality. The packaging and its
promotion also champion craft values and communicate the distilled essence of the drink, while
making the shade of Nova blue into a symbol of
its premium quality. In-store visibility is also
enhanced with this association between brand
and a particular color.

Infolge erfindungsreicher Ingenieurskunst wird während der Flaschenproduktion in einem exakt kalkulierten Moment dem Schmelzglas ein kobaltblauer Tropfen hinzugesetzt. Das führt zu wunderschönen blauen, einzigartigen Schlieren. Vier Millionen solcher Flaschen wurden für **Absolut Vodka** produziert und machen elegant auf diese Marke aufmerksam. Gleichzeitig repräsentiert jede einzelne den Geist der Originalität. Verpackung und Werbung verweisen auf die Handwerkskunst und kommunizieren die destillierte Essenz des Getränks. Als Symbol für die Premiumqualität steht der Farbton Nova-Blau. Dass die Marke mit einer bestimmten Farbe assoziiert wird, sorgt für erhöhte Sichtbarkeit im Laden.

Une prouesse d'ingénierie permet d'ajouter une goutte de cobalt bleu à du verre fondu au cours de la production de la bouteille, ce qui donne de superbes traînées azurées. Quatre millions d'unités ont été fabriquées pour **Absolut Vodka**, une façon élégante de promouvoir la marque et de démontrer un esprit d'originalité. L'emballage et sa promotion sont aussi la preuve d'un talent artisanal et expriment l'essence distillée de la boisson. La teinte bleu Nova incarne la qualité exceptionnelle, et la visibilité en magasins est assurée par l'association de la marque à une couleur spécifique.

Die angloamerikanische Agentur Turner Duckworth hat die **Coca-Cola-Flasche aus Aluminium** entworfen. Da eine so erfolgreiche Marke wie Coca-Cola im Laufe der Zeit immer vertrauter wird, ergänzt man sie am besten mit neuen grafischen Inhalten, um sie frisch zu halten. Doch im Laufe der Zeit verwässert sich womöglich auch dieser Effekt, und die Antwort könnte lauten, wieder zu den Grundlagen zurückzukehren. Genau das hat Turner Duckworth mit seiner Flasche gemacht: Man bewahrte die Form, jedoch in einem sehr modernen, aktuellen Material. Das Ergebnis ist eine Verpackung, die einem gleichzeitig vertraut und neu vorkommt. Es ist außerdem eine gute Möglichkeit, ein Design im Stil von „Weniger ist mehr" umzusetzen.

L'agence anglo-américaine Turner Duckworth a conçu la **bouteille en aluminium de Coca-Cola**. Une marque aussi connue que Coca-Cola finit par devenir trop familière, et lui donner un nouveau graphisme est une solution pour conserver sa fraîcheur. Mais l'effet peut se diluer avec le temps, et la réponse peut se trouver dans un retour à l'essentiel. C'est ce que Turner Duckworth a fait avec cette bouteille, en gardant la même forme, mais avec un nouveau matériau très contemporain. Le résultat est un packaging qui semble familier et nouveau à la fois. C'est aussi une bonne façon de mettre en pratique un design épuré à l'extrême.

The Anglo-American Turner Duckworth agency designed the **Coca-Cola aluminium bottle**. As a successful brand like Coca-Cola becomes ever more familiar, adding new graphics is an answer for keeping it fresh. But over time the effect can be diluted, and the answer can be a return to the basics. This is what Turner Duckworth has done with its bottle, keeping the same shape, but in a very contemporary new material. The result is packaging that feels familiar and new at the same time. It's also a good way of putting into practice a "Less is More" kind of design.

COCA-COLA
ALUMINIUM BOTTLE

Creative Direction:
David Turner, Bruce Duckworth
Design: Chris Garvey
Company: Turner Duckworth,
London & San Francisco
Country: UK/USA
Category: Best of the category
PLATINUM PENTAWARD 2008

COCA-COLA
SUMMER 2009 PACKAGING

Creative Direction:
David Turner, Bruce Duckworth
Design Direction: Sarah Moffat
Design: Rebecca Williams, Josh Michels
Company: Turner Duckworth,
London & San Francisco
Country: UK/USA
Category: Best of the category

PLATINUM PENTAWARD 2009

For this **Coca-Cola** can, Turner Duckworth used a red print on metal which features cheerful and feel-good images from summertime in the USA, culminating in the national holiday of the 4th of July: a BBQ, Raybans, a beach-ball, surfboards, stars and stripes. To add personality, the Coca-Cola logo is used with more freedom and creativity each time. Everything is also easily adaptable to all promotional material such as T-shirts, caps, beach towels, and so on, to create a perfectly integrated marketing campaign.

Bei dieser **Coca-Cola**-Dose arbeiteten Turner Duckworth mit einem roten Aufdruck auf Metall, der fröhliche und gutgelaunte Symbole der sommerlichen USA zeigt. Zusammen spielen sie auf den amerikanischen Nationalfeiertag an, den 4. Juli: ein Barbecue, Rayban-Sonnenbrillen, ein Beachball, Surfbretter und Stars and Stripes. Um allem noch mehr Persönlichkeit zu verleihen, wird das Logo von Coca-Cola stets freier und kreativer verwendet. Alles kann ganz einfach an verschiedene Werbematerialien wie T-Shirts, Baseballcaps, Strandtücher usw. angepasst werden, um eine perfekt integrierte Marketing-Kampagne zu schaffen.

Pour cette canette de **Coca-Cola**, l'agence Turner Duckworth a imprimé sur le métal rouge des images joyeuses et réconfortantes de l'été américain, dont le point fort est la fête nationale du 4 juillet : un barbecue, des Ray-Ban, un ballon de plage, des planches de surf, les rayures et étoiles du drapeau. Pour ajouter de la personnalité, le logo Coca-Cola est utilisé avec plus de liberté et de créativité dans chaque déclinaison. Le tout s'adapte aussi facilement à tous les supports promotionnels comme les t-shirts, les casquettes ou les serviettes de plage, pour créer une campagne marketing parfaitement intégrée.

HEINEKEN
STR BOTTLE

Design: Ramses Dingenouts,
Stéphane Castets (dBOD),
Pascal Duval (Iris Amsterdam)
Company: dBOD
Country: Netherlands
Category: Best of the category

PLATINUM PENTAWARD 2011

To catch the eye of an elite night-club clientele, the new STR bottle from **Heineken** really does light up the night. The special spot-UV ink is 100 percent invisible in daylight, but in a dark setting under UV the ink suddenly flares up on the bottle's surface revealing a brightly glowing design: a sky filled with shooting stars that makes club connoisseurs the star of the evening. With the smart, minimalist design on the aluminium bottle emphasising Heineken's broad appeal, the STR has been launched successfully in 40 markets around the world and featured widely in the press.

Als Blickfang für Gäste in elitären Nightclubs bringt die neue STR-Flasche von **Heineken** die Nacht zum Leuchten. Der Spezialaufdruck aus Spot-UV-Tinte ist bei Tageslicht unsichtbar, aber in dunkler Umgebung unter UV-Licht zeigt sich auf der Flaschenoberfläche ein strahlendes Design: Ein Himmel voller Sternschnuppen macht die Nightclubgäste zu Stars des Abends. Das clevere, minimalistische Design auf der Aluflasche betont die große Ausstrahlung von Heineken. Die STR-Flasche wurde erfolgreich auf 40 Märkten weltweit gelauncht und sorgte für breites Medienecho.

Pour attirer l'attention de la clientèle d'élite des établissements de nuit, la nouvelle bouteille STR de **Heineken** brille dans le noir. Son encre spéciale est 100 pour cent invisible à la lumière du jour, mais dans l'obscurité avec une lumière noire, elle s'illumine à la surface de la bouteille et révèle des motifs éclatants : un ciel rempli d'étoiles filantes qui convertit les noctambules avertis en astres de la soirée. Le graphisme élégant et minimaliste de la bouteille en aluminium souligne l'attrait de Heineken. La STR a été lancée avec succès sur 40 marchés dans le monde entier et a beaucoup fait parler d'elle dans la presse.

In einer Welt hauptsächlich in Dosen verkauf-
ter Biere ist es nicht einfach, sich durch Farbe,
Namen und Form deutlich von Rest abzuheben.
Als Metaphase Design Group ihre Dose in Form
einer Fliege für Frack oder Smoking vorstellte, war
dies etwas völlig Neues. Das Resultat beeindruckt
noch mehr, wenn man berücksichtigt, welche
technischen Schwierigkeiten zu bewältigen sind,
um Dosen in solch großen Mengen schnell zu
produzieren. Das Hauptziel war, eine visuell und
funktional noch attraktivere Dose zu schaffen und
so dem amerikanischen Klassiker neue Kunden zu
erschließen. Man braucht die **Budweiser**-Dose
nur in die Hand zu nehmen, um zu verstehen,
welchen Mehrwert die Marke der charakteristischen Form, die perfekt mit dem Logo harmoniert, verdankt. Das kann man nicht verbessern!

Si une marque se distingue des autres principalement par sa couleur, son nom et sa forme, il est
difficile de se réinventer dans le monde de la bière
où les canettes dominent le marché. Metaphase
Design Group a créé l'événement en inventant une
canette en forme de nœud papillon. Les difficultés
techniques ont su être maîtrisées, ce qui a permis la
production rapide de grandes quantités. L'objectif
premier était de créer une canette plus attrayante
et plus pratique afin de capter de nouveaux clients.
La prise en main de cette canette **Budweiser**
suffit à comprendre la valeur ajoutée de la marque,
grâce à sa forme en parfaite harmonie avec le logo :
difficile de faire mieux !

ANHEUSER-BUSCH INBEV
BUDWEISER

Design: Bryce Rutter, Jonathan Sundy, David
Kusch (Metaphase Design Group), Pat McGauley,
Lori Shambro, Thuy Vi Quach-Braig, Mark Viox,
Danielle Miller, Tim Buening, Lee Crossley
(AB InBev), Peter Kay (DCA)
Company: Metaphase Design Group
Country: USA
Category: Best of the category
PLATINUM PENTAWARD 2013

If a brand stands out from other brands chiefly
because of its color, name and shape, in the world of
beer, mainly sold in cans, it is not easy to break out.
So when Metaphase Design Group came up with a
can shaped like a bow-tie this was something quite
new, while overcoming the technical difficulties
of producing large quantities of such cans at speed
makes the result even more impressive. The primary aim was to create a more attractive can, both
visually and functionally, in order to attract new
customers to this American classic. Holding this
Budweiser can in your hand is enough to understand the added value to the brand, thanks to the
distinctive shape in perfect harmony with the logo.
You could not do better!

A long-standing Spanish winemaker wanted to enter the Chinese market. This process had to be as smooth as possible. French wines, which are the most popular in China, usually choose to keep their identity 100 percent, showing their authenticity. **Lascala** decided to merge Western and Eastern cultures; it is also the word the Chinese use for the theatre. A face all painted to imitate a theatre mask and with Eastern features to represent China, with the merger represented by La Peineta (the ornamental comb) Rosé Wine, El Abanico (the hand fan) White Wine, and La Bailaora de Flamenco (the Flamenco dancer) Red Wine. Products that are not originally manufactured in China cannot bear Chinese writing on the front packaging, so for the main label, the brand's text is displayed on a vertical axis, like traditional Chinese script.

LASCALA

Art Direction: Eduardo del Fraile
Design: Eduardo del Fraile, Manel Quilez
Company: Eduardo del Fraile
Country: Spain
Category: Best of the category
PLATINUM PENTAWARD 2010

Ein seit langem am Markt vertretener spanischer Produzent wollte seine Weine auch in China anbieten. In China sind französische Weine besonders begehrt. Ihre Produzenten entscheiden sich normalerweise dafür, die Identität der Weine hundertprozentig zu behalten und damit Authentizität zu verdeutlichen. Doch **Lascala** (diesen Begriff verwenden die Chinesen auch fürs Theater) beschloss, westliche und östliche Kultur zu verschmelzen. China wird durch eine Theatermaske mit fernöstlichen Gesichtszügen repräsentiert. Für Roséwein wird auf dem Etikett der Schmuckkamm La Peineta ergänzt, für den Weißwein der Fächer El Abanico und für den Rotwein La Bailaora de Flamenco (die Flamenco-Tänzerin). Produkte, die nicht ursprünglich in China hergestellt worden sind, dürfen auf der Vorderseite der Packung keine chinesischen Schriftzeichen tragen. Also werden die Buchstaben für das Hauptetikett in traditioneller chinesischer Schreibweise von oben nach unten aufgedruckt.

Un producteur de vin espagnol de longue tradition voulait pénétrer le marché chinois. Il fallait trouver comment préparer au mieux l'opération. Les vins français, qui sont les plus populaires en Chine, préfèrent habituellement garder leur identité sans rien y changer, pour montrer leur authenticité. La gamme **Lascala** fusionne les cultures occidentale et orientale. C'est par ailleurs le mot utilisé en Chine pour désigner le théâtre. L'identité visuelle se compose des visages asiatiques maquillés de blanc pour symboliser la Chine, et la fusion des cultures est symbolisée par La Peineta (peigne ornemental) pour le vin rosé, El Abanico (éventail) pour le vin blanc, et La Bailaora de Flamenco (danseuse de flamenco) pour le vin rouge. Les produits qui ne sont pas fabriqués en Chine ne peuvent pas arborer de lettres chinoises sur le devant de l'emballage. Pour l'étiquette principale, la marque est écrite verticalement, comme les lettres chinoises traditionnelles.

NONGFU SPRING MINERAL WATER FROM CHANGBAI MOUNTAIN

Design: Ian Firth, Sarah Pidgeon
Illustration: Natasha Searston
Company: Horse
Country: UK
Category: Best of the category

PLATINUM PENTAWARD 2015

Chinese bottled-water producer **Nongfu Spring** wanted to introduce a new premium mineral water aimed at high-end hotels, bars and restaurants. The design of the bottle conveys the quality of the water and communicates its source, an underground spring in the Changbai Mountains, a volcanic region between China and North Korea. The screen-printed designs depict species native to the area, including the Siberian tiger, Chinese merganser and Korean pine, accompanied by Chinese text providing facts about the region. Flora is used for the still variants, and fauna for the sparkling water, while the shape of the bottle is designed to resemble a hanging water droplet to suggest clarity and purity.

Der chinesische Tafelwasserproduzent **Nongfu Spring** wollte ein neues Premiummineralwasser einführen, das sich an hochwertige Hotels, Bars und Restaurants wendet. Das Design der Flasche lässt auf die hohe Wasserqualität schließen. Sie vermittelt die Herkunft aus einer unterirdischen Quelle in den Bergen von Changbai, einer vulkanischen Region zwischen China und Nordkorea. Die Siebdruckdesigns zeigen heimische Arten der Gegend, z. B. den Sibirischen Tiger, Schuppensäger oder die koreanische Kiefer. Chinesischer Text liefert Fakten über die Region. Auf den stillen Wasservarianten sind Pflanzen zu sehen und Tiere bei den sprudelnden Wassern. In Form eines hängenden Wassertropfens suggeriert die Flasche Klarheit und Reinheit.

Nongfu Spring est un producteur chinois d'eau en bouteille qui voulait lancer une nouvelle eau minérale haut de gamme destinée aux hôtels, bars et restaurants de luxe. La bouteille illustre la qualité de l'eau et informe de sa provenance, une source souterraine des montagnes de Changbai, région volcanique située entre la Chine et la Corée du Nord. Les motifs sérigraphiés représentent des espèces indigènes, notamment le tigre de Sibérie, le harle de Chine et le pin blanc de Corée, accompagnées d'informations sur la région en chinois. La flore est utilisée pour l'eau plate, et la faune pour l'eau pétillante. La forme de la bouteille évoque une goutte d'eau suspendue pour suggérer l'idée de pureté.

This special sake is named after the famous ornamental fish, the carp that is a symbol of Japan, and which has been bred for decades in the same Niigata prefecture where this **Nishikigoi** sake is manufactured. Considered a living jewel, the carp have beautiful red patterns on a white body, and this scheme has been adopted in the bottle design where the red is printed directly on to the white bottle. Japanese brush-work was used to create the red elements, while the outer box features a window in the shape of a fish. The combination of white, red and gold gives a luxury impression and makes it an excellent gift, while the packaging helps Nishikigoi stand out from other sake brands in Japanese and overseas markets.

IMAYOTSUKASA SAKE BREWERY

Art Direction/Design: Aya Codama
Project Direction: Masayuki Habuki
Project Management: Yosuke Tanaka
Calligraphy: Kasetsu
Printing: Yamaharu Glass, Taiyo Printing
Company: Bullet
Country: Japan
Category: Best of the category

PLATINUM PENTAWARD 2016

Dieser besondere Sake erhielt seinen Namen nach dem berühmten ornamentalen Koi-Karpfen. Schon seit Jahrzehnten wurde dieses japanische Symbol in der Präfektur Niigata gezüchtet, in der auch der **Nishikigoi**-Sake hergestellt wird. Mit seinen wunderschönen roten Mustern auf weißem Körper betrachtet man den Karpfen als lebendes Juwel. Auf der Flasche wird dieses Schema aufgegriffen und das Rot direkt auf die weiße Flasche gedruckt. Die roten Elemente sind in japanischer Pinselführung gestaltet, während der Karton ein fischförmiges Fenster aufweist. Weiß, Rot und Gold vermittelt kombiniert einen luxuriösen Eindruck und machen den Sake zu einem hervorragenden Geschenk. Mit seiner Verpackung hebt sich Nishikigoi von anderen Sake-Marken in Japan und den Märkten in Übersee ab.

Ce saké spécial porte le nom de la fameuse carpe koï, symbole du Japon, élevée depuis des décennies dans la préfecture de Niigata où le saké **Nishikigoi** est également fabriqué. Joyau vivant, cette carpe affiche de magnifiques motifs rouges sur un corps blanc. C'est ce même motif qui est reproduit ici, imprimé en rouge directement sur la bouteille blanche. Les éléments rouges ont été peints au pinceau japonais, et une ouverture en forme de poisson complète le concept. La combinaison du blanc, du rouge et de l'or donne une impression de luxe et en fait un excellent cadeau, tandis que le design différencie Nishikigoi des autres marques de saké.

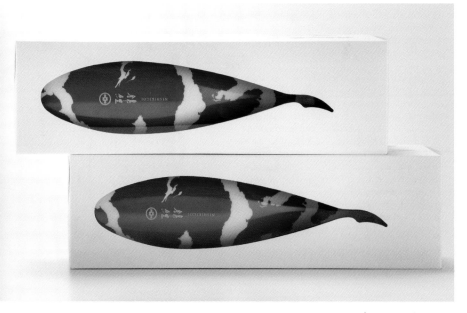

Seryab, a mineral water from Russia launched in summer 2010, takes its name from the Russian word for "silver", used in the filtration of artesian spring sources. To enhance its appeal a packaging design was developed to showcase the simple natural beauty of water, offset with the luxury of decanters and silverware. A new amphora-shaped container was found to be more pleasing to hold, and advantageously more material-efficient, whilst labels were dispensed with, the barcode and other information being printed on a heat-shrunk sleeve covering the cap. The curving design on the bottle's surface makes the water refract light and shine like crystal, additionally reinforcing the structure and so also saving material.

Das russische Mineralwasser **Seryab** startete im Sommer 2010. Der Name stammt vom russischen Wort für „Silber", das bei der Filterung artesischer Brunnen verwendet wurde. Die neue Verpackung stellt die natürliche Schönheit des Wassers heraus, verbunden mit dem Luxus von Dekantern und Silberbesteck. Die Form einer Amphore liegt deutlich angenehmer in der Hand und punktet besonders mit Materialeffizienz: Auf Etiketten wird verzichtet, der Strichcode und weitere Informationen finden mittels Wärmeschrumpffolie auf dem Deckel Platz. Die gekrümmte Oberfläche der Flasche bricht das Licht im Wasser und sorgt für kristallenes Funkeln. Zugleich verstärkt sie die Struktur und spart Material.

Seryab est une eau minérale russe lancée durant l'été 2010. Elle tient son nom du mot russe signifiant « argent », matériau utilisé pour le filtrage des puits artésiens. Pour la rendre plus séduisante, sa bouteille a été conçue de façon à mettre en valeur la beauté naturelle de l'eau, évoquant le luxe des carafes et de l'argenterie. La forme de l'amphore a été choisie parce qu'elle est plus agréable à prendre en main et qu'elle est plus efficiente du point de vue du matériau. Les étiquettes ont été éliminées ; le code-barres et les autres informations sont imprimés sur un manchon thermorétractable qui recouvre le bouchon. Les motifs en relief sur la bouteille réfléchissent la lumière et font briller l'eau comme du cristal, tout en renforçant la structure et en économisant du verre.

SERYAB

Creative Direction: Andrei Petrov
Design: Viktor Ryabov
Company: R2H (UK)
Country: Russia
Category: Water

GOLD PENTAWARD 2011

Deep Origin is a tear-drop-shaped, crystal-clear glass bottle, with dimple recesses positioned in parallel. These two 7/16 in-deep indentations on opposite sides of the bottle, resembling the bowl of a spoon in shape, not only function as an inviting grip for the hand, but also feature Deep Origin's company logo. To create a unique and functional package with low environmental impact Grenache Bottle Design chose packaging elements that used fewer resources and lent themselves to multiple reuse, or composting. The bottle's main label is in raised letters on the glass itself, reducing waste. The small biodegradable cellulose neck-label has water-soluble adhesive and is printed using vegetable-based inks.

DEEP ORIGIN

Design: Stephan Jelicich
Company: Grenache Bottle Design
Country: New Zealand
Category: Water
GOLD PENTAWARD 2010

Deep Origin ist eine kristallklare Glasflasche in Tropfenform mit parallelen Einkerbungen. Sie ist an zwei gegenüberliegenden Stellen 9 mm tief eingebuchtet. Diese Vertiefungen ähneln in der Form einem Löffel und dienen nicht nur als einladender Griff für die Hand, sondern tragen auch das Firmenlogo von Deep Origin. Um eine unverwechselbare und funktionale Verpackung möglichst ohne Umweltbelastungen zu schaffen, entschied sich Grenache Bottle bei der Verpackung für Elemente, die weniger Ressourcen verbrauchen und sich für Mehrfachverwendung oder Kompostierung eignen. Der Namenszug wird mit erhabenen Buchstaben auf das Glas selbst aufgebracht, was Abfall vermeidet. Das kleine Etikett, dessen Aufdruck aus pflanzlicher Druckfarbe besteht, ist biologisch abbaubar und wird mit wasserlöslichem Klebstoff befestigt.

Deep Origin est une bouteille en verre transparent comme le cristal, en forme de goutte, avec deux creux parallèles tels des fossettes. Ces deux renfoncements profonds de 9 mm de chaque côté de la bouteille prennent la forme de la partie concave d'une petite cuiller, et invitent à y placer les doigts pour saisir la bouteille, mais servent aussi à mettre en valeur le logo de Deep Origin. Pour créer un emballage original et fonctionnel tout en minimisant l'impact sur l'environnement, Grenache Bottle Design a choisi des éléments qui consomment moins de ressources et qui se prêtent à être réutilisés plusieurs fois, ou à être compostés. Le texte principal de la bouteille est inscrit en relief directement sur le verre pour réduire les déchets. La petite étiquette biodégradable en cellulose placée sur le col est collée avec un adhésif soluble dans l'eau et imprimée avec des encres végétales.

WATERHOUSE
EIRA

Creative Direction/Design: Bjørn Rybakken
Managing Direction: Line Støtvig
Account Management: Bente Hauge
Production Lead: Klaus Dalseth
Marketing Management:
Reidar Høidal (Waterhouse)
Managing Direction:
Torvald M. Jørstad (Waterhouse)
Company: Tangram Design
Country: Norway
Category: Water
BRONZE PENTAWARD 2012

PARIS BAGUETTE
EAU

Design: Karim Rashid
Company: Karim Rashid Inc.
Country: USA
Category: Water

SILVER PENTAWARD 2010

KIRIN
NATURAL MINERAL WATER

Art Direction: Kota Sagae,
Yukie Tamura
Company: Saga
Country: Japan
Category: Water

BRONZE PENTAWARD 2016

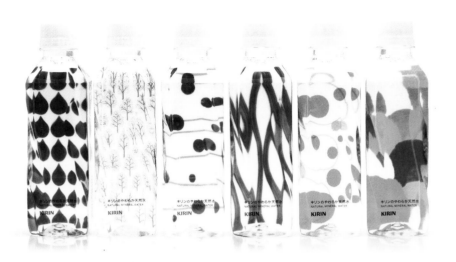

AIX LES BAINS
LES MOUSQUETAIRES
INTERMARCHÉ

Design: Damien Bourne,
Wilfried Hermel,
Laurent Lepoitevin
Company: Sidel
Country: France
Category: Water
BRONZE PENTAWARD 2013

ISKLAR

Executive Creative Direction: Martin Grimer
Design Direction: Reseigh Fooks; *Design Director Structure:* Guy Williams
Realisation Direction: Shaun Jones; *Account Direction:* Roger Hart
Company: Blue Marlin Brand Design
Country: UK
Category: Water

GOLD PENTAWARD 2009

Aqua achtet speziell darauf, dass Design allen Waren eine Seele verleihen kann, um die Kunden auf emotionaler Ebene anzusprechen. Dieses Design durchbricht die üblichen Codes seiner Kategorie. Die abgerundete vertikale Rippung und die dezente Grüntönung greifen das Spiel von Farbe und Licht auf, wie man es sonst bei Glasflaschen findet. Sanft und elegant fängt die Form Essenz und Licht des Mittelmeeres ein. Die Packung steht für Nachhaltigkeit, da sie aus Naturfaser-Polypropylen ohne Farbzusätze produziert ist und ein nur zweifarbig bedrucktes Etikett trägt. Außerdem hat man den Herstellungsprozess zugunsten einer signifikant reduzierten Klimabelastung angepasst.

Aqua a pour philosophie que le design confère une âme au produit et lui permet de connecter sur le plan émotionnel avec les consommateurs. Ici, le design rompt avec les codes habituels : des nervures verticales et un vert délicat imitent la réfraction et les tons plus souvent propres aux bouteilles en verre. Légère et élégante, la forme capte l'essence et la lumière de la Méditerranée : l'emballage prouve être durable, fait de polypropylène naturel sans colorants artificiels, et l'étiquette ne compte que deux couleurs. La fabrication a été personnalisée pour réduire de façon notable l'empreinte carbone.

AQUA
NATURAL MINERAL WATER

Design: Series Nemo team
Company: Series Nemo
Country: Spain
Category: Water

GOLD PENTAWARD 2014

Aqua maintains that through design all goods can have a soul and so connect with consumers at an emotional level. The design here breaks with the usual category codes and instead features rounded vertical ribs and a subtle green to suggest the refraction and tones more often found with glass bottles. Soft and elegant, the form also captures the essence and light of the Mediterranean, while the packaging does its bit for sustainability, using natural polypropylene with no color additives, and a label printed in just two colors. In addition, the manufacturing has been tailored to achieve a significant reduction in the carbon footprint.

GUMUS

Product Design Direction: Yesim Bakirkure (Ypsilon Tasarim)
Product Design: Yesim Bakirkure, Serpil Erden
Graphic Design Direction: Bulent Erkmen (Bek Tasarim)
Graphic Design: Haluk Tuncay, Baris Akkurt
Photography: Serdar Tanyeli
Company: Ypsilon Tasarim
Country: Turkey
Category: Water
SILVER PENTAWARD 2012

VITALIS

Creative Direction: Antonia Hayward
Client Managment: Sally Westlake
Company: Design Bridge
Country: UK
Category: Water

BRONZE PENTAWARD 2010

EVIAN

Design: Christophe Pradère, Adrien Vicario (Betc Design)
Marketing: Michael Aidan, Florence Bossard (Danone Waters)
Company: Evian (Danone Group)
Country: France
Category: Water

BRONZE PENTAWARD 2012

HOALIVE

Design: Kai-Ting Liu, Yu-Lin Hsu
Company: Dreamglobe Branding Design
Country: Taiwan
Category: Water

SILVER PENTAWARD 2015

SVALBARDI

Design: Rob Hall
Company: Studio H
Country: UK
Category: Water

SILVER PENTAWARD 2016

GLOJI

Design: Peter Kao
Company: Gloji
Country: USA
Category: Soft drinks, juices

GOLD PENTAWARD 2008

Apart from the light-bulb-shaped bottle, which represents energy, the idea for the **Gloji** packaging design was based on three related elements. First, the brand name "Gloji", second, the main ingredient "goji-berry juice", and third, the slogan "The juice that makes you glow". It visually tries to communicate the ideas of "Glowing and Healthy", and fits ergonomically in the consumer's hand.

Abgesehen von der Flasche in Glühbirnenform, die für Energie steht, basiert die Idee für das Verpackungsdesign von **Gloji** auf drei zusammengehörigen Elementen: erstens dem Markennamen „Gloji", zweitens der Hauptzutat „Gojibeerensaft" und drittens dem Slogan „Der Saft, der Sie zum Leuchten bringt". So wird versucht, den Gedanken von „leuchtend und gesund" visuell zu vermitteln, und das Produkt ist sehr ergonomisch auf die Hand des Verbrauchers abgestimmt.

Outre la bouteille en forme d'ampoule électrique qui symbolise l'énergie, l'idée qui se trouve derrière le packaging de **Gloji** est basée sur trois éléments connexes : le nom de la marque (« glow » signifie rayonner en anglais), l'ingrédient principal de « jus de baie goji », et le slogan « Le jus qui vous fait rayonner ». Le packaging essaie de communiquer visuellement la notion de rayonnement et de santé, et s'adapte ergonomiquement à la main du consommateur.

PASCUAL SELECCION
Design: Christophe Blin
Company: In Spirit Design
Country: Spain
Category: Soft drinks, juices
GOLD PENTAWARD 2010

SIS

Design: Stepan Azaryan
Company: Backbone Branding
Country: Armenia
Category: Soft drinks, juices
SILVER PENTAWARD 2016

Es ist schon ungewöhnlich, wenn ein Kunde mit einem Briefing für ein Getränk kommt, das seinen Namen von der Höhe der Flasche bezieht, in der es angeboten wird. Tritt dieser Fall ein, dann sollte man sich für eine solche Herausforderung wahrscheinlich etwas ganz Neues überlegen. Die Antwort für die **12-Inches**-Säfte lag in einem Etikett, das genau 12 Zoll lang ist und auf eine Banderole gedruckt wird, die in den Verkaufsstellen auch für die Beschilderung und die Warenwerbung eingesetzt werden kann.

Il est rare qu'un client vienne vous voir avec un produit baptisé d'après la hauteur de la bouteille qui le contient. Lorsque cela arrive, la mission appelle probablement une approche originale. Pour les jus **12 Inches,** une étiquette, qui mesure exactement 12 pouces (« inches ») de long et imprimée sur de l'adhésif d'emballage, peut aussi servir à la signalisation et au merchandising sur le point de vente.

12 INCHES

Design: Ivana Martinovic
Company: War Design
Country: Australia
Category: Soft drinks, juices

GOLD PENTAWARD 2009

It is unusual to have a client who comes with a briefing for a product named after the height of the bottle it comes in. When it happens, the challenge probably requires something different. The answer for the **12 Inches** juices was a label that was exactly 12 inches long, printed on to packaging tape, that could also be used as signage and merchandising in shops.

COCA-COLA
ARCTIC HOME

Creative Direction: Sarah Moffat, David Turner, Bruce Duckworth
Design: Butler Looney
Illustration: Darren Whittington
Design Direction: Pio Schunker, Frederic Kahn (The Coca-Cola Company)
Company: Turner Duckworth, London & San Francisco
Country: UK
Category: Soft drinks, juices

GOLD PENTAWARD 2012

Coca-Cola and the World Wildlife Fund (WWF) joined forces in a bold new campaign to help protect the polar bear's Arctic home. For the first time ever, **Coca-Cola** turned its familiar red cans white in honour of this endangered animal and committed some 3 million dollars to its conservation through the WWF. The can's distinctive red background was replaced with an all-white panorama, highlighted by the Coca-Cola script printed in red. The eye-catching design included the image of a mother bear and her two cubs making their way across the Arctic. A complementary red can was also released as part of this holiday season initiative.

Coca-Cola und der World Wildlife Fund (WWF) setzen sich mit vereinten Kräften in einer neuen Kampagne das Ziel, die Arktis als Heimat des Polarbären zu schützen. Zum ersten Mal überhaupt wählte **Coca-Cola** zu Ehren dieses vom Aussterben bedrohten Tieres anstatt seiner vertrauten roten Dosen die Farbe Weiß und spendete zu dessen Rettung etwa 3 Millionen Dollar an den WWF. Der typisch rote Hintergrund der Dose wurde durch ein klares weißes Panorama ersetzt, von dem sich der rote Coca-Cola-Schriftzug gut abhebt. Zum auffälligen Design gehört das Bild einer Bärenmutter und ihrer beiden Jungen, die sich durch die Arktis kämpfen. Als Teil dieser für die Urlaubszeit geplanten Aktion erschien auch eine entsprechende rote Dose.

Coca-Cola et le World Wildlife Fund (WWF) font équipe dans une nouvelle campagne audacieuse pour contribuer à la protection de l'habitat arctique de l'ours polaire. Pour la toute première fois, **Coca-Cola** a revêtu de blanc ses canettes traditionnellement rouges en l'honneur de cet animal en voie de disparition, et s'est engagé à verser quelque 3 millions de dollars au WWF pour sa protection. Le fond rouge caractéristique de la canette a été remplacé par un panorama tout blanc, rehaussé par les lettres de Coca-Cola imprimées en rouge. Ce graphisme accrocheur comprend l'image d'une ourse et de ses deux petits déambulant sur la banquise. En complément, une canette rouge a également été éditée pour les fêtes.

PARIS BAGUETTE
JUS
Design: Karim Rashid
Company: Karim Rashid Inc.
Country: USA
Category: Soft drinks, juices
SILVER PENTAWARD 2010

LIMO
Creative Direction: Bjørn Rybakken
Design: Alexandra Kloster
Managing Direction: Line Støtvig
Account Management: May Britt Lunde Baumann
Production Management: Henning Arnesen
Company: Tangram Design
Country: Norway
Category: Soft drinks, juices
BRONZE PENTAWARD 2014

Q TONIC
Design: Johan Liden
Company: Aruliden
Country: USA
Category: Soft drinks, juices
BRONZE PENTAWARD 2009

PEPSI
BIG BOLD BLUE

Design: PepsiCo Design & Innovation team, Tether
Company: PepsiCo Design & Innovation
Country: USA
Category: Soft drinks, juices
SILVER PENTAWARD 2015

PEPSI CO.

Chief Creative Officer: Stanley Hainsworth
Creative Direction: Steve Barrett
Design Direction: Sean Horita
Design Lead: Dave Schlesinger
Design: Jay Ostby, Ryan Maloney
Client: Pepsi R&D/Design
Company: Tether
Country: USA
Category: Soft drinks, juices
BRONZE PENTAWARD 2013

SUNTORY GOKURI BANANA

Creative Direction: Yoji Minakuchi (Suntory),
Hiroyuki Ishiura (Suntory)
Art Direction: Kiyono Morita (Suntory)
Design: Kotobuki Seihan Printing
Illustration: Shoji Waki
Company: Kotobuki Seihan Printing
Country: Japan
Category: Soft drinks, juices
BRONZE PENTAWARD 2013

COCA-COLA IBERIA MINUTE MAID LIMON&NADA MIEL

Creative Direction: Teresa Martín de la Mata
Company: Delamata Design
Country: Spain
Category: Soft drinks, juices
GOLD PENTAWARD 2015

In Japanese, "Cha" means tea, and the world's finest green tea comes from Kyoto, the ancient capital of Japan. It was there in 1790 that Iyemon Fukui founded the Fukujuen tea company. This family company still produces today its **Iyemon Cha Original Green Tea**, or "Sencha". For it, a special bottle shape was designed and shrink-wrapped, using different colors to differentiate the two flavours. Fine printing allowed subtle color gradations, and the mixture of both traditional Japanese calligraphy and Western typography gives the bottles a contemporary and yet classic feeling.

IYEMON CHA
ORIGINAL & ROASTED GREEN TEA
Creative Direction: Yoshio Kato
Art Direction: Yoji Minakuchi
Illustration: Kozo Hayashi
Logotype: Noriyuki Shimada
Company: Suntory
Country: Japan
Category: Tea (ready-to-drink)
GOLD PENTAWARD 2008

Auf Japanisch heißt Tee „Cha", und die besten grünen Tees stammen aus der vormaligen japanischen Hauptstadt Kyoto. Genau dort gründete Iyemon Fukui im Jahre 1790 die Teehandelsgesellschaft Fukujuen. Dieses Familienunternehmen produziert auch heute noch Sencha, den **Iyemon Cha Original Green Tea**. Dafür wurde eine spezielle Flaschenform gestaltet und in einer Schrumpffolienverpackung umgesetzt, wobei zwei Geschmackssorten anhand verschiedener Farben unterschieden werden. Durch spezielle Druckvorgänge waren subtile Farbverläufe möglich, die Mischung aus traditioneller japanischer Kalligraphie und westlicher Typographie verleiht den Flaschen ein modernes und gleichzeitig klassisches Flair.

En japonais, « Cha » signifie thé, et le meilleur thé vert du monde vient de Kyoto, l'ancienne capitale du Japon. C'est là-bas que Iyemon Fukui a fondé la compagnie de thé Fukujen en 1790. Aujourd'hui, cette entreprise familiale produit toujours son **thé vert original Iyemon Cha**, ou « Sencha ». Une bouteille spéciale a été conçue pour ce thé, avec un film de deux couleurs pour différencier les deux goûts. L'impression haut de gamme autorise des dégradés de couleur subtils, et le mélange de la calligraphie japonaise et de la typographie occidentale donne aux bouteilles un style contemporain et classique à la fois.

PARIS BAGUETTE
KOFFY

Design: Karim Rashid
Company: Karim Rashid Inc.
Country: USA
Category: Coffee, tea
(ready-to-drink)

GOLD PENTAWARD 2013

BLACK SHEEP COFFEE COLD BREW

Design: Cartils creative team
Company: Cartils
Country: Netherlands
Category: Coffee, tea (ready-to-drink)

SILVER PENTAWARD 2015

For the launch of this new brand of bottled milk tea on the Chinese market, a design was sought to present a consumer-friendly product with high aesthetics. Adopting a restrained and straightforward approach meant going back to basics for the simplest iconography for each of the product's components, using a cow for the milk and a tea-bag for the tea. When merged, these two ideas produced a design that can be understood universally, and the photo-realistic rendering makes it appear that there actually is such a tea-bag suspended inside the milky tea bottle. Colors are kept equally natural, and the coconut-flavor variety is distinguished by a light and cool shade of green on its bottle.

Für den Launch dieser neuen Marke mit Milchtees in Flaschen brauchte man auf dem chinesischen Markt ein Design, das ein verbraucherfreundliches Produkt mit hoher Ästhetik präsentiert. Jede Komponente des Produkts sollte möglichst dezent und unkompliziert vorgestellt werden. Dazu griff man auf die einfachste Ikonografie zurück und nahm eine Kuh für die Milch und einen Teebeutel für den Tee. Beides zusammen ergibt ein allgemeinverständliches Design. Die fotorealistische Darstellung lässt es wirken, als hinge in der milchigen Teeflasche tatsächlich ein Teebeutel. Die Farben sind ebenso natürlich gehalten, und die Sorte mit Kokosgeschmack erkennt man am hellen und kühlen Grünton der Flasche.

Pour le lancement de cette nouvelle marque de thé au lait en bouteille sur le marché chinois, il fallait un concept de produit attractif et esthétique. La démarche sobre et directe exprime un retour à l'essentiel et dégage l'idée la plus simple pour chacun des composants : une vache pour le lait et un sachet pour le thé. Ces deux idées ont créé un concept que tout le monde peut comprendre, et le réalisme photographique donne l'impression qu'il y a vraiment un sachet de thé suspendu dans la bouteille de lait. Les couleurs sont elles aussi naturelles, et la variété au goût noix de coco se distingue par la teinte vert clair de la bouteille.

UNI-PRESIDENT
ASSAM MILK TEA

Creative Direction: Greg Tsaknakis
Illustration: Kostas Kaparos, Ioanna Papaioannou
Logo Design: Thalassinos Anastasiou
Company: Mousegraphics
Country: Greece
Category: Coffee, tea (ready-to-drink)

GOLD PENTAWARD 2016

MATCHA MILK TEA

Creative Direction/Design: Gregory Tsaknakis
Illustration: Ioanna Papaioannou
Company: Mousegraphics
Country: Greece
Category: Coffee, tea (ready-to-drink)

SILVER PENTAWARD 2014

To promote these two new products, a black tea with milk and a premium type of matcha tea, amongst young, busy, everyday consumers in China who want a well-made, healthy tea that is also quick and easy to drink, an appropriate new packaging design was needed. Since both drinks are best whisked first, with the aid of a special Japanese bamboo tool, the shape of this implement was incorporated into the bottle's structure producing a completely distinctive yet natural-looking new form. Meanwhile, the graphics combined the Chinese and English words for tea around a T-shape, giving a smart, contemporary look to appeal to the target group.

Als Werbung für zwei neue Produkte – einem Schwarztee mit Milch und einem Matcha-Premiumtee – für junge, vielbeschäftigte chinesische Verbraucher, die einen gut zubereiteten, gesunden Tee wünschen, der schnell und einfach getrunken wird, brauchte es ein neues, passendes Verpackungsdesign. Weil beide Getränke am besten zuerst schaumig gerührt werden, griff man für die Struktur der Flasche die Gestalt dieses speziellen japanischen Rührbesens aus Bambus auf. Das ergab eine absolut charakteristische und doch natürlich wirkende neue Form. Außerdem wurden die chinesischen und englischen Zeichen für Tee in T-Form grafisch kombiniert, was einen smarten, aktuellen Look für die Zielgruppe ergibt.

Un nouveau design bien pensé s'imposait pour le lancement d'un thé noir au lait et d'un thé matcha raffiné auprès d'une clientèle jeune et active en Chine, demandeuse de thés sains et de qualité, mais aussi faciles et rapides à déguster. Les deux boissons étant meilleures si elles sont d'abord fouettées à l'aide d'un outil japonais spécial en bambou, la forme de cet accessoire a été intégrée à celle de la bouteille pour donner un objet original mais non pas moins naturel. Le graphisme mélange le mot thé en mandarin et en anglais autour d'une forme de T, ce qui confère une image contemporaine pertinente pour le public ciblé.

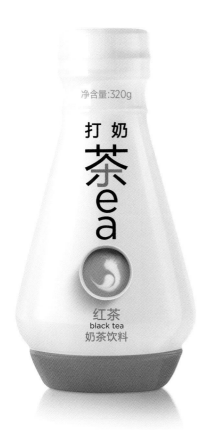

YOSHI-GO
HARUNA EUROPE

Art Direction: Jonas Lundin
Company: LA+B, Love for Art and Business
Country: Sweden
Category: Coffee, tea (ready-to-drink)

SILVER PENTAWARD 2009

SUNTORY COFFEE BOSS
SILKY BLACK

Creative Direction:
Yoshio Kato, Yoshiyasu Fujita
Art Direction: Hiroyuki Ishiura
Design: Satoshi Ito
Company: Suntory
Country: Japan
Category: Coffee, tea
(ready-to-drink)

SILVER PENTAWARD 2009

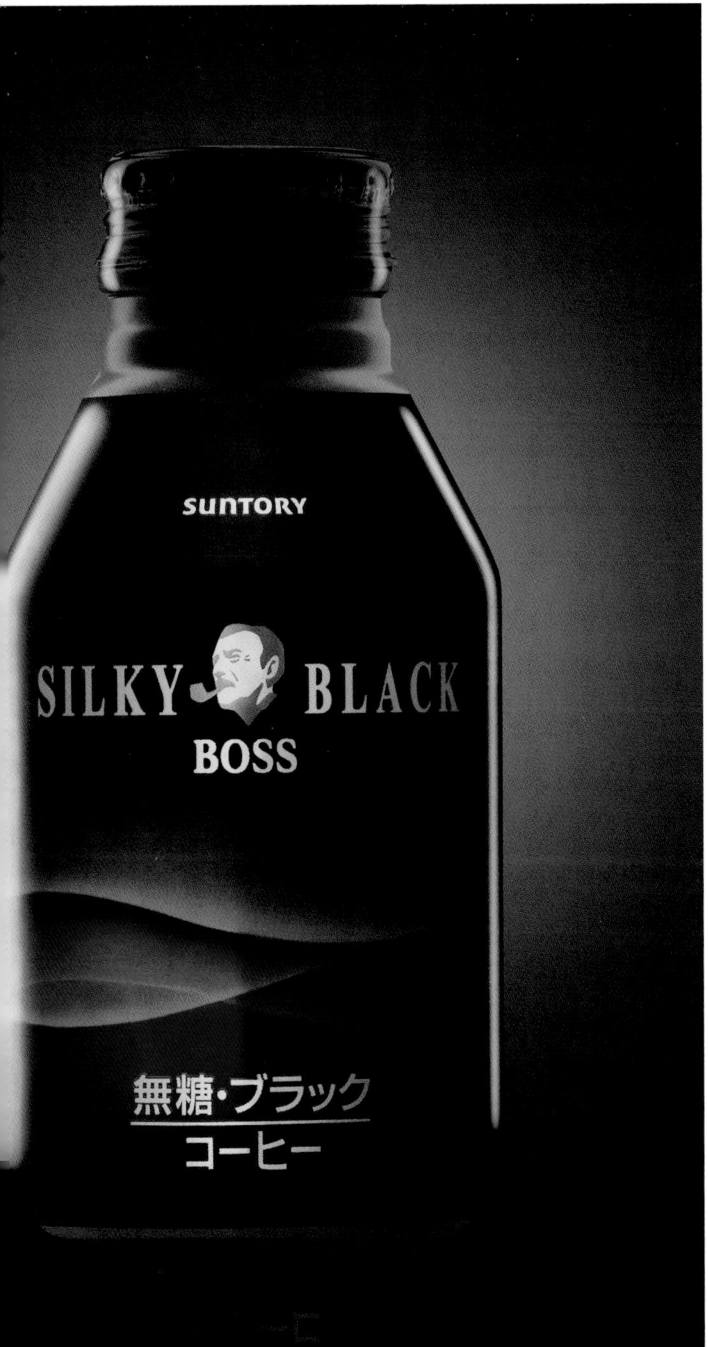
SUNTORY
SILKY BLACK
BOSS
無糖・ブラック
コーヒー

For Paris Baguette's Cheeky Tea, bursting with fresh peach flavour, a novel packaging was developed to represent its fruitiness. The container is designed to feel both organic and sensual, with the graphics intentionally a little provocative. The bulbous peach-like shape and clear plastic at the top hint at the flavour and source of the beverage within. The smooth curved base of the bottle makes it comfortable to carry and hold, whilst being shaped like a white pedestal it draws the eye up the bottle. The logo is as playful as the form, with **Cheeky** suggesting the shape of a peach, the human body and of the bottle itself, as well as the *chic* quality of the actual product, the tea.

Cheeky Tea von Paris Baguette platzt beinahe vor frischem Pfirsichgeschmack. Eine neuartige Verpackung sollte diese Fruchtigkeit verdeutlichen. Der Behälter fühlt sich gleichermaßen organisch und sinnlich an, wobei die grafische Gestaltung gewollt etwas anzüglich wirkt. Die bauchige, pfirsichförmige Flasche und der durchsichtige obere Bereich deuten Geschmack und Ursprung des Getränks darin an. Durch die glatte, gebogene Basis liegt die Flasche angenehm in der Hand, ihre Säulenform zieht Blicke auf sich. Das Logo ist verspielt wie die Form: **Cheeky** lässt an einen Pfirsich denken, an den menschlichen Körper und die Flasche selbst, aber auch an die elegante Qualität des eigentlichen Produkts: Tee.

Une bouteille originale a été mise au point pour représenter le goût fruité à la pêche fraîche du Cheeky Tea de Paris Baguette. Elle est conçue pour évoquer naturel et sensualité, et son graphisme est délibérément provocateur. En haut, la forme renflée comme une pêche en plastique transparent fait référence au goût et à l'origine de la boisson. La base lisse et ronde de la bouteille la rend agréable à prendre en main, mais c'est aussi un piédestal blanc qui guide le regard vers le haut. Le logo est aussi ludique que la forme. **Cheeky** (« effronté ») évoque la forme d'une pêche, du corps humain et de la bouteille elle-même, ainsi que le raffinement du produit.

PARIS BAGUETTE CHEEKY

Design: Karim Rashid
Company: Karim Rashid Inc.
Country: USA
Category: Coffee, tea (ready-to-drink)
GOLD PENTAWARD 2011

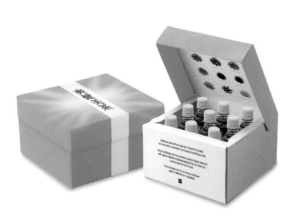

SOKENBICHA

Design: Glenn Geisendorfer, Gabe Goldman
Company: Platform
Country: USA
Category: Coffee, tea (ready-to-drink)

SILVER PENTAWARD 2011

BABA COFFEE
CARAMEL AFFOGATO
& SKINNY CAFFELATTE

Design: Choi Jin-kyu, Lee Sang-hee,
Heo In-sung, Lee you-na, Back Shin-young
Company: Woongjin Foods
Country: South Korea
Category: Coffee, tea (ready-to-drink)
BRONZE PENTAWARD 2012

NONG FU ORIENTAL LEAF

Creative Direction: Natalie Chung
Creative Partner: Jonathan Ford
Design: Sarah Pidgeon
Strategy: Tess Wicksteed
Copy: Sylvie Saunders
Illustration: Daisy Fletcher
Company: Pearlfisher
Country: UK
Category: Coffee, tea (ready-to-drink)
SILVER PENTAWARD 2012

IYEMON CHA REDESIGN

Creative Direction: Yoji Minakuchi
Art Direction/Design: Keiko Genkaku
Company: Suntory Business Expert
Country: Japan
Category: Coffee, tea (ready-to-drink)

SILVER PENTAWARD 2013

GAWATT
EMOTIONS

Art Direction: Stepan Azaryan
Design: Karen Gevorgyan
Illustration: Narine Manvelyan
Company: Backbone Branding
Country: Armenia
Category: Coffee, tea
(ready-to-drink)
BRONZE PENTAWARD 2015

CHAMELEON
COLD-BREW COFFEE

Design: Jeremy Dahl, Becky Nelson,
Daniela Anderson
Marketing Direction: Greg Fleishman
Company: Bex Brands
Country: USA
Category: Coffee, tea (ready-to-drink)
SILVER PENTAWARD 2016

UNI-PRESIDENT
LENTO COFFEE

Creative Direction: Greg Tsaknakis
Art Direction: Alexandros Mavrogiannis
Company: Mousegraphics
Country: Greece
Category: Coffee, tea (ready-to-drink)

SILVER PENTAWARD 2016

The classic Bialetti coffee-maker here serves as the model for the packaging of this ready-to-drink coffee, with the **Lento** brand-name also being adapted in the process. The name runs vertically up the side of the bottle, and the addition of extra visual elements to each letter creates a partial graphic echo of Chinese ideograms, both features being in respect of the brand's parent company. The packaging surface is otherwise left clean with only the use of silver color as in the original coffee-pot, apart from a few small drops of coffee to suggest the rich macchiato inside as well as the slow time ("lento") of its savoring. The latte variety is distinguished by its milky-white surface.

Der klassische Bialetti-Kaffeekocher dient als Modell für die Verpackung des trinkfertigen Kaffees. Der Markenname **Lento** hingegen läuft vertikal auf der Flaschenseite und schafft mit visuellen Elementen an jedem Buchstaben ein grafisches Echo chinesischer Ideogramme. Beides soll der Markenmutter Respekt zollen. Ansonsten bleibt die Packungsoberfläche frei. Nur die silberne Farbe erinnert an den ursprünglichen Kaffeekocher, und einige kleine Kaffeetropfen suggerieren den kraftvollen Macchiato darin und gemahnen an genussvolle Muße („lento" = langsam). Die Sorte Latte erkennt man an der milchig-weißen Oberfläche.

La classique cafetière Bialetti a servi de modèle pour l'emballage de ce café prêt-à-boire, et le nom de la marque **Lento** a également été adapté. Il est lisible à la verticale, et les éléments visuels ajoutés à chaque lettre créent un écho graphique des idéogrammes chinois. Ces deux caractéristiques font référence à l'entreprise mère de la marque. La surface est ultra simple en argenté, comme la cafetière originale, et quelques petites gouttes de café suggèrent la richesse du macchiato ainsi que la lenteur (« lento ») avec laquelle il doit être savouré. La variété latte se distingue par sa couleur blanche.

SUNTORY BLACK OOLONG TEA

Creative Direction: Yoji Minakuchi
Art Direction: Akiko Kirimoto
Design: Satoshi Abe
Company: Suntory
Country: Japan
Category: Coffee, tea (ready-to-drink)
SILVER PENTAWARD 2015

Seit 1997 arbeitet **Level Ground Trading** fair und direkt mit Kleinproduzenten in Entwicklungsländern zusammen und vermarktet deren Produkte in Nordamerika. Die Marke ermöglicht Konsumenten ethische Entscheidungen. Die enge Beziehung zu den Produzenten wurde Kern der Markenidentität, sobald das Unternehmen zu wachsen begann. Das Verpackungsdesign selbst zeigt die menschliche Note, der Hersteller wird zur eigentlichen Hauptperson. Fotos von lächelnden Bauern zieren authentische Taschen aus Kraftpapier. Die Beschriftung bezeugt die umfassenden Kenntnisse von Level Ground über Ursprung und Geschmacksprofil aller Kaffeesorten. Der Reißverschluss sichert die Frische des Produkts. Die Rückseite berichtet von einzelnen Pflanzern und Initiativen – als Zeugnis für den regen Austausch mit den Partnergemeinschaften.

Fondée en 1997, **Level Ground Trading** travaille équitablement et directement avec de petits producteurs de pays en voie de développement pour commercialiser leurs produits en Amérique du Nord, en proposant aux clients des choix éthiques. Au cours de la croissance de l'entreprise, cette relation étroite avec les fournisseurs est devenue le cœur de l'identité de la marque et apporte une touche d'humanité à l'emballage lui-même en donnant au producteur le rôle de protagoniste. Des photographies de fermiers souriants ornent les sachets en papier kraft authentique, et les étiquettes témoignent de la connaissance approfondie de Level Ground des origines de chaque variété de café ainsi que son profil gustatif. Les fermetures zip-lock garantissent la fraîcheur du produit, tandis que les étiquettes au dos présentent des histoires de chaque producteur et des initiatives pour illustrer l'interaction entre l'entreprise et les communautés partenaires.

LEVEL GROUND TRADING

Creative Direction: Roy White, Matthew Clark
Design: Matthew Clark, Roy White
Copy Text: Derek Perkins, Matthew Clark
Illustration: Matthew Clark
Photography: Hugo Ciro (Farmers)
Company: Subplot Design
Country: Canada
Category: Coffee, tea (dry and capsules)

GOLD PENTAWARD 2011

Founded in 1997, **Level Ground Trading** works fairly and directly with small-scale producers in developing countries to market their products in North America, offering customers ethical choices. This close relationship with suppliers became the brand identity's core as the company grew, and brings a human touch to the packaging design itself, making the producer the real hero. Photographs of smiling local farmers grace authentic kraft bags, with labels that declare Level Ground's deep knowledge of the origins and taste profiles of each variety of coffee. Zip-locks ensure re-sealable freshness, while back labels feature stories about individual growers and initiatives to give substance to how the company interacts with its trading-partner communities.

Um sich in einem Einzelhandelsbereich abzuheben, in dem sich oft ähnliche Sortimente oder visuelle Anreize zusammendrängen, muss eine Kaffeeverpackung Stil und Stärken jeder Mischung sowie die Premiumqualität von Marke und Produkt verkörpern. Ein aufgeräumtes und minimalistisches Schema repräsentiert jede **Rio**-Mischung, und mit der knackigen, freigestellten Bildgestaltung vor weißem Hintergrund entfaltet sie im Regal optische Kraft und Klarheit. Jede Tüte projiziert mit ihrem Design den Genuss der enthaltenen Kaffeemischung – vom kraftvollen Tritt eines Hengsts bis zum lässigen Komfort des Lehnstuhls. Die Bildgestaltung macht den Käufer kalkuliert neugierig und lädt ihn ein, seine Tüte mit der Lieblingsmischung zu wählen und sich mit deren Story zu beschäftigen.

Pour se démarquer dans un secteur surchargé où se répètent palettes de couleurs et repères visuels, les emballages de café doivent évoquer le style et la force de chaque mélange, ainsi que l'excellente qualité de la marque et du produit. Suivant une approche minimaliste, chaque mélange **Rio** est associé à des images sur un fond blanc pour un plus grand impact. Le design des sacs renvoie à l'expérience de dégustation du café qu'ils renferment, quelle qu'en soit l'intensité. Le visuel est pensé pour intriguer le consommateur et l'inviter à plonger dans l'histoire du mélange choisi.

RIO COFFEE

Creative Direction: Anthony De Leo,
Scott Carslake, Tom Crosby
Design: Tom Crosby
Company: Voice
Country: Australia
Category: Coffee, tea (dry and capsules)
GOLD PENTAWARD 2013

In order to stand out in a crowded retail sector, often using similar palettes or visual cues, coffee packaging needs to represent the style and strength of each blend, as well as the premium quality of brand and product. Based on a clean minimalist scheme, each of these **Rio** blends is represented with crisp, isolated imagery against a white background to achieve clarity and visual strength on the shelf. The design for each bag projects the coffee-drinking experience of the blend it contains, from the powerful kick of a stallion to the smooth comfort of an armchair, with the imagery being gauged to intrigue the consumer and invite them to pick this bag of their preferred blend and engage with its story.

ESPRESSO _____ riocoffee

COFFEE BEANS
500g Net

CLASSICO _____ riocoffee

COFFEE BEANS
500g Net

CREMA _____ riocoffee

COFFEE BEANS
500g Net

DECAF _____ riocoffee

COFFEE BEANS
500g Net

AURORA COFFEE – BEANS

Design: Motoki Koitabashi
Company: Akaoni Design
Country: Japan
Category: Coffee, tea
(dry and capsules)
BRONZE PENTAWARD 2015

RIO COFFEE

Creative Direction: Tom Crosby
Art Direction: Anthony De Leo,
Scott Carslake
Design: Tom Crosby
Illustration: Nate Williams
Copywriting: David Mackrell
Company: Voice
Country: Australia
Category: Coffee, tea
(dry and capsules)
SILVER PENTAWARD 2014

KUZHU BAMBOO LEAF TEA

Design: Chaohong Fu
Company: Chaohong Fu HD Design
Country: China
Category: Coffee, tea (dry and capsules)
BRONZE PENTAWARD 2016

YUN SHU CHUN

Design: Wen Jin Heng
Company: Shenzhen Lajiao Design
Country: China
Category: Coffee, tea (dry and capsules)
BRONZE PENTAWARD 2015

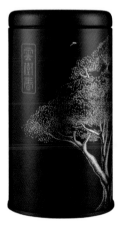

OLD MASTER'S PRIVATE TEA

Creative Direction: Kang Weijie
Design: SunL
Company: Shenzhen Oracle Creative Design
Country: China
Category: Coffee, tea (dry and capsules)

GOLD PENTAWARD 2015

GUIDING

Design: Shen Haijun
Company: Oracle Creativity Agencies
Country: China
Category: Coffee, tea (dry and capsules)

SILVER PENTAWARD 2014

XINLIN TEA
1793 CHAOSHAN OLD PORT
GONGFU TEA CULTURE

Design: Lin Shaobin
Company: Lin Shaobin Design
Country: China
Category: Coffee, tea (dry and capsules)

SILVER PENTAWARD 2014

MASTER FENG TENGCHONG

Design: Pan Hu
Company: TigerPan Packaging Design Lab
Country: China
Category: Coffee, tea
(dry and capsules)

SILVER PENTAWARD 2015

To plant itself in the consciousness of consumers this tea has been given a name, so that people may ask, "Who is **Master Feng**?" A real figure from history, he was a nobleman in Yunnan province in the time of the Republic of China, and is remembered along with his son for introducing the large-leaf Pu'er tea to the Gaoligong Mountain region. This is now a protected area and the old tea trees have become a source for this rare dark tea. The packaging design adopts the style of a newspaper from the period when the tea was first cultivated here, and recounts the story of Master Feng and his Pu'er.

Um diesen Tee im Bewusstsein der Konsumenten zu platzieren, bekam er einen Namen, sodass die Leute sich fragen: „Wer ist **Master Feng**?" Es handelt sich um eine reale Figur der chinesischen Geschichte – einen Edelmann aus der Provinz Yunnan in der Zeit der chinesischen Republik. Zusammen mit seinem Sohn wird er dafür geehrt, dass er den großblättrigen Pu-Erh-Tee in der Bergregion Gaoligong einführte. Sie steht nun unter Naturschutz, und die alten Teebäume dort liefern diesen seltenen dunklen Tee. Das Verpackungsdesign greift den visuellen Stil einer Zeitung der Periode auf, als der Tee zuerst kultiviert wurde, und erzählt die Geschichte von Master Feng und seinem Pu-Erh-Tee.

Pour qu'il s'implante dans l'esprit des consommateurs, ce thé a été baptisé afin que les gens puissent se demander « Qui est **Master Feng**? » Ce personnage historique était un noble de la province du Yunnan à l'époque de la République de Chine. Lui et son fils sont renommés pour avoir introduit le thé pu-erh à grandes feuilles dans la région des monts Gaoligong. Cette région est aujourd'hui protégée et les vieux arbres à thé sont devenus la source de ce thé sombre et rare. L'emballage adopte le style des journaux de l'époque, et raconte l'histoire de Master Feng et de son pu-erh.

TEA BAR

Creative Direction: Steven de Cleen
Design: Gertjan Muishout
Company: Proud Design
Country: Netherlands
Category: Coffee, tea
(dry and capsules)

BRONZE PENTAWARD 2014

JUNHE
KONGFU TEA

Company: Shenzhen Yuto Packaging Technology
Country: China
Category: Coffee, tea (dry and capsules)

SILVER PENTAWARD 2016

Die Marke **Teaforia** bricht alle Teekonventionen und kombiniert Vertrautes mit dem Unerwarteten. Damit präsentiert sie hervorragend schmeckende Tees in spannenden Formaten. Wechsel und Euphorie sollten direkt aus der neuen Verpackung und Positionierung der Marke spürbar werden. Dazu setzte man das Bild eines explodierenden Teeblatts als Blickfang: Der intensive Geschmack landet als gemahlener Tee in jeder Packung. Auf der Vorderseite deuten Blätter in kraftvollen Farben auf die verschiedenen Sorten hin, die sich im Regal deutlich abheben. Verschiedene Blattformen auf der Verpackung enthalten Infos für die Kunden und verleihen der Marke zusätzlich konstantes Auftreten.

Teaforia est la marque de thé qui brise toutes les règles, et allie le familier à l'inattendu pour offrir des thés savoureux dans des formats intéressants. Cette idée de changement et d'euphorie devait être traduite dans le repositionnement de la marque et son nouvel emballage, ici autour de l'image d'une feuille de thé dont la saveur intense explose pour se transformer en poudre. La couleur vive de la feuille indique les différentes variétés sur l'avant de l'emballage, bien visible dans les rayons, tandis que la forme de la feuille est utilisée pour présenter les informations et donner un résultat homogène.

TEAFORIA
GOURMET GROUND TEA

Design/Creative Direction/Illustration:
David Pearman
Company: This Way Up
Country: UK
Category: Coffee, tea (dry and capsules)

GOLD PENTAWARD 2016

Teaforia is the tea brand breaking all the rules, combining the familiar with the unexpected to present great-tasting teas in exciting formats. This sense of change and euphoria had to come right out with the brand's repositioning and new packaging, and the focus for it became the image of an exploding tea-leaf, bursting with intense flavor into the powdered ground-tea contents of each box. Vibrant-colored leaves indicate the different varieties on pack-fronts that stand out strongly on the shelf, while the leaf shape has been used across the pack to contain information and bring consistency to the branding.

NEWBY TEAS
SILKEN PYRAMIDS

Creative Direction: Mary Lewis
Design and Typography: Lucilla Lavender
Company: Newby Teas, Lewis Moberly
Country: UK
Category: Coffee, tea (dry and capsules)

SILVER PENTAWARD 2015

This range of teas and infusions, sold only by **Library Gyms**, is made from the best ingredients and blended for detox, relaxation and to refresh mind and body. The package design turns an object at hand into something newly functional: the jars are recycled wine bottles, simply cut and polished by hand. The individual lids, hand-lathed from carefully chosen local woods, are made by artisans in Central Africa, thus helping them to be self-sufficient. The environmentally and socially responsible design aims to raise the profile of locally made products worldwide and help alleviate poverty and raise self-esteem through talented crafted trade.

Dieses Tee- und Aufguss-Sortiment, exklusiv von **Library Gyms**, besteht aus besten Zutaten, die je nach Mischung zum Entgiften, zur Entspannung oder zur Erfrischung von Körper und Geist gedacht sind. Das Packungsdesign verwandelt ein Alltagsobjekt in etwas funktionell Neues: Recycelte Weinflaschen wurden einfach abgeschnitten und von Hand poliert. Die individuellen Verschlüsse aus sorgfältig ausgewählten heimischen Hölzern sind von Kunsthandwerkern in Zentralafrika gedrechselt, die dadurch autark bleiben können. Das nachhaltige und umweltbewusste Design zielt darauf, weltweit das Profil lokal produzierter Waren zu fördern, soll Armut lindern und durch talentiertes Kunsthandwerk das Selbstbewusstsein stärken.

Cette gamme de thés et d'infusions, uniquement vendus par **Library Gyms**, est faite à partir des meilleurs ingrédients ; les mélanges se veulent détoxifiants, relaxants et rafraîchissants pour le corps et l'esprit. Le design de l'emballage donne de nouvelles fonctions à des objets : les pots sont des bouteilles de vin recyclées, taillées et polies à la main. Des artisans d'Afrique centrale travaillent les couvercles dans du bois local choisi avec soin, et peuvent ainsi être autosuffisants. Le design responsable en matière d'environnement, par la promotion de produits locaux à l'échelle mondiale, mais aussi sur le plan social, vise à sortir des artisans de la pauvreté et à augmenter leur estime de soi.

LIBRARY LEAVES

Design: Karen Welman, Andrew Lyons, Peter Horridge,
Zana Morris, Corinne Spurrier, People of the Sun
Company: Pearlfisher
Country: UK
Category: Coffee, tea (dry and capsules)
GOLD PENTAWARD 2014

ÜBERSHOT

Design Direction: Ian Firth
Creative Direction: Natalie Chung
Creative Partner: Jonathan Ford
Company: Pearlfisher
Country: UK
Category: Functional drinks

GOLD PENTAWARD 2010

The brief was to create an identity and packaging for the new energy drink **Übershot** that would be launched in the UK with potential to roll out across Europe. The objective was to create a new category language. The logo is strong and striking with an arrow created out of the negative space. The aluminium packaging is a first in this category and creates stand-out next to the plastic bottles used by competitors. The formula was developed to avoid the usual crash that comes when normal energy drinks wear off.

Das Briefing lautete, für den neuen Energy-Drink **Übershot** Identität und Verpackung zu schaffen. Dieser Drink soll in Großbritannien auf den Markt kommen, verfügt aber über das Potenzial, auch in Europa vertrieben zu werden. Die Herausforderung bestand darin, die Sprache für eine neue Kategorie zu finden. Das Logo ist extrem wirksam: Aus einer Negativfläche entsteht ein nach oben gerichteter Pfeil. In dieser Kategorie gab es vorher keine Aluminiumverpackungen, was dieses Produkt von den Plastikflaschen der Konkurrenz abhebt. Mit der speziell entwickelten Rezeptur soll das typische Absacken nach dem Genuss normaler Energy-Drinks vermieden werden.

La mission était de créer une identité et un emballage pour la nouvelle boisson énergisante **Übershot** qui allait être lancée au Royaume-Uni, et peut-être dans toute l'Europe. L'objectif était de créer un nouveau langage pour la catégorie. Le logo a une présence forte, et son espace négatif dessine une flèche. La bouteille en aluminium est une première dans cette catégorie et se fait remarquer à côté des bouteilles en plastique des concurrents. La formule a été élaborée pour éviter la perte d'énergie que provoquent habituellement les autres boissons énergisantes lorsque leur effet s'estompe.

LOL

Design: Monique Pilley, Nigel Kuzimski
Company: Curious Design
Country: New Zealand
Category: Functional drinks
SILVER PENTAWARD 2009

POLA BURNING PLUS

Art Direction: Yushi Watanabe
Design: Hiromi Kobayashi
Company: Pola
Country: Japan
Category: Functional beverages

SILVER PENTAWARD 2013

CEETHREE'S IO

Creation/Lead Design: Jonas Lundin
Original Artwork: Martin Ring
Art Direction: Magdalena Adaktusson
Project Management: Elin Trogen, Frida Guldstrand
Company: LA+B, Love for Art and Business
Country: Sweden
Category: Functional beverages

BRONZE PENTAWARD 2011

SILK
SAKURA AND KOUJI

Art Direction: Koichi Sugiyama
Design: Minako Endo
Production: Yasutomo Ishii
Company: Maru
Country: Japan
Category: Functional beverages

BRONZE PENTAWARD 2014

1 ABOVE
AEROTONIC FLIGHT BEVERAGE

Design: Mike Tisdall, Simon Cairns,
Jamie McLellan, Mark di Somma,
Ben Reid, Tristan O'Shannessy
Client: Roger Boyd
Company: Insight Creative
Country: New Zealand
Category: Functional beverages

BRONZE PENTAWARD 2011

HAORENCHANG

Design: Alan Chen
Company: Shenzhen Thinkland/Alan Chen
Country: China
Category: Functional beverages

SILVER PENTAWARD 2015

NELSON BEER

Creative Direction: Reece Hobbins
Company: The Taboo Group
Country: Australia
Category: Beer
GOLD PENTAWARD 2009

Nelson beer is a lower-carb lager developed with the help of consumers and using Nelson Sauvin hops as the key ingredient. Creatives in parts of Melbourne and Sydney received their first taste of Nelson in August 2008. Using their feedback, Nelson returned in early 2009 with a name, labelling concept, and slightly different taste. From there, Nelson has continued to change by adopting the feedback of its drinkers. Welcoming audience feedback on the brew and inviting artists to design bottle imageryhas infused it with consumer ownership. Nelson's packaging was produced with the collaboration of illustrative duo Sonny & Biddy working to an open brief in creating the first bottle artwork.

Nelson beer ist ein kohlehydratarmes Lager, das unter Mitarbeit der Verbraucher entwickelt wurde und bei dem als wesentliche Zutat die Hopfensorte Nelson Sauvin eingesetzt wird. Kreative aus Melbourne und Sydney durften im August 2008 Nelson zum ersten Mal probieren. Nach ihrem Feedback kehrte Nelson Anfang 2009 mit einem neuen Namen, einem Konzept für die Etikettierung und einem leicht veränderten Geschmack auf den Markt zurück. Nelson hat sich weiterentwickelt, indem die Zielgruppe ihre Meinung über das Getränk äußern konnte und Künstler aufgefordert wurden, sich mit der Gestaltung der Flaschen auseinanderzusetzen. Das führte dazu, dass die Verbraucher sich diese Marke regelrecht angeeignet haben. Die Verpackung von Nelson wurde in Zusammenarbeit mit dem Illustratorenduo Sonny & Biddy produziert. Nach einem offenen Briefing haben sie an den ersten Illustrationen für die Flasche gearbeitet.

La **bière Nelson** est une bière pauvre en hydrates de carbone. Elle a été conçue avec l'aide des consommateurs et son ingrédient principal est le houblon Nelson Sauvin. La marque l'a fait goûter en avant-première à des créatifs de Melbourne et de Sydney en août 2008. Après avoir pris note de leurs commentaires, la bière est revenue début 2009 avec un nom, un concept d'étiquette et un goût légèrement différent. À partir de là, Nelson a continué de changer en fonction des commentaires de ses consommateurs. En prenant en compte les avis du public sur la bière et en invitant des artistes à créer des images pour la bouteille, la marque a donné aux consommateurs un sentiment de propriété sur le produit. Le packaging de la bière Nelson a été fabriqué avec la collaboration du duo d'illustrateurs Sonny & Biddy, qui ont eu carte blanche pour créer la première illustration de la bouteille.

MONTEITH'S SINGLE SOURCE

Creative Strategy: Michael Crampin
Creative Direction: Jef Wong
Design Lead: Damian Alexander
Company: Designworks
Country: New Zealand
Category: Beer

GOLD PENTAWARD 2011

Monteith's Single Source is a lager beer from New Zealand that respects tradition—true to the land and its people and batch-brewed with hand-picked ingredients. The black bottle helps to keep the contents fresh by blocking sunlight, but also enables it to stand out from other beers whilst providing a striking counterpoint to the labelling. The signature silhouette was retained to ensure its identification with the Monteith's family of beers. For the launch a special box was designed as a gift presentation for the first 100 bottles produced, all hand-signed and numbered by the brewer and closed with a wax seal.

DOSS BLOCKOS

Creative Direction: Josh Lefers,
Stephen Wools
Design: Kane Marevich
Company: Big Dog Creative
Country: Australia
Category: Beer

SILVER PENTAWARD 2011

Das Lagerbier **Monteith's** Single Source aus Neuseeland respektiert die Tradition – dem Land und seinen Menschen treu, aus handverlesenen Zutaten gebraut. Die schwarze Flasche schützt vor Sonnenlicht und hält den Inhalt länger frisch. Zugleich hebt sie sich so von anderen Biersorten ab und setzt einen spannenden Kontrast zum Etikett. Die charakteristische Silhouette blieb, um die Identifikation mit den Bieren der Monteith-Familie sicherzustellen. Bei Markteinführung wurden die ersten 100 produzierten Flaschen in besonders gestalteten Geschenkkartons verpackt, vom Braumeister handsigniert und nummeriert und mit Wachssiegel verschlossen.

La Single Source de **Monteith's** est une bière blonde néozélandaise qui respecte la tradition (elle est fidèle à la terre et à ses gens), et est brassée par lots avec des ingrédients soigneusement sélectionnés. La bouteille noire aide à conserver la fraîcheur de son contenu en bloquant la lumière du jour, mais permet également au produit de se démarquer des autres bières tout en créant un contraste net avec l'étiquetage. La silhouette caractéristique des bouteilles de la marque a été conservée afin de favoriser l'association du produit à la famille de bières de Monteith's. Pour le lancement, un coffret-cadeau spécial a été conçu pour les 100 premières bouteilles produites, signé et numéroté par le brasseur et fermé par un sceau en cire.

DOLINA

Design: Daniel Morales, Javier Euba
Company: Moruba
Country: Spain
Category: Beer
SILVER PENTAWARD 2014

Dolina, the first artisanal beer from Burgos (Spain), is named after Gran Dolina, one of Europe's foremost archeological sites. Taking this as the design's leitmotif, together with searching and discovery, an interesting experimental result came about in which the consumers themselves are able to make a find. The beer-drinker's reflex scratching at a bottle label resembles the work of archeologists at a dig, but here as the label is scratched away the skull of *Homo heidelbergensis* is revealed. Scratching off the back label reveals this to be the world's most intact fossilized human skull, whose discovery at Dolina proved revolutionary.

Dolina, das erste hausgemachte Bier aus dem spanischen Burgos hat seinen Namen von Gran Dolina, einer der wichtigsten archäologischen Grabungsstätten Europas. Darauf bezieht sich auch das Designleitmotiv: Der Kunde gelangt durch Suchen und Entdecken zu einem interessanten experimentellen Resultat. Das reflexhafte Kratzen vieler Biertrinker am Flaschenetikett ähnelt der Arbeit eines Archäologen bei Ausgrabungen: Wenn man das Etikett abkratzt, stößt man auf den Schädel des *Homo heidelbergensis*. Rubbelt man dann noch die Rückseite frei, erfährt man, dass es sich hier um den am besten erhaltenen fossilen Menschenschädel handelt, dessen Entdeckung in Dolina eine Sensation war.

Dolina, la première bière artisanale fabriquée à Burgos (Espagne), tire son nom de Gran Dolina, l'un des sites archéologiques les plus célèbres d'Europe. Tel est le leitmotiv du design, qui joue avec les notions de fouilles et de découvertes et permet aux consommateurs de faire eux-aussi une trouvaille. Le réflexe qu'un buveur de bière a de gratter l'étiquette de la bouteille s'apparente au travail des archéologues : ici toutefois, c'est le crâne d'un *Homo heidelbergensis* qui apparaît petit à petit. Il s'agit du fossile humain le plus intact au monde qui a été exhumé lors d'une découverte exceptionnelle sur le site de Dolina.

MILLER LITE

Executive Creative Direction:
David Turner, Bruce Duckworth
Creative Direction: Mark Waters
Design: Miles Marshall, David Thompson,
Jennie Spiller, Jamie Nash, Mike Harris
Production: James Norris, Will Rawlings
Illustration: Geoffrey Appleton
Retouching: Peter Ruane
Account Management: Kate Elkins
Company: Turner Duckworth,
London & San Francisco
Country: UK, USA
Category: Beer
GOLD PENTAWARD 2015

Although **Miller Lite** was the original light beer, increased competition from craft beers and a decline in the category as a whole has led to falling sales. A revamp of the packaging was intended to bring back consumers by restoring the historical message that this was a beer with a great taste but only half the calories. Based on its earlier format, the redesigned Miller Lite 1974 heritage can and bottle provided a template for an overall identity that includes tap handles, glassware, special editions and promotional features. Packaging design was also assisted by the redesigned Germanic typography and the beer crest, which promotes the beer's status and high-quality ingredients.

Zwar war **Miller Lite** das erste Light-Bier, doch durch zunehmende Konkurrenz der Craft-Biere und den Rückgang der Sparte insgesamt kam es zu sinkenden Verkaufszahlen. Die Neugestaltung der Verpackung sollte die Konsumenten wieder zurückgewinnen und die historische Botschaft unterstreichen, dass dieses Bier hervorragend schmeckt, aber nur halb so viele Kalorien hat. Die neu gestaltete Miller-Lite-1974-Traditionsdose und -flasche basiert auf der originalen Form und liefert die Vorlage für die gesamte Identität, zu der Zapfhähne, Gläser, Sondereditionen und Werbematerialien gehören. Ergänzt wird die Gestaltung durch die neu designte germanische Typografie und das Bierwappen, den Status und die qualitativ hochwertige Zutaten des Biers bewirbt.

Bien que la **Miller Lite** soit la toute première bière light, la concurrence croissante des bières artisanales et le déclin de cette catégorie dans son ensemble ont causé une chute des ventes. Il fallait renouveler l'emballage pour intéresser les consommateurs en restaurant le message historique, une bière savoureuse avec deux fois moins de calories. Basées sur le format précédent, la canette et la bouteille Miller Lite 1974 ont servi de modèle pour une identité globale qui comprend les manettes de tireuse, les verres, des éditions spéciales et des éléments promotionnels. La typographie germanique et l'écusson, qui vante le statut de la bière et la qualité de ses ingrédients, ont également été revus.

SAN MIGUEL 1516

Creative Direction:
Antonia Hayward, Matt Thompson
Project Direction: Edward Mitchell
Design Direction: Emma Follet
Design: Sarah Bustin, Hayley Barrett
3D Creative Direction:
Laurent Robin-Prevallee
3D Design: Ben Davey
Company: Design Bridge
Country: UK
Category: Beer

SILVER PENTAWARD 2012

San Miguel 1516 is founded on the principles of the Germanic beer purity law of 1516 and is produced only with water, malt, hops and yeast. To avoid confusion with a strong beer and instead convey its purity and carve out a position in the premium beer market, the brewer required an appropriate new packaging design. The bottle's smooth new profile echoes the San Miguel logo and in place of a label "1516" has been formed in the glass itself along with the message "according to the law of purity"—a self-assured bespoke finish to appeal to the brand's consumers. Each bottle carries a red seal, certifying the simplicity of its ingredients.

VICTORIA PALE LAGER

Creative Design: Julian Ditchburn (O-I)
Concept Design: Cowan Design
Company: O-I
Country: USA
Category: Beer

BRONZE PENTAWARD 2012

San Miguel 1516 wird, basierend auf den Prinzipien des deutschen Reinheitsgebots von 1516, nur aus Wasser, Malz, Hopfen und Hefe gebraut. Um sich vom Starkbier abzugrenzen und vor allem die Reinheit des Bieres zu betonen, wünschte die Brauerei ein passendes neues Verpackungsdesign, mit dem man sich eine gute Position im Markt der Premiumbiere erkämpfen wollte. Im glatten, neuen Profil der Flasche klingt das Logo von San Miguel an. Das „1516" erscheint ohne Etikett auf dem Glas selbst, ebenso die Botschaft „Nach dem Reinheitsgebot gebraut". Diese maßgeschneidert selbstbewusste Lösung spricht die Zielgruppe besonders an. Jede Flasche ziert ein rotes Siegel als Zertifikat für die Reinheit seiner Inhaltsstoffe.

San Miguel 1516 est fondée sur les principes de la loi germanique de 1516 sur la pureté de la bière et est produite uniquement avec de l'eau, du malt, du houblon et de la levure. Pour éviter toute confusion avec une bière forte, transmettre l'idée de pureté et se faire une place sur le marché de la bière haut de gamme, le brasseur avait besoin d'une nouvelle bouteille. Son nouveau profil lisse fait écho au logo de San Miguel, et en guise d'étiquette, l'inscription « 1516 » a été travaillée en relief dans le verre avec le message « conformément à la loi sur la pureté ». C'est une touche finale pleine d'assurance pour séduire les consommateurs de la marque. Chaque bouteille est garnie d'un sceau rouge qui certifie la simplicité de ses ingrédients.

GUINNESS AFRICA SPECIAL

Creative Direction: Tim Vary
Design Direction: John Wigham, Phil Dall
Client Services Direction: Debbie Barber
Senior Client Management: Jemima Wilson
Client Management: Molly Thornberry
Production Implementation: Talitha Watson
Company: Design Bridge
Country: UK
Category: Beer
GOLD PENTAWARD 2016

Packaging for this new chill-filtered, ginger-infused stout, aimed at young Africans, had to marry the **Guinness** identity with the bold vibrancy of modern Africa. The bespoke design, based on traditional Ankara wax print fabrics, was created to wrap around the familiar packaging forms. The pattern combines the Swahili symbols for greatness, charisma and leadership with stringed instruments and radiating circles, like a bass bin speaker. The flowing cloth harmonizes with the angle of the harp-strings, with color accentuating the overlaps and set against the black background, like bright fabrics worn on dark African skin. The custom-designed embossed lettering has orange accents to hint at the kick of the ginger.

Die **Guinness**-Identität sollte für ein neues Stout mit der kraftvollen Lebendigkeit des modernen Afrika verschmolzen werden. Kalt gefiltert und mit Ingwer versetzt, richtet sich dieses dunkle Bier an die Jugend Afrikas. Das maßgeschneiderte Design basiert auf traditionellen Batikarbeiten und kleidet die vertrauten Packungsformen. Die Muster zeigen die Suaheli-Symbole für Erhabenheit, Charisma und Führerschaft, kombiniert mit Saiteninstrumenten und strahlenförmigen Kreisen wie Basslautsprechern. Der fließende Stoff harmoniert mit den angewinkelten Harfensaiten. Die Farben akzentuieren Überlappungen und sind gegen den schwarzen Hintergrund abgesetzt, wie leuchtende Stoffe auf dunkler afrikanischer Haut. Die eigens erstellte geprägte Schrift hat orangefarbene Akzente und verweist damit auf den Ingwerkick.

L'emballage de cette nouvelle stout filtrée à froid et infusée de gingembre, qui cible les jeunes Africains, devait marier l'identité de **Guinness** et la vitalité bouillonnante de l'Afrique moderne. Le concept, basé sur les tissus de cire traditionnels Ankara, a été créé pour épouser les formes familières de la bouteille. Le motif contient les symboles swahilis de la grandeur, du charisme et du leadership, avec des instruments à corde et des cercles concentriques tels des ondes de basse. Le tissu fluide suit l'angle des cordes de la harpe, et la couleur accentue les superpositions sur le fond noir. Le lettrage embossé est souligné d'orange pour évoquer le piquant du gingembre.

HAMOVNIKI BEER

Design: DDH creative team
Company: Dutch Design House
Country: Russia
Category: Beer

BRONZE PENTAWARD 2013

ANHEUSER-BUSCH INBEV BUDWEISER

Managing Direction: Sara Hyman
Creative Direction: Tosh Hall
Design Direction: Daniel D'Arcy,
Paul Sieka, Andy Baron
Company: Jones Knowles Ritchie
Country: USA
Category: Beer
SILVER PENTAWARD 2016

To reinvigorate a brand as well known as **Budweiser** to catch the attention of consumers today meant a makeover for its screw-top aluminum bottles to produce a fresh and vibrant redesign that drinkers would want to be seen enjoying. By deconstructing the elements of the beer's central iconography, the label, and then re-imagining them in a bold contemporary style, a striking new design was obtained using all-new custom typography which expressed the desired balance between old values and new.

ANHEUSER-BUSCH INBEV BUDWEISER

Design: Tosh Hall, Daniel D'Arcy,
Saskia Naidu, Ian Brignell
Managing Direction: Sara Hyman
Company: Jones Knowles Ritchie
Country: USA
Category: Beer
SILVER PENTAWARD 2015

Um eine so bekannte Marke wie **Budweiser** neu zu beleben und die Aufmerksamkeit heutiger Verbraucher zu wecken, muss man das Äußere gründlich überarbeiten. So gelang für die Aluflaschen mit Schraubverschluss ein frisches und lebendiges Neudesign, das die Konsumenten auch wirklich schätzen. Dazu wurden Elemente der zentralen Bierikonografie und das Etikett dekonstruiert und in einem mutigen, modernen Stil neu aufgesetzt. Das ergab ein bestechendes Design mit völlig neuer spezieller Typografie, was die gewünschte Balance zwischen alten und neuen Werten ausdrückt.

Pour redynamiser une marque aussi connue que **Budweiser** et attirer l'attention des consommateurs actuels, il fallait rhabiller les bouteilles en aluminium à bouchon vissé et leur donner un look que les consommateurs seraient fiers de tenir en main. C'est en déconstruisant l'élément central de l'iconographie de la bière, l'étiquette, et en lui conférant un style contemporain qu'est né ce nouveau concept, avec une typographie qui exprime l'équilibre souhaité entre les valeurs d'antan et celles actuelles.

ST STEFANUS

Design: Hamish Shand,
Chris Noakes, David Beard
Company: Brandhouse
Country: UK
Category: Beer

GOLD PENTAWARD 2013

GOLD MINE BEER
Creative Direction: Andrey Kugaevskikh
Design: Sergey Gerasimenko
Company: Svoe Mnenie
Country: Russia
Category: Beer
GOLD PENTAWARD 2014

JAW DROP COOLERS

Design: Laurie Millotte,
Bernie Hadley-Beauregard
Illustration: Gary Bullock
3D: Paul Sherstobitoff
Company: Brandever
Country: Canada
Category: Ciders, low-alcohol drinks

BRONZE PENTAWARD 2012

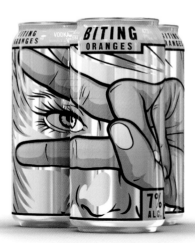

LT WATERS
BEACH, SPORT, NIGHT

Design: Xavier Corretje, Ana Hernando, Bruno Andrez
Company: Corretjé Comunicació Gràfica
Country: Spain
Category: Ciders, low-alcohol drinks

GOLD PENTAWARD 2010

CHIYONOKAME SOURYU

Creative Direction/Art Direction/Design: Yoshiki Uchida
Design: Shohei Onodera
Art: Manuela Paul-Cavallier
Calligraphy: Ukyo Kamigori
Photography: Takaomi Watanabe
Company: Cosmos
Country: Japan
Category: Ciders, low-alcohol drinks

SILVER PENTAWARD 2016

BROOKS DRY CIDER

Creative Direction/Design: Tosh Hall
Strategy: Allison Hung
Illustration: Luke Dixon
Client: Brooks Bennett
Company: Hall
Country: USA
Category: Ciders, low-alcohol drinks
GOLD PENTAWARD 2015

Die Weine von **JAQK Cellars** sind das Resultat einer Zusammenarbeit zwischen den Gründern von Hatch Design und einer renommierten Winzerei aus Napa Valley. Die Buchstabenfolge JAQK bezieht sich auf die Bildkarten in einem Skatspiel (englisch Jack, Ace, Queen und King), und JAQK Cellars hat sich als neue Firma das Spielen zum Motto gemacht. Die Namen und Designs aller acht Weine aus dem Einführungsangebot beschwören Reiz und Raffinesse in der Welt der Glücksspiele: High Roller (Glücksspieler), Soldiers of Fortune (die Buben), Black Clover (Kreuzkarten), Pearl Handle (der Revolver, der die Spielsaloons zähmte), 22 Black (Roulette), Bone Dance (Würfelspiel), Her Majesty (die Königin) und Charmed (je mehr Glück, desto besser).

Les vins des **caves JAQK** sont le fruit d'une collaboration entre les fondateurs de Hatch Designs et un viticulteur renommé de Napa Valley. Baptisées d'après les valets, as, reines et rois (Jack, Ace, Queen et King) d'un jeu de cartes, les caves JAQK sont une nouvelle entreprise qui a pris le jeu pour thème central. Les noms et designs des huit vins de la gamme inaugurale évoquent le style et la sophistication du monde du jeu : High Roller (grand parieur), Soldiers of Fortune (les valets), Black Clover (trèfle), Pearl Handle (le nom du pistolet Derringer qui faisait la loi dans les saloons), 22 Black (roulette), Bone Dance (dés), Her Majesty (la reine), et Charmed (pour la chance).

JAQK CELLARS

Creative Direction:
Katie Jain, Joel Templin
Design: Eszter T. Clark, Ryan Meis
Company: Hatch Design
Country: USA
Category: Wines
GOLD PENTAWARD 2009

JAQK Cellars wines are the offspring of a collaboration between Hatch Design founders and a renowned Napa Valley winemaker. Named after the Jack, Ace, Queen, and King in a deck of cards, JAQK Cellars is a new company dedicated to play. The names and designs of all eight wines in the inaugural offering evoke the allure and sophistication of the world of gaming: High Roller, Soldiers of Fortune (the Jacks), Black Clover (clubs), Pearl Handle (the derringer that tamed the gambling saloons), 22 Black (roulette), Bone Dance (dice), Her Majesty (the Queen), and Charmed (the luckier the better).

Paperboy is about as green as it's possible to make a wine bottle. Each one is made from compressed recycled paper, printed with natural inks and with a recyclable sleeve inside just as you find in a wine-box. The bottles are nevertheless rigid and strong, even ice bucket-safe for three hours, and require only 15 percent of the energy normal bottles take to produce. They weigh only an ounce when empty and so save a considerable amount of energy in shipping. In aiming to be the most environmentally friendly wine around, the bottle's form targets those who are already aware while the brand name and retro graphics are directed to early adopters.

Die Weinflasche **Paperboy** wird so grün wie nur irgend möglich produziert. Jede Flasche besteht aus gepresstem Recyclingpapier, bedruckt mit naturbelassener Tinte, darin eine recycelbaren Hülle wie in einem normalen Weinkarton. Die Flaschen sind dennoch stabil und widerstandsfähig. Man kann sie sogar bis zu drei Stunden ins Eisfach stellen. Die Herstellung benötigt nur 15 Prozent der für normale Flaschen verbrauchten Energie. Leer wiegen sie gerade 30 Gramm und sparen damit bei der Auslieferung beträchtlich Energie. Die Zielsetzung lautete, der umweltfreundlichste Wein überhaupt zu sein. Dafür richtet sich die Form der Flasche an jene, die bereits umweltbewusst sind, während Markenname und Retro-Grafik sich an die Early Adopters wenden.

Paperboy est aussi écologique que peut l'être une bouteille de vin. Chacune est fabriquée en papier recyclé, imprimée avec des encres naturelles et accompagnée d'un manchon recyclable comme ceux présents dans les coffrets de vins. Les bouteilles sont toutefois rigides et résistantes, peuvent rester plongées dans un seau à glace pendant trois heures et ne demandent que 15 pour cent de l'énergie habituellement nécessaire pour fabriquer des bouteilles standard. Leur poids à vide est de 30 grammes, ce qui réduit l'énergie dépensée en transport. Visant à être le vin le plus respectueux de l'environnement, la forme de la bouteille convainc ceux déjà responsables, alors que le nom et le graphisme rétro parlent aux acheteurs qui veulent s'aventurer.

TRUETT HURST PAPERBOY WINE

Art Direction: Kevin Shaw
Design: Cosimo Surace
Company: Stranger & Stranger
Country: UK
Category: Wines
GOLD PENTAWARD 2014

MAQUINA & TABLA GRAND CRU & VINS DU VILLAGE LINES

Design: Joan Josep Bertran
Illustration: Error Design
Company: JJ Bertran Studio
Country: Spain
Category: Wines

GOLD PENTAWARD 2016

These **Maquina & Tabla** wines present graphic portrayals of the struggle between man and nature. The look and feel of each bottle rests on the perceived quality of the print finish on the labels, with the apparent sentimentality of old-style engraving being abruptly offset by a modern take on the macabre. The range is divided into two distinct varieties, with the single vineyard wines being represented by an animal native to that area and hence significant to the people living there too, while the vins du village reflect their combined but related origins in illustrations of the landscapes where these vineyards are found, such as arid settings for the D. O. Toro or the Sierra de Gredos for the D. O. Castilla.

Die Weine von **Maquina & Tabla** werden anhand der Darstellungen vom Kampf zwischen Mensch und Natur präsentiert. Aussehen und Eindruck jeder Flasche basieren auf der Qualität des Etikettendrucks. Erkennbar sentimental greifen sie altmodische Kupferstiche auf, in denen abrupt moderne Spielarten des Makabren erkennbar werden. Das Sortiment teilt sich in zwei Varianten auf. Die Weine der einzelnen Weingärten sind durch ein in dieser Gegend beheimatetes Tier dargestellt, das für dortige Menschen bedeutsam ist. Vins du Village hingegen spiegeln durch Illustrationen der Landschaften die kombinierten, aber nicht zusammenhängenden Ursprünge wider, in denen sich diese Anbaugebiete befinden, z. B. die trockenen Gegenden für D. O. Toro oder die Sierra de Gredos für D. O. Castilla.

Les vins **Maquina & Tabla** offrent une représentation graphique de la lutte entre l'homme et la nature. La personnalité de chaque bouteille repose sur le contraste brutal entre la sentimentalité apparente de la gravure ancienne et une nouvelle interprétation du macabre. La gamme se divise en deux variétés. Les vins provenant d'un vignoble unique sont représentés par un animal originaire de cette région, qui a donc une signification pour les habitants, tandis que les vins du village évoquent leurs origines mixtes à l'aide des paysages de ces vignobles, comme le paysage aride du D. O. Toro ou la sierra de Gredos pour le D. O. Castilla.

BARCELONA BRANDS
PORRÓN MOLÓN

Design: Series Nemo team
Company: Series Nemo
Country: Spain
Category: Wines

SILVER PENTAWARD 2016

Porrón Molón is a Mediterranean way of sharing, derived from the use of the historic *porrón* which let people drink a stream of wine flowing from a spout with no need for their mouth to touch the vessel, which also served as the bottle. This hygienic custom was common in the Spanish Mediterranean from the late 14th century onwards but has now mostly fallen into disuse. Its resurrection here involves modern craftsmanship to update this tradition, employing a smooth design and different materials (ceramic and cork) alongside technical improvements (an anti-drip feature) to produce a versatile object which offers a clean and simple drinking experience.

Porrón Molón ist eine mediterrane Weise des gemeinsamen Teilens, abgeleitet vom historischen *porrón*: Mit diesem Krug labt man sich gemeinsam an einem Wein, ohne mit den Lippen das Gefäß zu berühren, das gleichzeitig als Flasche dient. Diese hygienische Sitte war seit Ende des 14. Jahrhunderts an der spanischen Mittelmeerküste üblich, ist aber heute weitgehend außer Mode. Seine Wiederauferstehung beinhaltet moderne Handwerkskunst, um diese Tradition ins Heute zu bringen. Hier werden glattes Design in verschiedenen Materialien eingesetzt (Keramik und Kork) und technische Verbesserungen (Tropfschutz) eingeführt, sodass ein vielseitiges Objekt entsteht, das eine saubere und einfache Trinkerfahrung verschafft.

Porrón Molón est une tradition méditerranéenne de partage, dérivée de l'utilisation du *porrón* : les convives boivent un jet de vin coulant du bec du récipient, qui sert aussi de bouteille, sans le toucher avec la bouche. Cette coutume hygiénique était répandue dans la Méditerranée espagnole du XIVe siècle, mais est aujourd'hui pratiquement tombée en désuétude. Ici, sa renaissance s'appuie sur l'artisanat moderne pour actualiser cette tradition à l'aide d'un concept épuré et de différents matériaux (céramique et liège) alliés à des améliorations techniques (antigoutte) pour obtenir un objet polyvalent qui offre un geste de boisson propre et simple.

Tyto alba
PORTUGAL
VINHAS PROTEGIDAS

COMPANHIA
DAS LEZÍRIAS

Tyto alba
PORTUGAL
VINHAS PROTEGIDAS
Tinto, Red Wine
2011

COMPANHIA DAS LEZÍRIAS

TYTO ALBA

Art Direction: Rita Rivotti
Design: Rita Rivotti, Sara Correia
Box Design: Rita Rivotti,
Companhia das Lezírias
Client: Companhia das Lezírias
Company: Rita Rivotti – Wine Branding & Design
Country: Portugal
Category: Wines
SILVER PENTAWARD 2015

Companhia das Lezírias has long been an active supporter of environmental research, including the TytoTagus project which manages the distribution of barn owl nesting-boxes in forests in Portugal. The region now has the largest known concentration in the world, making the barn owl the ideal symbol for the estate's wine. The distinctive forward-looking owl face stares out from the label, as the "face" of the wine, and the name comes from the bird's Latin name. Moreover, the traditional wooden box used for wines was modified so that it doubles as an actual nesting-box, which can be put up in the garden. This highly individual design stands out strongly in the market while conveying clear and engaging messages about the environment.

Companhia das Lezírias unterstützt schon lange aktiv Forschungen zur Umwelt. Dazu gehört auch das Projekt TytoTagus, das sich um die Verteilung von Nistkästen für Schleiereulen in den Wäldern Portugals kümmert. Diese Region beherbergt jetzt die größte bekannte Schleiereulenpopulation der Welt, was sie zum idealen Symbol für dieses Weingut macht. Das markante Eulengesicht auf dem Etikett schaut einen als das „Gesicht" des Weins direkt an. Der Name leitet sich von der lateinischen Bezeichnung des Vogels ab. Überdies wurde der traditionelle Holzkasten für Weine so modifiziert, dass er im Garten tatsächlich als Nistkasten aufgehängt werden kann. Dieses höchst individuelle Design sticht auf dem Markt besonders hervor und vermittelt klare, anregende Botschaften über die Umwelt.

Companhia das Lezírias soutient depuis longtemps la recherche environnementale, notamment à travers le projet TytoTagus qui gère la distribution de nichoirs pour chouettes effraies dans les forêts du Portugal. La région possède aujourd'hui la plus grande concentration connue de ces oiseaux dans le monde, ce qui fait de la chouette effraie le symbole idéal du vin du domaine. L'oiseau de l'étiquette regarde par le trou et devient le « visage » du vin, baptisé d'après le nom latin de la chouette effraie. De plus, le coffret traditionnel en bois a été modifié de façon à pouvoir être accroché dans le jardin et servir de nichoir. Ce concept très individuel se distingue sur le marché tout en communiquant un message clair et convaincant sur l'environnement.

FRITZ MÜLLER

Design: Schmidt/Thurner/von Keisenberg
Büro für visuelle Gestaltung
Photography: Anja Prestel
Company: Fritz Müller
Country: Germany
Category: Wines

GOLD PENTAWARD 2010

VIVANZA

Art Direction/Design: Eduardo del Fraile
Company: Eduardo del Fraile
Country: Spain
Category: Wines

BRONZE PENTAWARD 2010

PURE DROPS

Design: Bob Studio design team
Company: Bob Studio
Country: Greece
Category: Wines

SILVER PENTAWARD 2014

LONGVIEW VINEYARD
W. WAGTAIL

Creative Direction: Anthony De Leo
Design: Shane Keane
Company: Voice
Country: Australia
Category: Wines
SILVER PENTAWARD 2012

BODEGAS CARCHELO
ALTICO, CARCHELO, VEDRÉ

Design: Eduardo del Fraile
Company: Eduardo del Fraile
Country: Spain
Category: Wines

SILVER PENTAWARD 2009

UPROOT WINE

Creative Direction: David Turner,
Bruce Duckworth, Sarah Moffat
Design Direction: Robert Williams,
Rebecca Au Williams
Design: Mike Gertz, Georgiana Ng
Production Direction: Craig Snelgrove
Company: Turner Duckworth,
London & San Francisco
Country: UK, USA
Category: Wines

SILVER PENTAWARD 2014

CRIANZAS Y VIOEDOS R. REVERTE

Creative Direction: Alexey Fadeev
Art Direction: Alexandr Zagorskiy
Illustration: Vadim Bryksin
Calligraphy: Julia Zhdanova
Design: Alexandr Kishchenko
Copywriting: Ekaterina Lavrova
Company: Depot WPF
Country: Russia
Category: Wines

BRONZE PENTAWARD 2014

À LA PETITE FERME

Design: Erika Barbieri, Henrik Olssøn
Company: Designers Journey
Country: Norway
Category: Wines

BRONZE PENTAWARD 2009

TENTENUBLO
ESCONDITE DEL ARDACHO

Creative Direction: Sergio Aja
Design: Raúl Barrio
Company: Calcco
Country: Spain
Category: Wines

GOLD PENTAWARD 2015

GIGANTE
ROSSO DEL VIGNETO NUOVO

Creative Direction: Mirco Onesti
Structural Design: Gustavo Messias
Graphics: Fiona Martin, Luca Mazzoleni
Illustration: Fiona Martin
Photo Retouching: Antonella Iozzolino
Photography: Thomas Libis
Company: Reverse Innovation
Country: Italy
Category: Wine as bag-in-box
BRONZE PENTAWARD 2015

VERNISSAGE

CHARDONNAY
VIOGNIER

VIN DE PAYS D'OC

PRODUCT OF FRANCE

VERNISSAGE
Design: Sofia Blomberg, Takis Soldatos
Company: Oenoforos
Country: Sweden
Category: Wine as bag-in-box
GOLD PENTAWARD 2010

RAWAL GIN

Company: Dorian
Country: Spain
Category: Spirits

GOLD PENTAWARD 2015

In creating a distinctive design to package this gin made by Pesca Salada, a small bar in Barcelona, it was important to mark it off from other brands found in supermarkets and to instill some association with the bar, the only place where it's available. As the name suggests, "salt fish" used to be sold on the premises, and since the bar has kept this maritime theme the bottle's design connects the liquid content with the image of the swimmer on the outside. The production was done by screen-printing the bottle itself, giving a better result than using a transparent label, and as the bottle empties and the level of the gin drops a visual game results according to the swimmer's position.

Dieser Gin wird von Pesca Salada produziert, einer kleinen Bar in Barcelona. Für das charakteristische Design war es wichtig, ihn von Supermarktmarken abzugrenzen und die Verbindung zur Bar zu suggerieren, denn nur dort kann man ihn kaufen. Wie der Name schon sagt, wurden in diesem Haus „Salzfische" verkauft. Weil die Bar dieses maritime Thema bewahrte, schlägt das Flaschendesign mit dem Bild des Schwimmers die Brücke zum flüssigen Inhalt. Die Grafik wurde im Siebdruckverfahren außen auf die Flasche gebracht, was bessere Ergebnisse liefert als transparente Etiketten. Beim Leeren der Flasche verringert sich der Ginspiegel und spielt optisch mit der Position des Schwimmers.

Afin de créer un concept distinctif pour ce gin fait par Pesca Salada, un petit bar de Barcelone, il était important de le distinguer des autres marques vendues en supermarché et de l'associer au bar, le seul endroit où il est disponible. Comme le nom le suggère, du « poisson salé » était jadis vendu dans ce local, et puisque le bar a conservé ce thème marin, la bouteille fait le lien entre le contenu liquide et l'image de nageur sur l'extérieur. L'illustration est sérigraphiée directement sur le verre, ce qui donne un meilleur résultat qu'une étiquette transparente, et au fur et à mesure que la bouteille se vide, le niveau de gin qui descend crée un jeu visuel avec la position du nageur.

ALKKEMIST

Design: Series Nemo team
Company: Series Nemo
Country: Spain
Category: Spirits
SILVER PENTAWARD 2014

ABSOLUT VODKA
ABSOLUT CRAFT
BARTENDER'S COLLECTION

Executive Client Direction: Jonas Andersson
Design Direction: Henrik Billqvist
Client Direction: Felicia Leksell, Alfred Alfred
Client Management: Britt-Marie Möller
Project Management: Jonas Westius (No Picnic)
Creative Direction: Thomas Schaad
Industrial Design: Urban Ahlgren (No Picnic)
Client: The Absolut Company
Global Direction Design Strategy: Anna Kamjou
Senior Management Global on Premise Strategy:
Miranda Dickson
Global Management Design Strategy:
Caroline Mörnås
Company: Brand Union
Country: Sweden
Category: Spirits
GOLD PENTAWARD 2013

When **Absolut** wanted to raise its profile amongst bartenders around the world, and to promote itself as an inspiration for creating cocktails, an elegant design was settled on which reflected the focus and craftsmanship of the mixologist Nick Strangeway. The strong silhouette of the bottle recalls the brand's heritage and expertise in distillation, as is also stated by the alchemical symbol positioned at the neck. The color coating on the glass is inspired by 17th-century apothecary jars and also serves to protect the natural ingredients. The design clearly differentiates this range as something new and distinct from Absolut.

Absolut schickte sich an, unter den Barkeepern weltweit sein Profil zu schärfen und sich als Inspiration für die Kreation von Cocktails ins Spiel zu bringen. Dazu entschied man sich für ein elegantes Design, das die Kunst des Mixologen Nick Strangeway reflektieren und fokussieren sollte. Die kraftvolle Silhouette der Flasche ruft Erinnerungen an das Erbe der Marke und deren Expertise im Destillieren hervor. Das wird außerdem im alchemistischen Symbol am Flaschenhals aufgegriffen. Der Farbüberzug des Glases ist von den Apothekergefäßen des 17. Jahrhunderts inspiriert und dient ebenfalls dem Schutz der natürlichen Zutaten. Das Design hebt sich eindeutig als etwas Neues und im Sortiment von Absolut Einzigartiges ab.

Quand **Absolut** a décidé de se faire valoir auprès des barmans de la planète et de s'afficher comme une inspiration à l'élaboration de cocktails, la marque a misé sur un design élégant reflétant l'approche et le savoir-faire du mixologue Nick Strangeway. La silhouette franche de la bouteille rappelle l'héritage et l'expertise en matière de distillation, comme l'indique aussi le symbole alchimique sur le goulot. Le verre teinté rappelle les flacons d'apothicaire du XVIIᵉ siècle, tout en protégeant les ingrédients naturels de la lumière. Le design crée la nouveauté avec cette offre inédite signée Absolut.

Die Hauptproduktlinie von Karloff nennt sich **Tatratea**. Das sind aus Tee hergestellte Kräuterliköre, für die eine neue Flasche geschaffen werden sollte, bei der ein moderner Look mit traditionellen Elementen kombiniert wird. Beim Design ging man von einfachen und ursprünglichen Formen aus, ergänzt durch einen übergreifenden, vom slowakischen Tatra-Gebirge abgeleiteten Namen sowie lokale Traditionen. Die Tatratea-Flasche bekam eine Form wie eine Thermosflasche. Das darauf abgebildete große T wird aus Elementen geformt, die aus den slawischen Symbolen für den Zyklus des Lebens, Liebe und Glück sowie traditionellen slowakischen Künsten bestehen. Die Farben werden je nach Geschmacksvariante in einer passenden Tönung direkt auf die Flasche gedruckt.

Pour sa gamme principale, les liqueurs à base de thé **Tatratea**, Karloff souhaitait créer une nouvelle bouteille combinant un look moderne et des éléments traditionnels. Pour le design, les critères de départ étaient une forme simple et originale, un nom emprunté aux montagnes Tatras, et la tradition locale. La bouteille Tatratea a donc été dotée de la forme d'une gourde isotherme, avec un grand T composé d'éléments inspirés par les symboles slaves du cercle de la vie, de l'amour, du bonheur et de l'artisanat. L'impression est faite directement sur la bouteille, avec une palette de couleurs étudiée pour chaque parfum.

TATRATEA
HERBAL LIQUEURS

Creative Direction/Graphic Design:
Juraj Demovic (Pergamen Trnava)
Concept/Graphic Design:
Livia Lorinczova (Pergamen Trnava)
Product Creation:
Jan Semanak, MD (Karloff)
Photography: Jakub Dvorak
(Pergamen Trnava)
Company: Karloff
Country: Slovakia
Category: Spirits

GOLD PENTAWARD 2010

For its main product range, **Tatratea** tea-based liqueurs, Karloff wished to create a new bottle combining a modern look and traditional elements. The design criteria started with a simple and original shape, a global name taken from the Tatra Mountains, and local tradition. The Tatratea bottle was thus given a thermos-flask shape together with a large initial T made out of elements inspired by Slavic symbols of the circle of life, love, and happiness, and traditional Slovak crafts. Colour-printed directly on to the bottle, in an appropriate color scheme for all flavor variations.

TWO JAMES
Art Direction: Kevin Shaw
Design: Cosimo Surace
Company: Stranger & Stranger
Country: UK
Category: Spirits
SILVER PENTAWARD 2014

PAZO DE VALDOMIÑO
Design: Series Nemo team
Company: Series Nemo
Country: Spain
Category: Spirits
SILVER PENTAWARD 2011

AYAKIKU SHUZO HONTAKACHU

Client: Ayakiku Shuzo
Brand Management: Miyatake Kazutoshi
Design: Kuroyanagi Jun
Printing Direction: Nakayama Hideki
Company: Kuroyanagi Jun
Country: Japan
Category: Spirits
BRONZE PENTAWARD 2014

GRATON DISTILLING COMPANY
BENHAM'S GIN

Design: Stranger & Stranger
Company: Stranger & Stranger
Country: UK
Category: Spirits
SILVER PENTAWARD 2016

SHIXINTANG
NATIONAL PRECIOUSNESS
NATIONAL STANDARD

Design: Liang Wenfeng design team
Company: China (Shenzhen)
Superman Valley Marketing
Country: China
Category: Spirits
SILVER PENTAWARD 2016

VL92 GIN

Design: Sietze Kalkwijk, Rick de Zwart
Company: Rare Fruits Council
Country: Netherlands
Category: Spirits
BRONZE PENTAWARD 2013

TANQUERAY NO. TEN

Executive Creative Direction: Graham Shearsby
Creative Direction: Emma Follett
3D Creative Direction: Laurent Robin-Prevallee
3D Design: Ben Davey (senior), Jiah Lee
Realization: Ed Mitchell
Creative Direction Brand Language: Holly Kielty
Client Direction: Claire Riley (senior), Debbie Barber
Client: Jeremy Lindley, Montserrat De Rojas (Diageo)
Company: Design Bridge
Country: UK
Category: Spirits
GOLD PENTAWARD 2014

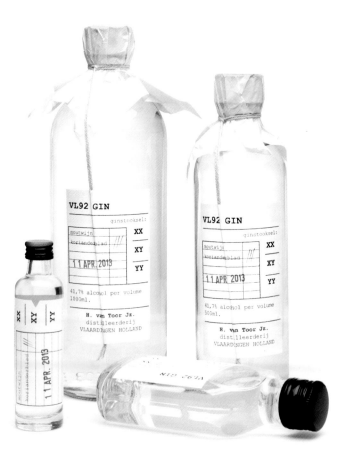

DISTILLERIE DEINLEIN 8TH TRIBE

Creative Direction: Nigel Kuzimski
Design: Monique Pilley
Company: Curious Design
Country: New Zealand
Category: Spirits

SILVER PENTAWARD 2010

THE KRAKEN

Design: Kevin Shaw
Company: Stranger & Stranger
Country: UK
Category: Spirits

SILVER PENTAWARD 2010

BEEFEATER 24

Design: Graham Shearsby, Antonia Hayward,
Laurent Robin-Prevalle, Claire Dale, Emma Warner
Company: Design Bridge
Country: UK
Category: Spirits

SILVER PENTAWARD 2009

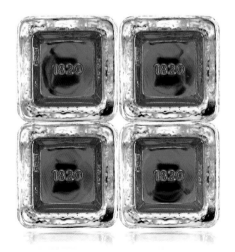

BERRY BROS. & RUDD
Nº3

Design: David Beard,
Pip Dale, Bronwen Edwards,
Keely Jackman
Company: Brandhouse
Country: UK
Category: Spirits

GOLD PENTAWARD 2011

SKYY SPIRITS EL ESPOLÓN

Executive Creative Direction:
Nicolas Aparicio
Design: Tony Rastatter,
Anastasia Laksmi (senior designer)
Company: Landor Associates
Country: USA
Category: Spirits
BRONZE PENTAWARD 2011

YUN JIU

Design: Mercury Team
Company: Shenzhen Baixinglong
Creative Packaging
Country: China
Category: Spirits
BRONZE PENTAWARD 2016

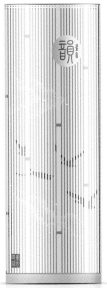

JACK DANIEL'S

Creative Direction: Roger Akroyd
Design Direction: Barry Gillibrand
Account Direction: Charlie Bosworth
Production Direction: Andrew Smith
Production Development:
Joey Schmissrauter, Chris Hallam
Company: Mayday
Country: UK
Category: Limited editions,
limited series, event creations
GOLD PENTAWARD 2009

The main thrust of this project's brief was to strengthen the brand's design presence, and aim to become associated with "best in class" design. Specific aims for the **Jack Daniel's** Mayday packaging within this framework were to maintain and reassert the brand's premium pricing and brand image, and, moreover, to reinforce the brand's iconic status and successfully cut through to consumers in a competitive and cluttered environment.

Die Haupttriebkraft für dieses Projekt-Briefing war es, die Designpräsenz der Marke zu stärken: Sie sollte mit einem „Best in class"-Design verknüpft werden. Die speziellen Ziele für die Mayday-Verpackung von **Jack Daniel's** innerhalb dieses Rahmens lauteten, die Preisgestaltung und das Markenimage dieser Premium-Marke zu bewahren und ihr erneut Geltung zu verschaffen. Obendrein sollte der Kultstatus der Marke verstärkt und die Konsumenten in einem hart umkämpften Umfeld mit Überangebot direkt erreicht werden.

L'idée maîtresse de ce projet était de renforcer la présence de la marque sur le terrain du design, et d'être ainsi associée aux meilleurs dans ce domaine. Les objectifs spécifiques du packaging que l'agence Mayday a créé pour **Jack Daniel's** étaient en outre de réaffirmer le prix et l'image de la marque, de renforcer son statut emblématique et d'arriver à atteindre les consommateurs dans un environnement concurrentiel et encombré.

JA

Te

SOU

WH

DISTIL

JACK DA

LEM MO

LYNCHBUF

ES

TENNESSEE

Jack Daniel

NOT JUST A BARREL-OUR -BARREL-

An important part of making our quality whiskey is making a quality barrel. That's why we devote the same care and attention to barrel making as we do to making and maturing our charcoal mellowed sipping whiskey. We start by selecting the very best white oak for the barrel staves. Our craftsmen fit the staves together by hand then carefully toast and char the inside of the barrel to caramelize the wood's natural sugars. It's from the toasted oak the whiskey draws its rich amber color, distinctive flavor and finish. While some are content to store their whiskey in used barrel's, Jack Daniel's only entrusts its slowly mellowed whiskey to new oak.

The barrel's quality is so important to us that we're the only distiller that goes to the extra effort and expense to craft our own.

J&B Rare Scotch Blend Whisky kam Mitte des 19. Jahrhunderts in London zur Welt, etwa zur gleichen Zeit, als in der Stadt Tätowierungen bei Bewohnern aller Schichten in Mode kamen – von Seeleuten bis in die oberen Klassen, selbst bei König Edward VII. Um die Londoner Wurzeln dieses geistreichen Getränks zu würdigen, ließ J&B tatsächlich 25 Flaschen tätowieren. Um die Illusion noch mehr zu vervollkommnen, wurden sie zuerst in eine hautfarbene Latexhülle eingewickelt – ähnlich jener, die man bei der Ausbildung von Tätowierern nutzt. Der Pariser Tätowierkünstler Sébastien Mathieu ging dann an die Arbeit, ohne zu ahnen, wie schwer seine Aufgabe war: Denn an jeder Flasche saß er etwa 20 Stunden. Hier wurde ein einfaches Grunddesign eingesetzt, doch jede Flasche ist ein Unikat.

Au milieu du XIXᵉ siècle, le whisky **J&B Rare Scotch** a vu le jour à Londres ; à cette époque, les tatouages ont commencé à devenir célèbres en ville, des marins aux classes supérieures, y compris le propre Edward VII. Pour célébrer les origines londoniennes du spiritueux, J&B a commandé 25 bouteilles véritablement tatouées. Elles ont d'abord été recouvertes d'un film en latex, comme celui utilisé par les tatoueurs, de couleur chair pour parfaire l'illusion. Le tatoueur parisien Sébastien Mathieu s'est ensuite attelé à la tâche, loin d'imaginer la difficulté de l'ouvrage : chaque bouteille a demandé environ 20 heures de travail. Le design choisi est simple, mais chaque bouteille est unique.

J&B
REAL TATTOOED BOTTLES

Chief Creative Officer: Kay Hes
Chief Salientist Officer: William Black
Tattoo: Sébastien Mathieu
Company: Button Button
Country: France
Category: Limited editions, limited series, event creations

GOLD PENTAWARD 2014
SLEEVER PRIZE

J&B Rare Scotch blend whisky was born in London in the mid-19th century, about the same time that tattoos began to spread through the city, from sailors to the upper classes and even Edward VII. To mark the spirit's London origins in a memorable way J&B commissioned 25 bottles to be tattooed for real. Firstly, they were covered with a latex skin, like that used in tattoo practice and the color of human skin to highlight the illusion. Paris-based tattooist Sébastien Mathieu then set to work, little knowing how hard it would be: each bottle took around 20 hours to be completed. A single basic design was used, but each bottle is unique.

This summer design to reinvigorate **Budweiser** in the eyes of today's consumers entailed a special partnership with the National Parks Foundation and led to a truly colossal design, matching the ultimate symbol of freedom with this great American beer. Both the Statue of Liberty and Budweiser were founded in 1876 and the design was able to exploit this within the newly simplified visual identity. Bold graphics sit against a field of red and white stripes, with Lady Liberty herself as the star, portrayed by renowned French illustrator Malika Favre in a nod to the statue's French origins. On release, Bud Liberty stemmed the brand's North American sales decline for the first time in over a decade.

Um **Budweiser** im Bewusstsein heutiger Verbraucher neu zu beleben, greift dieses Sommerdesign eine spezielle Partnerschaft mit der National Parks Foundation auf. Als Ergebnis bringt ein wahrlich kolossales Design das ultimative Symbol der Freiheit mit diesem großartigen amerikanischen Bier zusammen. Sowohl die Freiheitsstatue als auch Budweiser wurden 1876 gegründet. Im Design wird beides in einer neuen vereinfachten visuellen Identität zusammengeführt. Kraftvolle Grafiken liegen auf einem roten und weißen Streifenfeld. Lady Liberty höchstpersönlich ist der Star, porträtiert von der bekannten französischen Illustratorin Malika Favre mit Referenz auf ihre französischen Wurzeln. Bud Liberty bremste bei seinem Erscheinen den Rückgang der Verkäufe in Nordamerika erstmals seit einem Jahrzehnt aus.

Cette action estivale destinée à redynamiser l'image de **Budweiser** dans l'esprit des consommateurs a demandé un partenariat spécial avec la National Parks Foundation et généré un concept véritablement colossal, associant le symbole de liberté par excellence à cette grande bière américaine. Cette identité visuelle simplifiée s'inspire du fait que la Statue de la Liberté et Budweiser sont toutes deux nées en 1876. La figure se détache sur un fond de rayures rouges et blanches, création de la célèbre illustratrice française Malika Favre en référence à l'origine française de la statue. La sortie de Bud Liberty a enrayé le déclin des ventes nord-américaines de la marque pour la première fois en plus d'une décennie.

ANHEUSER-BUSCH INBEV BUDWEISER LIBERTY

Managing Direction: Sara Hyman
Creative Direction: Tosh Hall
Global Account Direction: Matt Bevington
Design Direction: Daniel D'Arcy
Account Direction: Phil Buhagiar
Design: Gus Cook
Illustration: Malika Favre
Company: Jones Knowles Ritchie
Country: USA
Category: Limited editions, limited series, event creations

GOLD PENTAWARD 2016

COCA-COLA
SUMMER 2010 PACKAGING

Creative Direction: David Turner, Bruce Duckworth, Sarah Moffat
Design: Emily Charette, Josh Michels
Design Direction: Pio Schunker, Vince Voron, Frederic Kahn
(Coca-Cola North America)
Company: Turner Duckworth, London & San Francisco
Country: USA
Category: Limited editions, limited series, collectors' items

GOLD PENTAWARD 2011

COCA-COLA
2010 WINTER OLYMPICS
PACKAGING AND PREMIUMS

Creative Direction: David Turner, Bruce Duckworth
Design Design: Tetsuya Takenomata, Josh Michels
Direction: Sarah Moffat
Illustration: John Geary
Company: Turner Duckworth, London & San Francisco
Country: UK/USA
Category: Limited editions, limited series, event creations
SILVER PENTAWARD 2010

ORANGINA
MISS O

Design: Fabrice Peltier and team
Company: Diadeis
Country: France
Category: Limited editions,
limited series, collectors' items

BRONZE PENTAWARD 2012

PEPSI PERFECT

Design: PepsiCo Design & Innovation
Company: PepsiCo Design & Innovation
Country: USA
Category: Limited editions,
limited series, event creations

BRONZE PENTAWARD 2016

IYEMON CHA
TEA CEREMONY IN AUTUMN

Creative Direction: Yoji Minakuchi
Art Direction: Keiko Genkaku
Design: Keiko Genkaku/Chiso
Company: Suntory
Country: Japan
Category: Limited editions,
limited series, event creations

SILVER PENTAWARD 2010

EVIAN
BY ISSEY MIYAKE

Design: Issey Miyake
Company: Evian (Danone Group)
Country: France
Category: Limited editions,
limited series, collectors' items

BRONZE PENTAWARD 2011

EVIAN
PAUL SMITH

Design: Paul Smith
Company: Evian (Danone Group)
Country: France
Category: Limited editions,
limited series, event creations

GOLD PENTAWARD 2010

VELKOPOPOVICKY KOZEL

Art Direction/Design: Yurko Gutsulyak
Company: Yurko Gutsulyak Studio
Country: Ukraine
Category: Limited editions, limited series,
event creations

BRONZE PENTAWARD 2013

WILLIAMSON TEA

Creative Direction: Moyra Casey
Design: Sue Bicknell
Company: Springetts Brand Design Consultants
Country: UK
Category: Limited editions, limited series,
event creations

GOLD PENTAWARD 2013

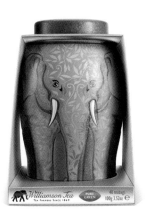

PACEÑA CARNIVAL CANS

Design: Pierini Partners
Company: Pierini Partners
Country: Argentina
Category: Limited editions, limited series,
event creations

SILVER PENTAWARD 2015

COCA-COLA SELFRIDGES
Design: Coca-Cola UK, Selfridges
Company: Sleever International
Country: France
Category: Limited editions,
limited series, event creations
BRONZE PENTAWARD 2010

MALIBU
Design: The Brand Union Paris,
MJC, Delta for Ricard
Company: Brand Union
Country: France
Category: Limited editions,
limited series, event creations
BRONZE PENTAWARD 2009

HEINEKEN
THE 2012 HEINEKEN
LIMITED EDITION GIFT-PACK

Art Direction: Ramses Dingenouts (dBOD),
Pascal Duval (Iris Amsterdam)
Design: Janneke Visser (dBOD),
Glenn Doherty (Iris Amsterdam)
Copy: Ady Thomas (Iris Amsterdam)
Account Direction: Evelyn Hille (dBOD)
Project Management: Kim Hogenbirk (dBOD)
Account: Chris Friends, Matt Atherton
(Iris Amsterdam)
Company: dBOD
Country: Netherlands
Category: Limited editions,
limited series, collectors' items

SILVER PENTAWARD 2012

BEYONCÉ FUTURE POP
PEPSICO 2013 MUSIC CAMPAIGN

Creative Direction: Christopher Stern
Associate Creative Direction: Adam Walko
Art Direction: JP Elliot, Grace Kao
Account Direction: Cynthia Davies
Account Management: Colleen Drake
Photography: Patrick Demarchelier
Company: Safari Sundays
Country: USA
Category: Limited editions,
limited series, event creations

SILVER PENTAWARD 2013

Coca-Cola
daftcoke.com
Coca-Cola
Inspired by
DAFT PUNK's
original bottle*
daftcoke.com
Coca-Cola
daftcoke.com
Coca-Cola
Inspired by
DAFT PUNK's
original bottle*
daftcoke.com

COCA-COLA CLUB COKE
Design Direction: Laurent Moreau,
Virgil Reboul (Pixelis)
Design: Brice Marchelidon (Pixelis)
Company: Coca-Cola France
Country: France
Category: Limited editions,
limited series, collectors' items
BRONZE PENTAWARD 2011

COCA-COLA
HISTORIC GLASS BOTTLES
Design: Mia Vojnic, Thomas Portenseigne,
Eric Kaddari, Argiris Dabanlis,
Daniela Zahariea, Saskia Goeteyns
Company: Coca-Cola Services
Country: Belgium
Category: Limited editions,
limited series, collectors' items
BRONZE PENTAWARD 2012

TRUETT HURST
SAFEWAY BOTTLE SLEEVES

Creative Direction: Kevin Shaw
Design: Cosimo Surace, Ewa Oliver
Company: Stranger & Stranger
Country: UK
Category: Distributors'/Retailers' own brands

GOLD PENTAWARD 2013

These eye-catching bottle sleeves were launched with the specific aim of spicing up the appearance of the wine shelves. The patented design features everything from quotes and recipes to retro imagery and even different ties at the top. Amongst rows of glass bottles the sleeves really stand out, adding interest for shoppers and making these bottles ideal gifts. The increased sleeve area offers possibilities to engage with customers in a way a tiny back label never could—everyone just wants to pick them up and read them. Feedback from both the retailer and customers has been incredible and has resulted in plans to extend the range.

Diese auffälligen Flaschenhüllen sollten speziell dem Ziel dienen, die Wirkung im Weinregal zu optimieren. Das patentierte Design zeigt alles Mögliche: Zitate und Rezepte bis hin zu Retrobildern und sogar unterschiedliche Krawatten oder Bänder am Flaschenhals. Stehen die Flaschen im Regal, fallen ihre Hüllen wirklich sehr auf und wecken das Interesse der Käufer, was sie zum idealen Geschenk macht. Durch die großzügige Gestaltung bietet die Hülle weitere Möglichkeiten, die Kundschaft auf eine Weise einzubeziehen, die mit winzigen Etiketten auf der Rückseite nie möglich wäre – man fühlt sich förmlich genötigt, die Flasche in die Hand zu nehmen und lesen. Die begeisterten Rückmeldungen von Händlern und Kunden gleichermaßen führten zu Planungen für ein erweitertes Sortiment.

Ces manchons de bouteilles pleins d'originalité ont été lancés dans le but d'égayer les rayonnages de vins. Le design breveté inclut des citations, des recettes, une imagerie rétro et différentes fermetures au col. Au milieu des rangées de bouteilles, les manchons se distinguent clairement et se présentent comme un cadeau idéal. Leur taille a été augmentée et les rend plus attirants encore : les clients sont intéressés à les toucher et à les observer, ce qui n'est pas le cas avec une étiquette standard. Les avis des magasins comme des clients ont été très positifs, au point d'envisager d'étendre la gamme.

DELHAIZE 365

Design: Nacho Lavernia,
Alberto Cienfuegos
Company: Lavernia & Cienfuegos
Country: Spain
Category: Distributors'/
Retailers' own brands

GOLD PENTAWARD 2012

THE DELI GARAGE
POWERFUEL

Creative Direction: Kathrin Oeding
Art Direction: Reginald Wagner
Copywriting: Katharina Trumbach
Graphic Design: Jan Simmerl
Illustration: Heiko Windisch
Company: Kolle Rebbe
Country: Germany
Category: Distributors'/
Retailers' own brands

SILVER PENTAWARD 2009

FRESH & EASY
NEIGHBOURHOOD MARKET RANGE

Art Direction: Phil Curl, Simon Pemberton, Adrian Whitefoord
Company: Pemberton & Whitefoord
Country: UK
Category: Distributors'/
Retailers' own brands

SILVER PENTAWARD 2009

BELVEDERE VODKA
ICE CRUSH

Creative Direction: Jean-Sébastien Blanc,
Vincent Baranger
Design: Martin Lefèvre
Company: 5.5 designstudio
Country: France
Category: Casks, cases, gift boxes,
ice buckets

SILVER PENTAWARD 2014

ARDBEG
ESCAPE PACK

Design: Pocket Rocket
Creative Direction/Production: Dapy
Company: Dapy/Do International
Country: France
Category: Casks, cases, gift boxes,
ice buckets

SILVER PENTAWARD 2014

RICARD DUO
BY JAKOB+MACFARLANE

Design: Dominique Jakob,
Brendan MacFarlane
Company: Ricard
Country: France
Category: Casks, cases, gift boxes,
ice buckets

GOLD PENTAWARD 2014

STOCKING FILLER CHRISTMAS WINE

Design: Tim Wilson, Ash Higginbotham, Stephnie Croft, Gary Scott, Tim Warren
Company: Cowan Design
Country: Australia
Category: Self-promotion

GOLD PENTAWARD 2011

THANKSGIVING WINE

Creative Direction: Stan Church
Design: Bird Tubkam, Chung-Tao Tu
Company: Wallace Church & Co.
Country: USA
Category: Self-promotion

GOLD PENTAWARD 2008

Every year Wallace Church designs a
Thanksgiving wine bottle as a gift for clients
and friends. For 2008's design, the solution was
a simple twist on a classic fork, creating a fanciful
turkey face. The message was: Thanksgiving, a
turkey feast enjoyed with a good wine.

Jedes Jahr gestaltet Wallace Church zu
Thanksgiving als Geschenk für Kunden und
Freunde eine Weinflasche. Beim Design des Jahres
2008 bestand die Lösung einfach darin, die Zinke
einer Gabel umzuknicken, wodurch sehr fantasie-
voll und einfach der Kopf eines Truthahns entstand.
Die Botschaft lautete: Thanksgiving ist ein Fest, bei
dem man zum Truthahn einen guten Wein genießt.

Chaque année, Wallace Church crée une bouteille de vin que l'agence offre à ses clients et amis
à l'occasion de **Thanksgiving**. La solution choisie
pour l'année 2008 était la réinterprétation d'une
fourchette classique modifiée pour évoquer une
dinde stylisée. Le message : Thanksgiving, un festin
de dinde savouré avec un bon vin.

Mit dieser Verpackung wollten wir unseren Kunden ein einzigartiges Weihnachtsgeschenk präsentieren und gleichzeitig unser neues Angebot vorstellen. Wir erinnern unsere Kunden daran, wer wir sind und wie viele lange Stunden in unserer Arbeit stecken. Außerdem soll damit unser gesamtes Personal mit seiner Kreativität und seinem Humor vorgestellt werden. Zu jedem Teammitglied gibt es ein entsprechendes Etikett. Der Kunde wird ermuntert, aus den verschiedenen Gesichtselementen ein neues Gesicht zu schaffen: **BYO** – Build Your Own!

Le but de cet emballage était de créer un cadeau de Noël original pour nos clients, tout en servant également de support de présentation sur le marché. Il devait leur rappeler qui nous sommes, ainsi que les longues heures que nous investissons dans notre travail. Il devait aussi représenter toute notre équipe, et refléter notre créativité et notre sens de l'humour. Chaque étiquette s'inspire d'un membre de l'équipe et se compose d'éléments de son visage. Le client est invité à faire de même : **BYO** (Build Your Own – Fabriquez le vôtre).

THE CREATIVE METHOD
BYO - BUILD YOUR OWN

Creative Direction: Tony Ibbotson
Design: Andi Yanto
Company: The Creative Method
Country: Australia
Category: Self-promotion

GOLD PENTAWARD 2010

The aim of this packaging was to create a unique gift to give our clients at Christmas and to act as a new business introduction. It needed to remind them of who we are and the long hours that we put into our work. It also needed to feature all of our staff, and reflect our creativity and sense of humour. Each label was based on one staff member and included a number of facial features and the client was encouraged to **BYO** – Build Your Own.

Milk*

*pinot noir

A milk bottle?
Yes, we know that you have
never received this kind of gift.
That's why we've packed our
finest Pinot Noir in this
bottle of milk.
Enjoy it!

ampro design

AMPRO DESIGN

Creative Direction: Irinel Ionescu
Design/3D: Alin Patru
Art Direction/Copy: Francesca Muresan
Production: Danubiu Birzu
Company: Ampro Design Consultants
Country: Romania
Category: Self-promotion

GOLD PENTAWARD 2012

Ampro Design schuf dieses ganz spezielle Urlaubsgeschenk für seine Kunden und bekräftigte damit die eigene Reputation für Kreativität und ideenreiches Querdenken in Designlösungen. Zwar dürfen viele internationale Kunden keine Geschenke annehmen, aber man umging dies geschickt durch die Frage „Wer hätte schon etwas dagegen, eine Milchflasche zu erhalten?". Natürlich hatte kein Kunde ein Präsent wie dieses erwartet. Für eine noch größere Überraschung sorgte der Inhalt: ein ausgezeichneter Pinot Noir.

To reinforce its reputation for creativity and "out of the box" design solutions, **Ampro Design** developed this special holiday gift for its clients. With many of its international trade customers not being allowed to receive gifts for various reasons, this was neatly circumvented by asking: "who would be upset to receive a bottle of milk?" Of course, no client would expect to receive a gift like this, even more so when it was discovered that the bottle in fact contains a fine Pinot Noir.

Ampro Design a créé cet original cadeau de Noël pour ses clients dans le but de renforcer sa réputation basée sur la créativité et les solutions inédites. Nombre de ses clients internationaux n'étant pas autorisés à recevoir des cadeaux, pour des raisons diverses, ce problème a été astucieusement contourné en posant la question : « quel problème pourrait-il y avoir à recevoir une bouteille de lait ? » Évidemment, aucun client ne pourrait s'attendre à recevoir un tel cadeau. Surtout que la bouteille contient en fait un grand Pinot Noir.

HOLY WATER LABEL

Design: Tony Ibbotson
Artwork: Greg Coles
Account Direction: Jess McElhone
Creative Direction: Tony Ibbotson
Illustration: Jason Paulos (The Drawing Book)
Company: The Creative Method
Country: Australia
Category: Self-promotion

BRONZE PENTAWARD 2012

CREATIVITY ON YOUR DOORSTEP

Design: Shaun Green
Company: SMR Creative
Country: UK
Category: Self-promotion

BRONZE PENTAWARD 2011

TEA IN A BOX

Design: Jure Leko
Company: The Grain
Country: Australia
Category: Self-promotion

BRONZE PENTAWARD 2011

GATORADE ON THE GO

Design: Cadú Gomes
Company: Cadú Gomes Design
Country: UK
Category: Packaging concept
GOLD PENTAWARD 2012

With a more than 40-year track record in helping to rehydrate athletes and people in physical training, **Gatorade**'s specially designed formula is a proven sports drink. By taking the brand's identity and literally putting it in the hands of the consumer, a smart re-working of the initial "G" of the logo has produced a unique structural design with instant recognition and a team of walking (well, running) advertising boards for the drink. Whether you're an amateur, athlete or pro, now you can recover on the go.

Mit seiner über 40-jährigen Erfolgsbilanz als isotonisches Sportlergetränk hat sich die speziell entwickelte Formel von **Gatorade** wahrhaft bewährt. Die Identität der Marke wird dem Verbraucher buchstäblich in die Hand gegeben: Man setzte den Anfangsbuchstaben des Logos pfiffig in ein unverwechselbar strukturiertes Design um. So auffällig wird es sofort erkannt, und die Verbraucher laufen buchstäblich Werbung für das Getränk. Egal ob Sie Amateur, Athlet oder Profi sind – nun können Sie sich schon beim Laufen erholen.

Avec plus de 40 ans d'expérience dans le domaine de la réhydratation des athlètes, la formule spéciale de **Gatorade** a fait ses preuves dans le secteur des boissons sportives. Le « G » du logo a été astucieusement retravaillé et l'identité de la marque est littéralement mise entre les mains du consommateur. Ce design permet une identification instantanée et produit une armée de supports publicitaires vivants pour la boisson. Que vous soyez amateur, athlète confirmé ou pro, vous pouvez maintenant reprendre des forces n'importe où, n'importe quand.

DAILY DOSE

Design: Ivan Pierre,
Laurent Lepoitevin,
Damien Bourne
Company: Sidel
Country: France
Category: Packaging concept

SILVER PENTAWARD 2012

BOSS
CUP-CAN

Design: Hiroyuki Ishiura
Company: Suntory
Country: Japan
Category: Packaging concept
GOLD PENTAWARD 2015

Canned coffee with milk and sugar has become one of the most popular drinks in Japan. Being convenient, casual and masculine, it has been especially loved by blue-collar workers for a long time. **Boss** coffee was launched in 1992 with this market in mind and so named for targeting those who take pride in their work and can say, like the man in the logo, "I am the Boss in my field." The cup-can here was specifically designed for executive workers, with the clean gold finish being a symbol of success. The neat addition of a handle allows the drink to be held like a real cup of coffee.

Gesüßter Kaffee mit Milch in Dosen gehört zu den beliebtesten Getränken Japans. Weil sie so praktisch, zwanglos und männlich sind, lieben Arbeiter sie besonders. Der **Boss**-Kaffee erschien 1992 für diese Zielgruppe auf dem Markt. Der Name richtet sich an jene, die auf ihre Arbeit stolz sind und wie der Mann im Logo sagen können: „In meinem Bereich bin ich der Boss." Die Becherdose mit ihrem sauberen goldenen Finish als Symbol des Erfolgs ist speziell für Vorarbeiter gedacht. Durch den schmucken Henkel wird die Dose wie eine echte Tasse Kaffee gehalten.

Le café au lait sucré en canette est devenu l'une des boissons les plus populaires au Japon. Pratique, décontractée et masculine, elle est particulièrement appréciée depuis longtemps des cols bleus. Le café **Boss** a été lancé en 1992 avec ce segment pour cible, et ainsi baptisé pour plaire à ceux qui sont fiers de leur travail et peuvent dire, comme l'homme du logo « Je suis le boss dans mon domaine ». Cette canette-tasse a été conçue spécifiquement pour les exécutifs, la finition dorée étant un symbole de succès. L'ajout d'une anse permet de tenir la canette comme une vraie tasse de café.

ORANGINA SPIRAL PEEL

Design: Yuko Takagi
Company: Suntory
Country: Japan
Category: Packaging concept

GOLD PENTAWARD 2016

ARCTIC ICE WATER

Concept: Vlad Mikhailov
Creative Direction: Nadie Parshina
Design: Marina Malygina
Company: Ohmybrand
Country: Russia
Category: Packaging concept

SILVER PENTAWARD 2016

This pure **Arctic Water** comes from glaciers located above the Arctic Circle, bordering on the Barents Sea and the Kara Sea. The water is taken directly from the mass of ice with minimal use of mechanized labor, and the details of each production site are given on the individual blocks. Following its excavation the ice is packed in biodegradable 2,2 lb bags and delivered to stores frozen. The customer then buys 2,2 lb of water, takes it home and out of the package and puts it into a special flask where the ice melts naturally at room temperature. A photocell built into the bottom of the flask is activated when the glass is approached, giving a gentle glow to this freshest of water.

Dieses reine **Arctic Water** stammt von Gletschern, die oberhalb des Polarkreises an Barentssee und Karasee grenzen. Das Wasser wird mit minimalem maschinellen Aufwand direkt den Eismassen entnommen. Die einzelnen Blöcke zeigen Details jeder Produktionsstätte. Nach dem Aushub wird das Eis in biologisch abbaubare 1-kg-Tüten gefüllt und gefroren an die Läden geliefert. Die Kunden kaufen das Wasser dann in 1-kg-Portionen und legen es zu Hause in eine spezielle Flasche, in der das Eis auf natürliche Weise bei Zimmertemperatur schmilzt. Eine in den Flaschenboden integrierte Fotozelle wird aktiviert, wenn das Glas näher kommt, und lässt dieses unvergleichlich frische Wasser sanft leuchten.

Arctic Water est une eau pure qui provient de glaciers situés au-dessus du cercle arctique, au bord de la mer de Barents et de la mer de Kara. Elle est prélevée directement dans la masse de glace, avec une mécanisation minimale, et les détails de chaque site de production sont indiqués sur chaque bloc. La glace est emballée dans des sacs d'1 kg biodégradables et livrée en magasin congelée. Le client achète alors 1 kg d'eau, et une fois chez lui, la sort de l'emballage et la met dans un récipient spécial où la glace fond naturellement à température ambiante. Au fond, une photocellule s'active lorsque le verre en est approché, ce qui confère un doux éclat à cette eau pure.

RISE & SHINE

Design: Cristian Stancu, Viorel Rusu
Company: Remark Studio
Country: Romania
Category: Packaging concept
BRONZE PENTAWARD 2013

VOLKSBIER

Design: Cristian Stancu, Viorel Rusu
Company: Remark Studio
Country: Romania
Category: Packaging concept
GOLD PENTAWARD 2014

Packaging for beer has become more and more involved in recent years, so this design aimed for a simpler approach, based on two trends on the Romanian market: a general increase in the consumption of beer, and the use of PET bottles or aluminum cans. As beer has now become more popular than wine in Romania, especially beers of German origin, **Volksbier** was chosen as a distinctive new brand name while the eye-catching container is based on a pint glass. Transparent cans are already used for soft drinks and the same PET material here gets very close to glass in its appearance.

Die Verpackung von Bieren wurde in den letzten Jahren immer aufwendiger. Darum verfährt dieses Design nach einem ganz einfachen Ansatz, der zwei Trends auf dem rumänischen Markt aufgreift: den steigenden Bierkonsum und die Verwendung von PET-Flaschen oder Aludosen. Da Bier in Rumänien mittlerweile beliebter ist als Wein, vor allem jenes aus deutscher Herstellung, nannte man die neue Marke **Volksbier** und wählte als Blickfang für das Behältnis einen Bierhumpen. Für Softdrinks werden bereits transparente Dosen eingesetzt, und das PET-Material hier wirkt schon sehr wie Glas.

À l'heure où l'emballage de bières est chaque fois plus élaboré, ce design parie sur une approche simple fondée sur deux tendances actuelles en Roumanie : la consommation croissante de bières et l'emploi répandu de bouteilles PET ou de canettes d'aluminium. La bière (notamment d'origine allemande) s'étant imposée au vin sur le marché roumain, **Volksbier** a été adopté pour rebaptiser le produit, et l'original emballage rappelle une pinte en verre. Les canettes transparentes sont déjà utilisées pour les boissons rafraîchissantes et le PET simule ici parfaitement le verre.

BEER COLORS

Design: Txaber Mentxaka
Company: Txaber
Country: Spain
Category: Packaging concept
SILVER PENTAWARD 2015

REAL DRINKS
GENUINE DRINKS
Design: Kyungmin Park
Company: Imkm Design
Country: South Korea
Category: Packaging concept
SILVER PENTAWARD 2014

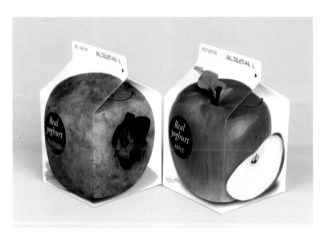

SQUEEZE & FRESH

Design: Stepan Azaryan
Company: Backbone Branding
Country: Armenia
Category: Packaging concept
SILVER PENTAWARD 2016

NUDE
JR FLAVOURED MILK

Design: Andrianto Kwan (student)
School: Billy Blue College of Design
Country: Australia
Category: Packaging concept
SILVER PENTAWARD 2012

KISS,
PURÉE OF VEGETABLES AND FRUITS

Design: Alexandra Istratova
Company: Alexandra Istratova
Country: Russia
Category: Packaging concept

GOLD PENTAWARD 2013

EAT.

PARSNIP
BEETROOT &
CARROT CRISPS

100% NATURAL INGREDIENTS

40g ℮

Best of the category
Cereals
Dairy or soya products
Spices, oils, sauces
Fish, meat, poultry
Fruit, vegetables
Soups, ready-to-eat dishes

food

Confectionery, sweet snacks
Savoury snacks
Pastry, biscuits, ice-cream, desserts, honey, sugar
Food trends
Fast-food restaurants
Limited editions, limited series, event creations, collectors' items
Distributors'/Retailers' own brands, private labels
Cross-category ranges
Packaging concept

KANPYO UDON

Design: Nosigner
Company: Nosigner
Country: Japan
Category: Best of the category
PLATINUM PENTAWARD 2009

The Nosigner agency in Tokyo had to design the packaging for a new type of **Udon** noodles, which are actually made from dried vegetable marrow, and not from wheat flower. The packaging design was turned into an amusing combination which mixed the shape of a pumpkin and fresh noodles that evokes a non-industrial product, quite luxurious, and yet still affordable. This design has broken the mold of what has traditionally been done in Japan for this type of product, although using traditional Japanese paper and calligraphy.

Die Agentur Nosigner aus Tokio sollte die Verpackung einer neuen Sorte **Udon**-Nudeln gestalten, die nicht aus Weizen-, sondern aus Kürbismehl hergestellt werden. Die Verpackung wurde als amüsante Kombination gestaltet, in der eine Kürbisform und frische Nudeln zusammengeführt werden. Sie weckt Assoziationen an ein nicht-industrielles Produkt, das recht luxuriös, aber doch erschwinglich ist. Diese Gestaltung sprengt die Form dessen, was traditionell in Japan für diese Art von Produkt gemacht wurde, obgleich dabei traditionelles japanisches Papier und Kalligraphie eingesetzt werden.

L'agence tokyoïte Nosigner devait créer le packaging d'un nouveau type de nouilles **Udon**, fabriquées à partir de courge déshydratée au lieu de farine de blé. Le design du packaging est une combinaison amusante qui allie la forme d'une citrouille aux nouilles fraîches et suggère un produit non industriel, assez luxueux, et pourtant abordable. Le design s'éloigne de ce qui se fait traditionnellement au Japon pour ce genre de produit, mais emploie la calligraphie et le papier japonais traditionnels.

TESCO TORTILLA CHIPS

Design: Simon Pemberton,
Lee Newham, Barry Crombie
Company: Pemberton & Whitefoord
Country: UK
Category: Best of the category
PLATINUM PENTAWARD 2008

The Pemberton & Whitefoord agency of London developed a range of tortilla chips for the British retailer Tesco by creating "the Bandito", a comical character who changes outfit and accessories according to the type of chips, bringing a touch of humour to the product. Moreover, the strong color codes aim to increase the display impact.

Die Londoner Agentur Pemberton & White-foord entwickelte für den britischen Händler Tesco verschiedene Tortilla-Chips. Dazu spannte sie die spaßige Figur des „Banditos" ein, der sein Äußeres und seine Accessoires je nach Art der Chips ändert. So verleiht er dem Produkt einen humorvollen Touch. Überdies verstärken die kräftigen Farb-codes der Verpackung die Wirkung im Regal.

L'agence londonienne Pemberton & Whitefoord a conçu une gamme de chips tortillas pour les magasins anglais Tesco en créant le « Bandito », un personnage comique qui change de vêtements et d'accessoires en fonction du type de chips, et ajoute par la même occasion une touche d'humour au produit. Les couleurs fortes visent à augmenter l'effet visuel en rayon.

EGGS FOR SOLDIERS

Creative Direction: Moyra Casey
Design: Jon Vallance
Company: Springetts Brand Design Consultants
Country: UK
Category: Best of the category
PLATINUM PENTAWARD 2012

The introduction of a new brand of eggs into the market also offered through its design an opportunity to help raise awareness for the Help for Heroes charity. By calling them **Eggs for Soldiers** the familiar way of eating boiled eggs with toast soldiers also referred to the charitable intent. Strong use of coloring helps with identification, along with the weave of military uniforms, while the photographic image doubles in its suggestion of a medal. After a successful launch in May 2011, the brand is now worth £2.3m and has so far donated £250,000 to its charity.

Bei der Lancierung dieser neuen Eiermarke sollte über das Design auf die Charity-Organisation Help for Heroes aufmerksam gemacht werden. Die Bezeichnung **Eggs for Soldiers** spielt einerseits auf den typisch englischen Snack an, bei dem man Toaststifte in ein weichgekochtes Ei dippt (die sogenannten Toast Soldiers), zugleich wird für den karitativen Zweck geworben. Die kraftvolle Farbgebung und die militärisch anmutende Gewebeart verstärken die Identifikation, die Abbildung des Eis spielt deutlich auf militärische Orden an. Nach dem erfolgreichen Start im Mai 2011 ist die Marke nun 2,3 Millionen Pfund wert und hat bisher 250.000 Pfund an Spenden eingebracht.

Le lancement d'une nouvelle marque d'œufs a également été l'occasion, à travers la conception de son emballage, de contribuer à faire connaître l'organisation caritative Help for Heroes. Le nom **Eggs for Soldiers** fait référence aux « mouillettes » trempées dans l'œuf à la coque, appelées « soldiers » en Angleterre, mais aussi à cette œuvre charitable. Le choix de la couleur facilite l'identification, tout comme la trame de toile militaire, tandis que la photographie de l'œuf évoque également une médaille. Après un lancement réussi en mai 2011, la marque vaut aujourd'hui 2,3 M £, et elle pour l'instant reversé 250 000 £ à la cause qu'elle défend.

QIAN'S GIFT
黔之礼赞

In southeast Guizhou, people still follow the age-old ways of growing rice, rejecting chemical products in favor of letting nature look after things and so ensuring the best-quality organic rice is grown. In thus avoiding industrialization the rice packaging too abandons modern manufacturing methods and prefers traditional, high plant-fiber wrappers made by local paper-makers. Indigo is used in the region for dyeing cloth so this was adopted for printing the information on the packaging, all applied by hand without resort to machinery. The distinctive design both respects the environment and goes back to the roots of craft production methods.

In Guizhou im Südwesten Chinas wird der Reis immer noch nach uralter Tradition angebaut. Die Bauern lehnen den Einsatz von Chemikalien ab und lassen der Natur ihren Lauf. Somit produzieren sie einen organischen Reis bester Qualität. Da man Industrialisierung meidet, werden auch bei der Reispackung keine modernen Herstellungsmethoden eingesetzt. Man bevorzugt traditionelle Hüllen aus Pflanzenfasern, von örtlichen Papierherstellern produziert. In dieser Region färbt man Stoffe mit Indigo. Dieser Naturstoff wird auch bei den Produktinfos der Verpackung verwendet – alles per Hand ohne Maschineneinsatz. Das charakteristische Design respektiert die Umwelt und greift auf ursprüngliche Produktionsmethoden zurück.

Dans la province chinoise de Guizhou, les habitants appliquent encore d'anciennes techniques de culture du riz, en bannissant les produits chimiques et en laissant la nature faire son travail pour donner le meilleur des riz biologiques. Pas d'industrialisation, donc pas non plus de méthodes de fabrication modernes pour l'emballage : l'enveloppe en fibre végétale est la création de fabricants de papier locaux. L'indigo est employé dans cette région pour teindre les vêtements ; il a aussi été retenu pour imprimer les informations sur le paquet, le tout à la main sans la moindre machine. Ce design original est respectueux de l'environnement et renvoie aux origines de production artisanale.

QIAN'S GIFT

Company: Pesign Design
Country: China
Category: Best of the category
PLATINUM PENTAWARD 2014

PANDA LIQUORICE

Design: David Pearman, Hayley Bishop
Company: Cowan Design
Country: UK
Category: Best of the category

PLATINUM PENTAWARD 2011

MAN CAVE MEATS

Design: CBX design team
Company: CBX
Country: USA
Category: Best of the category
PLATINUM PENTAWARDS 2016

WALKERS
TIGER NUTS

Design: David Annetts, Hayley Barrett, Felicity Walker,
Alice Douglas Deane, Jim Burton, Lisa Mathews,
Debbie Barber, Michelle Connolly, David Clabon,
Rosie Marlow, Chris Mitchell, Chris Weir
Company: Design Bridge
Country: UK
Category: Best of the category
PLATINUM PENTAWARD 2013

In the jungle that is the world of crisps, crackers and nuts sold in bags, it is imperative to stand out. Amidst fierce competition from national brands on one side and private labels on the other, the Walkers brand (Lay's in many countries) is the market leader in crisps but sought a similar position in the nuts market. To this end, the packs were given a general design representing the face of a tiger in which can be read, as a subliminal image, the name **Tiger Nuts**, cleverly and creatively formed in the distinctive black stripes of a tiger's fur.

Im Dschungel der in Tüten angebotenen Kartoffelchips, Kräckern und Nüssen muss man sich von der Konkurrenz abheben. Mitten im Wettstreit nationaler Marken auf der einen und Eigenmarken auf der anderen Seite ist Walkers (in vielen Ländern bekannt als Lay's) Marktführer beim Knabbergebäck, strebt aber im Segment der Nusssnacks eine ähnliche Position an. Zu diesem Zweck verlieh man den Verpackungen ein Gestaltungskonzept in Form eines Tigerkopfes, in dem man als subliminales Bild die Worte **Tiger Nuts** lesen kann, sehr geschickt und kreativ eingebettet als Streifen des Tigerfells.

Dans la jungle des chips, biscuits salés et fruits secs vendus en sachets, il est crucial de se démarquer. Au milieu de cette féroce concurrence des marques nationales d'une part et des labels privés d'autre part, la marque Walkers (Lay's dans de nombreux pays) domine le marché des chips. En quête d'une présence similaire pour les fruits secs, les emballages ont été entièrement repensés, avec une tête de tigre faite, tel un message subliminal, des lettres de **Tiger Nuts** pour représenter les bandes noires de la fourrure de l'animal.

RICE GARDEN
EIGHT TREASURES
OF HAPPINESS

Design: Victor Branding creative team
Company: Victor Branding Design Corp.
Country: Taiwan
Category: Cereals
GOLD PENTAWARD 2011

Eight Treasures of Happiness was the theme chosen for the packaging for this range of different flavoured rice, personified through eight different experts in the business of rice production: grain-polisher, quality-controller, supervisor for organic standards, environmental protection officer, simple farmer, and so on. With these eight all contributing their expertise to the process, excellent quality rice is the result, delivering the taste of happiness to consumers. To bring this process home each package was personalised with one of the key production personnel, using cartoon-style illustrations for the design.

Die **Acht Schätze des Glücks** waren das auserwählte Thema für die Verpackungen dieser Produktpalette Reis verschiedener Geschmacksrichtungen, personifiziert durch acht Experten der Reisproduktion: den Entspelzer, den Qualitätskontrolleur, den Kontrolleur für die organischen Standards, den Umweltschutzbeamten, den einfachen Bauern usw. Weil alle acht ihr Fachwissen in den Prozess einbringen, entsteht ein hervorragender Qualitätsreis und schenkt den Konsumenten den „Geschmack des Glücks". Um diesen auch bis ins eigene Heim spürbar zu machen, wurden alle Packungen durch Illustrationen im Cartoonstil von Schlüsselfiguren der Produktion personalisiert.

Huit trésors du bonheur est le thème choisi pour l'emballage de cette gamme de riz parfumé, personnifiée par huit experts de la production du riz : polisseur de grain, contrôleur qualité, superviseur des normes biologiques, agent de protection de l'environnement, simple fermier, etc. Grâce à l'expertise de ces huit métiers, le résultat est un riz d'excellente qualité qui a le goût du bonheur. Pour communiquer cette idée, chaque paquet a été illustré avec l'un de ces métiers clés de la production dans un style proche de celui des dessins animés.

FENGFAN FARM PRODUCTS
FISH N RICE

Design: Li Sun
Company: Rong Design
Country: China
Category: Cereals

Fengfan Farm Products is based in Jintan, a traditional village in south China that has long relied on its agriculture. The land is held in high regard and Fengfan aims to supply the local organic farm products to the wider market. Since the word for "abundance" in Mandarin has the same sound as the word for "fish" people wish each other "fish every year" in blessing, especially at harvest festival. By combining this cultural history with reuse and ease of carrying a smart new design was developed for this 22 lb rice bag. The one-piece canvas bag is naturally balanced and formed as a double fish, using screen-printed graphics that also include details of rice and wheat to indicate the contents.

Fengfan Farm Products befindet sich in Jintan, einem traditionellen Dorf im Süden Chinas, das sich schon lange auf seine Landwirtschaft verlässt. Grund und Boden werden besonders geschätzt, und Fengfan will für die lokal biologisch angebauten Produkte einen größeren Markt erreichen. Weil das Wort „Fülle" in Mandarin so klingt wie „Fisch", wünschen sich die Leute als Segensgruß „Fisch das ganze Jahr", vor allem beim Erntedankfest. Diese kulturelle Anekdote wurde in einem raffinierten neuen Design mit der Idee kombiniert, einen 10-kg-Reisbeutel einfach tragen und wiederverwenden zu können. Dessen Segeltuchtasche ist gut ausbalanciert und geformt wie ein doppelter Fisch. Die Siebdruckgrafik außen verweist mit Details von Reis und Weizen auf den Inhalt.

Fengfan Farm Products est basé à Jintan, un village traditionnel dans le sud de la Chine qui dépend depuis longtemps de son agriculture. La terre y est une ressource tenue en haute estime, et Fengfan distribue les produits biologiques locaux sur un marché plus large. En mandarin, le mot « abondance » a le même son que le mot « poisson ». Les gens se souhaitent donc « du poisson chaque année » lors de la fête des moissons. C'est en s'inspirant de cette tradition culturelle qu'est né le concept d'un sac de riz de 10 kg. D'une seule pièce et en tissu, il est naturellement équilibré et représente un double poisson sérigraphié avec des motifs de riz et de blé pour indiquer le contenu.

WAHAHA
Design: Yunfeng Wang
Company: Hang Zhou Wahaha Group
Country: China
Category: Cereals
SILVER PENTAWARD 2010

JIN MAI LANG
LANDSCAPE VERMICELLI

Design: Xiaohui Xi
Company: CAC 110 Creativity Advertising
Country: China
Category: Cereals
SILVER PENTAWARD 2011

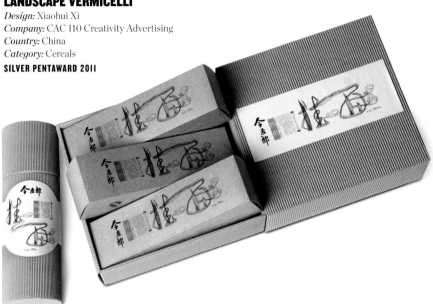

PERACH
CEREAL CAKES

Design: Efrat Mizrahi
Illustration: Efrat Mizrahi
Creative Direction: Ayelet Sadé
Company: Sadowsky Berlin
Country: Israel
Category: Cereals
BRONZE PENTAWARD 2016

QINGYINONGNONG GO HOME FOR DINNER

Design: Jingfang Mei
Company: Hangzhou Dongyun
Advertising Design
Country: China
Category: Cereals
BRONZE PENTAWARD 2016

SHISHANG SANMING ECOLOGICA RICE

Design: Jia Tian
Company: Jia Tian
Country: China
Category: Cereals
SILVER PENTAWARD 2016

PIZZA SHIGARAKI
RICE FLOUR PIZZA

Creative Direction/Design: Masahiro Minami
Executive Creative Direction: Shota Noto
Company: Masahiro Minami Laboratory
Country: Japan
Category: Cereals

SILVER PENTAWARD 2015

ASO MILK

Design: Hideaki Iwai
Company: Ohesono Design Works
Country: Japan
Category: Dairy products
GOLD PENTAWARD 2011

The pasteurised milk produced at the Abe dairy farm, in **Aso** in Kumamoto, is delivered without any involvement from middlemen, with the milk going directly from the farm to the consumer. It is delivered daily, with the empty bottles being collected, so to distinguish it the design concentrates on the bottle itself – it has a simple, classic shape, easily identifiable, but made individual by the red stripe design which forms a red cross when the bottle is empty!

Die pasteurisierte Milch aus dem Abe-Milchbetrieb der Stadt **Aso** in der Präfektur Kumamoto gelangt ohne Zwischenhandel direkt vom Bauernhof zum Konsumenten. Die Milchflaschen werden täglich ausgeliefert und geleert abgeholt. Um beides zu unterscheiden, konzentriert sich das Design auf die Flasche selbst: Sie hat eine einfache, klassische Form und ist leicht identifizierbar – aber das Design mit den roten Balken, die bei leerer Flasche zu einem roten Kreuz werden, macht sie individuell.

Le lait pasteurisé produit à la laiterie Abe, à **Aso**, dans la préfecture de Kumamoto, est livré sans aucun intermédiaire, directement de la ferme au consommateur. La répartition se fait chaque jour et les bouteilles sont consignées. Afin de mieux les distinguer, le concept est centré sur la bouteille elle-même : sa forme simple et classique est facilement reconnaissable, et individualisée grâce aux bandes rouges qui forment une croix lorsqu'elle est vide !

SKY-HIGH

Creative Direction: Alexey Fadeev
Design: Vera Zvereva
Copywriting: Anastasia Tretyakova
Account Management: Ksenia Parkhomenko
Company: Depot WPF
Country: Russia
Category: Dairy products

GOLD PENTAWARD 2013

In Russia today almost every variety of milk available to buy in stores has a period for extended consumption. As a result the taste is not natural, owing to the large number of preservatives that have been added. Thus, in the consumer's opinion there is no "true" milk. In order to counter this impression a new brand of milk was created, one that was bright and emotionally associated with childhood. The design depicts a world as seen by children, playful, energetic and uncomplicated, and in this way conveys the message that here is a true product with nothing to hide.

In Russland ist heutzutage praktisch jede im Laden erhältliche Sorte Milch verlängert haltbar. Als Folge davon schmeckt sie wegen der großen Zahl zugesetzter Konservierungsstoffe nicht mehr natürlich. Somit gibt es in der Wahrnehmung der Verbraucher keine „echte" Milch mehr. Um diesem Eindruck zu begegnen, wurde eine neue Milchmarke geschaffen, die fröhlich wirkt und emotional mit Kindheit verknüpft ist. Das Design zeigt die Welt, wie sie von Kindern gesehen wird: spielerisch, voller Energie und unkompliziert. So vermittelt es die Botschaft, hier handle es sich um ein Produkt, das nichts zu verbergen hat.

Dans la Russie actuelle, presque tous les types de lait disponibles en magasins ont une date limite de consommation éloignée, et le goût n'est pas naturel en raison des nombreux conservateurs qui ont été ajoutés. Dans l'esprit du consommateur, il n'existe donc pas de « véritable » lait. Pour combattre cette impression, une nouvelle marque de lait a été lancée avec une évocation de l'enfance. Le design illustre le monde tel que vu par les petits : ludique, dynamique et sans complications. Le message transmis est celui d'un produit authentique, qui n'a rien à cacher.

BRIE BISTRO

Design: Emma Ringsberg, Per Hallin, Mr. Golv
Company: ID kommunikation
Country: Sweden
Category: Dairy products

GOLD PENTAWARD 2010

MLK
ORGANIC DAIRY RANGE
Creative Direction: Alexey Fadeev
Strategic Planning Direction: Inna Likhacheva
Art Direction: Aram Mirzoyants, Vadim Briksin
Company: Depot WPF
Country: Russia
Category: Dairy products
SILVER PENTAWARD 2011

KALATHAKI LEMNOS
Creative Direction: Alexis Nikou,
Vaggelis Liakos, Yiannis Charalambopoulos,
Photography: Kostas Pappas
Company: Beetroot Design Group
Country: Greece
Category: Dairy products
SILVER PENTAWARD 2011

NATURAL PLAN

Design: Park Sang-Hyun, Kwon Min-Jung,
Park Moon-Soon, Jeon Sun-Young,
Lee Moon-Yong, Jung Ju-Hee, Jeon Hye-Lim
Company: Korea Yakult
Country: South Korea
Category: Dairy products
SILVER PENTAWARD 2013

LURPAK SLOW CHURNED

Chief Creative Officer: Jonathan Ford
Creative Direction: Natalie Chung
Design: Vicki Willatts
Realization: Shaun Jones
Strategy: Rory Fegan
Account Direction: Nicci Cooper
Company: Pearlfisher
Country: UK
Category: Dairy products
SILVER PENTAWARD 2014

**MENGNIU
HI!MILK**

Creative Direction: Guanru Li
Design: Guanru Li, Shubin Zhang, Zheng Dong
Illustration: Sixue Liu
Marketing Direction: Hao Chen
Product Management: Tuo Zeng
Company: L3 Branding Experience
Country: China
Category: Dairy or soya-based products
GOLD PENTAWARD 2016

SOSOFACTORY
SOSO

Design: Eduardo del Fraile, Aurelia Gonzalez
Company: Eduardo del Fraile
Country: Spain
Category: Spices, oils, sauces

GOLD PENTAWARD 2009

Soso is the name of a high-quality salt brand from Spain, and means "lacking salt or short of salt" in Spanish. The client was looking for a distinguished container that could be used both to store salt and as a salt-cellar. Inspired by the egg, Eduardo del Fraile used the form of its shell for the packaging of the container, and an egg-box tray to serve as the product's base and support. Moreover, both shape and colour are very unusual in this category of products.

Soso ist der Name einer qualitativ hochwertigen spanischen Salzmarke. Auf Spanisch bedeutet Soso etwa „ungesalzen" in der Bedeutung von „fade" oder „langweilig". Der Auftraggeber suchte nach einem charakteristischen Behälter, mit dem man Salz nicht nur verpacken, sondern den man auch als Salzstreuer verwenden kann. Eduardo del Fraile ließ sich von Eiern inspirieren und nutzte die Form der Eierschale für die Verpackung des Containers und ein Tablett mit Eierkartons, das als Basis und Support für das Produkt dienen soll. Überdies sind sowohl Form als auch Farbe in dieser Produktkategorie sehr ungewöhnlich.

Soso est le nom d'une marque espagnole de sel haut de gamme, et signifie « qui manque de sel » en espagnol. Le client voulait un récipient distingué qui pourrait servir à entreposer et conserver le sel. Eduardo del Fraile s'est inspiré de l'œuf et a repris la forme de sa coquille pour le packaging : il a aussi créé une boîte d'œufs qui fait office de base et de support du produit. Cette forme et ces couleurs sont en outre très inhabituelles dans cette catégorie de produits.

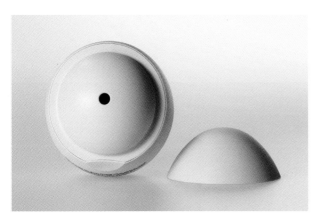

KRAFT
BULL'S-EYE

Design: Kai Muller
Account Direction: Ben Blaber
Company: Davis
Country: Canada
Category: Spices, oils, sauces

GOLD PENTAWARD 2010

Die Neugestaltung des Designs für **Bull's-Eye** sollte aktuell, maskulin und einfach sein, um die Marke mit neuem Leben zu erfüllen und das Kundeninteresse neu zu entfachen. Dazu sollte authentisch all das Grillfachwissen vermittelt werden, das der Marke Bull's-Eye eigen ist. Erzielt wurde dies durch eine kraftvolle Typografie, eine veränderte Oberflächenbeschaffenheit und die Neugestaltung des Stiers als Markensymbol.

To revitalise **Bull's-Eye** and reignite consumer interest, the redesign needed to be contemporary, masculine, unpretentious, and genuinely convey the BBQ expertise that is inherent in the Bull's-Eye brand. This was achieved through bold typography, distressed textures, and a reinvention of the brand's icon of the Bull.

Pour revitaliser **Bull's-Eye** et relancer l'intérêt des consommateurs, la refonte du design se devait d'être contemporaine, masculine, sans prétention, et d'exprimer avec authenticité l'expertise en barbecue qui est au cœur de la marque. C'est chose faite avec une typographie originale, des textures vieillies, et une réinvention du taureau emblème de la marque.

VERSTEGEN
SPICES & SAUCES
HERB AND SPICE SHAKERS

Design: Erik de Graaf, Robert Stakenburg
Company: Millford
Country: The Netherlands
Category: Spices, oils, sauces

SILVER PENTAWARD 2009

Guzman y Gomez brachten ihre eigene Auswahl an Saucen auf den Markt, die in Restaurants und ausgewählten Supermärkten verkauft werden sollten. Für das Design wurden Fotos von mexikanischen Geschäftsinhabern verwendet, die zeigen, wie sie die Saucen probieren. Dabei entsprechen ihre Gesichtsausdrücke der Menge an Chili in der jeweiligen Sauce beziehungsweise deren Schärfegrad. Dieser Ansatz verlieh den Saucen sofort eine Persönlichkeit, und das Produkt erschloss sich schnell.

Guzman y Gomez a lancé sur le marché sa propre gamme de sauces, qui devait être vendue en restaurants et dans des supermarchés sélectionnés. Sur les bouteilles, on voit les visages de gérants mexicains de filiales de la marque, photographiés en train de goûter aux sauces. Leur expression reflète la quantité de chili ou d'épices dans chaque variété. Cette approche confère de la personnalité aux sauces et transmet instantanément des informations sur le produit. Sur le côté de la bouteille, un petit texte décrit les impressions que la personne photographiée a ressenties en goûtant la sauce, ce qui donne une grande authenticité et affirme encore davantage la personnalité du produit.

MARUSAN FOODS ICHIMARU SOY SAUCE

Executive Creative Direction: Junichi Nakazawa
Creative Direction: Yoichi Kondo
Design: Rika Anpo
Account Management: Tamotsu Koizumi
Company: J Inc./Enjin
Country: Japan
Category: Spices, oils, sauces

BRONZE PENTAWARD 2016

GUZMAN Y GOMEZ

Creative Direction: Tony Ibbotson
Design: Andi Yanto
Artwork: Paul Rumens
Company: The Creative Method
Country: Australia
Category: Spices, oils, sauces

GOLD PENTAWARD 2008

Guzman y Gomez were releasing their own range of sauces to be sold in restaurants and selected supermarkets. The design used the faces of Mexican store managers and photographed them tasting the sauces, their expressions reflecting the amount of chilli or heat in each one. This approach gave the sauces immediate personality and quick communication of the product. Along with using the images of the staff there is also a blurb on the side of each bottle that describes the person's experience with it, which gives great authenticity and adds further personality.

GINO'S GARDEN

Conceptual Design: Marios Karystios
Structural Design: Christina Laouri
Ceramics: Stelios Laskaris
Photography: Roger Moukarzel
Printing: Lefteris Kontorousis
Company: Marios Karystios
Country: Cyprus
Category: Spices, oils, sauces
GOLD PENTAWARD 2015

Gino's Garden organic olive oil comes from the region of Rihaneh in Lebanon, with a small quantity being produced each year. The olives are picked by hand in a grove belonging to Gino Haddad and cold-pressed within six hours, making a fine-quality oil. To indicate the organic methods and limited production, a custom-made bottle was specially designed in two different types of olive-shaped finish. The ceramic forms were achieved using mathematical techniques to calculate the irregular shape and volume, and then produced with either a black gloss or green matte glaze. Designed in Cyprus, produced in Greece and enjoyed in Lebanon and elsewhere, a small piece of art and not just another bottle.

Das biologische Olivenöl von **Gino's Garden** stammt aus der Region Rihaneh im Libanon. Jährlich wird nur eine kleine Menge produziert. Handgepflückt in einem Wäldchen, das Gino Haddad besitzt, werden die Oliven innerhalb von sechs Stunden zu einem Öl in feiner Qualität kalt gepresst. Um die biologischen Methoden und die limitierte Produktion zu verdeutlichen, gestaltete man für die Flasche zwei verschiedene olivenförmige Varianten. Für die Keramik nutzte man mathematische Techniken, um die unregelmäßige Form und Größe zu berechnen, die dann entweder mit schwarzer Glanz- oder grüner Mattglasur produziert wurden. Designt in Zypern, produziert in Griechenland und vertrieben im Libanon und anderswo, ist dies nicht einfach nur eine Flasche, sondern ein kleines Kunstwerk.

L'huile d'olive biologique de **Gino's Garden** provient de la région de Rihaneh, au Liban, et seule une petite quantité est produite chaque année. Les olives sont récoltées à la main dans une oliveraie qui appartient à Gino Haddad, et pressées à froid dans les six heures qui suivent pour obtenir une huile de grande qualité. Une bouteille en forme d'olive a été conçue tout spécialement pour souligner la production biologique et à petite échelle. Les formes en céramique ont été obtenues à l'aide de techniques mathématiques pour calculer le volume irrégulier, puis produites en noir brillant ou en vert mat. Conçue à Chypre, produite en Grèce et vendue au Liban et ailleurs, c'est une véritable petite œuvre d'art.

SOLIGEA

Creative Direction/Art Direction: Greg Tsaknakis
Company: Mousegraphics
Country: Greece
Category: Spices, oils, sauces

BRONZE PENTAWARD 2015

Soligea Premium is a superior standard Extra Virgin Olive Oil produced using both modern technology and long-established family tradition. Extracted only by selected olive fruits naturally grown, harvested and pressed in the aromatic pineland of Soligea in Corinth, this fine product of extremely low acidity captivates their full flavor and richness. Enjoy its unique balance of mild fruity notes with spicy accents in all salads and gourmet dishes for the ultimate culinary experience.

Average nutrional value
per 100ml of product

Energy	3389kj / 824kcal
Proteins	0g
Carbohydrates	0g
_Sugars	0g
Fat	91.6g
_Saturated	12.8g
_Monounsaturated	70.5
_Polyunsaturated	8.3
Cholesterol	0g
Dietary fibres	0g
Sodium	0g

Cold extraction
Product of Greece

500ml (16,9 fl.oz)

Bottled by PAMAR Ltd.
Solatati Korinthias,
20100 Korinthos, Greece.
www.soligea.gr

This product may become cloudy at less than 8°C but will clear at room temperature. Store in cool and dark place. Do not expose to direct sunlight.

Best before end:

PREMIUM

Soligea™

Greek extra virgin olive oil

0.5L

JENS EIDE

Design: Eia Grødal
Creative Lead/Design: Morten Throndsen
Company: Strømme Throndsen Design
Country: Norway
Category: Fish, meat, poultry
GOLD PENTAWARD 2011

Jens Eide, a well-known butcher's in Agder, Norway, offers high-quality meat and sausages but lacked the means to communicate this added value to the consumer and so missed out on doing better business. To convey this sense of quality the shop was re-branded as a specialist outlet, offering expert skills and knowledge, and a wide variety of meat products. The design was based on the values of competence, quality and local pride and resulted in a simple yet powerful identity that stated "Butcher handcraft from the heart of Agder".

Jens Eide aus dem norwegischen Agder ist ein bekannter Fleischereibetrieb, der hohe Qualität anbietet. Aber es fehlten die finanziellen Mittel, um das zu kommunizieren, und der Umsatz stagnierte. Um diesen Qualitätsanspruch zu transportieren, wurden die Filialen als Fachgeschäfte neu definiert, in denen man Qualitätsarbeit und Fachberatung findet, außerdem ein breites Angebot. Das Design basiert auf den Werten Kompetenz, Qualität und Lokalstolz und führt zu der einfachen und doch kraftvollen Identität mit der Aussage „Fleischerhandwerk aus dem Zentrum von Agder".

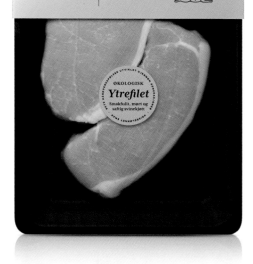

Jens Eide, un boucher renommé à Agder, en Norvège, vend de la viande et des saucisses de qualité, mais n'avait pas les moyens de communiquer cette valeur ajoutée aux consommateurs et perdait donc l'occasion de faire croître son activité. Pour transmettre cette idée de qualité, la stratégie de marque a été revue afin de faire de la boucherie un magasin spécialisé offrant des compétences et connaissances d'expert ainsi qu'une grande variété de produits de boucherie. Le graphisme est basé sur les valeurs de compétence, de qualité et de fierté locale. Le résultat confère une identité simple mais efficace qui indique « Boucher artisanal au cœur d'Agder ».

TZUKUAN FISHERIES ASSOCIATION

Design: Wu Chun Chung
Company: Bosin Design
Country: Taiwan
Category: Fish, meat, poultry

SILVER PENTAWARD 2012

In designing the packaging for this seafood pastry the main motif was fishing culture, with each design shaped like a different fish or shrimp, which also helps protect the fragile contents nicely. The sectional shape allows two or three to be bundled together with twine as a gift set, or packaged just as fishermen in olden days put the dry fish together for sharing with friends and family. In the same way that **Tzukuan** is a fishing village rich in both harvest and happiness, in which the fishermen shared along with their catch, nowadays people can enjoy that too by sharing this delicious seafood pastry.

SEAFOOD MONSTER
GOT ONE!! WILD MULLET CATCH

Design: Ching Wei Liu
Company: Devours Bacon
Country: Taiwan
Category: Fish, meat, poultry
GOLD PENTAWARD 2016

Das Verpackungsdesign dieser Pasteten aus Meeresspezialitäten bezieht seine Hauptmotive aus der Fischereikultur. Jede Verpackung zeigt dem Inhalt entsprechend unterschiedliche Fisch- oder Shrimpsorten und schützt gleichzeitig die Ware sehr gut. Wegen der angeschnittenen Form können zwei oder drei Packungen mit einer Schnur als Geschenk zusammengebunden oder so verschnürt werden, wie früher die Fischer ihren getrockneten Fisch an Freunde und Familie weitergereicht haben. **Tzukuan** ist ein fröhliches Fischerdorf mit reichhaltigem Fangergebnis, in dem alle Fischer ihren Ertrag miteinander teilten. Auf gleiche Weise können heutzutage andere Menschen diese köstlichen Pasteten gemeinsam genießen.

Pour la conception de cet emballage pour des spécialités aux fruits de mer, le thème principal est la culture de la pêche. Chaque élément est en forme de poisson ou de crevette, ce qui aide aussi à protéger le fragile contenu. La forme modulaire permet d'attacher ensemble deux ou trois éléments avec de la ficelle pour faire un cadeau, tout comme les pêcheurs d'antan attachaient les poissons séchés pour les partager avec leurs amis et leur famille. **Tzukuan** est un village où les pêcheurs avaient la coutume de faire profiter de leurs prises. Aujourd'hui nous pouvons faire de même en partageant ces délicieuses spécialités aux fruits de mer.

DAMN TASTY

Creative Direction: Andrey Kugaevskikh
Art Direction/Design: Sergey Trushevsky
Company: Svoe Mnenie
Country: Russia
Category: Fish, meat, poultry

GOLD PENTAWARD 2015

The **Damn Tasty** range of pork products
revives Russian recipes from the 18th century, and
uses the popular lubok style of print to get this
idea across. The simple graphic form was used to
illustrate popular tales and religious stories and
since the Devil was a common feature in Russian
folklore a similar image has been employed for
the brand's visuals and as a reference in its name.
The somewhat crude imagery and provocative
name might prove shocking to some people, but
the result is both eye-catching and authentically
Russian, at the same time conveying the idea of
this Russian delicatessen.

Mit ihren Schweinefleischprodukten lässt **Damn Tasty** russische Rezepte aus dem 18. Jahrhundert wieder aufleben und setzt sich mit den beliebten Lubok-Druckstil in Szene. Diese einfache grafische Form verwendete man zur Illustration beliebter Geschichten und religiöser Erzählungen. Weil der Teufel in der russischen Folklore häufig vorkommt, griff man ihn visuell auf und spielte auch mit dem Produktnamen darauf an. Die recht ungehobelte Bildsprache und der provokative Name schockieren sicher einige. Doch das Ergebnis sticht ins Auge und ist, da es gleichzeitig die Idee dieser nationalen Delikatesse vermittelt, authentisch russisch.

La gamme de viandes de porc **Damn Tasty** ressuscite des recettes russes du XVIIIᵉ siècle, et utilise le style des estampes loubki pour illustrer ce concept. Cette forme graphique simple illustrait les contes populaires et religieux, et sachant que le diable était un personnage courant dans le folklore russe, une image similaire a été utilisée pour les visuels de la marque, et comme référence dans son nom. L'imagerie assez grossière et le nom provocateur pourront en choquer certains, mais le résultat est visuellement réussi, authentiquement russe et transmet parfaitement l'idée du produit.

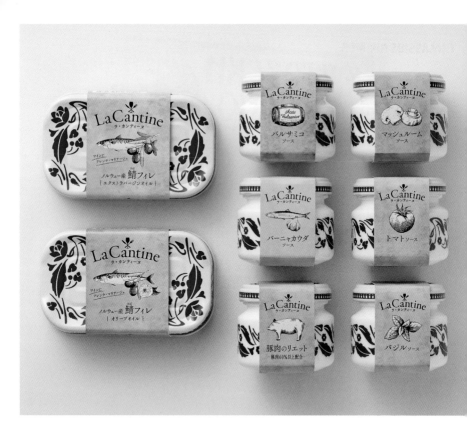

LA CANTINE

Creative Direction: Akiyama Takahiro
Creative Art Direction: Tani Saori
Art Direction: Okabe Maki
Design: Kakizaki Yumiko
Client: Maruha Nichiro
Company: GK Graphics
Country: Japan
Category: Fish, meat, poultry
SILVER PENTAWARD 2015

THALASSIOS KOSMOS

Creative Direction/Design: Gregory Tsaknakis
Company: Mousegraphics
Country: Greece
Category: Fish, meat, poultry

SILVER PENTAWARD 2014

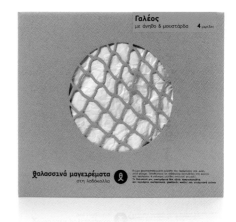

JEALOUS FRUITS
CANADIAN CHERRIES

Design: Bernie Hadley-Beauregard,
Laurie Millotte, Sarah King
Company: Brandever
Country: Canada
Category: Fruit, vegetables

SILVER PENTAWARD 2009

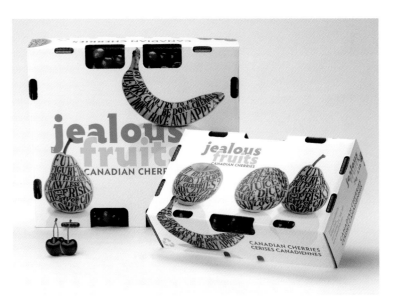

ORTOROMI
INSAL'ARTE

Creative Direction/Graphic Design: Mirco Luzzi
Photography: Gaetano De Rosa
Copywriting: Martina Boromello
Company: DeOfficina
Country: Italy
Category: Fruit, vegetables

SILVER PENTAWARD 2015

SUNFEEL

Creative Direction: Vladimir Fedoseev
Art Direction: Arina Yushkevich
Design: Suzanna Belkina, Elena Kobeleva
Company: Otvetdesign
Country: Russia
Category: Fruit, vegetables

SILVER PENTAWARD 2015

LOKALE HELTER

Art Direction: Morten Throndsen
Design: Linda Gundersen
Typography: Richard Dawson
Company: Strømme Throndsen Design
Country: Norway
Category: Soups, ready-to-eat dishes
SILVER PENTAWARD 2009

K&K
SOZAI GOHAN NO MOTO

Creative Direction/Art Direction:
Masayuki Okabe
Design: Natsuki Hara
Company: L&C Design
Country: Japan
Category: Soups, ready-to-eat dishes
BRONZE PENTAWARD 2015

L'ARTIGIANO

Management Direction: Emmanouela Bitsaxaki
Graphic Design: Eleni Pavlaki
Studio Management: Alexandra Papaloudi
Company: 2yolk Branding & Design
Country: Greece
Category: Soups, ready-to-eat dishes

BRONZE PENTAWARD 2012

Bei diesem so eigenartigen und höchstwahr-scheinlich einzigartigen Produkt spricht die Ver-packung eher mutige und tapfere Verbraucher mit süßem Zahn und Entdeckernase an. Die exzentri-sche Kombination von Verpackung und Produkt spielt mit Medium und Botschaft. Sie präsentiert vor allem für neugierige Augen ein „Außen-Innen"-Spiel der Illusionen. Ein paradoxerweise süßer, essbarer, sogar appetitlicher Kieselstein, das wun-derschöne Bild einer offenen Frucht mit ihrem verblüffend realistischen Fruchtfleisch, echt wir-kende Kirschen, die wie auf den antiken Gemälden des Zeuxis sogar die Vögel verlocken, an ihnen zu knabbern – all dies ein Hochgenuss für den Geist und ersonnen für Verbraucher in einer Umgebung der durchs Design gesteigerten Realität.

Avec un produit aussi étrange, et certainement unique, l'emballage devait attirer les consomma-teurs les plus audacieux, portés sur les sucreries et avides de découvertes. L'association excentrique de l'emballage et du produit joue sur la relation entre le support et le message et présente un jeu d'illusions « intérieur-extérieur » à l'intention des curieux. Le paradoxe d'un galet sucré, comestible, et même appétissant, la superbe image d'un fruit ouvert, avec sa chair étonnamment réaliste, de fausses cerises qui peuvent tromper les oiseaux et les inviter à les grignoter, comme dans les peintures antiques de Zeuxis : toutes ces friandises de l'esprit ont été concoctées pour le consommateur dans un environnement graphique en réalité augmentée.

HATZIYIANNAKIS DRAGEES

Creative Direction: Gregory Tsaknakis
Art Direction: Kostas Vlachakis
Illustration: Ioanna Papaioannou
Company: Mousegraphics
Country: Greece
Category: Confectionery, sweet snacks

GOLD PENTAWARD 2012

With a product so strange and quite likely unique, its packaging should attract the bolder and braver consumer, with a sweet tooth and a nose for discoveries. Playing on the relationship between medium and message, the eccentric coupling of package and product presents an "outer-inner" game of illusions especially for the eyes of the curious. The paradox of a sweet, edible, even appetising pebble, the beautiful image of an open crop, with its startlingly realistic flesh, fake cherries which can fool birds into coming down to nibble at them like in the ancient paintings of Zeuxis: all these are mind-treats concocted for the consumer within a heightened-reality design environment.

BIOKIA

Creative Direction/Concept: Renne Angelvuo
Graphic Design: Tiina Achrén
Illustration: Mikael Achrén
Company: Win Win Branding
Country: Finland
Category: Confectionery, sweet snacks

SILVER PENTAWARD 2012

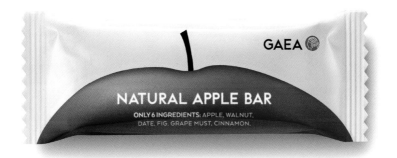

GAEA FRUIT BARS

Creative Direction: Greg Tsaknakis
Art Direction/Design: Greg Tsaknakis, Kostas Kaparos
Illustration: Kostas Kaparos
Company: Mousegraphics
Country: Greece
Category: Confectionery, sweet snacks

SILVER PENTAWARD 2015

NA! NATURE ADDICTS

Creative Direction: Cécile Lacoste,
Jérôme Lanoy
Art Direction: Lise Fenouil
Company: Logic Design
Country: France
Category: Confectionery, sweet snacks
GOLD PENTAWARD 2014

As a 100 percent natural and guilt-free snack,
and a playful alternative to eating actual fruit, this
juice range in squeezable pouches took advantage
of new fruit-processing technology to revamp its
packaging. The "fruit+ process" moves from pick-
ing to blending in just 24 hours, with no cooking;
the package design follows this sense of directness
and, based on the idea that a picture says more
than 1,000 words, expresses immediately what the
product is: pure blended fruit. It does this by making the packaging into the form of the fruit itself,
exactly as it would be found at the produce store.

CHUPA CHUPS
GIFT PACK

Design: Bak Sang-hee, Oh Hye-mi,
Bae Hong-cheol
Company: Nongshim Communications
Country: South Korea
Category: Confectionery, sweet snacks
SILVER PENTAWARD 2012

Als 100 Prozent natürlicher Snack ohne schlechtes Gewissen und als unbeschwerte Alternative zum Genuss echter Früchte nutzt dieses Saftsortiment im Druckbeutel aktuelle Fortschritte der Fruchtverarbeitung. Der Prozess der Weiterverarbeitung zwischen Pflücken und Verschneiden benötigt weniger als 24 Stunden – ohne Kochen. Das Verpackungsdesign greift diese Direktheit auf: Ein Bild sagt mehr als 1000 Worte, und so drückt die Packung sofort aus, um was es hier geht: um reinsten Fruchtsaft! Dafür wird die Verpackung zur Frucht selbst, als hätte man sie gerade beim Obsthändler gefunden.

Cet en-cas sain et 100 pour cent naturel est une nouvelle façon amusante de consommer des fruits frais. La gamme de jus se présente dans des gourdes souples et l'emballage relooké s'inspire du nouveau procédé de traitement des fruits. Le cycle allant de la cueillette au mélange prend seulement 24 heures et n'implique aucune cuisson. Le design obéit à l'esprit de transparence et partant du principe qu'une image vaut plus que mille mots, il montre sans détour ce qu'il renferme: un mélange de fruits pur. L'emballage a la forme du propre fruit, comme sorti de l'étal du maraîcher.

Cacao Barry produziert feinste Schokolade für Restaurants und Süßwarenläden, aber die Papppackungen haben diese Qualität nie so recht aufgegriffen und vermittelt. Charles Barry reiste 1842 nach Afrika und entdeckte die Geschmacksvielfalt der Kakaobohnen verschiedener Plantagen. Diese Reise wurde Grundlage einer „Periodentabelle des Geschmacks", um die vielen komplexen Noten des Sortiments darzustellen. Jede Zutatengruppe wurde dann von unterschiedlichen Künstlern charakteristisch illustriert. Durch Verweise auf spezielle Menschen und Orte, Geologie und Klimazonen sowie Verarbeitung und Techniken präsentiert man Küchenchefs und anderen Verbrauchern neue Anregungen.

Cacao Barry produit du chocolat fin pour la restauration et la confiserie, mais l'emballage en carton ne reflétait pas cette qualité. Le concept est basé sur le voyage de Charles Barry en Afrique en 1842, lors duquel il découvrit la diversité des arômes des fèves de cacao provenant de différentes plantations. Un « tableau périodique des arômes » a été mis au point pour représenter les notes nombreuses et complexes de la gamme, et chaque ensemble d'ingrédients a été illustré par différents artistes. Le résultat fait référence à des personnes, endroits, terrains, climats, processus et techniques spécifiques, et apporte une toute nouvelle proposition.

Cacao Barry produces fine-grade chocolate for the restaurant and confectionery markets, but it was felt this quality was neither preserved nor communicated by its cardboard packaging. Based on Charles Barry's original journey to Africa in 1842, when he discovered the variety of flavors within cocoa beans from different plantations, a 'periodic table of flavor' was developed to represent the many complex different notes across the range and each set of ingredients was then illustrated by distinctly different artists. By referring to specific people and places, geology and climates, and processes and techniques, the result presents a new proposition for chefs and other consumers.

CACAO BARRY
CHOCOLATE DE COUVERTURE

Senior Design: Marloes Oomen
Client Management: Valentina Baraldi
Executive Creative Direction: Claire Parker
Creative Direction: Zayne Dagher
Print Direction: Oscar Flier
Implementation Project Management: Marijn Ham
Creative Artwork: Richard Rigby, Remco Moneiro
Client Direction: Sander Tóth
Company: Design Bridge Amsterdam
Country: Netherlands
Category: Confectionery, sweet snacks

GOLD PENTAWARD 2016

LOTTE
BLACK BLACK FLAVONO

Art Direction: Yoichi Kondo
Creative Direction: Yukio Okada
Copy Text: Endoh 2nd
Design: Yoichi Kondo, Kaoru Ogawa,
Kana Mashiko
Planning Direction: Seiichi Nishikawa
Production: Isao Tomizawa
Company: Enjin
Country: Japan
Category: Confectionery, sweet snacks

BRONZE PENTAWARD 2011

LE CHOCOLAT DES FRANÇAIS

Creative Direction/Art Direction:
Paul-Henri Masson, Matthieu Escande
Illustration: Marie Assénat, Edith Carron,
Soba, Serge Bloch, Gaston de Lapoyade,
Cléa Lala, Maud Begon, Laurène Boglio,
Laureline Galliot, Steffie Brocoli
Company: Le Chocolat des Français
Country: France
Category: Confectionery, sweet snacks

GOLD PENTAWARD 2015

Le chocolat des Français — Noir 70% cacao / Dark 70% cocoa — MADE IN FRANCE

Le chocolat des Français — Noir 70% cacao / Dark 70% cocoa — MADE IN FRANCE

Le chocolat des Français — Noir 70% cacao / Dark 70% cocoa — MADE IN FRANCE

Le chocolat des Français — Lait crémeux / Creamy milk — MADE IN FRANCE

Le chocolat des Français — Lait crémeux / Creamy milk — MADE IN FRANCE

Le chocolat des Français — Lait Caramel et sel — MADE IN FRANCE

Le chocolat des Français — Lait crémeux / Creamy milk — MADE IN FRANCE

Le chocolat des Français — Lait Caramel et sel — MADE IN FRANCE

Le chocolat des Français — Lait crémeux / Creamy milk — MADE IN FRANCE

Le chocolat des Français — Lait crémeux / Creamy milk — MADE IN FRANCE

Le chocolat des Français — Lait Caramel et sel — MADE IN FRANCE

Le chocolat des Français — Lait crémeux / Creamy milk — MADE IN FRANCE

IMURAYA GROUP
GOOD LUCK YOKAN

Design: Kaori Takimoto, Miki Imai,
Kanako Matsuyama, Eri Inamura, Shihomi Ikeda
Company: Rengo
Country: Japan
Category: Confectionery, sweet snacks

BRONZE PENTAWARD 2014

MAROU
FAISEURS DE CHOCOLAT

Design: Chi-An De Leo, Joshua Breidenbach
Company: Rice Creative
Country: Vietnam
Category: Confectionery, sweet snacks

BRONZE PENTAWARD 2012

HANDS OFF MY CHOCOLATE

Design: Kim Kamperman
Company: Yellow Dress Retail
Country: Netherlands
Category: Confectionery, sweet snacks

SILVER PENTAWARD 2014

SULTRY SALLY

Creative Direction: Tony Ibbotson
Illustration: Mark Sofilas
Artwork: Tanya Walker
Company: The Creative Method
Country: Australia
Category: Savoury snacks
GOLD PENTAWARD 2008

The **Sultry Sally** potato chips range was new to the market, so it needed to have immediate cut-through, personality, and standout. The Vargas girls illustrations of the 1940s were used as a basis because, like the chips, they were high in flavor, had immediate character, and the figures of women from this era were slimmer as there was less fat in the diet. A plain matted foil was used for most of the pack surface, and by using color, each flavor is distinguished with an individual feel and story through its pack design.

Die Kartoffelchips der Marke **Sultry Sally** kamen neu auf den Markt. Sie mussten also sofort durchschlagenden Erfolg haben, brauchten eine eigene Persönlichkeit und Alleinstellungsmerkmale. Die Illustrationen mit den Vargas-Girls der 1940er-Jahre wurden als Grundlage verwendet, weil sie wie die Chips voller Geschmack sind und unmittelbar als Persönlichkeiten wirken. Außerdem waren die Frauen dieser Ära schlanker, weil ihre Ernährung fettärmer war. Für den Großteil der Verpackungsoberfläche wurde eine einfache, mattierte Folie eingesetzt. Die Farbgestaltung der Packungen verleiht jeder Sorte einen individuellen Touch und hebt sie durch eigene Geschichten voneinander ab.

La gamme de chips de pomme de terre **Sultry Sally** était nouvelle sur le marché. Il fallait donc qu'elle atteigne sa cible immédiatement en se démarquant et grâce à sa personnalité. Des illustrations de pin-ups Vargas des années 1940 ont été choisies comme base car comme le produit, elles sont pleines de saveur, elles ont du caractère, et les silhouettes des femmes de cette époque étaient plus minces car leur régime contenait moins de graisse. Le reste de la surface du sachet est une feuille métallisée mate, et chaque parfum se distingue des autres grâce à la couleur employée et à un style et une histoire différents déclinés sur tout le paquet.

BULLET MEAL
MOBILE HUNGER STOPPERS
PROTEIN AND ENERGY MEALS

Design: Packlab team
Company: Packlab
Country: Finland
Category: Savory snacks

GOLD PENTAWARD 2016

Bullet Meal is a Finnish start-up brand with the big ambition to redefine the market for ready-meals. Offering a market first with their savory protein bars, this is a high-quality selection of convenient energy snacks for people on the go everywhere. The design takes a playful approach, creating an accessible brand and enabling easy translation to social media campaigns, promotion and advertising. When someone is seen eating one of these products, the image on the pack interacts with their face, giving them a cow's nose, a chicken's neck or a carrot sticking out of their mouth.

BEAUTIFOOD
OINK, OINK

Creative Direction: Paco Adin
Account Direction: Lourdes Morillas
Account Management: Susana Seijas
Company: Supperstudio
Country: Spain
Category: Savory snacks

GOLD PENTAWARD 2015

Bullet Meal ist eine ehrgeizige finnische Start-up-Marke, die den Markt der Fertiggerichte neu definieren will. Zuerst kamen ihre schmackhaften Proteinriegel auf den Markt als qualitativ hochwertige Auswahl praktischer Energiesnacks für Menschen, die viel unterwegs sind. Das spielerische Design schafft eine leicht zugängliche Marke und ermöglicht die einfache Umsetzung in Kampagnen für soziale Medien, Reklame und Werbung. Beobachtet man jemanden beim Genießen dieser Produkte, dann interagiert das Bild auf der Packung mit dessen Gesicht und gibt ihm die Nase einer Kuh, den Hals eines Hühnchens oder lässt eine Möhre aus seinem Mund ragen.

Bullet Meal est une jeune marque finlandaise qui veut redéfinir le marché des repas préparés. Elle a innové avec ses barres protéinées salées, et cette sélection d'en-cas énergétiques haut de gamme et pratiques pour la vie moderne. Le design ludique crée une marque accessible car il est facile à transposer en campagnes sur les réseaux sociaux, promotions et publicité. Lorsqu'une personne mange l'un de ces produits, l'image sur l'emballage se superpose à son visage et lui donne un museau de vache, un cou de poulet ou une carotte plantée dans la bouche.

MÖVENPICK
NESTLE SUPER PREMIUM

Design: Marie Thys
Company: Future Brand
Country: France
Category: Pastry, biscuits, ice-cream, desserts, honey, sugar

GOLD PENTAWARD 2009

FutureBrand's key objective was to clearly position the brand in the Super Premium area, to determine and reflect the new brand essence and be strongly different from premium ice-cream competitors. The design principle was to create the most ice-cream super premium brand which would incarnate "The Art of Swiss Ice-Cream", born from a passion for gastronomy, combined with Swiss perfection.

FutureBrand hatte das Ziel gesetzt bekommen, die Marke eindeutig im Bereich der Super-Premiumprodukte zu positionieren und sie deutlich von den Konkurrenten auf dem Eiscreme-Markt unterscheidbar zu machen. Außerdem sollten die wesentlichen Merkmale dieser neuen Marke festgelegt und umgesetzt werden. Das Prinzip für das Design lautete: Es soll die maximale Super-Premiummarke für Eiscreme geschaffen werden. Diese Marke soll die „Eiscremekunst der Schweiz" verkörpern, die aus einer Leidenschaft für die Gastronomie geboren ist und mit Schweizer Perfektion kombiniert wird.

L'objectif essentiel de FutureBrand était de positionner clairement la marque dans la catégorie « super premium », de définir et de communiquer sa nouvelle essence et de la différencier fortement de ses concurrents haut de gamme. Le principe du design était de créer la marque de crème glacée par excellence, qui incarnerait « l'art de la crème glacée suisse », né d'une passion pour la gastronomie et combiné à la perfection suisse.

GELATI SKY

Brand Strategy: Peter Singline
Creative Direction: David Ansett
Design Direction: Anton Drazevic
Design: Lachlan McDougall, Cassandra Gill
Typography/Illustration: Lachlan McDougall, Cassandra Gill, Anton Drazevic
Copywriting: David Ansett, Peter Singline
Finish Art: Rachel O'Brien
Company: Truly Deeply
Country: Australia
Category: Pastry, biscuits, ice-cream, desserts, honey, sugar

SILVER PENTAWARD 2010

This super-premium, all-wood packaging was developed not so much as a pack for the honey jar, but as an object that may become a permanent piece of a household's kitchenware. In so doing it completely reinvents the idea of the domestic honey-pot. The packaging comprises a cap, a base and four smoothly sanded rings in the middle, all threaded together with a rope handle to create the charming appearance of a beehive, with the jar of honey inside. The region of Armenia it comes from is known for its high-quality honey, produced from meadows no fertilizer has ever touched, thus making this new brand the perfect gift.

Diese Superpremium-Verpackung aus Vollholz wurde weniger als Hülle für ein Honigglas konzipiert, sondern eher als Objekt, das auch dauerhaft in der eigenen Küche nutzbar ist. Dazu erfand man die Idee des häuslichen Honigtopfs komplett neu. Die Verpackung besteht aus Deckel, Basis und vier glattgeschmirgelten, über ein Band miteinander verbundenen Ringen. Zusammen erscheinen sie als bezaubernder Bienenkorb mit Honigglas darin. Die armenische Region, aus der das Lebensmittel stammt, ist für ihren qualitativ hochwertigen Honig bekannt, der auf Wiesen produziert wird, die keinen Kunstdünger kennen. Das macht diese neue Marke zum perfekten Geschenk.

Cet emballage en bois d'extrême qualité a été conçu non pas tant comme une protection pour le pot de miel, mais comme un objet pouvant trouver sa place dans une cuisine ; l'idée du pot de miel familial est ainsi complètement revisitée. L'emballage en bois poncé compte un couvercle, une base et un corps fait de quatre anneaux. Une corde passe par tous ces éléments et finit en poignée, rappel évident d'une ruche, avec le pot de miel à l'intérieur. La région d'Arménie dont il provient est réputée pour son miel d'excellente qualité, produit dans des prairies qui n'ont jamais reçu d'engrais. Le produit forme un cadeau idéal en soi.

BZZZ

Design: Stepan Azaryan, Matt Bartelsian
Company: Backbone Branding
Country: Armenia
Category: Pastry, biscuits, ice-cream,
desserts, honey, sugar

GOLD PENTAWARD 2013

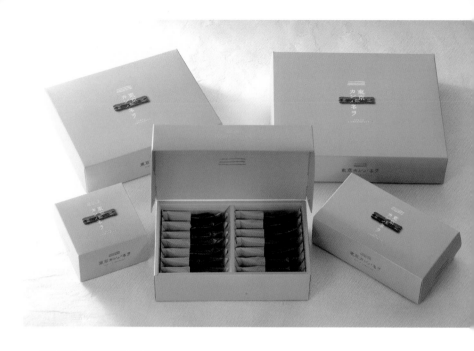

TOKYO CAMPANELLA

Design: Fumi Sasada
Company: Bravis International
Country: Japan
Category: Pastry, biscuits,
ice-cream, desserts, honey, sugar

GOLD PENTAWARD 2008

ZENKASHOIN
"ZEN" CASTELLA

Art Direction: Shigeno Araki
Design: Toshiyuki Murayama, Mizuho Tada
Company: Shigeno Araki Design & Co.
Country: Japan
Category: Pastry, biscuits, ice-cream, desserts, honey, sugar

GOLD PENTAWARD 2010

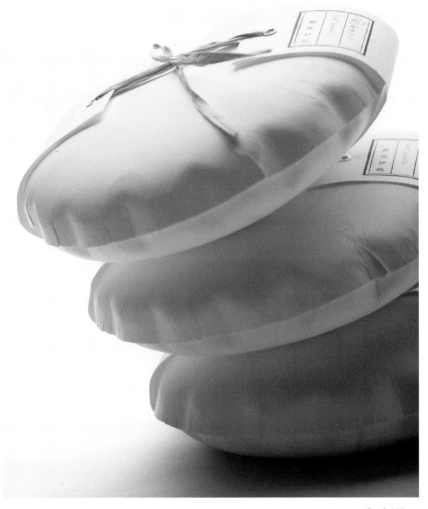

MARAIS

Design: Kazuaki Kawahara
Company: Latona Marketing
Country: Japan
Category: Pastry, biscuits, ice-cream,
desserts, honey, sugar

SILVER PENTAWARD 2016

CISHAN FOCUS
BANANA PIE

Design: Wu Chun Chung
Company: Bosin Design
Country: Taiwan
Category: Pastry, biscuits,
ice-cream, desserts, honey, sugar

BRONZE PENTAWARD 2011

JOHNNY DOODLE
CHOCOLATE & FUDGE

Concept: Arthur van Hamersveld,
Jantine Knijnenburg
Art Direction: Arthur van Hamersveld,
Femke van Zijl
Design and Typography: Femke van Zijl
Company: Brandnew
Country: Netherlands
Category: Pastry, biscuits, ice-cream,
desserts, honey, sugar

GOLD PENTAWARD 2016

FOODSCROSS

*Creative Direction and
Art Direction:* Greg Tsaknakis
Illustration: Si Scott,
Thalassinos Anastasiou
Company: Mousegraphics
Country: Greece
Category: Pastry, biscuits,
ice-cream, desserts, honey, sugar
BRONZE PENTAWARD 2015

HARMONIAN

Creative Direction: Gregory Tsaknakis
Design: Joshua Olsthoorn
Company: Mousegraphics
Country: Greece
Category: Food trends
SILVER PENTAWARD 2014

KALLØ

Creative Direction: Perry Haydn Taylor
Company: Big Fish
Country: UK
Category: Food trends
GOLD PENTAWARD 2014

Kallø makes natural, healthy alternatives to things like cakes, biscuits, bread and stock-cubes, but their packaging has in the past been typically rather anonymous. With customers who are intelligent and like to be in control of what they eat it was also important to move on from the old packaging which made them feel like they had "special needs" rather than being foodies free to enjoy natural nibbles. The revamped design was thus intended to liberate Kallø consumers from any negative feelings and instead give them something to love and be proud of, with these cheerful packs decorated with poems and illustrations.

Kallo bietet eine natürliche, gesunde Alternative für Kekse, Biskuits, Brot oder auch Brühwürfel, doch deren Verpackung war früher oft recht anonym. Für intelligente Kunden, die unbedingt wissen wollen, was sie essen, war es aber auch wichtig, sich von der alten Verpackung zu lösen. Die alte Packung hatte das Gefühl vermittelt, irgendwie bedürftig zu sein, anstatt den Feinschmecker in den Vordergrund zu rücken, der gerne natürlichen Knabberspaß genießt. Das umgestaltete Design sollte somit die Kallø-Kunden von negativen Gefühlen befreien und ihnen mit den fröhlichen Verpackungen, geschmückt mit Gedichten und Illustrationen, etwas an die Hand geben, das sie lieben und worauf sie stolz sein können.

Kallø fabrique des gâteaux, des biscuits, du pain et, des cubes de bouillon à la fois sains et naturels ; ses emballages étaient toutefois sans personnalité. Les consommateurs étant de plus en plus attentifs et soucieux de ce qu'ils mangent, il était important pour la marque d'évoluer vers un design en accord avec les besoins des clients qui préfèrent être considérés des gourmets amateurs d'en-cas naturels plutôt qu'ayant des besoins spéciaux. La refonte du design a donc cherché à libérer les consommateurs de Kallø de sentiments négatifs en leur offrant des produits agréables, aux emballages colorés et décorés de poèmes et d'illustrations.

www.mcwhopper.com

BURGER KING MCWHOPPER

Head of Design: David Turner,
Bruce Duckworth
Creative Direction: Clem Halpin (TD),
Tom Paine (Y&R NZ)
Design: Christian Eager, Jamie Nash,
Adam Cartwright (TD)
SeniorAccount Management: Nicola Eager (TD)
Chief Creative Management:
Josh Moore (Y&R NZ)
Company: Turner Duckworth/Y&R NZ
Country: UK, USA, New Zealand
Category: Fast-food restaurants
GOLD PENTAWARD 2016

To raise awareness of World Peace Day, **Burger King** called for a "burger wars ceasefire" with old rival McDonald's, proposing the two join forces to sell the McWhopper: a symbolic hybrid burger containing key ingredients of the Big Mac and the Whopper. Knowing how likely McDonald's was to decline the idea, a campaign strategy sought to ensure maximum coverage for the McWhopper in PR and social media, complete with logo and finished identity. The peaceful union of the two brands was expressed in the coalition of their respective logos and color schemes, and the resulting image was quickly circulated to popular acclaim; McDonald's drew widespread criticism from media when they rejected the offer.

Um für den Weltfriedenstag zu werben, rief **Burger King** den alten Konkurrenten McDonald's zu einem „Waffenstillstand der Burgerbrater" auf. Beide sollten sich zusammentun und den „Mc-Whopper" verkaufen: Dieser symbolische Hybridburger enthält die Hauptzutaten von Big Mac und Whopper. Klar war, dass McDonald's die Idee möglicherweise ablehnen würde, und deshalb griff man zu einer Kampagnenstrategie komplett mit Logo und eigenständiger Identität, die dem Mc-Whopper maximale Resonanz bei PR und Social Media ermöglicht. Die friedvolle Vereinigung dieser beiden Marken drückte sich im Verbund beider Logos und ihrer Farbgebung aus. Das Ergebnis zirkulierte schnell und erhielt positiven Zuspruch; McDonald's zog sich die allgemeine Kritik der Medien zu, als man das Angebot ablehnte.

À l'occasion de la Journée internationale de la paix, **Burger King** a appelé au « cessez-le feu dans la guerre des hamburgers » avec son vieux rival McDonald's, et a proposé que les deux marques unissent leurs forces pour vendre le McWhopper : un hybride symbolique entre le Big Mac et le Whopper. Sachant que McDonald's refuserait sûrement l'idée, une stratégie de campagne chercha à assurer une diffusion maximum sur les réseaux sociaux du McWhopper, avec logo et identité complète. L'union pacifiste des deux marques est exprimée par l'association de leurs logos et couleurs, et l'image résultante a rapidement et largement été diffusée et acclamée par le public. McDonald's s'est attiré les foudres des médias en déclinant l'offre.

WAGAMAMA
TAKEOUT EXPERIENCE

Chief Creative Direction: Jonathan Ford
Managing Direction: Darren Foley
Design Direction: Fiona John
3D Design Direction: Mike Beauchamp
Senior Technical Project Management: Jenny Cairns
Senior Creative Strategy: Jack Hart
Client Management: Ally Tyger
Plastics: Anson Food Packaging
Boards: Matthews Printers
Distribution: Bunzl Catering Supplies
Company: Pearlfisher
Country: UK
Category: Fast-food restaurants
BRONZE PENTAWARD 2016

BURGER KING
HALLOWEEN WHOPPER

Design Direction: David Turner,
Bruce Duckworth
Creative Direction: Clem Halpin
Design: David Blakemore, Boyko Taskov
Illustration: Geoffrey Appleton
Production: James Norris
Senior Account Management: Nicola Eager
Company: Turner Duckworth,
London & San Francisco
Country: UK, USA
Category: Fast-food restaurants

SILVER PENTAWARD 2016

VAN DER **BURGH**
CHOCOLAAD
HANDGEMAAKTE CHOCOLADE

PURE CHOCOLADE
72% CACAO
100 GRAM

VAN DER **BURGH**
CHOCOLAAD
HANDGEMAAKTE CHOCOLADE

PURE CHOCOLADE
54% CACAO
100 GRAM

VAN DER **BURGH**
CHOCOLAAD
HANDGEMAAKTE CHOCOLADE

MELK CHOCOLADE
MET HELE HAZELNOOT
40% CACAO
100 GRAM

VAN DER **BURGH**
CHOCOLAAD
HANDGEMAAKTE CHOCOLADE

MELK CHOCOLADE
MET AMANDEL
40% CACAO
100 GRAM

VAN DER BURGH CHOCOLAAD JHERONIMUS BOSCH

Design: Jeroen Hoedjes, Paul Roeters
Company: Studio Kluif
Country: Netherlands
Category: Limited editions, limited series, event creations

GOLD PENTAWARD 2015

In 2016 the city of 's-Hertogenbosch commemorates the 500th anniversary of the death of the painter Hieronymus Bosch, its most famous son. His utterly distinctive style and fantastic imagery are the basis for the **jHEROnimus** brand, which markets contemporary products inspired by the artist's works. Amongst a variety of different items to be sold in museum-shops around the world, the jHEROnimus chocolate has been handmade by the Van der Burgh Chocolaad company. A limited edition, its wrapper incorporates details from Bosch's works alongside simple graphic wallpaper motifs.

2016 gedenkt die holländische Stadt 's-Hertogenbosch des 500. Todestags von Hieronymus Bosch, dem berühmtesten Sohn der Stadt. Sein außerordentlich charakteristischer Stil und die fantastischen Gemälde bilden die Basis der Marke **jHEROnimus**, unter der moderne, vom Werk des Künstlers inspirierte Produkte vermarktet werden. Neben vielfältigen verschiedenen Artikeln, die in Museumsshops in aller Welt verkauft werden, stellt die Firma Van der Burgh Chocolaad die Schokolade jHEROnimus per Hand her. Die limitierte Edition zeigt Details der Werke von Bosch neben einfachen Tapetenmustern.

En 2016, la ville de Bois-le-Duc a commémoré le 500ᵉ anniversaire de la mort du peintre Jérôme Bosch, son enfant le plus célèbre. Son style tout à fait distinctif et ses images fantastiques sont la base de la marque **jHEROnimus**, qui vend des produits contemporains inspirés par les œuvres de cet artiste. Les différents articles qui seront vendus dans les musées du monde entier comprennent aussi le chocolat jHEROnimus, fabriqué à la main par la société Van der Burgh Chocolaad. En édition limitée, son emballage associe des détails des œuvres de Bosch à des motifs de papier peint graphique.

KIT KAT
75TH ANNIVERSARY
Design: Abt Dylan
Company: ARD Design Switzerland
Country: Switzerland
Category: Limited editions,
limited series, event creations

SILVER PENTAWARD 2010

KAHVE DÜNYASI
ISTANBUL 2010 CHOCOLATE TABLETS
Creative Direction: Bülent Erkmen, Yesim Bakirküre
Design: Bülent Erkmen
Company: Bek Tasarim, Ypsilon Tasarim
Country: Turkey
Category: Limited editions,
limited series, event creations

BRONZE PENTAWARD 2010

CRISTAL UNION DADDY SUCRE "PRISONNIERS"

Design: CB'a design team
Company: Sleever International
Country: France
Category: Limited editions, limited series, event creations

GOLD PENTAWARD 2013

CRISTAL UNION DADDY SUCRE

Design: CB design team
Company: Sleever International
Country: France
Category: Limited editions, limited series, event creations

SILVER PENTAWARD 2014

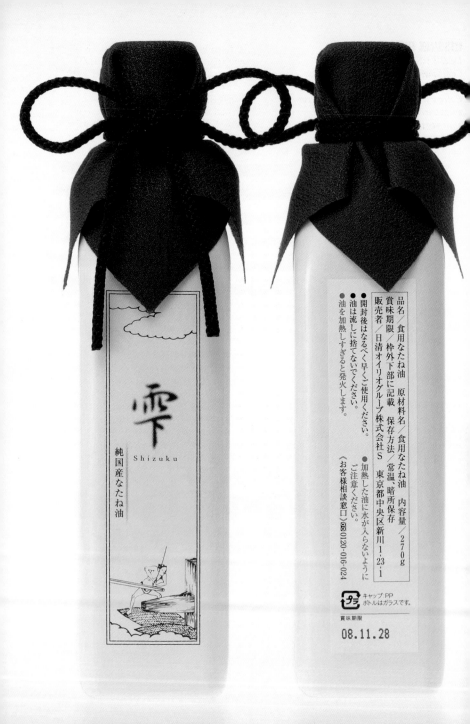

雫
Shizuku

純国産なたね油

品名／食用なたね油
原材料名／食用なたね油　内容量／270g
賞味期限／枠外下部に記載　保存方法／常温、暗所保存
販売者／日清オイリオグループ株式会社S　東京都中央区新川1・23・1

● 開封後はなるべく早くご使用ください。
● 油は流しに捨てないでください。
● 油を加熱しすぎると発火します。
● 加熱した油に水が入らないように
　ご注意ください。

《お客様相談窓口》☎0120-016-024

キャップ：PP
ボトルはガラスです。

賞味期限
08.11.28

NISSHIN OILLIO

Design: Hanae Yamamuro
Company: Deziro
Country: Japan
Category: Limited editions, limited series,
event creations
GOLD PENTAWARD 2008

Nisshin Oillio is a pure, domestically-produced
canola oil, and a limited supply of it was produced
to celebrate the 290th anniversary of a famous
Japanese department store. The glass bottle was
coated using an ancient spray-technique for porcelain ware, so that it feels like a porcelain bottle,
suggesting that the oil is a relic of ancient Japan.

Nisshin Oillio ist ein reines Rapsöl aus ein-
heimischer Produktion. Ein Teil davon wurde
in begrenzter Auflage hergestellt, um den 290.
Geburtstag eines berühmten japanischen Waren-
hauses zu feiern. Die Glasflasche wurde mittels
einer altertümlichen Sprühtechnik für Porzellan
bedeckt, damit sie sich wie eine Porzellanflasche
anfühlt und somit den Eindruck vermittelt,
das Öl sei ein Relikt des alten Japans.

Nisshin Oillio est une huile de colza pure
produite au Japon. Une quantité limitée en a été
produite pour célébrer le 290ᵉ anniversaire d'un
grand magasin japonais renommé. La bouteille
en verre a été recouverte à l'aide d'une technique
ancienne de pulvérisation pour la vaisselle en porcelaine, afin de suggérer que l'huile est un vestige
du Japon ancien.

AGROVIL
ILIADA

Design: Gregory Tsaknakis,
Ioanna Papaioannou,
Vassiliki Argyropoulou
Company: Mousegraphics
Country: Greece
Category: Limited editions,
limited series, event creations
SILVER PENTAWARD 2009

BOLLING COFFEE FORTNUM & MASON
300TH ANNIVERSARY COFFEE METAL TIN

Design: Fortnum and Mason
Company: Crown Speciality Packaging
Country: France
Category: Limited editions, limited series,
event creations
BRONZE PENTAWARD 2009

CADBURY FAVOURITES

Creative Direction: Chris Wilson
Strategic Direction: Nina Kelly
Design: Sam Holliss
Company: Brand Society
Country: Australia
Category: Limited editions, limited series,
event creations

SILVER PENTAWARD 2016

BISCUITERIE JULES DESTROOPER

Creative Direction: Jürgen Hûughe
Concept/Design: Joseph Robinson
Company: Quatre Mains
Country: Belgium
Category: Limited editions, limited series,
event creations

SILVER PENTAWARD 2016

2479 PRISONER PRODUCT

Executive Creative Direction:
Somchana Kangwarnjit
Creative Direction:
Orawan Jongpisanpattana
Design: SKJ, Pongpipat Jetsadalak
Company: Prompt Design
Country: Thailand
Category: Private labels

GOLD PENTAWARD 2015

The striped theme for this range of wines, condiments and foodstuffs is taken from the prisoner's uniform of horizontal black and white bands, with the addition of a prisoner's number common to all items. The number **2479** corresponds to the year in the Buddhist calendar (= 1936) when the Penitentiary Act was amended to improve the conditions of inmates, while on the back of the packaging the hands on the "cell bars" of the bar code sit beneath a pair of hands extended in handshake, to represent reintegration in society. Currently programs are in place to grant training to prisoners, providing them with skills for life after release and with many of the products from this work, from furniture to food, being available in certain outlets.

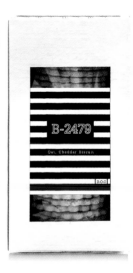

Dieses Wein-, Gewürz- und Lebensmittelsortiment bedient sich mit seinen horizontalen schwarzweißen Streifen bei Gefangenenuniformen. Überdies trägt jeder Artikel eine Gefangenennummer. Die Zahl **2479** korrespondiert mit dem Jahr des buddhistischen Kalenders (= 1936), in dem das Strafvollzugsgesetz zur Verbesserung der Haftbedingungen geändert wurde. Auf der Rückseite der Packung greifen Hände in die „Schwedischen Gardinen" des Strichcodes. Die einander ergreifenden Hände darüber repräsentieren die Reintegration in die Gesellschaft. Aktuelle Programme sollen die Gefangenen in Schulungen auf das Leben nach der Haft vorbereiten; behilflich sind dazu viele Produkte dieser Arbeit, von Möbeln bis zu Lebensmitteln, die in bestimmten Läden verkauft werden.

Le thème à rayures de cette gamme de vins, condiments et aliments provient de l'uniforme rayé noir et blanc des prisonniers, avec un matricule commun à tous les articles. Le chiffre **2479** correspond à l'année du calendrier bouddhiste (= 1936) durant laquelle l'Acte pénitentiaire a été amendé afin d'améliorer la situation des détenus. Au dos de l'emballage, des mains sur les « barreaux de cellule » du code-barres sont situées en dessous d'une paire de mains tendues pour représenter la réintégration sociale. Des programmes sont actuellement menés pour offrir aux prisonniers une formation qui leur servira après leur libération, et nombre des produits de ce travail, qui vont des meubles ou aliments, sont disponibles dans certains points de vente.

AMBAR
SHOPPING LIST

Creative Direction: Alexandr Zagorsky
Copywriting: Fara Kuchkarov,
Ekaterina Lavrova
Art Direction: Tatyana Mikolaevskaya
Project Lead: Anna Smirnova
Company: Depot WPF
Country: Russia
Category: Private labels

SILVER PENTAWARD 2016

Here is a packaging design that strips the concept down to its absolute essentials, marketing this private-label brand according to the simplest criterion of all from a consumer's point of view, the shopping list. The design scheme for the whole range is as plain and clear as can be, based on the awareness that consumers are busy and might often prefer not to have to waste time on thousands of logos, colors and images, particularly when buying such basics as milk, eggs or honey. There should be no distractions, they just need to follow the shopping list!

Dieses Verpackungsdesign streicht das Konzept auf die wesentlichsten Bestandteile zusammen und vermarktet diese Privatmarke über das aus Sicht des Verbrauchers einfachsten Kriterium von allen: die Einkaufsliste. Das Designschema für das gesamte Sortiment ist so einfach und klar wie möglich und basiert auf dem Wissen, wie eilig es die Verbraucher haben und oft lieber keine Zeit mit Tausenden Logos, Farben und Bildern verschwenden, vor allem wenn's um den Kauf solch grundlegender Nahrungsmittel wie Milch, Eier oder Honig geht. Keine Ablenkung, man folgt einfach nur seiner Einkaufsliste!

Voici un concept d'emballage qui revient à l'essentiel, et articule cette marque de distributeur autour du critère le plus simple du point de vue du consommateur, à savoir la liste de courses. Le design de toute cette gamme est aussi simple et clair que possible, et se base sur l'idée que les consommateurs sont occupés et préfèrent souvent ne pas perdre de temps avec des milliers de logos, couleurs et images, surtout lorsqu'ils cherchent des produits de base tels que du lait, des œufs ou du miel. Adieu les distractions, il suffit de suivre la liste de courses !

THE DELI GARAGE
OIL CHANGE

Creative Direction: Kathrin Oeding
Art Direction: Reginald Wagner
Copywriting: Katharina Trumbach
Graphic Design: Jan Simmerl
Company: Kolle Rebbe
Country: Germany
Category: Distributors'/Retailers' own brands
GOLD PENTAWARD 2009

Oil Change (Ölwechsel) ist ein Premium-Olivenöl, das mit Chili, Koriander und Limone geschmacklich verfeinert wurde. Damit die Öle den gewünschten Werkstattcharakter bekommen, wurden sie in kleinen Fläschchen verpackt, wie sie auch für Motoröle verwendet werden. Das Öl spritzt man aus diesen Flaschen direkt auf die Lebensmittel. Die Illustrationen auf den Flaschen suggerieren Ölflecken. Wenn man durch die Flasche hindurch schaut, erzeugen sie außerdem den Eindruck, als würden sie Monster in sich tragen. **The Deli Garage** als Hersteller dieses Produkts unterstützt auch kleine und einheimische Erzeuger.

Oil Change is a premium olive oil flavoured with chilli, coriander, and lemon. To fit the garage character, the oils were packaged in the little oil bottles used for motor oil, and could be squeezed from them on to food. The illustrations on the bottles also suggest oil stains, and have the effect that when they are looked at through the bottle it's as if monsters are emerging from them. **The Deli Garage**, the maker of the product, also supports small and local manufacturers.

Oil Change (vidange) est une huile haut de gamme parfumée au piment rouge, au romarin et au citron. Pour rester dans l'esprit « garage », les huiles ont été conditionnées dans de petites bouteilles similaires à celles utilisées pour l'huile de moteur. Ces bouteilles permettent de verser l'huile sur les aliments d'une simple pression de la main. Les illustrations évoquent également des taches d'huile et donnent l'impression, quand on les regarde à travers la bouteille, de voir apparaître des monstres. **The Deli Garage**, qui produit ces huiles, soutient également les petits producteurs locaux.

MORRISONS SAVERS

Creative Direction: Stephen Bell
Design: Craig Barnes, Carolyn Sweet
Account Management: Andy Hellmuth
Company: Coley Porter Bell
Country: UK
Category: Distributors'/Retailers' own brands

GOLD PENTAWARD 2012

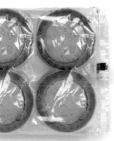

M savers

12 Fairy Cakes
Ready to decorate

Seasonal Salad

14 Normal Incontinence Pads

14 Ultra Towels

Sweetcorn

Whisky

Vodka

Brandy

Gin

40 Plasters

10 All Purpose Cloths

Orange Juice
from concentrate
1 Litre

D
Carbon Zinc
batteries

AAA
Carbon Zinc
batteries

9v
Carbon Zinc
batteries

20 Nappies
size 4

72 Fragrance Free
Baby Wipes

Shaving Foam
250ml

Hair Mousse
400ml

GARANT BY AXFOOD
ECOLOGICAL PRODUCTS

Art Direction/Design: Stefan Sundstrom
Artwork/Design: Malin Ringsby,
Linn Svensson, Mathias Jonsson,
Karl Mattisson, Johan Haag
Creative Direction: Marie Wollbeck
Account Direction: Susanne Oberg Dimic
Strategic Direction: Torbjorn Nordkvist
Project Management Design:
Jenny Wenngren (Axfood)
Photography: Fabian Bjornstjerna
Company: BAS
Country: Sweden
Category: Cross-category ranges

SILVER PENTAWARD 2013

TESCO FINEST
GROCERY

Design: Melanie Kendall, Jesse Moran, Helena Bland, Jon Sleeman, Paul Watson
Art Direction: Simon Pemberton
Company: Pemberton & Whitefoord
Country: UK
Category: Cross-category ranges

GOLD PENTAWARD 2014

GOGOL MOGOL

Creative Direction: Kirill Konstantinov
Design: Evgeny Morgalev
Company: Kian Branding Agency
Country: Russia
Category: Packaging concept

GOLD PENTAWARD 2012

With **gogol mogol** eggs an ambitious project for the future introduces a new way of cooking, storing and packing eggs. Sold in shops on a three-storey pedestal, this also takes up less space in a shopping-bag. Each egg is packaged individually in recycled cardboard with further layers beneath—the second constitutes the catalyst, beneath which is a membrane separating it from a third layer made of smart material. When the membrane is pulled out (by means of a tag), a chemical reaction occurs between the catalyst and the smart material, and the egg begins to heat up. After a few minutes, when the lid of the packaging is lifted off, a boiled egg is ready for an easy breakfast.

Die **gogol mogol**-Eier führen ein ehrgeiziges zukunftsorientiertes Projekt ein, das neue Wege beim Zubereiten, Lagern und Verpacken von Eiern vorstellt. In den Läden werden sie in einer Art dreiteiligen Säule verkauft, die auch in Einkaufstüten weniger Platz benötigt. Jedes Ei wird einzeln in recyceltem Karton verpackt. In der Schicht darunter befindet sich der Katalysator und darunter, getrennt durch eine Membran, eine dritte Schicht aus einem intelligenten Material. Wenn die Membran mittels eines kleinen Etiketts herausgezogen wird, löst das eine chemische Reaktion zwischen Katalysator und intelligentem Material aus, und das Ei wird erhitzt. Nach wenigen Minuten kann man den Deckel der Verpackung öffnen und erhält ein perfektes Frühstücksei.

Les œufs **gogol mogol** sont un projet d'avenir ambitieux qui présente une nouvelle façon de cuire, stocker et emballer les œufs. Vendus en magasin sur un présentoir à trois étages, ils prennent aussi moins de place dans les sacs à provisions. Chaque œuf est emballé individuellement dans du carton recyclé avec plusieurs couches internes : la deuxième est le catalyseur, et une membrane la sépare d'une troisième couche faite d'un matériau intelligent. Lorsqu'on ouvre la membrane (à l'aide d'une languette), une réaction chimique se produit entre le catalyseur et le matériau intelligent, et l'œuf commence à chauffer. Quelques minutes plus tard, lorsqu'on soulève le couvercle, l'œuf à la coque est prêt pour le petit-déjeuner.

EAT&GO

Design: Olga Gambaryan,
Diana Gibadulina,
Alexander Kischenko,
Andronik Poloz (students)
School: British Higher School
of Art & Design (Moscow)
Country: Russia
Category: Packaging concept
SILVER PENTAWARD 2013

Just Laid

6 MEDIUM FREE RANGE EGGS

JUST LAID

Design: Kevin Daly
Illustration: Peter O'Connor
Company: Springetts Brand Design Consultants
Country: UK
Category: Packaging concept
GOLD PENTAWARDS 2014

In order to promote the idea of sustainability for this general foodstuff the emphasis was put squarely on its freshness by means of the design showing an egg being "just laid". The three images of hens a-laying indicate the three different sizes of eggs available. The use of the standard egg-box helps to convey the idea of freshness, with the fastening bump becoming a representation of the egg itself so that consumers can better understand the natural process of egg-laying.

Um für dieses Grundnahrungsmittel das Konzept der Nachhaltigkeit in den Vordergrund zu stellen, bestimmt die Frische des Produkts das Design: Die Verpackung zeigt ein „frisch gelegtes" Ei. Drei Bilder von Hennen im Legeeinsatz kennzeichnen die verschiedenen Eiergrößen. Das Standardformat der Eierkartons hilft die Frische unmittelbar zu vermitteln. Der Kartonverschluss selbst repräsentiert bereits das Produkt. Dem Verbraucher wird so der natürliche Prozess des Eierlegens näher gebracht.

Pour mettre en avant, l'idée de développement durable de cet aliment de base, l'accent est mis sur la fraîcheur par l'image de l'oeuf pondu « en direct ». Les trois images de poules en train de pondre correspondent aux trois tailles d'oeufs disponibles. L'utilisation de la boîte standard véhicule l'idée de fraîcheur ; le système de fermeture est symbolisé par un œuf afin que les consommateurs perçoivent mieux encore le processus naturel de ponte.

SPROUT

Creative Direction: Moyra Casey
Design: Kelly Bennett
Visualization: Peter O'Connor
Company: Springetts Brand Design Consultants
Country: UK
Category: Packaging concept

GOLD PENTAWARD 2013

Sprout set out to break new ground in the baby food category with the introduction of a fresh, chilled range of part-prepared baby food, similar to formats available for adult consumption. This would allow parents to make up the meals quickly and easily at home. The name is intended to convey the integrity of the ingredients and how the right food is key to healthy development. Building on this idea, the creative execution is a playful, literal expression of "you are what you eat". The baby is shown as happy, healthy and flourishing with the help of nature's best ingredients, an image designed to be both reassuring and emotionally engaging, as well as making people smile.

Sprout macht sich daran, in der Kategorie Babynahrung Neuland zu betreten, und führte ein frisches, gekühltes Sortiment mit teilweise vorge-kochter Babynahrung ein. Solche Formate gibt es bereits als Produkte für Erwachsene. So können Eltern die Mahlzeiten schnell und einfach zu Hause zubereiten. Der Name soll die Integrität der Zutaten vermitteln und richtige Nahrung als Schlüssel zu einer gesunden Entwicklung. Die kreative Ausführung greift dieses Konzept auf und setzt den Spruch „Du bist, was du isst" spielerisch und buchstäblich um. Man sieht das gesunde und glückliche Baby, das mithilfe bester natürlicher Zutaten wächst und gedeiht. Dieses Bild verleiht Bestätigung, schafft emotionale Bindung und entlockt ein Lächeln.

Sprout cherchait à innover dans le domaine des aliments pour bébés en lançant une gamme de préparations au design frais et dans des formats semblables à ceux pour les adultes. L'idée était de permettre aux parents de préparer rapidement les repas. Le nom vise à évoquer l'intégrité des ingrédients et à faire savoir qu'une alimentation saine est la clé d'une bonne croissance. Le résultat est l'expression littérale de « vous êtes ce que vous mangez » : les bébés apparaissent contents, en bonne santé et épanouis grâce aux meilleurs ingrédients qu'offre la nature. L'image est conçue pour être rassurante et stimulante, mais aussi pour faire sourire.

HOT MAGIC CUP BOWL

Design: Saki Murai
Company: Toyo Seikan
Country: Japan
Category: Packaging concept
GOLD PENTAWARD 2015

The special packaging for this instant miso soup features an outer layer whose shape changes when hot water is poured into it. A heat-contraction film sealed inside the two-layer paper cup shrinks with the heat of hot water, causing the outside layer of the cup to take the form of a bowl. The delicate curving lines are produced by flexible strips of paper which give the simple cup a shape similar to traditional Japanese soup bowls, and means that the miso may be enjoyed in an authentic way by holding the bottom and side of the bowl.

In der Verpackung für diese Miso-Instantsuppe gibt es eine spezielle Schicht, deren Form sich ändert, sobald heißes Wasser eingegossen wird. Ein zwischen den beiden Schichten des Papierbechers versiegelter Film schrumpft durch die Wärme und lässt die Verpackung die Form einer Schale annehmen. Flexible Papierstreifen sorgen für die zarte Krümmung, die den einfachen Becher in eine traditionelle japanische Suppenschale verwandelt. Hält man den Becher nun seitlich von unten, kann man die Misosuppe auf authentische Weise genießen.

L'emballage spécial de cette soupe miso instantanée est doté d'une couche extérieure qui change de forme lorsqu'on y verse de l'eau chaude. Entre les deux couches du gobelet en papier, un film se contracte sous l'effet de la chaleur et fait prendre à la surface extérieure la forme d'un bol. Les délicates lignes incurvées sont créées par des bandes de papier flexible qui évoquent un bol à soupe japonais classique et signifient que l'on peut boire la soupe miso à la manière traditionnelle, en tenant le bol par le fond et le côté.

A POUCH WITH DECORATIVE HOLES

Design: Takashi Nomura
Company: Toyo Seikan
Country: Japan
Category: Packaging concept
BRONZE PENTAWARD 2015

POTATO CHIPS

Design: Mina Matsuhiro
Company: Toyo Seikan
Country: Japan
Category: Packaging concept
BRONZE PENTAWARD 2016

JAMÓN IBÉRICO

LOMO IBÉRICO

DEMARIA
Design: Gaizka Ruiz
Creative Direction: Enric Aguilera
Company: Enric Aguilera Asociados
Country: Spain
Category: Packaging concept
BRONZE PENTAWARD 2013

YOUR WAY JERKY
Design: Oleg Safronov (student)
School: British Higher School
of Art & Design (Moscow)
Country: Russia
Category: Packaging concept
SILVER PENTAWARD 2014

DINO ICE

Design: Sasha Perelman,
Katya Mushkina (students)
School: British Higher School
of Art & Design (Moscow)
Country: Russia
Category: Packaging concept

SILVER PENTAWARD 2016

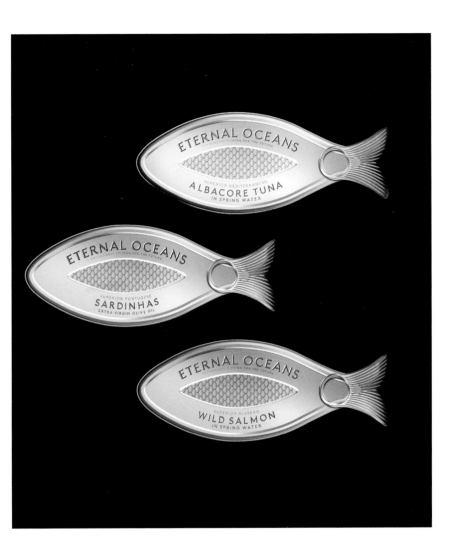

ETERNAL OCEANS
Design: Sara Jones
Company: Anthem
Country: Netherlands
Category: Packaging concept
GOLD PENTAWARD 2016

Best of the category
Clothing, garments
Health care
Body care

body

Beauty
Perfumes, cosmetics
Distributors'/Retailers' own brands, private labels
Packaging concept

Görtz 17 suchte für die Converse-Kollektion nach einem innovativen Verpackungsdesign, das Konsumenten am Point of Sale ansprechen sollte – wohl wissend, dass die Linie dieser stylishen Schuhe selbst bereits ein Kultprodukt ist. Um dem Verkauf nachzuhelfen und die Marke noch begehrenswerter erscheinen zu lassen, wurde als erstes Werk dieser Art ein recycelbares Schuhbehältnis entwickelt, das Plastiktüten überflüssig macht. Das minimalistische Design lenkt das Augenmerk auf die Tragegriffe, die man herausziehen und als zusätzliches Paar Schnürsenkel verwenden kann. Die Serie besteht aus fünf farbigen Schnürsenkeldesigns, die zu jedem der Schuhe aus der Kollektion passen.

Görtz 17 voulait pour sa collection Converse un emballage innovant qui attirerait l'attention des clients sur le lieu de vente, sachant que sa ligne de chaussures était déjà un produit culte. Pour stimuler les ventes et rendre la marque encore plus séduisante, une boîte à chaussures recyclable qui rend les sacs en plastique inutiles a été imaginée et est unique en son genre. Son graphisme minimaliste attire l'attention sur les anses, que l'on peut détacher et utiliser comme paire de lacets supplémentaire. La série compte cinq couleurs de lacets qui peuvent être portés avec n'importe quelle paire de chaussures de la collection.

GÖRTZ 17
SHOELACE BOX

Design: Loved, Heiko Freyland
Creative Direction: Tim Belser,
Heiko Freyland
Copywriting: Tim Belser
Design: Christiane Eckhardt,
Peter Ruessmann
Photography: Alexander Kate (cmp)
Company: Kempertrautmann
Country: Germany
Category: Best of the category

PLATINUM PENTAWARD 2011

Görtz 17 sought an innovative packaging design for its Converse Collection that would engage consumers at the point of sale, knowing that its line of stylish shoes was already something of a cult product. To boost sales and make the brand even more desirable a recyclable shoebox that makes plastic bags unnecessary was developed, the first of its kind. Its minimalist design draws attention to the handles, which can be removed and used as an extra pair of shoelaces. The series consists of five lace-color designs that can be worn with any of the shoes in the collection.

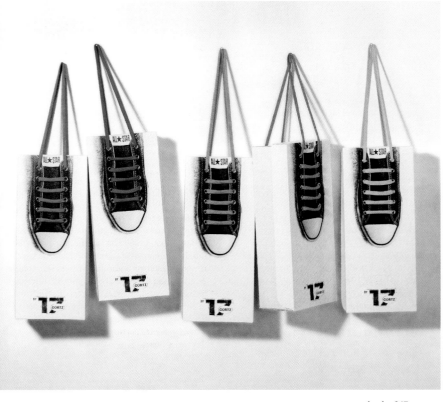

ETUDE HOUSE
HANDS UP DEODORANT/
DEPILATORY

Design: Jung Mi Jung, Sul Se Mi,
Lee Mi Jin (Etude),
Kim Hee, Kim Jeun (Purun Image)
Company: Etude
Country: South Korea
Category: Best of the category
PLATINUM PENTAWARD 2012

Etude is a beauty and cosmetic brand with
nearly 30 years' experience in catering for girls in
the 16-22 age-group. The various products in the
Hands Up range have all been designed with an
arm-shaped outer casing to express the message
that users can raise their arms with full confidence.
An extra detail is found in the tear-off strip when
customers first open the container, a humorous
reference to depilatory waxing. The range is sold
through outlets in about a dozen countries in Asia,
and at reasonable prices, with the younger customers in mind.

Etude besitzt als Beauty- und Kosmetikmarke eine fast 30-jährige Erfahrung mit Angeboten für junge Frauen zwischen 16 und 22. Den Verpackungen der verschiedenen Produkte aus der Palette Hands Up entwachsen Arme und vermitteln so die Botschaft, dass Verbraucher vertrauensvoll ihre Arme hochnehmen können. Der Abreißstreifen, mit dem das Behältnis beim ersten Mal geöffnet wird, liefert dem Kunden eine humorvolle Anspielung auf die Enthaarung mit Wachs. Die in Asien in etwa einem Dutzend Ländern erhältliche Produktserie nimmt durch ihre vernünftige Preisgestaltung Rücksicht auf die jüngere Zielgruppe.

Etude est une marque de cosmétiques et de produits de beauté qui possède près de 30 ans d'expérience sur le segment des jeunes filles de 16-22 ans. Les différents produits de la gamme Hands Up ont tous été dotés d'un emballage externe avec des bras pour faire comprendre que les utilisatrices peuvent lever les bras en toute tranquillité. Lorsque les clientes ouvrent le produit pour la première fois, elles trouvent un détail supplémentaire, une référence humoristique à l'épilation à la cire. La gamme est vendue dans une dizaine de pays en Asie à des prix raisonnables, pensés pour les jeunes consommatrices.

LIVING PROOF
NO FRIZZ

Creative Direction: Todd Simmons
Design: Tiziana Haug, Sung Kim
Production Direction: Beth Kovalsky
Production Management: Michele Miller
Copywriting: Mary Ellen Muckerman,
Carmine Montalto
Strategy: Mary Ellen Muckerman
Account Direction: Veronica Otto
Account Management: Erin Roh
Company: Wolff Olins
Country: USA
Category: Best of the category
PLATINUM PENTAWARD 2009

For the **Living proof** range of packaging, Wolff Olins of New York dove deep into the world of beauty, ran diagnostic profiles of the competition, and went well beneath the skin of consumer needs to discover real insights. They observed that on many occasions the industry didn't pay attention to the basic needs of consistency, simplicity, confidence, truth, and responsibility. **Living proof**, **no frizz** is a line of silicone-free, hair-care straightening products. The design is very refined and sober, as too is the lettering. It draws inspiration from up-market cosmetics, and uses shiny white covers and a mouse-grey, matt background, thus differing from other hair products available on the market or in hairdressing salons.

Für die Verpackungsserie **Living proof** vertiefte sich Wolff Olins aus New York in die Welt der Schönheit, führte diagnostische Profile der Wettbewerbssituation durch und hinterfragte peinlich genau die Anforderungen der Verbraucher, um einen echten Erkenntnisgewinn zu erzielen. So stellte sich heraus, dass die Branche vielfach kaum auf grundlegende Bedürfnisse wie Konsistenz, Einfachheit, Vertrauen, Wahrheit und Verantwortung achtete. **Living proof**, **no frizz** ist eine silikonfreie Pflegelinie zum Glätten der Haare. Das Design ist wie die Beschriftung sehr edel und nüchtern. Es lässt sich von Kosmetikartikeln der gehobenen Preisklasse inspirieren und arbeitet mit glänzend weißen Deckeln und einem mausgrauen, mattierten Korpus. Dadurch unterscheidet es sich von den Haarprodukten, die im freien Handel oder in Friseursalons erhältlich sind.

Pour le packaging de la gamme **Living proof**, l'agence new-yorkaise Wolff Olins a plongé dans le monde de la beauté, a analysé les profils des concurrents et est allée bien au-delà des besoins de base des consommateurs pour découvrir de nouvelles perspectives. Les designers ont ainsi remarqué que le secteur négligeait souvent les besoins de base en termes de cohérence, de simplicité, de confiance, de vérité et de responsabilité. **Living proof**, **no frizz** est une gamme de soins capillaires lissants sans silicone. Le design est très raffiné et sobre, tout comme la typographie. Il s'inspire des cosmétiques haut de gamme, avec des bouchons blancs brillants et un fond gris souris mat, ce qui le différencie des autres produits capillaires disponibles sur le marché ou dans les salons de coiffure.

STRONG NUTRIENTS

Design: Karen Welman
Illustration: Andy Lyons, Handsome Frank
Company: Pearlfisher
Country: UK
Category: Best of the category
PLATINUM PENTAWARD 2013

Strong is a brand of high-quality supplements developed to promote health and beauty at the cellular level for a younger, stronger and more dynamic body. The design's objective was to stand out from functional brands and create the concept of "beauty from within" by evoking the ultimate benefits of choosing Strong over other products. The labeling showcases a range of beautiful and elegant birds (as well as Pegasus) which are known for their hidden strength, with the illustrations rendered in a stylized and timeless manner. The resulting designs are visually striking, creating high visibility for both retail and e-commerce.

Strong ist eine Marke qualitativ hochwertiger Nahrungsergänzungsmittel. Für einen jüngeren, stärkeren und dynamischeren Körper stärken sie Gesundheit und Aussehen auf zellulärer Ebene. Die Designvorgabe war, sich von funktionalen Marken abzuheben und das Konzept einer „Schönheit von innen" zu schaffen. Dazu betonte man die ultimativen Vorteile von Strong gegenüber anderen Produkten. Die Etiketten zeigen verschiedene schöne und elegante Vögel (zudem einen Pegasus), die für ihre verborgene Kraft bekannt sind. Die Illustrationen sind in stilisierter und zeitloser Art ausgeführt. Im Ergebnis sind die Designs visuell überzeugend und sorgen sowohl im Einzel- als auch im Onlinehandel für einen hohen Wahrnehmungsgrad.

Strong est une marque de compléments alimentaires de grande qualité élaborés comme source de santé et de beauté au niveau cellulaire, avec la promesse d'un corps plus jeune, plus fort et plus dynamique. L'objectif du design était de se distinguer des marques fonctionnelles et de créer un concept de « beauté de l'intérieur » en expliquant tous les bienfaits de Strong comparé à la concurrence. L'étiquetage présente une série d'oiseaux élégants (ainsi que Pégase), connus pour leur force cachée. Les illustrations sont reproduites de façon stylisée et intemporelle, avec un fort impact visuel et une grande visibilité, en magasin comme en ligne.

In developing this new skincare line for middle- to upper-class consumers, a name was sought that would express its equal blend of the aesthetic and the scientific. Inspired by art history, the word **Beatific** was chosen, meaning blessed and indicating a communion with the divine, so as to be able to share its spiritual light and glory. With this name then signposting the meeting-point of Beauty and Science, the rest of the design followed accordingly: the abstract and ethereal light patterns on the packaging; the use of semi-transparent, translucent material; the 4-color iridescent palette; and the elegant and sober typography.

In der Entwicklung dieser neuen Hautpflegelinie für Kunden aus der Mittel- und Oberklasse suchte man einen Namen, der Ästhetik und Wissenschaft in ausgewogener Mischung verdeutlicht. Inspiriert durch die Kunstgeschichte entschied man sich für **Beatific**, das auf Seligkeit anspielt und auf die Verbindung mit dem Göttlichen verweist, als könne man dessen spirituelles Licht und Herrlichkeit teilen. Im Namen schon verschmelzen also Schönheit und Wissenschaft, und dem schließt sich das restliche Design an: die abstrakten und ätherischen Lichtmuster der Verpackung, das halbtransparente, durchscheinende Material, die schillernde Vierfarbpalette mit ihrer eleganten und nüchternen Typografie.

Pour cette nouvelle ligne de produits cosmétiques s'adressant à une clientèle de classe moyenne à supérieure, le nom devait transmettre l'équilibre entre esthétique et science. Synonyme de béni, **Beatific** s'inspire de l'histoire de l'art et traduit la communion avec le Divin, capable de faire partager sa lumière spirituelle et sa gloire. Ce mariage entre beauté et science a dicté le reste du design : un graphisme abstrait et éthéré, un matériau d'emballage translucide et semi-transparent, une palette de 4 couleurs irisées et une typographie sobre et élégante.

Beatific™
Youth Elixir
face serum

BEATIFIC

Creative Direction/Design: Gregory Tsaknakis
Illustration: Kostas Kaparos
Company: Mousegraphics
Country: Greece
Category: Best of the category

PLATINUM PENTAWARD 2014

Beatific™
Extreme Anti-Aging
face cream

Beatific™
Hydrating Comfort
serum

Beatific™
Instant Beauty Booster
face mask

In Japan ist es Tradition, dass Firmen und Läden ihren Stammkunden eine Rolle Toilettenpapier als Geschenkartikel überreichen, um sich erkenntlich zu zeigen. Vor diesem Hintergrund wurde **Fruit Toilet Paper** so gestaltet, dass die verspielte Verpackung Kunden anzieht und amüsiert – überraschend, aber für solche Gelegenheiten perfekt. Dieses Set weist vier Designs mit Kiwi, Erdbeere, Wassermelone und Orange mit einer Schutzverpackung aus bedrucktem Papier auf.

Au Japon, il est devenu courant pour de nombreuses entreprises et boutiques d'offrir à leurs clients un rouleau de papier toilette en signe d'appréciation. C'est dans cet esprit que **Fruit Toilet Paper** a été conçu, pour attirer et amuser les clients grâce à son emballage ludique, inattendu mais idéal pour ce type d'occasion. La gamme compte quatre variantes (kiwi, fraise, pastèque et orange) et l'emballage est en papier imprimé.

THE FRUIT TOILET PAPER

Design: Kazuaki Kawahara
Company: Latona Marketing
Country: Japan
Category: Best of the category

PLATINUM PENTAWARD 2015

In Japan it has become something of a tradition with many companies and stores to offer customers and patrons a roll of toilet paper as a novelty gift to show their appreciation. With this in mind, **Fruit Toilet Paper** has been designed to attract and amuse customers with its playful packaging, unexpected but perfect for such occasions. There are four designs in the range (kiwi, strawberry, watermelon and orange) and the wrappers are made of printed paper.

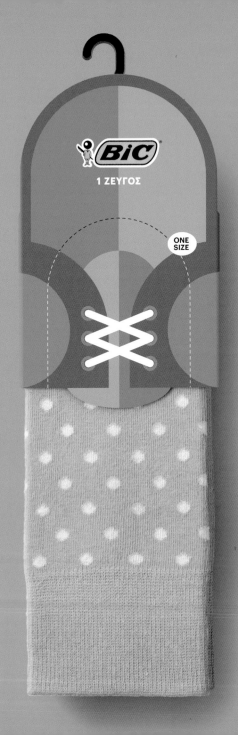

BIC SOCKS

Creative Direction: Greg Tsaknakis
Illustration: Ioanna Papaioannou
Art Direction: Alexandros Mavrogiannis
Company: Mousegraphics
Country: Greece
Category: Best of the category

PLATINUM PENTAWARDS 2016

A fresh packaging idea here brings a number of **Bic** products together by the use of a smart but simple concept and its variations: if socks dress the feet and shoes complete the process, then socks for sale on the shelf can also be 'dressed' in shoes in a playful manner that catches the eye right away. The packaging for each style features the image of a type of shoe (women's, men's, sports, casual) that is paired to match with the sock. Within the brand's range this creates a discrete category that is easy to identify (shoes) while also providing a unifying principle.

Verschiedene **Bic**-Produkte werden anhand einer unverbrauchten Verpackungsidee zusammengeführt. Das einfache, aber clevere Konzept mit seinen Varianten lautet: Wenn Strümpfe die Füße bekleiden und dies mit den Schuhen vollendet wird, kann man Strümpfe zum Verkauf auch spielerisch mit Schuhen im Regal „bekleiden" und sie so als Blickfang aufwerten. Die Verpackung für jeden Stil bildet eine Schuhsorte ab (Damen- und Herrenschuhe, Sport- und Freizeitschuhe), die zur Socke passt. Innerhalb des Markensortiments sorgt dies für eine eigenständige, leicht erkennbare Kategorie (Schuhe), die trotzdem nach einem einheitlichen Prinzip arbeitet.

Une idée innovante rassemble plusieurs produits de **Bic** à l'aide d'un concept astucieux mais simple, décliné en différentes variantes : si les chaussettes habillent le pied dans la chaussure, les chaussettes mises en rayon peuvent aussi être « habillées » de chaussures de façon ludique pour attirer le regard. L'emballage de chaque variante montre l'image du type de chaussure (homme, femme, sport, décontracté) qui correspond à la chaussette. Il s'agit d'une catégorie à part dans la gamme de la marque, facile à identifier (chaussures) tout en obéissant à un principe unificateur.

SOC is a Japanese brand of socks whose slogan is "An inspiration born from your foot". The package has been designed so that it is able to contain socks of all sizes and display the different styles, and was created according to the art of traditional Japanese folding, so that it may be opened without destroying the packaging. The form is compact and uses a minimum of paper, is reusable after purchase, inexpensive to produce and is still attractive: much like the values of SOC itself.

Die japanische Strumpfmarke **SOC** wirbt mit dem Slogan „inspiriert von deinen Füßen". Das Design kann Socken in allen Größen aufnehmen, und die verschiedenen Styles bleiben sichtbar. Es wurde in der Kunst des japanischen Papierfaltens geschaffen: So kann man die Verpackung öffnen, ohne sie zu beschädigen. In kompakter Form und mit wenig Papierverbrauch kann sie nach dem Kauf anderweitig verwendet werden, ist preisgünstig in der Herstellung und trotzdem attraktiv – genau diese Werte verkörpert auch SOC selbst.

SOC est une marque japonaise de chaussettes dont le slogan est « Une inspiration née de votre pied ». L'emballage a été pensé pour contenir des chaussettes de toutes les tailles et présenter les divers styles disponibles. Il a été créé selon le traditionnel art du pliage japonais pour s'ouvrir sans être abimé. Sa forme est compacte, demande un minimum de papier, il est réutilisable, sa production est bon marché et le résultat est attrayant : telles sont aussi les valeurs de SOC.

SOC TOKYO
Art Direction/Design: Keiko Akatska
Printing Direction: The Pack
Client: Old Fashion
Company: Keiko Akatsuka & Associates
Country: Japan
Category: Garments
GOLD PENTAWARD 2014

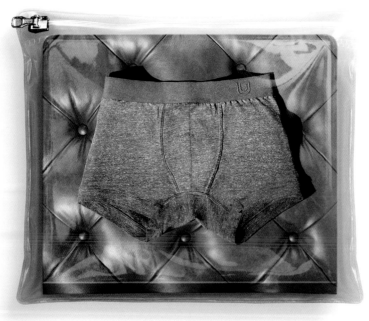

362

UNDAMENTALS

Design: Moyra Casey,
Kelly Bennett, Chris McDonald
Company: Afterhours
Country: UK
Category: Garments
GOLD PENTAWARD 2016

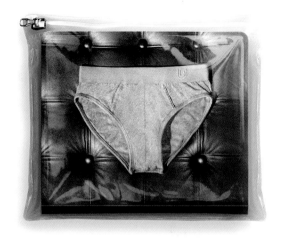

Bei **Shiseido** lässt sich von einer Art „Buchstaben im Shiseido-Stil" sprechen. Deren Formen hat man für Produkte und Werbung eingesetzt und im Laufe der Jahre von Designer-Generationen immer wieder neu zeichnen und anpassen lassen. Als Furoshiki bezeichnet man die Tradition, Geschenke oder andere Gegenstände in ein tragbares Tuch zu wickeln. Gut zu sehen sind die mit der Yuzen-Färbetechnik aus Kyoto aufgebrachten zarten Farben und kräftigen Linien. So werden ursprünglich in dekorativen Kombinationen verwendete Buchstaben nun zu wunderschönen abstrakten Mustern. Überdies packt man die Furoshiki jeweils in nur ein Blatt Papier, das im gleichen Stil per Hand gefaltet ist.

Chez **Shiseido**, il existe ce que l'on pourrait appeler une « police de caractère maison », une typographie utilisée pour les produits et les campagnes publicitaires, conçues et adaptées depuis des années par des générations de designers. Le furoshiki est une méthode traditionnelle pour l'emballage de cadeaux à l'aide d'un morceau de tissu. Les couleurs douces et les lignes franches emploient les techniques de teinture yuzen de Kyoto. Résultat : les lettres qui étaient utilisées dans des arrangements décoratifs forment désormais de superbes motifs abstraits. Le papier enveloppant chaque furoshiki n'a qu'une feuille d'épaisseur, pliée à la main dans le même style.

SNUG AS A BUG WRAPS
Design: Leanne Balen
Creative Direction: Geoff Bickford, Tracy Kenworthy
Company: Dessein
Country: Australia
Category: Garments
BRONZE PENTAWARD 2015

SHISEIDO FUROSHIKI

Creative Direction: Yoji Nobuto
Art Direction/Design: Ippei Murata
Typography: Yutaka Kobayashi
Production: Kumiko Suzuki
Company: Shiseido
Country: Japan
Category: Garments

SILVER PENTAWARD 2014

At **Shiseido**, there is what could be called the "Shiseido style of letters," a set of letter forms used for products and advertising which have been redrawn and adapted over the years by new generations of designers. The furoshiki is a traditional way of wrapping and carrying gifts using a single piece of cloth, while the delicate colors and bold lines shown here employ yuzen dyeing techniques from Kyoto. The result is that letters that were originally used in decorative combinations now become beautiful abstract patterns. Furthermore, the paper used to package each furoshiki itself uses just one sheet of paper, hand-folded in the same style.

MARUJU
HANDKERCHIEF OF MENPU MASDA

Design: Hidekazu Hirai
Company: Peace Graphics
Country: Japan
Category: Garments

SILVER PENTAWARD 2016

In a bid to combat declining sales, the venerable **Maruju** factory developed this packaging so that the different styles of their handkerchief patterns could be seen through a window that also makes each handkerchief a part of the cover design. At the same time, the different illustrations in the range show how the contents can be used, for example, to mop the face on a hot day, or as a place mat at lunchtime. The packaging is formed out of a single piece of cardboard, folded in half and held in position with a white rubber-band. In Japan, handkerchiefs are often sold unpacked, so this colorful packaging is a more attractive choice for those who want to give one as a gift.

In ihrem Kampf gegen nachlassende Verkaufszahlen entwickelte die altehrwürdige Firma **Maruju** diese Verpackung. Dabei sind die verschiedenen Taschentuchmuster durch ein Fenster sichtbar, so wird jedes Tuch Teil der Hüllengestaltung. Gleichzeitig illustriert das Sortiment, wie man den Inhalt nutzen kann, um sich z. B. an heißen Tagen das Gesicht abzutupfen oder es als Platzdeckchen zum Essen zu verwenden. Die Verpackung besteht aus einem einzigen Karton, halb gefaltet und durch ein weißes Gummiband zusammengehalten. In Japan werden Taschentücher oft unverpackt verkauft. Diese farbenfrohe Verpackung spricht auch jene an, die eines verschenken möchten.

Pour enrayer le déclin des ventes, la vénérable usine **Maruju** a mis au point cet emballage afin que les différents motifs de ses mouchoirs soient visibles à travers une fenêtre qui intègre aussi le mouchoir au graphisme. En même temps, les différentes illustrations de la gamme montrent comment le contenu peut être utilisé, par exemple pour éponger le visage par grande chaleur, ou comme set de table à l'heure du déjeuner. Fait d'un seul morceau de carton, l'emballage est plié en deux et maintenu par un élastique blanc. Au Japon, les mouchoirs sont souvent vendus sans emballage, ce concept est donc séduisant pour ceux qui veulent en offrir un en cadeau.

MARUJU
GAUZE OF MENPU MASDA
Design: Hidekazu Hirai
Company: Peace Graphics
Country: Japan
Category: Garments
SILVER PENTAWARD 2015

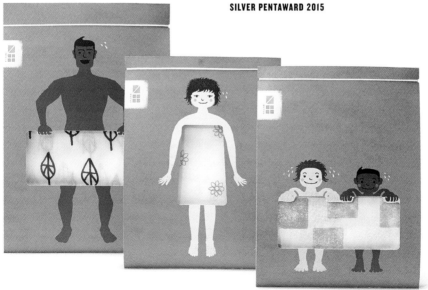

HERE! SOD T-SHIRT PACKAGING

Design: Somchana Kangwarnjit,
Passorn Subcharoenpun,
Chidchanok Laohawattanakul,
Mathurada Bejrananda
Company: Prompt Design
Country: Thailand
Category: Clothing

GOLD PENTAWARD 2010

Here! Sod T-Shirt Packaging takes design clues from food packaging used to sell groceries and, as here, presents a new line of T-shirts sold in a simple and distinctive way to look like the food packaging found in supermarkets. Each shirt in the product line is sold in a different form of packaging to make them more eye-catching and to create a more engaging shopping experience.

Die von **Here! Sod T-Shirt** gestaltete Verpackung von T-Shirts greift das Design von Umverpackungen für Lebensmittel auf. Hier wird auf einfache, aber unverwechselbare Weise eine neue Produktlinie mit T-Shirts präsentiert, indem man sie wie Produkte aus dem Supermarkt aussehen lässt. Jedes T-Shirt dieser Kollektion wird in einer andersartigen Verpackungsform angeboten: Das fällt ins Auge und bietet eine unterhaltsame Kauferfahrung.

L'emballage des tee-shirts **Here! Sod T-Shirt** s'inspire des ceux utilisés dans l'alimentation et, comme ici, présente une nouvelle ligne de tee-shirts avec simplicité et originalité, en leur donnant l'aspect des denrées alimentaires que l'on trouve en supermarché. Chaque tee-shirt de la ligne est vendu dans un emballage différent, pour attirer l'œil et rendre le processus d'achat plus ludique.

ITO
KOBO ORIZA

Art Direction: Hirokazu Kobayashi, Haruna Yamada
Design: Hirokazu Kobayashi, Haruna Yamada, Satoko Manabe
Management: Riho Kokubu
Company: Spread
Country: Japan
Category: Clothing

SILVER PENTAWARD 2010

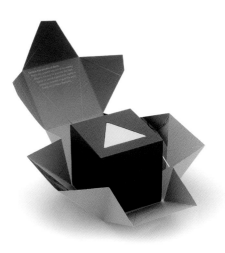

ANON

Creative Direction: Natalie Chung
Creative Partner: Jonathan Ford
Design: Will Gladden
Strategy: Georgia Levison
Copywriting: Sylvie Saunders
Company: Pearlfisher
Country: UK
Category: Clothing
BRONZE PENTAWARD 2010

AHLENS

Concept Direction: Ulf Berlin
Art Direction: Cajsa Bratt
Photography: Niclas Alm
Design: Cajsa Bratt, Henrik Billqvist
Production Management: Anna Harrysson, Ida Stagles
Production Design: Monica Holm
Company: Designkontoret Silver
Country: Sweden
Category: Clothing
GOLD PENTAWARD 2011

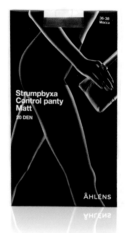
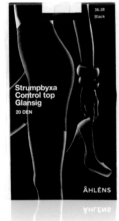
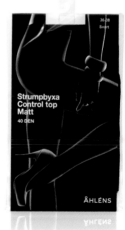

DARKDESIGN PACKAGING FOR T-SHIRT COLLECTION

Design: Dima Zeibert, Larisa Mamleeva
Company: Dark Design Group
Country: Russia
Category: Clothing

SILVER PENTAWARD 2009

BABYQSHOP
Design: Chow Kar Wo
Company: BabyQ Shop
Country: China
Category: Clothing
SILVER PENTAWARD 2011

DUO

Creative Direction: Greg Tsaknakis
Art Direction and Design: Joshua Olsthoorn,
Alexandros Mavrogiannis
Company: Mousegraphics
Country: Greece
Category: Health care

GOLD PENTAWARD 2015

In giving **Duo** an update in order to make it a continued force in the market and to appeal to new target audiences, the logo was redesigned from the earlier isolated oval to smoother lettering that was better integrated with the rest of the packaging design, which was now redirected to the circle, a fundamental shape which is also the sectional view of a condom. The different varieties in the Duo range could then be represented in a playful lexicon of simple, colored graphic forms, with each type of condom subtly indicated by minimal variation of the circle set against a strong black background.

KLEENEX BRAND SPRING EDITION

Design: Christine Mau, Jody Douglas, Jennifer Brock, Katie Hinrichs, Cinzah Merkens
Company: Kimberly-Clark
Country: USA
Category: Health care
SILVER PENTAWARD 2012

Damit **DUO** weiterhin eine wirksame Kraft am Markt bleibt und neue Zielgruppen erschließt, bekam das Logo ein Update. Das ehemals isolierte Oval erhielt einen glatteren, besser ins restliche Packungsdesign integrierten Schriftzug. Das Design wurde mehr auf den Kreis umgestellt, und diese fundamentale Form bildet auch die Schnitt-ansicht eines Kondoms. Die verschiedenen Varian-ten des Duo-Sortiments wurden dann in verspiel-ten einfachen und farbigen Grafiken repräsentiert, bei dem sich alle Kondomsorten subtil durch minimale Varianten des Kreises vor einem kraft-vollen schwarzen Hintergrund unterscheiden.

L'actualisation de **Duo** visait à pérenniser sa présence sur le marché et à séduire de nouveaux publics cibles. L'ancien logo ovale a été redessiné et les lettres sont plus lisses, mieux intégrées au reste du concept d'emballage, qui se base mainte-nant sur le cercle, une forme fondamentale et la vue en coupe d'un préservatif. Les différentes variantes de la gamme Duo peuvent alors être représentées par un lexique de formes graphiques simples et colorées, chaque type de préservatif étant subtilement indiqué par une variation mini-male des cercles sur fond noir.

KLEENEX
DIVINE DESSERT WEDGES

Creative Direction: Christine Mau
Design: Jennifer Brock, Katie Hinrichs
Brand Design Management: Jody Douglas
Illustration: Hiroko Sanders
Company: Kimberly-Clark
Country: USA
Category: Health care

GOLD PENTAWARD 2011

JOHNSON & JOHNSON
FIRST AID KIT

Design: Harry Allen
(Johnson & Johnson, Global Design Strategy Office)
Company: Harry Allen Design
Country: USA
Category: Health care
BRONZE PENTAWARD 2009

IA
OPTICAL RANGE FOR PHARMACIES

Creative Direction: Eduardo del Fraile
Design: Eduardo del Fraile, Antonio Marquez
Company: Eduardo del Fraile
Country: Spain
Category: Health care
SILVER PENTAWARD 2013

ia
interapothek

SPRAY
LIMPIAGAFAS
CON GAMUZA MICROFIBRA

EYEGLASS CLEANER SPRAY
WITH MICROFIBER CLOTH
SPRAY DE LIMPEZA PARA ÓCULOS
COM CAMURSA MICROFIBRA
SPRAY DE NETTOYAGE POUR
LUNETTES AVEC CHAMOISINE

EFECTO ANTINAHO
TODO TIPO DE LENTES

20 ml

ia
interapothek

TOALLITAS
LIMPIAGAFAS

TOWELS GLASSES CLEANER
TOALHITAS LIMPA ÓCULOS
LINGETTES NETTOYANTES
POUR LUNETTES

ANTI-RAYADO
EFECTO ANTINAHO
TODO TIPO DE LENTES

12 UNIDADES

R.D.G.F.P.S.: 8842-CS

Envasado por B-30597249

20 ml

MORAZ COSMETICS

Creative Direction: Ayelet Sad'e
Design: Ayelet Sad'e, Efrat Mizrahi
Illustration: Alex Melik-Adamov
Company: Sadowsky Berlin
Country: Israel
Category: Body care

GOLD PENTAWARD 2015

This new cosmetic line from **Moraz** offers products developed from the best 1+1 plant extractions to suit all skin types. Ingredients include pomegranate, shea butter and achillea, extracted in concentrated form to ensure the gels and lotions are as potent as can be. A clean design and white background fit this aim, with the plants made central on the front panels, in vivid illustrations linked with the plus sign to indicate directly the active ingredients of each particular product. With the plants up front like this it is also clear this is an all-natural cosmetic line.

Diese neue **Moraz**-Kosmetikreihe enthält Produkte, entwickelt aus den besten 1+1-Pflanzenextrakten, um alle Hauttypen zu bedienen. Als Zutaten wurden Granatapfel, Sheabutter und Schafgarbe in konzentrierter Form extrahiert, damit die Gels und Lotionen optimal wirken. Ein klares Design und der weiße Hintergrund dienen diesem Ziel: Die leuchtenden Illustrationen in der Mitte der Verpackungsvorderseite sind mit dem Pluszeichen verbunden, um direkt die aktiven Ingredienzien eines bestimmten Produkts anzuzeigen. Weil die Pflanzen so direkt und deutlich gezeigt werden, ist sofort klar, dass es sich um eine ganz natürliche Kosmetikreihe handelt.

Cette nouvelle ligne cosmétique de **Moraz** offre les meilleurs extraits de plante 1+1 pour s'adapter à tous les types de peau. Les ingrédients comprennent la grenade, le beurre de karité et l'achillée, extraits sous forme concentrée pour un effet plus puissant. Le concept épuré et le fond blanc restent dans cet esprit, et les plantes sont illustrées avec réalisme sur l'avant des boîtes avec un signe plus pour indiquer directement les ingrédients actifs de chaque produit. La place de choix accordée aux plantes signifie clairement qu'il s'agit d'une ligne de cosmétique entièrement naturelle.

CHICCO ARTSANA
PURE.BIO

Creative Direction: Chiara Sozzi Pomati
Design: Marta Mapelli
Account Management: Alessandra Mauri
Company: CMGRP Italia, Future Brand
Country: Italy
Category: Body care
SILVER PENTAWARD 2011

LIESE
IRON MAKE COLLECTION

Creative Direction: Masako Hirasawa
Art Direction/Design: Akiko Saito
Design: Yohei Shimura
Company: Kao Corporation
Country: Japan
Category: Body care

SILVER PENTAWARD 2010

TROJAN

Structural Design: Peter Clarke, Jesse Kruska
Graphic Design: Colangelo, Jim O'Neill
Company: Product Ventures
Country: USA
Category: Body care
SILVER PENTAWARD 2013

MAYBREEZE

Design: JooHyun Sohn, BoGyeong Jung (K-C Design), Woofer Design
Company: Yuhan-Kimberly; *Country:* South Korea
Category: Body care
BRONZE PENTAWARD 2010

MANDOM
LUCIDO-L HAIR MAKE SUPPLEMENT

Creative Direction/Art Direction: Zenji Hashimoto
Design: Midori Hirai, Anna Kuramochi
Account Management: Koichi Furusawa
Company: Cloud8
Country: Japan
Category: Body care

SILVER PENTAWARD 2012

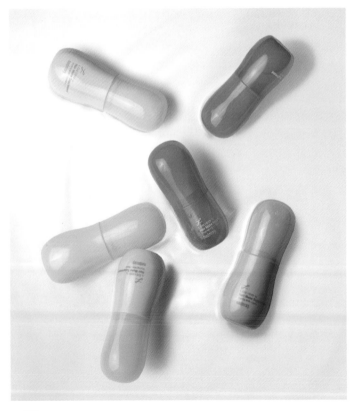

MR. PARKER

Creative Direction: Morten Throndsen
Design: Sandro Kvernmo,
Bendik Høibraaten
Company: Strømme Throndsen Design
Country: Norway
Category: Body care
GOLD PENTAWARD 2014

Mr. Parker is a new range that provides the discerning modern gentleman with everything needed for the best possible shave. It consists of a ready-fitted razor, replacement blade cartridges and a soothing shaving foam. The use of clean typography reflects a clean shave, and is combined with solid colors in bands which correspond to the international code for barbershops. The use of a moustache is a smart signature for the friendly logo and presents the range as a product with a highly personable appearance.

Mr. Parker ist ein neues Sortiment, das dem anspruchsvollen modernen Gentleman alles für die bestmögliche Rasur liefert. Enthalten sind ein einsatzbereiter Rasierer, Ersatzklingen und milder Rasierschaum. Die klare Typografie entspricht einer sauberen Rasur, kombiniert mit kraftvollen, zum internationalen Code der Friseurläden passenden Farbbändern. Der Schnurrbart ist ein smartes Element in dem freundlichen Logo, welches dem gesamten Sortiment ein höchst sympathisches Auftreten ermöglicht.

Mr. Parker est une nouvelle ligne de produits offrant à l'homme moderne exigeant tout ce dont il a besoin pour un rasage parfait. Elle se compose d'un rasoir prêt à l'emploi, de cartouches de lames de rechange et d'une mousse de rasage apaisante. Le recours à une typographie franche annonce un rasage de près, et la combinaison de couleurs vives en bandes rappellent le code international des enseignes de barbiers. La moustache est un logo amusant bien trouvé, symbole d'une gamme de produits très avenante.

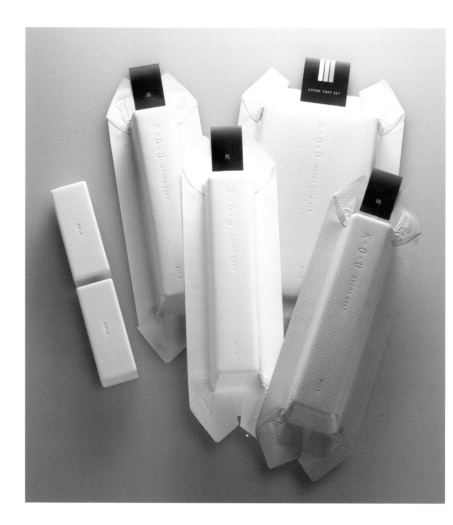

POLA K-O-U

Creative Direction: Takeshi Usui
Art Direction: Nobuyuki Shirai
Design: Kentaro Ito
Company: Pola
Country: Japan
Category: Body care

GOLD PENTAWARD 2010

HOLIKA HOLIKA
ALOE

Design: Enprani design team
Company: Enprani
Country: South Korea
Category: Body care

GOLD PENTAWARD 2016

LUCIDO-L POWDER IN MILK

Creative/Art Direction: Zenji Hashimoto
Design: Midori Hirai, Chiaki Nomi,
Anna Kuramochi
Account Management: Koichi Furusawa
Company: Cloud8
Country: Japan
Category: Body care
SILVER PENTAWARD 2014

ETUDE HOUSE
MILK TALK BODY WASH

Design: Jung Mi Jung, Sul Se Mi,
Kim Min Hee, Choi Ji Yee
Company: Etude
Country: South Korea
Category: Body care
BRONZE PENTAWARD 2012

LUCIDO-L DESIGNING POT

Design: Zenji Hashimoto
Company: Cloud8
Country: Japan
Category: Body care

SILVER PENTAWARD 2009

BIC
SOLEIL SHAVE & TRIM

Design: A Touch of Mojo
Design Development Lead: BIC France
Client: BIC USA Brand Design
Company: BIC USA
Country: USA
Category: Body care

BRONZE PENTAWARD 2013

LEIF

Design: Brenan Liston, Jonnie Vigar, Mark Evans
Company: Container
Country: Australia
Category: Body care

BRONZE PENTAWARD 2010

USPA

Design: Brenan Liston, Jonnie Vigar,
Todd Gill, Mark Evans
Company: Container
Country: Australia
Category: Body care

BRONZE PENTAWARD 2009

PRISMOLOGIE

Creative Direction: Garrick Hamm
Design Direction/Design: Fiona Curran
Account Direction: Wybe Magermans
Photography: Iain Crawford
Production Direction: Gary Morris
Company: Williams Murray Hamm
Country: UK
Category: Perfumes, cosmetics
GOLD PENTAWARD 2015

The packaging for this new range of premium body-care products takes its inspiration from color therapy and the way that different colors can influence or shape our moods, for example, the cleansing purity of white, the positive energy of yellow, and the power and passion of red. In accordance with these basic correspondences each individual pack has been given its own color identity, so that its properties are expressed through the use of action and texture as well as the color itself. This luxury brand is aimed at women aged 40+ in a range of markets across Europe and beyond.

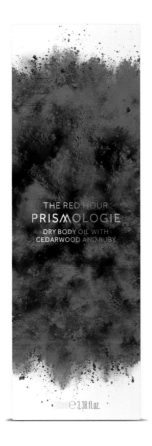

Die Verpackung für dieses neue Sortiment Premiumkörperpflegeprodukte ließ sich von Farbtherapie und der Weise inspirieren, wie Farben unsere Stimmung formen und beeinflussen, z. B. die reinigende Klarheit von Weiß, die positive Energie von Gelb und die Kraft und Leidenschaft von Rot. Im Einklang mit diesen grundlegenden Bedeutungen verfügt jede Einzelpackung über eine eigene Farbidentität, um durch Einsatz von Aktion und Textur ihre Eigenschaften genauso auszudrücken wie mit der Farbe selbst. Diese Luxusmarke richtet sich an Frauen über 40 auf verschiedenen europäischen Märkten sowie weltweit.

L'emballage de cette nouvelle gamme de produits de soin du corps puise son inspiration dans la chromathérapie et l'influence que les couleurs peuvent avoir sur nos humeurs, comme la pureté du blanc, l'énergie positive du jaune ou la puissance et la passion du rouge. Chaque article a sa propre identité couleur en fonction de ces correspondances de base afin que ses propriétés s'expriment à travers l'utilisation et de la texture, mais aussi de la couleur elle-même. Cette marque de luxe est destinée aux femmes de 40 ans et plus, sur différents marchés en Europe et dans le monde.

ORIFLAME
VERY ME

Creative Direction: André Hindersson
Art Direction: Cajsa Bratt
Production Design: Monica Holm
Production Management: Christine Schönborg
Company: Designkontoret Silver
Country: Sweden
Category: Beauty

BRONZE PENTAWARD 2010

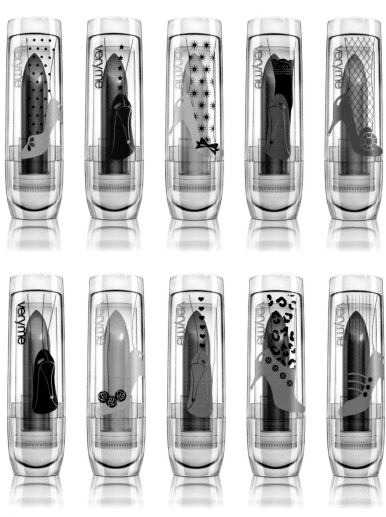

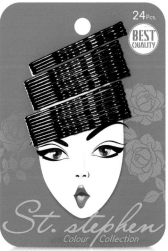

ST. STEPHEN

Creative Direction: Somchana Kangwarnjit
Design: Chalita Chaipibul
Company: Prompt Design
Country: Thailand
Category: Beauty

SILVER PENTAWARD 2012

ETUDE
FEDORA HAIR WAX

Design: Jung Mi Jung,
Lee Jae Myung, Sul Semi, Min Anna
Company: Etude
Country: South Korea
Category: Beauty

SILVER PENTAWARD 2013

EPIQUAL

Creative Direction: Youngha Park
Design: Junsu Lim
Company: Dipco
Country: South Korea
Category: Body care
BRONZE PENTAWARD 2016

ETUDE
ETOINETTE LINES

Design: Jung Mi Jung, Mijin Lee, Sylvie de France
Marketing: Hye Yeon Ji
Company: Etude
Country: South Korea
Category: Beauty
BRONZE PENTAWARD 2013

AREA FOUNDY

Creative Direction/Art Direction: Yuji Tokuda
Design: Mayuko Kato, Koji Fujii
Copywriting: Maco Taguchi
Photography: Keisuke Minoda
Client: Flowfushi
Company: Canaria
Country: Japan
Category: Beauty
SILVER PENTAWARD 2016

POLA
B.A.

Creative Direction: Takashi Matsui
Art Direction: Haruyo Eto
Design: Kei Ikehata, Shingo Isobe,
Karin Mai Kamiyama
Company: Pola
Country: Japan
Category: Beauty

GOLD PENTAWARD 2016

Warew („authentisch japanischer Stil") ist ein Hautpflegesortiment, das innere Schönheit zum Leuchten bringen will. Dafür nutzt es natürliche, lokale Ingredienzen und setzt somit neue Standards auf dem japanischen Markt. Da Schönheit in der Einfachheit oder im unsichtbaren Geist existiert, wählte man als Markenfarben ein dunkles Zinnoberrot und Weiß. Die Farben basieren auf dem Shiromuku-Kimono, den eine Frau dann angelegt, wenn sie am schönsten ist: zur Hochzeit. Auch die Idee der Geste wird aufgegriffen, indem die schönen Shosa-Bewegungen wie bei den subtilen Handlungen der Teezeremonie im Design der Verpackung anklingen. Das Logo spielt sowohl auf die japanische Flagge als auch einen Handspiegel an und reflektiert somit die Essenz japanischer Schönheit.

Warew signifie « style japonais authentique » ; c'est aussi une ligne de produits cosmétiques faits d'ingrédients locaux naturels et cherchant à révéler la beauté intérieure. La marque crée en cela un précédent sur le marché japonais. Il existe une beauté dans la simplicité et dans l'invisible : le blanc et un vermillon intense ont été retenus pour l'identité, tel le shiromuku, ce kimono que portent les femmes le jour de leur mariage. La gestuelle est également présente en évoquant le mouvement shosa, tel le déroulement d'une cérémonie du thé. Le logo rappelle à la fois le drapeau national et un miroir de poche reflétant toute l'essence de la beauté japonaise.

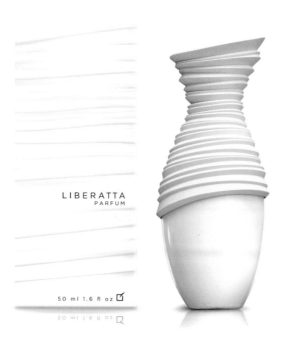

LIBERATTA
PARFUM

50 ml 1.6 fl oz

YANBAL LIBERATTA
Design: Malú Goñi,
Cynthia Becerra, Betsy Nishimura
Company: Unique
Country: Peru
Category: Perfumes, cosmetics
SILVER PENTAWARD 2015

WAREW

Creative/Art Direction:
Eisuke Tachikawa (Nosigner)
Design: Eisuke Tachikawa,
Takeshi Kawano
Photography: Hatta,
Takeshi Kawano
Company: Nosigner
Country: Japan
Category: Beauty
GOLD PENTAWARD 2014

Warew, meaning "authentic Japanese style,"
is a range of skincare products that seek to bring
out the inner beauty, using natural, local ingredients
and thus setting new standards in the Japanese
market. As beauty exists in simplicity or in the
invisible spirit, deep vermilion and white were
chosen as the brand colors based on the shiromuku,
a kimono worn when a woman is at her most beautiful, a bride. The idea of gesture is present too with
the packaging designed to evoke the beautiful shosa
movement, like the subtle steps of a tea ceremony.
The logo recalls both the national flag and a hand
mirror, reflecting the essence of Japanese beauty.

21 DROPS

Creative Direction: Kelly Kovack, Larry Paul
Graphic Design: Mi Rae Park
Company: Purpose-Built
Country: USA
Category: Beauty
GOLD PENTAWARD 2011

21 Drops is a line of therapeutic-grade essential oil blends catering for 21 universal complaints through 21 blended aromatherapy solutions. To broaden such a product's appeal to retailers as well as consumers a brand identity was developed based on qualities of transparency, quality and product design. A contemporary sensibility has been matched with the heritage of aromatherapy which helps recall the artisanal nature of the product. The packaging employs a vibrant colour palette and font-driven numerical graphics combined with embossed patterns on wholesome card, all chosen to be specifically tactile and memorable while the copy and naming system is evocative yet straightforward and informative.

21 Drops ist eine Produktlinie ätherischer Öle in therapeutischer Reinheit, die 21 universelle Beschwerden anhand von 21 Aromatherapielösungen beheben soll. Damit ein solches Produkt für Händler wie Kunden ansprechend wirkt, wurde eine Markenidentität entwickelt, die auf den Prinzipien Transparenz, Qualität und Produktdesign beruht. Neben das zeitgenössische Empfinden hat man das Erbe der Aromatherapie gestellt und die handwerkliche Natur des Produkts in Erinnerung gerufen. Für die Verpackung werden neben einer leuchtenden Farbpalette und charakteristischen Schriften für die Zahlengrafiken auch gestanzte Muster auf umweltfreundlichem Karton eingesetzt. Alles ist so gewählt, dass es besonders taktil und erinnernswert scheint, während Produkttexte und das Namenssystem aussagekräftig, aber doch unkompliziert und informativ sind.

21 Drops est une gamme de mélanges thérapeutiques à base d'huiles essentielles destinés à traiter 21 problèmes universels grâce à 21 solutions d'aromathérapie. Afin de rendre le produit plus attrayant pour les détaillants ainsi que pour les consommateurs, l'identité de marque a été développée autour des idées de transparence, de qualité et de conception de produit. La sensibilité contemporaine s'allie à l'héritage traditionnel de l'aromathérapie pour aider à rappeler la nature artisanale du produit. L'emballage emploie une palette de couleurs vives et différentes polices de caractères pour les numéros, combinées à des motifs en relief sur du carton brut. Tout cela a été choisi expressément pour offrir une impression tactile et mémorable. Les textes et le système pour les noms sont évocateurs, directs et informatifs.

MERCADONA SOLCARE

Design: Nacho Lavernia,
Alberto Cienfuegos, Raul Edo
Company: Lavernia & Cienfuegos
Country: Spain
Category: Distributors'/Retailers' own brands

GOLD PENTAWARD 2012

A redesign of this sun-care range was undertaken with an eye on optimising costs but without any perceived loss in quality or product recognition. The resulting blow-moulded bottles in two varieties may be fitted with different lids and standard dosing mechanisms: pump, spray or disc-top. This solution dealt with the logistics of production and packaging while still offering a differentiated range of products, each with its own identity. The coloring distinguishes the sub-ranges of sunscreen, tanning-aid and after-sun, supported by clean and succinct graphics. These are linked to a prominent numeral that indicates the protection factor, a key element in the purchase decision but which also strengthens the personality of the range.

FPS BAJA · SPF LOW
06
BRONCEADOR
LECHE SOLAR
PIELES MUY BRONCEADAS
ACEITE DE PALMA ROJA Y VITAMINA E
ACELERADOR DEL BRONCEADO
FILTROS UVA-UVB

SUNSCREEN BRONZE MILK
DEEP TANNED SKIN

solcare

50+
FPS MUY ALTA
SPF VERY HIGH
LECHE SOLAR
PIELES INFANTILES Y
SENSIBLES AL SOL
CON ALOE Y VITAMINA E
FILTROS UVA-UVB

SUNSCREEN MILK
FOR CHILDREN/SENSITIVE SKIN

solcare

30
FPS ALTA
SPF HIGH
LECHE SOLAR
PIELES CLARAS Y PRIMERAS
EXPOSICIONES AL SOL
CON ALOE Y VITAMINA E
FILTROS UVA-UVB

SUNSCREEN MILK
LIGHT SKIN AND FIRST DAYS
OF SUN EXPOSURE

solcare

Das Redesign dieser Sonnenschutzmittel berücksichtigt die Kostenoptimierung ohne merkbare Verluste bei Qualität oder Produktwahrnehmung. Das Ergebnis sind blasgeformte Flaschen in zwei Varianten, die man mit unterschiedlichen Verschlüssen und Dosiermechanismen ausstatten kann: Pumpe, Spray oder Disc-Top. Das löst die Logistik von Produktion und Verpackung und bietet gleichzeitig klar erkennbare Unterschiede zwischen den Produkten, die alle ihre eigene Identität aufweisen. Durch Farbgebung und die klaren, prägnanten Grafiken lassen sich die Gruppen Sonnenschutz, Bräunungsmittel und After Sun leicht unterscheiden. Bei den Grafiken wird mit prominent dargestellten Ziffern gearbeitet, die auf den Schutzfaktor verweisen. Dieses Schlüsselelement für die Kaufentscheidung stärkt auch die Persönlichkeit der Palette.

Le remodelage de cette gamme de produits solaires avait pour but d'optimiser les coûts tout en évitant toute perte perçue en terme de qualité ou de reconnaissance du produit. Les deux modèles de bouteille soufflée peuvent être assortis de différents bouchons et de mécanismes de dosage standard : pompe, spray ou bouchon disc top. Cette solution répond aux besoins logistiques de production et d'emballage tout en permettant de proposer une gamme de produits différenciés qui ont chacun leur propre identité. Les sousgammes solaires, aide au bronzage et après-soleil se différencient grâce à leurs couleurs et à un graphisme épuré et succinct. Un grand chiffre indique le facteur de protection, élément essentiel dans la décision d'achat, et renforce également la personnalité de la gamme.

ETNIA
LUXURY SKIN CELLS

Art Direction: Nacho Lavernia,
Alberto Cienfuegos
Graphics: Alberto Cienfuegos
Package Design: Raúl Edo
Company: Lavernia & Cienfuegos
Country: Spain
Category: Private labels

GOLD PENTAWARD 2016

The aim of this design was to create a product range that would announce its own individuality while keeping to the quality standards and general concept of the other Luxury Skin Cells items. With the key notes of elegance, sophistication and exclusivity, **Etnia** chose to combine a number of different finishes to the packaging to convey premium quality as well as a series of direct messages. Organic shapes and metallic surfaces for the jars are both intended to suggest the idea of cells, which extends to the individual box designs where the same skin tones again help to keep the range unified. The text is also blind embossed, without ink, so that the 'cells' remain the prime focus of the design.

Das Design zielt auf eine Produktpalette, die durch ihre Individualität hervorsticht und gleichzeitig den hohen Qualitätsstandards und dem allgemeinen Konzept der anderen Artikel von Luxury Skin Cells genügt. **Etnia** entschied sich für eine Kombination verschiedener Oberflächen unter den Hauptaspekten Eleganz, Raffinesse und Exklusivität, um sowohl Premiumqualität als auch verschiedene klare Botschaften zu vermitteln. Die organischen Formen und metallischen Oberflächen der Tiegel sollen die Idee von Zellen transportieren. Das greift auch auf die Gestaltung einzelner Schachteln über, wo die gleichen Hauttöne das Sortiment vereinheitlichen sollen. Der Text ist farbfrei blind geprägt, damit die „Zellen" der Hauptfokus des Designs bleiben.

Le but de ce concept était de créer une gamme de produits qui afficherait son individualité tout en préservant les exigences de qualité et l'approche générale des autres articles Luxury Skin Cells. Autour d'une idée d'élégance, de sophistication et d'exclusivité, **Etnia** a choisi de combiner diverses finitions sur l'emballage afin de symboliser la qualité haut de gamme, ainsi que toute une série de messages directs. Les formes organiques et les surfaces métalliques des pots suggèrent l'idée de la cellule, qui s'applique aussi à chaque boîte, où le même ton chair contribue à unifier la gamme. Le texte est travaillé en relief, sans encre, afin que les « cellules » restent les grandes vedettes du concept.

BATH & BODY WORKS
JAPANESE CHERRY BLOSSOM

Executive Creative Direction:
Sam O'Donahue
Design/Creative Direction:
Pierre Jeand'heur
Design: Felix de Voss, Valeria Bianco
Company: Established
Country: USA
Category: Distributors'/Retailers' own brands
BRONZE PENTAWARD 2012

ZARA BABY BOY & BABY GIRL

Creative Direction: Nacho Lavernia, Alberto Cienfuegos
Design: Steve Casquero
Company: Lavernia & Cienfuegos
Country: Spain
Category: Private labels
SILVER PENTAWARD 2015

IN-KIND

Creative Direction: Mark Christou
Client Development Direction: Cynthia Davies
Company: Pearlfisher
Country: USA
Category: Distributors'/Retailers' own brands
SILVER PENTAWARD 2011

UNIQLO
SHOES

Design: Uniqlo creative team
Company: Uniqlo
Country: Japan
Category: Private labels

BRONZE PENTAWARD 2016

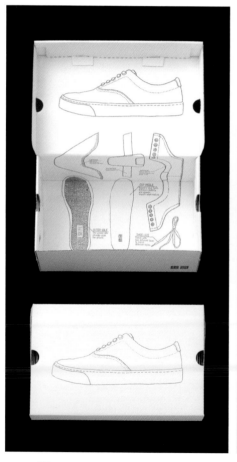
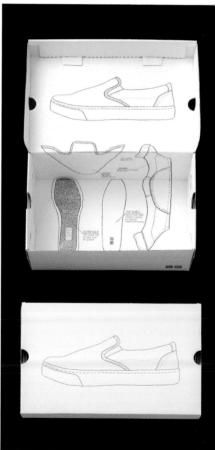

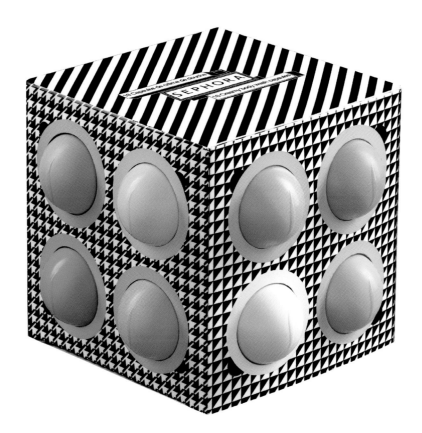

SEPHORA
BATH

Design: Marie-Christine Gendron
Company: Sephora
Country: France
Category: Distributors'/Retailers' own brands

BRONZE PENTAWARD 2013

body **413**

HINOKI

Design: Axel Brechensbauer,
Isabelle Dahlborg Lidström,
Lachlan Bullock, Andreas Linnell,
Henrik Lundblad
Company: Nine
Country: Sweden
Category: Packaging concept
GOLD PENTAWARD 2016

Hinoki is a range of travel-size, organic skin-care products in biodegradable paper packages. The concept is based on simplicity and a respect for the materials of single-use consumer items, with each flat sachet bottle being created using origami. A single piece of laminated paper is folded and pressed into shape, with a tear-off corner revealing a cap made of hinoki wood. This tree is also present in the structural design as well as the active ingredients and the scent of the products, resulting in a natural skin-care range with a premium value derived not from artificial inflation but rather an honest representation and respect for the value of the packaging materials and the product itself.

NAKED

Design: Stas Neretin (student)
School: British Higher School
of Art & Design (Moscow)
Country: Russia
Category: Packaging concept
GOLD PENTAWARD 2015

Hinoki ist ein Sortiment von organischen Hautpflegeprodukten in Reisegrößen, verpackt in biologisch abbaubares Papier. Schlichtheit ist die Konzeptbasis und auch der Respekt für das Material dieser Einmalartikel. Jede flache Beutelflasche wurde mit Origamitechnik hergestellt: Ein Stück laminiertes Papier wird gefaltet und in Form gepresst, und wenn man eine Ecke abreißt, zeigt sich ein Verschluss aus Hinoki-Holz. Dieser Baum gehört sowohl zum strukturellen Design als auch zu den Zutaten und dem Duft der Produkte. Das sorgt für den Premiumwert dieser natürlichen Hautpflegeserie, der sich nicht von einer künstlichen Aufwertung ableitet. Vielmehr ist es eine ehrliche Repräsentation des Verpackungsmaterials und des Respekts für den Wert des Produkts selbst.

Hinoki est une gamme de produits de soin bio pour la peau en format voyage, présentée dans des emballages en papier biodégradable. Le concept est basé sur la simplicité et le respect des matériaux des articles à usage unique. Chaque sachet plat est une création d'origami. Une seule feuille de papier contrecollé est pliée et pressée, avec un angle à déchirer révélant un bouchon en bois d'hinoki. Cet arbre est également présent dans la conception structurelle, ainsi que dans les ingrédients actifs et le parfum des produits, ce qui donne une gamme de soins naturels dont la valeur ajoutée n'est pas le fruit d'une approche artificielle, mais d'une représentation honnête et du respect des matériaux d'emballage et du produit en soi.

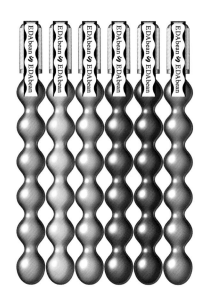

EDA BEANS
EDAMAME CONTAINER
Design: Mutsushi Hirano, Sayaka Shiraishi
Company: Toyo Seikan
Country: Japan
Category: Packaging concept
BRONZE PENTAWARD 2014

UNDER*
(there)
WEAR

COTTON FEEL PADS WITH TABS
Care what you wear under there.

CARE WHAT YOU **WEAR UNDER** (there)

FOOTSTEPS

Design: Mychko Yuliana (student)
School: British Higher School of Art & Design (Moscow)
Country: Russia
Category: Packaging concept
GOLD PENTAWARD 2014 BIC STUDENT PRIZE

UNDER THERE WEAR

Design: Kelly Bennett,
Chris MacDonald, Moyra Casey
Company: Afterhours
Country: UK
Category: Packaging concept
SILVER PENTAWARD 2014

Best of the category
Perfumes, cosmetics, body care
Spirits
Fine wines, champagne

luxury

Casks, coffrets, gift boxes, ice buckets, glorifiers
Gourmet food
Limited editions, limited series, event creations, collectors' items
Packaging concept

PERNOD RICARD
L'OR DE JEAN MARTELL

Design: Angelique Lecussan
Company: Dragon Rouge
Country: France
Category: Best of the category

PLATINUM PENTAWARD 2009

Created by Dragon Rouge Paris, **L'Or de Jean Martell** is a very luxuriously designed bottle for a rare cognac. With this conspicuously up-market product Martell pursues its development strategy in the luxury market to meet the demands of elite customers distributed in different cultural environments such as Russia and Asia. The bottle is the combination of creative and technical prowess, developed in cooperation with the Cristallerie de Sèvres. By building on the concept of perfect harmony as expressed through the "golden number" the agency imagined a bottle fashioned from pure crystal in which the precious liquid is concentrated in a single droplet suspended by an arch decorated with arabesques in gold. Produced in a very limited edition, each bottle is sold for € 3,000.

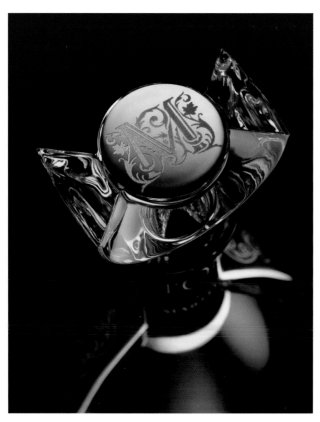

L'Or de Jean Martell wurde von Dragon Rouge in Paris geschaffen und ist eine außergewöhnlich luxuriös gestaltete Flasche für einen seltenen Cognac. Mit diesem auffallenden Produkt für ein gehobenes Marktsegment treibt Martell seine Entwicklungsstrategie im Markt der Luxusgüter voran. Hier soll den Anforderungen der Elitekunden entsprochen werden, die in verschiedenen kulturellen Kontexten wie Russland und Asien leben. Die Flasche ist eine Kombination aus kreativem und technischem Können und wurde in Zusammenarbeit mit der Cristallerie de Sèvres entwickelt. Hier setzt man auf das Konzept einer perfekten Harmonie, wie beim „Goldenen Schnitt". Die Agentur stellte eine aus reinem Kristall gefertigte Flasche vor, in der die kostbare Flüssigkeit von einem einzigen Tropfen umschlossen wird, der unterhalb eines mit goldenen Arabesken dekorierten Bogens hängt. Jede Flasche erscheint in einer sehr begrenzten Auflage und kostet 3.000 €.

Créée par Dragon Rouge Paris, **L'Or de Jean Martell** est une bouteille au design extrêmement luxueux pour un cognac rare. Avec ce produit ostensiblement très haut de gamme, Martell poursuit sa stratégie de développement sur le marché du luxe pour répondre aux besoins d'une clientèle d'élite qui évolue dans des environnements culturels divers, notamment en Russie et en Asie. La bouteille allie prouesse créative et technique, et a été élaborée en collaboration avec la Cristallerie de Sèvres. En partant du concept d'harmonie parfaite exprimé par le « nombre d'or », l'agence a imaginé une bouteille en cristal pur, où le précieux liquide est concentré en une goutte suspendue à une arche décorée d'arabesques en or. Chaque bouteille de cette édition très limitée est vendue 3 000 €.

THE BALVENIE 50

Creative Partner: Mark Paton
Design: Andy Giddings
Company: Here Design
Country: UK
Category: Best of the category

PLATINUM PENTAWARD 2013
LUXEPACK PRIZE

David Stewart is known around the world by lovers of Scotch whisky and to celebrate the 50th anniversary of his arrival at the Balvenie distillery a limited edition of 88 bottles, with a sale price of £20,000, was produced from a rare cask of **Balvenie** single malt distilled in 1962. Scottish cabinetmaker Sam Chinnery was employed to make a cylinder to hold the bottle composed of 49 layers of wood, from local trees, and one of brass, on which was engraved the history of this exceptional single malt. Inside, a certificate of authenticity was inserted beneath a brass plate. Significant dates in the production of this whisky were mentioned on the label of the bottle, made of blown glass, and the wooden stopper was also handmade by the craftsman.

David Stewart ist bei Liebhabern von Scotch-Whisky weltweit bekannt. Um den 50. Jahrestag seines Eintritts in der Balvenie Distillery zu feiern, wurde eine Sonderauflage von 88 Flaschen mit einem Verkaufspreis von 20.000 £ produziert. Die Abfüllung stammt aus einem seltenen Fass mit einem 1962 gebrannten **Balvenie** Single Malt. Der schottische Kunsttischler Sam Chinnery fertigte für die Flasche einen Zylinder, der aus 49 Holzschichten aus Bäumen der Region besteht sowie einer Messingscheibe, in der die Geschichte dieses außergewöhnlichen Single Malt eingraviert ist. Im Inneren wurde das Echtheitszertifikat unter einer Messingplatte eingefügt. Das Etikett auf der Flasche aus mundgeblasenem Glas erwähnt wesentliche Daten zur Produktion dieses Whiskys, und auch der hölzerne Verschluss stammt von Chinnery.

David Stewart est connu dans le monde entier par les amateurs de Scotch. Pour célébrer le 50ᵉ anniversaire de son arrivée à la distillerie Balvenie, une édition limitée de 88 bouteilles (prix de vente : 20 000 £) a été produite à partir d'un fût rare de single malt **Balvenie** distillé en 1962. L'ébéniste écossais Sam Chinnery a été sollicité pour fabriquer un cylindre comptant 49 couches de bois d'arbres locaux et une couche de laiton sur laquelle est gravée l'histoire de cet exceptionnel single malt. À l'intérieur, un certificat d'authenticité a été glissé sous une plaque en laiton. Les principales dates de production de ce whisky sont inscrites sur l'étiquette de la bouteille en verre soufflé ; le couvercle en bois a également été fabriqué à la main par l'artisan.

PERNOD-RICARD
MARTELL TRICENTENAIRE

Design: Gérald Galdini, François Takounseun,
Emilie Etchelecou, Aurélie Sidot
Company: Partisan du Sens
Country: France
Category: Best of the category

**PLATINUM PENTAWARD 2015
LUXEPACK PRIZE**

Martell celebrates its 300th anniversary with
this exclusive blend of three exceptional eaux-de-vie:
Grande Champagne, Fins Bois and Borderies,
each evoking a different period in the history of
the cognac house according to its aromatic profile.
The bottle is presented in a wooden box decorated
with a three-tone inlay, echoing the ingredients
of the blend, while the bottle design is a faithful
reproduction of the traditional flasks that were
used to present samples to the Cellar Master. Each
of the 3,708 limited-edition bottles is numbered,
and aimed at faithful connoisseurs, being sold to
them directly by the VIP sales manager to impart
the full sense of occasion.

Martell feiert mit dieser exklusiven Mischung
aus den drei außergewöhnlichen Branntweinen
Grande Champagne, Fins Bois und Borderies
seinen 300. Geburtstag. Sie rufen je nach ihren
aromatischen Profilen Erinnerungen an verschiedene Perioden der Geschichte des Cognac-Hauses
wach. Die Flasche präsentiert sich in einem Holzkasten, dekoriert mit einer dreifarbigen Einlege-
arbeit, die auf die gemischten Inhalte anspielt. Das
Flaschendesign ist eine naturgetreue Reproduktion der traditionellen Glasflaschen, mit denen
Kellermeister ihre Trinkproben präsentierten.
Jede der 3.708 Flaschen der Sonderedition ist
nummeriert und für treue Connaisseurs gedacht.
Sie werden durch VIP-Salesmanager direkt verkauft und vermitteln so diesen besonderen Anlass
durch und durch.

Martell célèbre son 300ᵉ anniversaire avec
cet assemblage exclusif de trois eaux-de-vie excep-
tionnelles : Grande Champagne, Fins Bois et
Borderies, évoquant chacune une période différente dans l'histoire de la maison de cognac. La
bouteille est présentée dans un coffret en bois
décoré d'une incrustation à trois tons pour faire
écho aux ingrédients de l'assemblage, tandis que la
bouteille est une reproduction fidèle des flasques
traditionnelles qui étaient utilisées pour présenter
les échantillons au maître de chai. Chacune des
3 708 bouteilles de cette édition limitée est numé-
rotée et destinée à être vendue directement par le
directeur commercial VIP à un connaisseur fidèle.

CHIVAS REGAL
THE ICON

Creative Direction: Richard Clayton
Company: Coley Porter Bell
Country: UK
Category: Best of the category

**PLATINUM PENTAWARDS 2016
LUXEPACK PRIZE**

Chivas Regal was the first Scotch to be exported to the rest of the world, in 1909, and became known as a luxury whisky from this time. For this new ultra-prestige product, the pinnacle of the range (retailing at $ 3,500), the brand's essence needed to be reconceived in its most sublime form. This resulted in a return to the original 1909 bottle, a green crystal decanter with a classic, elegant form, together with touches of red throughout the packaging and the image of the ship on the badge in homage to the brand's export story. The presentation case was made by specialist cabinet-makers and each decanter was mouth-blown and hand-finished by the master craftsmen at Dartington Crystal.

Chivas Regal war 1909 der erste Scotch, der in die restliche Welt exportiert wurde, bekannt als der Luxuswhisky jener Zeit. Da dieses neue Ultraprestigeprodukt als Spitze des Sortiments mit 3.500 $ angeboten wird, musste die Essenz der Marke in ihrer nobelsten Form neu konzipiert werden. Was uns zurück zur Originalflasche des Jahres 1909 führt: die grüne Kristallkaraffe mit einer klassischen, eleganten Form, zusammen mit den Rottönen der Verpackung und dem Bild eines Schiffes auf dem Emblem als Hommage an die Exportgeschichte der Marke. Der Präsentations-koffer wurde von Spezialschreinern hergestellt. Jede Karaffe ist mundgeblasen und handwerklich vollendet durch die Meister von Dartington Crystal.

Chivas Regal a été le premier Scotch exporté vers le reste du monde en 1909, et est depuis connu comme un whisky de luxe. Pour ce produit de grand prestige, le summum de la gamme (vendu à 3 500 $), l'essence de la marque devait être réinterprétée sous sa forme la plus sublime. Cela se traduit par un retour à la bouteille originale de 1909, une carafe en verre vert à la ligne classique et élégante, avec des touches de rouge réparties sur tout l'emballage et l'image du bateau sur le badge en hommage à la tradition d'exportation de la marque. Le coffret de présentation est l'œuvre d'ébénistes spécialisés et chaque carafe a été soufflée à la bouche et finie à la main par les maîtres-artisans de Dartington Crystal.

Dieser in Scheiben geschnittene Premium-Schinken benötigte eine prestigeträchtige, neue Verpackungsform. Denn dieses Topprodukt von **Extrem** sollte im selben Moment, als sich die Marke in Gourmetgeschäften weltweit gerade neu positionierte, auch als Geschenk gekauft werden können. Die Verpackung musste die besonders hohe Qualität des Produkts vermitteln, damit es verglichen mit anderen Top-Köstlichkeiten wie Kaviar und Foie Gras dem Kunden sofort ins Auge springt. Das resultierende Design in mattem Schwarz mit dem kontrastierenden goldenen Griff in Schweine-Form dient gleichzeitig als elegante Servierschale, um den besten iberischen Schinken außergewöhnlich smart zu präsentieren.

Produit phare d'**Extrem**, ce jambon en tranches de qualité supérieure méritait un nouvel emballage prestigieux digne d'un présent, alors que la marque tentait de se repositionner dans les épiceries fines du monde entier. L'emballage devait être à la hauteur de la qualité exceptionnelle du produit pour le mettre au niveau d'autres aliments raffinés comme le caviar et le foie gras. D'un noir mat sur lequel tranche la poignée dorée en forme de cochon, le design imaginé sert également de plateau de service pour présenter en toute élégance le meilleur du jambon ibérique.

AGRICULTURAS DIVERSAS SLU EXTREM

Creative Direction:
Alberto Cienfuegos, Nacho Lavernia
Design: Raul Edo
Company: Lavernia & Cienfuegos
Country: Spain
Category: Best of the category

PLATINUM PENTAWARD 2014
LUXEPACK PRIZE

A prestigious new packaging was required for this premium sliced ham so that **Extrem**'s top product could be bought as a special gift at the same time as the brand was repositioning itself in gourmet stores around the world. The packaging needed to convey the product's extremely high quality in order for it to stand comparison with other high-end delicacies, such as caviar and foie gras. The resulting design, in matt black and with a contrasting golden handle in the form of a pig, doubles as an elegant serving-tray for presenting the finest cuts of Iberian ham in the very smartest style.

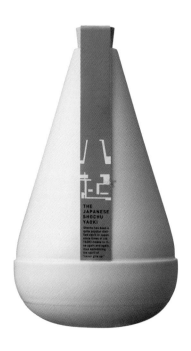

Dieses von Dentsu Kyushu entwickelte Projekt wurde von **Yaoki** Sake in Auftrag gegeben und führte zu einer sehr eleganten Flasche mit einer raffinierten weißen Form und einer runden Basis. Aufgrund dieser Form stellt sie sich immer wieder von selbst auf. Das Getränk wird aus Kartoffeln hergestellt. Die Flasche besteht aus dem berühmten Arita-Porzellan von der japanischen Insel Kyushu. Die Botschaft leitet sich von dem alten Sprichwort ab: „Wenn du siebenmal hinfällst, stehe auch das achte Mal wieder auf."

Ce projet développé par Dentsu Kyushu a été commandé par **Yaoki** Sake et son résultat est une bouteille très élégante, aux formes raffinées, de base arrondie et qui reprend sa position verticale toute seule. Ce Sake est obtenu à partir de pommes de terre, et la bouteille est fabriquée en porcelaine Arita, de l'île japonaise de Kyushu. Le message est tiré d'un proverbe ancien : « Si tu tombes sept fois, relève-toi la huitième fois ».

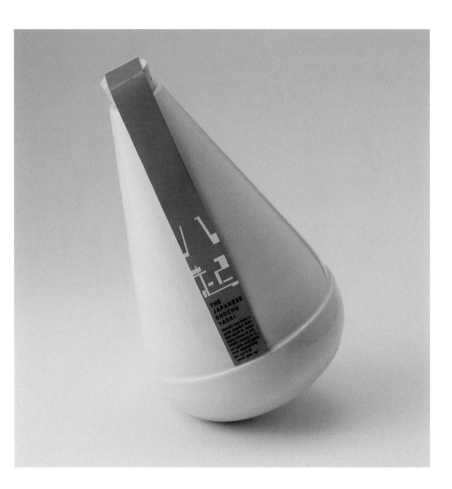

YAOKI

Design: Tadashi Cho
Copywriting: Iku Nara
Planning: Shinji Kaneko
Company: Dentsu Kyushu Inc.
Country: Japan
Category: Best of the category

PLATINUM PENTAWARD 2008

This project developed by Dentsu Kyushu was commissioned by **Yaoki** Sake and resulted in a very elegant bottle, with a white refined shape and a rounded base, allowing it to regain its vertical position by itself. The product is made from potatoes, and the packaging is made from the famous Arita porcelain, from the Japanese island of Kyushu. The message was drawn from an ancient proverb that says "If you fall down seven times, get up the eighth time".

ORIENS
VAN CLEEF & ARPELS

Design: Joël Desgrippes, Eric Douane
Company: Brandimage – Desgrippes & Laga
Country: France
Category: Best of the category

PLATINUM PENTAWARD 2010

In order to continue to boost Van Cleef & Arpels' high-end image in the perfume industry in line with the famous jeweller's positioning, the objective of this new package was to pursue the story initiated in 2008 with Féerie in the gems perfume territory, with a new fragrance emphasising the universe of precious stones dear to **Van Cleef & Arpels**. For the design of this baroque bottle Brandimage – Desgrippes & Laga drew inspiration from the brand's heritage, taking up the luxurious shapes of a high-end jewellery ring and its rare tourmaline sparkle. Oriens was launched in March 2010 (in the US exclusively at Bergdorf Goodman and Neiman Marcus stores).

Um das Top-Image von Van Cleef & Arpels in der Parfümbranche zusammen mit seiner Positionierung als berühmte Juweliere weiter zu fördern, lautete der Auftrag bei dieser Verpackung, die 2008 im Bereich von Edelsteinen und Parfüms mit Féerie initiierte Story auszubauen. Dazu sollte ein neuer Duft das Universum kostbarer Steine betonen, an denen **Van Cleef & Arpels** besonders gelegen ist. Für das Design dieser barocken Flasche ließ man sich vom traditionellen Erbe dieser Marke inspirieren: Brandimage – Desgrippes & Laga griff die luxuriösen Formen eines Topklasse-Rings und das Funkeln seines seltenen Turmalins auf. Oriens kam im März 2010 auf den Markt (in den USA exklusiv in den Luxuskaufhäusern Bergdorf Goodman und Neiman Marcus).

Pour continuer à renforcer l'image haut de gamme de Van Cleef & Arpels sur le marché des parfums, en cohérence avec le positionnement du joaillier, l'objectif de ce nouvel emballage était de poursuivre le fil narratif né en 2008 avec Féerie sur le territoire des parfums bijoux, avec une nouvelle fragrance qui reprend l'univers des pierres précieuses, si cher à **Van Cleef & Arpels**. Pour concevoir ce flacon baroque, Brandimage – Desgrippes & Laga a tiré son inspiration de l'héritage de la marque, et lui a emprunté les formes voluptueuses d'une bague de luxe et l'éclat rare de la tourmaline. Oriens a été lancé en mars 2010 (aux États-Unis exclusivement dans les magasins Bergdorf Goodman et Neiman Marcus).

MARC JACOBS
BANG

Design: Harry Allen
Company: Harry Allen Design
Country: USA
Category: Best of the category

PLATINUM PENTAWARD 2011
LUXEPACK PRIZE

In developing a form for the new fragrance from Marc Jacobs the packaging had to reflect the brand image and stand out to the young male target audience whilst also responding to the given name, **Bang**. Metal sheets struck with hammers and rocks retain the form of the impact, a literal visualisation, and one such piece was translated by computer to produce the design for the bottle. Slightly ambiguous, masculine but not over-designed, this template was then given over to the engineering team to produce in glass, the other initial criterion.

Das Design für den neuen Duft von Marc Jacobs sollte das Image der Marke widerspiegeln und für das junge, männliche Zielpublikum hervorstechen, gleichzeitig den Namen **Bang** aufgreifen. Mit Hammer oder Stein deformiertes Metall bewahrt diese Form – eine buchstäbliche Visualisierung. Ein solches Ergebnis wurde vom Computer für das Flaschendesign umgerechnet. Dezent mehrdeutig und maskulin, aber nicht überdesignt, wurde diese Vorlage dann ans Ingenieursteam weitergegeben, um die Produktion in Glas auszuführen – das war ein weiteres Eingangskriterium.

Pour le nouveau parfum de Marc Jacobs, l'emballage devait refléter l'image de la marque et se faire remarquer auprès de sa cible d'hommes jeunes, tout en faisant écho au nom choisi, **Bang**. Une feuille de métal frappée par un marteau ou une pierre conserve la forme de l'impact. C'est cette visualisation littérale qui a été traduite numériquement pour produire la forme de la bouteille. Légèrement ambigu, masculin mais pas trop travaillé, ce modèle a ensuite été transféré à l'équipe d'ingénieurs afin de le fabriquer en verre, une autre condition décidée dès le départ.

DAVIDOFF CHAMPION

Design: Alnoor Design
Company: Objets de Convoitises, Alnoor Design
Country: France
Category: Perfumes

GOLD PENTAWARD 2011

VAN CLEEF & ARPELS
FÉERIE

Creative Direction: Joël Desgrippes
Art Direction/3D: Eric Douane
Art Direction/2D: Sylvie Verdier
Company: Brandimage – Desgrippes & Laga
Country: France
Category: Perfumes

GOLD PENTAWARD 2009

Féerie by Van Cleef & Arpels was first launched in August 2008, and the perfume range was later extended with a new Eau de Toilette. The exclusive bottle, faceted like a precious stone, displays the colour of night and illuminates the heavenly mystery of the luxurious Van Cleef & Arpels perfumery. The package's most distinguished feature is its unexpected oversized silver cap bearing an iconic fairy resting delicately in a graceful, impish pose atop a moonflower.

Féerie, ein Parfüm von Van Cleef & Arpels, kam erstmals im August 2008 auf den Markt und wurde von einem neuen Eau de Toilette begleitet. Der exklusive Flakon, facettiert wie ein kostbarer Edelstein, stellt die Farbe der Nacht dar und erhellt das himmlische Geheimnis der Luxusparfümerie Van Cleef & Arpels. Die auffallendste Eigenschaft der Verpackung ist ihr unerwartet großer silberner Verschluss, der symbolisch eine Fee darstellt, die feingliedrig in einer eleganten und kecken Haltung auf einer Mondblume sitzt.

Féerie est un parfum de Van Cleef & Arpels. Initialement lancée en août 2008, la gamme s'est agrandie avec l'arrivée d'une nouvelle eau de toilette. Le flacon exclusif, taillé comme une pierre précieuse, est couleur nuit et illumine le divin mystère des parfums luxueux de Van Cleef & Arpels. La caractéristique la plus originale du packaging est un bouchon surdimensionné portant une fée gracieuse et espiègle assise sur une trompette des anges.

K BY KILIAN
THE ART OF LOVE COLLECTION

Creative Direction: Franck Basset
Art Direction: Dimitri Rastorgoueff
Company: Carré Basset
Country: France
Category: Perfumes

GOLD PENTAWARD 2015

The Art of Love is a new collection of four perfumes from **K by Kilian** launched exclusively on the Russian market. The oval bottle is a modern version of the classic Fabergé egg, with the adaptation that it stands freely upside down, with the cap serving as support. To achieve the beautiful and flawless shiny surface in conjunction with this unstable shape presented several technical difficulties, while the use of high-gloss black metallization manages to magnify the flame-polished shape. Into this surface the name of each perfume has been cut by laser: Kisses Don't Lie, Criminal of Love, Killing Me Slowly, and Dangerously in Love.

The Art of Love ist eine neue Kollektion mit vier Düften von **K by Kilian**, exklusiv für den russischen Markt. Die ovale Flasche ist ein modernes Fabergé-Ei und so angepasst, dass sie frei auf dem Kopf steht und die Verschlusskappe als Halterung dient. Um mit der instabilen Form diese schöne und makellos glänzende Oberfläche zu erzielen, mussten verschiedene technische Herausforderungen gemeistert werden. Der hochglänzenden schwarzen Metalliclackierung gelingt es, die getemperte Form zu vergrößern. Mit Laser sind die Namen der Parfüms in diese Oberfläche eingraviert: Kisses Don't Lie, Criminal of Love, Killing Me Slowly und Dangerously in Love.

The Art of Love est une nouvelle collection de quatre parfums de **K by Kilian** lancée exclusivement sur le marché russe. Le flacon ovale est une version moderne de l'œuf Fabergé classique, qui tient debout tête en bas, en s'appuyant sur le bouchon. Il a fallu surmonter plusieurs difficultés techniques pour obtenir cette magnifique surface brillante sur la forme instable de l'objet, polie au feu et mise en valeur par la métallisation laquée noir. Le nom de chaque parfum a été gravé au laser sur cette surface : Kisses Don't Lie, Criminal of Love, Killing Me Slowly et Dangerously in Love.

GIVENCHY ANGE OU DÉMON

Design: Angela Summers, Vincent Villéger
Company: Villéger Summers Design
Country: UK
Category: Perfumes
GOLD PENTAWARD 2008

Villéger Summers Design received the brief from Givenchy to design a luxurious bottle, linking with its original design, and the main inspiration for it arose from the crystal chandelier. This refillable version is complemented by a chain of beads, and additional facets give an increased feeling of luxury. Originally meant to be disposable, the bottle was thought too good to throw away, prompting **Givenchy** to introduce a soft disposable refill. In this case, the challenge was that the graphics had also to provide a luxurious aspect for a format usually associated with lower-end products.

Givenchy gab Villéger Summers Design das Briefing an die Hand, einen luxuriösen Flakon zu gestalten und dabei eine Verbindung zum ursprünglichen Design herzustellen. Inspirieren ließ man sich dafür hauptsächlich von einem Kronleuchter. Diese nachfüllbare Version wird durch eine Glasperlenkette ergänzt. Außerdem bekommt das Gefäß durch zusätzliche Facetten noch ein sehr luxuriöses Flair. Eigentlich war diese Flasche als Einwegartikel gedacht, aber man fand, sie sei zu gut zum Wegwerfen. So sah **Givenchy** sich veranlasst, eine Soft-Nachfüllpackung anzubieten. Hier bestand die Herausforderung darin, bei einem Format, das man eher mit geringwertigen Produkten assoziiert, das äußere Erscheinungsbild ebenfalls erstklassig wirken zu lassen.

Givenchy a chargé Villéger Summers Design de concevoir une bouteille luxueuse qui devait établir un lien avec le design original, et la principale inspiration a été le chandelier en cristal. Cette version rechargeable est complétée par une chaîne de perles, et les facettes augmentent encore la sensation de luxe. À l'origine, la bouteille devait être jetable, mais elle a été considérée trop réussie pour finir à la poubelle, ce qui a poussé **Givenchy** à lui ajouter une recharge jetable dans un packaging souple. Dans ce cas, le défi était que le graphisme devait également transmettre la notion de luxe, pour un format habituellement associé à des produits plus bas de gamme.

SELECTIVE BEAUTY
JOHN GALLIANO

Creative Direction: Elie Papiernik
Creative Team: Katja Liebig, Guozheng Jiang,
Nathalie Pierre, Cécile Cazanova
Company: Centdegrés
Country: France
Category: Perfumes

SILVER PENTAWARD 2009

MARC JACOBS
DAISY DREAM

Creative Direction: Sam O'Donahue
Design: Peter Ash, Felix De Voss
Company: Established
Country: USA
Category: Perfumes

GOLD PENTAWARD 2014

The light and airy delicacy of **Daisy Dream** is inspired by the boundless spirit of blue skies and meadow flowers. At the same time, this floral, fruity fragrance reflects an irresistible mixture of intricate details, elegance and femininity which delivers a fresh interpretation of the daisy motif. The glass bottle design is enveloped in a shawl of laced daisies and is topped with a silver cap adorned with further flowers with gold centers.

Daisy Dream mit seiner leichten und luftigen Zartheit lässt sich von der grenzenlosen Weite des blauen Himmels und den Wiesenblumen inspirieren. Gleichzeitig spiegelt der florale und fruchtige Wohlgeruch die unwiderstehliche Mischung diffiziler Details, Eleganz und Weiblichkeit. Die Glasflasche dicht von Gänseblümchen ummantelt, obenauf sitzt einsilbernen Verschluss, verziert mit weiteren Blüten mit goldenem Stempel.

Le design aérien et délicat de **Daisy Dream** s'inspire des étendues de ciel bleu et de prairies en fleurs. Ce parfum à la fois floral et fruité diffuse un mélange irrésistible de détails complexes, d'élégance et de féminité pour une réinterprétation de la marguerite. Le flacon en verre est enveloppé d'un châle de marguerites entrelacées et chapeauté d'un bouchon argenté orné de ces fleurs au cœur d'or.

HOUSE OF SILLAGE
GECKO

Design: Brian Hassine, Philip Azzolina
Company: Laguna Made
Country: USA
Category: Perfumes
SILVER PENTAWARD 2015

COTY-MARC JACOBS DECADENCE

Design: Sam O'Donahue
Company: Established
Country: USA
Category: Perfumes
GOLD PENTAWARD 2016

In a typically bold departure for packaging concepts in the luxury market, this innovative design from **Marc Jacobs** presents the bottle for Decadence in the shape of a glamorous handbag, combining a nod to the aesthetic of the parent fashion label with an unashamedly indulgent package. The accessorizing details of the python-skin fold at the top, the chunky gold chain and silk tassel all sit coolly against the deep green of the glass to declare this scent's sexy sophistication and opulence.

Mit seiner typischen mutigen Abkehr von Verpackungskonzepten im Luxusmarkt präsentiert dieses innovative Design von **Marc Jacobs** die Flasche für Decadence in Form einer glamourösen Handtasche. Damit zieht sie den Hut vor der Ästhetik des Muttermodelabels und zeigt gleichzeitig eine unverhohlen maßlose Verpackung. Sehr cool, wie sich die Accessoiredetails wie der Verschluss aus Pythonhaut oben, die klobige Goldkette und die Seidenquaste vom Tiefgrün des Glases abheben, um die sexy Eleganz und Opulenz dieses Dufts zu verkünden.

Avec ce concept d'emballage d'une originalité qui convient parfaitement au marché du luxe, **Marc Jacobs** présente le flacon du parfum Decadence sous forme de sac à main glamour, référence claire à l'esthétique de la maison de mode avec un flacon délibérément hédoniste. Les détails du rabat en python, de la grosse chaîne dorée et du gland en soie se détachent nonchalamment sur le vert profond pour signifier la sophistication sensuelle et l'opulence de cette fragrance.

POLA B.A. THE CREAM

Creative Direction: Takeshi Usui
Art Direction: Chiharu Suzuki
Design: Haruyo Eto, Taishi Ono
Company: Pola
Country: Japan
Category: Cosmetics

GOLD PENTAWARD 2010

By employing advanced resin formation and vapour deposition technologies in the shape of this new packaging for **Pola B.A.** the result is a new, dynamic, and dazzling life created by cellular division. The container opens and closes with a unique screw mechanism, an engineering feat stemming from an ingenious combination of practical use and smart design. The inner container can be replaced, creating a stylish and welcome touch that preserves natural resources.

Bei der Gestaltung dieser neuen Verpackung für **Pola B.A.** wurden fortschrittliche Techniken der Kunstharzformung und Aufdampfverfahren eingesetzt. Das Produkt sorgt für ein neues, dynamisches und glanzvolles Leben, das durch Zellteilung geschaffen wird. Der Behälter wird mit einem einzigartigen Schraubverschluss geöffnet. Diese technische Meisterleistung kombiniert praktischen Nutzen und cleveres Design auf ausgeklügelte Weise. Der innere Behälter kann ausgetauscht werden und schafft somit eine stilvolle und willkommene Note, mit der natürliche Ressourcen bewahrt werden.

La forme de ce nouvel emballage pour **Pola B.A.** est le fruit de technologies de pointe dans le moulage de la résine et la vaporisation. Le résultat est une nouvelle vie dynamique et éclatante créée par division cellulaire. Le pot s'ouvre et se ferme grâce à un mécanisme à vis original, une prouesse technique qui opère une alliance ingénieuse entre commodité d'utilisation et conception intelligente. Le pot interne peut être remplacé, une touche élégante et bienvenue qui permet de préserver les ressources naturelles.

KENZO
UNIDENTIFIED

Design: Ron Arad
Company: Kenzo Parfums
Country: France
Category: Perfumes

SILVER PENTAWARD 2009

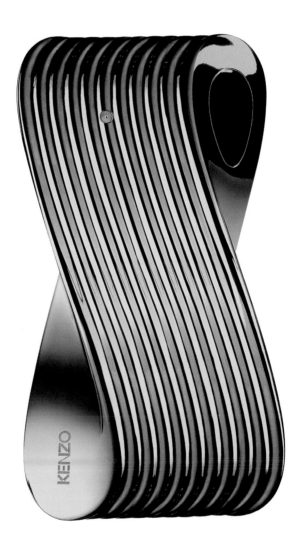

MARC JACOBS
DOT
Design: Sayuri Shoji
in collaboration with Marc Jacobs
Company: Sayuri Studio
Country: Japan
Category: Perfumes
SILVER PENTAWARD 2013

VALENTINO
PARFUM & EXQUISITE BODY MILK
Design: Ian Carnduff, Nice design team
Company: Nice
Country: USA
Category: Perfumes
SILVER PENTAWARD 2010

JEAN-PAUL GAULTIER
SILVER MY SKIN

Creative Direction: Sébastien Servaire
Art Direction: Justine Dauchez
Company: Servaire & Co
Country: France
Category: Perfumes

BRONZE PENTAWARD 2012

DIPTYQUE
EAU DE PARFUM

Creative Direction: Sébastien Servaire
Design: Candido de Barros
Graphic Design: Justine Dauchez, Yael Audrain
Company: Servaire & Co
Country: France
Category: Perfumes

SILVER PENTAWARD 2013

DIPTYQUE
ELECTRIC DIFFUSER

Art Direction: Caroline Colin
Art Direction Animation/
Illustration: Juliette Lavat
Marketing Direction:
Sébastien Servaire
Product Development Direction:
Erwann Pivert
Company: Servaire & Co
Country: France
Category: Perfumes
SILVER PENTAWARD 2014

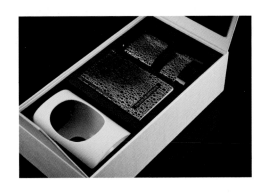

CLÉ DE PEAU BEAUTÉ
ROSE SYNERGIQUE

Creative Direction: Izumi Matsumoto
Art Direction: Mao Komai
Design: Benoît-Pierre Emery,
Damian O'Sullivan, Mao Komai
Company: Shiseido
Country: Japan
Category: Perfumes
SILVER PENTAWARD 2014

CHRISTIAN SIRIANO SILHOUETTE

Design: Karim Rashid
Company: Karim Rashid Inc.
Country: USA
Category: Perfumes

BRONZE PENTAWARD 2015

SHISEIDO EVER BLOOM

Creative Direction: Yoji Nobuto
Art Direction and Design: Mao Komai
Company: Shiseido
Country: Japan
Category: Perfumes

SILVER PENTAWARD 2016

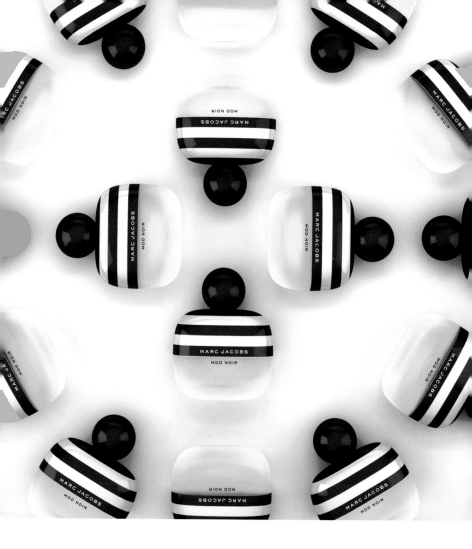

MARC JACOBS
MOD NOIR

Creative Direction: Sam O'Donahue
Senior Design: Peter Ash
Company: Established
Country: USA
Category: Perfumes

SILVER PENTAWARD 2015

COSME DECORTE
AQMW SKINCARE SERIES

Art Direction: Marcel Wanders
Creative Direction: Tatsuo Kannami
Design: Gabriele Chiave, Kazuhiro Niikura
Company: Kosé Corporation
Country: Japan
Category: Cosmetics

GOLD PENTAWARD 2011

To commemorate the 40th anniversary of Cosme Decorte the **AQMW** Skincare Series was given some very special packaging. An elegant pattern of flowers in full bloom, interwoven with buds and overlaying a vibrant garden planted with an evergreen tree that stays in leaf all year round, was the motif chosen to represent skin regeneration and wellbeing. Transferring the design to the container in the form of a relief involved considerable technical difficulty, with two-dimensional patterns being pasted evenly over the surface using high-end three-dimensional modeling and advanced molding techniques.

Anlässlich des 40. Geburtstags von Cosme Decorte wurde die Hautpflegeserie **AQMW** auf ganz besondere Weise verpackt. Ein elegantes Muster voller blühender Blumen, mit Knospen verschlungen und einen lebendigen Garten überlagernd, worin ein immergrüner Baum das ganze Jahr über seine Blätter trägt – dieses erwählte Motiv sollte die Regeneration der Haut und Wohlgefühl darstellen. Die Übertragung des Designs auf den Behälter in Form eines Reliefs stellte eine beträchtliche technische Herausforderung dar, wobei das zweidimensionale Muster anhand von dreidimensionaler Highend-Modellierung und fortschrittlicher Formungstechniken gleichmäßig auf die Oberfläche aufgebracht wurde.

Pour célébrer le 40ᵉ anniversaire de Cosme Decorte, la gamme **AQMW** Skincare Series méritait de nouveaux flacons très spéciaux. Un élégant motif de fleurs en plein floraison entrelacé avec des bourgeons, superposé à un beau jardin orné d'un arbre qui ne perd jamais ses feuilles, a été choisi pour représenter la régénération de la peau et le bien-être. Pour transférer ce motif en relief sur le flacon, il a fallu surmonter des difficultés techniques considérables : les traits bidimensionnels ont été appliqués uniformément sur la surface à l'aide d'un procédé de modelage tridimensionnel dernier cri et de techniques de moulage complexes.

IPSA
THE TIME RESET

Design: Aoshi Kudo, Shuichi Ikedalo, Helmut Schmid
Company: Communication Design Laboratory
Country: Japan
Category: Cosmetics

SILVER PENTAWARD 2009

POLA WHITISSIMO

Creative Direction: Takeshi Usui
Art Direction: Chiharu Suzuki
Design: Taishi Ono, Haruyo Eto
Company: Pola
Country: Japan

SILVER PENTAWARD 2011

SHISEIDO BIO-PERFORMANCE

Creative Direction: Yoji Nobuto
Art Direction: Mao Komai
Design: Akira Muraoka
Company: Shiseido
Country: Japan
Category: Make-up, body care, beauty products

GOLD PENTAWARD 2016

IPSA
PREMIER LINE

Art Direction/Design: Aoshi Kudo
Creative Direction: Shuichi Ikeda
Logo Design: Helmut Schmid
Company: Communication Design Laboratory
Country: Japan
Category: Make-up, body care, beauty products

SILVER PENTAWARD 2014

IPSA
ME

Art Direction/Creative Direction/Design:
Aoshi Kudo
Company: Communication Design Laboratory
Country: Japan
Category: Make-up, body care, beauty products

SILVER PENTAWARD 2016

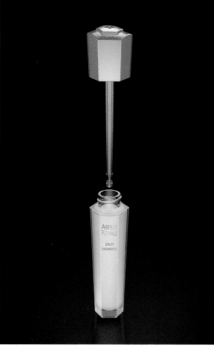

GUERLAIN

Art Direction: Sébastien Servaire
Design: Candido De Barros
Account Management: Virginie Bourgoin
Illustration: Yael Bibliowicz
Company: Servaire & Co
Country: France
Category: Cosmetics
SILVER PENTAWARD 2010

The agency created a new premium anti-ageing skin-care serum for **Guerlain**. Mixing technology and brand heritage to create a mythic product for the ultra-competitive market, the agency was inspired by one of the most essential life-forms in nature: the bee. Since its creation, Guerlain has used the bee as a symbol of the brand in its perfumes and fragrances. Given that one-third of human food supply depends on insect pollination, bees are a key factor in sustaining life and constitute a major type of pollinator in ecosystems. The agency developed unique packaging which translates the bee universe into reality, by adding a complementary element (Beehive) to an existing brand code (Bee).

Die Agentur schuf für **Guerlain** ein neues Premium-Produkt: ein neuartiges Hautpflegeserum gegen Hautalterung. Dabei ließ sie sich von einer der grundlegendsten Lebensformen der Natur inspirieren: von der Biene. Seit seiner Entstehung hat Guerlain bei dieser Marke die Biene als Symbol für seine Parfüms und Duftstoffe eingesetzt. Wenn man bedenkt, dass ein Drittel der menschlichen Nahrungsversorgung auf Befruchtung durch Insekten beruht, sind Bienen ein zentraler Faktor für den Erhalt des Lebens. Sie dienen in unseren Ökosystemen als besonders wichtige Bestäuber. Die Agentur entwickelte eine charakteristische Verpackung, über die die Welt der Bienen in die Realität umgesetzt wird: Dem vorhandenen Code der Marke (die Biene) wird ein ergänzendes Element hinzugefügt, nämlich der Bienenstock.

L'agence a créé un nouveau sérum anti-âge haut de gamme pour **Guerlain**. Elle a allié la technologie et l'héritage de la marque pour créer un produit mythique sur un marché ultra concurrentiel, et s'est inspirée de l'une des formes de vie les plus essentielles dans la nature : l'abeille. Elle est le symbole des parfums de la marque depuis sa création. Étant donné qu'un tiers des aliments consommés par les humains dépend de la pollinisation des insectes, et que les abeilles sont un agent majeur de pollinisation dans les écosystèmes, elles jouent un rôle clé pour la vie sur la planète. L'agence a imaginé un emballage original qui traduit l'univers des abeilles dans notre réalité, en ajoutant un élément complémentaire (la ruche) à un code qui existait déjà pour la marque (l'abeille).

CLÉ DE PEAU BEAUTÉ CREAM

Creative Direction: Katsuhiko Shibuya
Art Direction: Chieko Yamamoto
Art Direction/Design: Mao Komai
Company: Shiseido
Country: Japan
Category: Make-up, body care, beauty products
BRONZE PENTAWARD 2016

PERNOD RICARD
ROYAL SALUTE 62 GUN SALUTE

Design Direction: Stuart Humm
Company: Coley Porter Bell
Country: UK
Category: Spirits

GOLD PENTAWARD 2011

Royal Salute is a super-premium whisky brand, relatively new to customers, which competes primarily with Cognac in its core markets (Asia). It is the pinnacle of luxury whisky and retails at $ 2,200 a bottle. In order to stand out amongst such top-end spirits, whilst retaining the brand's distinctive visual style, keeping the bottle shape was key before embellishing it with a crest and an ornate crown-like stopper. The porcelain flagon usually associated with the brand was, however, retired in favor of the greater luxury of cut crystal. The new decanter is hand-blown and cut by master craftsmen at Dartington Crystal, each one taking over 40 hours to make, and conveys a sense of nobility and allure which helps set it apart from Cognac.

Royal Salute ist eine Whiskymarke der Super-premium-Klasse und für Kunden relativ neu – sie konkurriert auf ihren (asiatischen) Kernmärkten primär mit Cognac. Sie stellt den Gipfel der luxuriösen Whiskysorten dar und wird pro Flasche für $ 2.200 angeboten. Damit dieses Produkt neben den anderen Top-End-Spirituosen hervorsticht und gleichzeitig der charakteristische visuelle Stil der Marke gewahrt bleibt, war es essenziell, die Flaschenform zu bewahren, bevor sie mit Wappen und kronenähnlichem Verschluss geschmückt wird. Normalerweise kennt man die Marke in einer Flasche aus Porzellan, aber um des größeren Luxus willen wurde hier einem Gefäß aus geschliffenem Kristall der Vorzug gegeben. Der neue Dekanter wurde bei den Meisterhandwerkern von Dartington Crystal mundgeblasen und geschliffen. Jede Flasche erfordert über 40 Arbeitsstunden und vermittelt das Gefühl von Adel und Faszination, was sie noch besser vom Cognac abhebt.

Royal Salute est une marque de whisky très haut de gamme, relativement nouvelle pour les clients, qui fait principalement concurrence au cognac sur ses principaux marchés (Asie). C'est le summum du whisky de luxe, et son prix de vente atteint 2 200 $ par bouteille. Pour se faire remarquer aux côtés des spiritueux les plus exclusifs, tout en préservant le style visuel qui caractérise la marque, il était essentiel de conserver la forme de la bouteille avant de l'embellir avec des armoiries et un bouchon orné en forme de couronne. La bouteille en porcelaine habituellement associée à la marque a cependant été remplacée par du cristal taillé, plus luxueux. La nouvelle carafe est soufflée à la bouche et taillée par les maîtres-artisans de Dartington Crystal. Chaque unité nécessite plus de 40 heures de travail et transmet un sentiment de noblesse et d'élégance qui aide à démarquer ce produit du cognac.

ANESTASIA SENSATIONAL SPIRIT

Design: Karim Rashid
Company: Karim Rashid Inc.
Country: USA
Category: Spirits

GOLD PENTAWARD 2013

Anestasia vodka creates a new taste sensation by making the mouth tingle and feel cool, relieving the usual burn of alcoholic spirits. The remarkable bottle design reflects this perfectly with the crystalline and obliquely faceted surface giving it an ultra-futuristic feel. The hard-edged and asymmetrical form also proves to be easy to grip and comfortable for the hand, while the bottle's beauty makes it an ideal tabletop piece, accenting any environment with a look which embodies cutting-edge style.

DIAGEO
JOHNNIE WALKER
THE JOHN WALKER
Design: Linea design team
Company: Linea
Country: France
Category: Spirits
SILVER PENTAWARD 2010

Anestasia Wodka sorgt für ein neues Geschmackserleben, weil er im Mund kribbelt und kühlt. So wird der normalerweise brennende Geschmack bei hochprozentigen Getränken gelindert. Dem entspricht perfekt das bemerkenswerte Design mit seiner kristallinen Oberfläche und den schrägen Facetten, was der Flasche eine ultrafuturistische Note verleiht. Nimmt man die kantige und asymmetrische Form in die Hand, wirkt sie grifffreundlich und angenehm, während die Flasche durch ihre Schönheit zu einem idealen Schmuckstück für den Tisch wird, das jeder Umgebung den Touch hochmodernen Stils verleiht.

La vodka **Anestasia** offre une nouvelle saveur qui chatouille les papilles et rafraîchit la bouche, loin de la sensation de brûlure des spiritueux. L'impressionnant design de la bouteille évoque parfaitement cette expérience, avec une surface cristalline à facettes donnant un air très futuriste. La forme asymétrique permet une agréable prise en mains, et la beauté de la bouteille en fait un objet décoratif apportant une touche clairement avant-gardiste à n'importe quel intérieur.

TESSERON
TRÉSOR SIGNATURE COLLECTION
Design: Linea design team
Company: Linea
Country: France
Category: Spirits
SILVER PENTAWARD 2014

FINE & SPIRITS
FLEUR COGNAC
Design: Linea design team
Company: Linea
Country: France
Category: Spirits
SILVER PENTAWARD 2012

DOMAINE DE CANTON
Design: John Cooper
Producer: Cameo Metal Products
Country: USA
Category: Spirits
GOLD PENTAWARD 2008

COGNAC DE LUZE
Design: Sébastien Schalchli
Brand Positioning: Laurent Berriat
Management: Stéphane Aussel,
Robert Eastham (Cognac De Luze)
Company: Toscara
Country: France
Category: Spirits
SILVER PENTAWARD 2011

妻有
清酒

天神囃子

特別本醸造

TENJIN-BAYASHI

Design: Uonuma Sake Brewery,
Kuroyanagi Jun
Company: Kuroyanagi Jun
Country: Japan
Category: Spirits

SILVER PENTAWARD 2010

CIROC X

Creative Direction:
Laurent Hainaut, J. B. Hartford
Art Direction: Kristin Buchanan
Structural Art Direction: William Kang
Account Direction: Leigh von Boetticher
Company: Force Majeure Design
(former Raison Pure NYC)
Country: USA
Category: Spirits

GOLD PENTAWARD 2015

WILD TURKEY
MASTER'S KEEP

Commercial Direction: Jonathan Ford
Executive Direction: Mike Branson
Creative Direction: Hamish Campbell
Realization: Brandi Parker
Design Direction: Sissy Emmons Hobizal
Company: Pearlfisher
Country: USA
Category: Spirits
SILVER PENTAWARD 2016

CHANGYU

Design: Wu Kuanfu, Tang Sisi
Company: Shenzhen Excel Package Design
Country: China
Category: Spirits
BRONZE PENTAWARD 2014

JOHNNIE WALKER PRIVATE COLLECTION

Design: Jason Barney, Jeremy Roots
Company: Sedley Place
Country: UK
Category: Spirits
SILVER PENTAWARD 2015

THE MACALLAN 1824 SERIES

Design: Elie Hasbani
Company: Brandimage – Desgrippes & Laga
Country: France
Category: Spirits
BRONZE PENTAWARD 2015

TRUETT HURST
DRY CREEK VALLEY
VML

Design: Kevin Shaw, Cosimo Surace
Company: Stranger & Stranger
Country: USA
Category: Fine wines, champagne
GOLD PENTAWARD 2012

Biodynamic winemaking may well sound like organic farming but actually has its roots in pagan mythology and alchemy—early winemakers would bury stag heads and bladders filled with petals as part of their manufacturing. Even so, label design for this class of wines is conspicuously dull and undistinguished, which left an opening to introduce some magic into the sector. With certain practices still today that sound like witchcraft, the biodynamic winemaker could be shown on labels as head of a coven, surrounded by her faithful worshippers.

Biodynamischer Weinbau – das hört sich vielleicht nach organischer Landwirtschaft an, aber tatsächlich wurzelt der Weinbau in heidnischer Mythologie und Alchemie: Die ersten Bauern vergruben in ihren Weinbergen Hirschköpfe und mit Blütenblättern gefüllte Blasen. Doch trotz dieses Wissens ist die Etikettengestaltung für diese Klasse Weine oft auffallend langweilig und recht mittelmäßig – eine Lücke, die man durch etwas Magie füllen kann. Auch heute noch gibt es bestimmte Praktiken, die nach Hexerei klingen. So wird der biodynamische Weinbauer auf den Etiketten passenderweise als Herr eines Hexenzirkels gezeigt, umgeben von treuen Anbetern.

La viticulture biodynamique peut sembler avoir beaucoup en commun avec l'agriculture organique, mais elle prend en fait ses racines dans la mythologie païenne et dans l'alchimie. Les premiers viticulteurs enterraient des têtes de cerf et des vessies remplies de fleurs. Pourtant, les étiquettes de ce type de vin brillent par leur manque d'imagination, une porte ouverte pour introduire un peu de magie dans le secteur. Les viticulteurs biodynamiques utilisent aujourd'hui encore certaines pratiques qui ressemblent à de la sorcellerie, c'est pourquoi l'étiquette les représente sous les traits de sorciers entourés de fervents adorateurs.

BLACKBIRD WINES

Design: Vanja Cuculic
Illustration: Tomislav Tomi
Company: Studio Cuculic
Country: Hungary
Category: Fine wines, champagne

SILVER PENTAWARD 2010

AFIP DIAMOND

Design: Wu Kuan Fu
Company: Shenzhen Excel Package Design
Country: China
Category: Fine wines, champagne

GOLD PENTAWARD 2010

RONGZI

Design: Kuan Fu Wu
Company: Shenzhen Excel Package Design
Country: China
Category: Fine wines, champagne
SILVER PENTAWARD 2012

800 LOVE LETTERS WINE

Design: Wu Shao Nan
Company: Shenzhen Excel Package Design
Country: China
Category: Fine wines, champagne

SILVER PENTAWARD 2013

YANGYANG INTERNATIONAL WINERY HE BRAND LIKOUBEI SERIES

Design: Kuanfu Wu
Company: Shenzhen Excel Brand Design Consultant
Country: China
Category: Fine wines, champagne
SILVER PENTAWARD 2016

Für sein Ziel, eine „Avantgarde-Champagner-marke" zu entwickeln, bricht das Design dieser Flasche Konventionen, da es kein Frontetikett aufweist und Name sowie Symbol direkt in Gold aufs Glas gedruckt werden. Die Flaschenform selbst ergab sich ebenfalls aus verschiedenen Innovationen bei der traditionellen Champagner-produktion. Der ungewöhnlich lange, schlanke Hals der Flasche hilft, dass sich die Aromen des Cuvée entwickeln. Die rote Schärpe schließlich wurde tatsächlich zu einem echten Band transfor-miert und in einer technologischen Meisterleis-tung ins Glas geprägt.

Ce concept de bouteille rompt avec les conven-tions en se passant d'étiquette, et en imprimant en doré le nom et le symbole directement sur le verre, pour créer une « marque de champagne d'avant-garde ». La forme de la bouteille est également le résultat d'une série d'innovations apportées au processus traditionnel de production du cham-pagne, et son col inhabituellement long et mince contribue à l'épanouissement des arômes de la cuvée. Enfin, prouesse technologique, le ruban rouge est un vrai ruban incrusté dans le verre.

MUMM GRAND CORDON

Design: Ross Lovegrove
Cellars Master: Didier Mariotti
Brand Direction: Louis de Fautereau
Marketing Management: Ludivine Catrice
Purchase and Development Direction:
Jean-Pascal Martin Festa
Glassmaker: Selective Line by Verallia
Production: Dekorglass (Poland),
Sparflex (France), Billet (France)
Company: Maison Mumm
Country: France
Category: Fine wines, champagne

GOLD PENTAWARD 2016

With the aim of developing an "avant-garde champagne brand" this bottle design breaks with convention by having no front label, instead printing the name and symbol directly on to the glass in gold. The shape of the bottle too is the result of a series of innovations to the traditional champagne production process, and the bottle's unusually long, slender neck serves to help the development of the aromas of the cuvée. Lastly, the red sash has been transformed into a real ribbon, which—in a feat of technology—is actually indented into the glass.

CHATEAU RUBAN

Graphic Design: Juraj Vontorcik,
Juraj Demovic, Livia Lorinczova
Illustration: Igor Benca
Company: Pergamen Trnava
Country: Slovakia
Category: Fine wines, champagne
BRONZE PENTAWARD 2014

CROCHET

Design: Rita Rivotti, João Miranda
Company: Rita Rivotti – Wine Branding & Design
Country: Portugal
Category: Fine wines, champagne

GOLD PENTAWARD 2014

ABSOLUT VODKA
TUNE

Creative Direction: Patrick Gebhardt
Executive Client Direction: Jonas Andersson
Client Management: Camilla Sand, Frida Frisén
Client Direction: Alfred Alfred
Project Management: Jonas Westius (No Picnic)
Industrial Design: Anna-Carin Neale, Thomas Schaad (No Picnic)
Visualization: Stefan Wennerström (No Picnic)
Creative Direction: Urban Ahlgren (No Picnic)
Global Marketing Management: Tamara Urukalo
Global Direction Design Strategy: Anna Kamjou
Global Direction Innovation: Nina Gillsvik
Company: Brand Union
Country: Sweden
Category: Fine wines, champagne

BRONZE PENTAWARD 2013

BITRI
EACH BOTTLE HAS A SECRET

Art Direction: Eduardo Aires
Design: Ana Simões
Company: White Studio
Country: Portugal
Category: Fine wines, champagne

SILVER PENTAWARD 2013

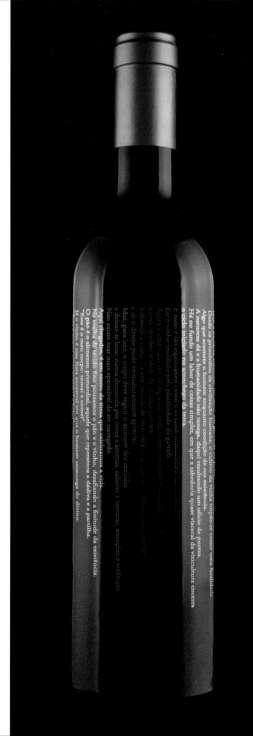

PIQUENTUM

Creative Direction: Jelena Fiskus, Sean Poropat
3D Design: Eugen Slavik
Company: Studio Sonda
Country: Croatia
Category: Fine wines, champagne
BRONZE PENTAWARD 2016

JIULAN MOUNTAIN GIFT OF NATURE

Design: Zhou Jingkuan
Company: Left and Right Design
Country: China
Category: Fine wines, champagne
SILVER PENTAWARD 2015

THE CHANGYU FAMILY COLLECTION

Design: Jian Wei Miao, Sun Xiao
Company: Jian Wei Miao
Country: China
Category: Fine wines, champagne
SILVER PENTAWARD 2014

VEGAMAR SELECCIÓN

Creative Direction: Nacho Lavernia, Alberto Cienfuegos
Company: Lavernia & Cienfuegos
Country: Spain
Category: Fine wines, champagne

SILVER PENTAWARD 2015

VALENTINA PASSALACQUA WINERY LITOS

Design: Mario Di Paolo
Company: Spazio Di Paolo
Country: Italy
Category: Fine wines, champagne
BRONZE PENTAWARD 2016

Rooted in Puglia's white stony subsoil, the vines in the **Valentina Passalacqua Winery** thrive, and from this comes the rock layering effect on the label using three types of paper in three shades of white. The sophisticated overlapping of the separate labels is actually the result of much work behind the scenes, and specific equipment had to be designed and built to cope with production. The resulting three-layered, self-adhesive labels, with their concentric overlays, had never been done before using automated production, but once the system had been designed manufacturing costs could be lowered while perfectly identical labels were produced every time.

Die Weine der **Valentina Passalacqua Winery** wachsen und gedeihen im weißen, steinigen Untergrund von Puglia. Dessen Steinschichtungen hat man sich für die drei Papiersorten in verschiedenen Weißtönen abgeguckt. Die ausgefeilten Überlappungen der verschiedenen Etiketten ist tatsächlich das Ergebnis einer Menge Arbeit hinter den Kulissen. Spezielle Gerätschaften mussten für dieses Design und die Produktion konstruiert werden. Das resultierende dreischichtige selbstklebende Etikett mit der mittigen Überlagerung kam noch niemals zuvor bei einer automatischen Produktion zum Einsatz. War das Systems erst mal etabliert, konnten die Herstellungskosten gesenkt und bei jedem Durchgang exakt identische Etiketten produziert werden.

Les vignes de **Valentina Passalacqua Winery** poussent dans un sol de pierres blanches de la région des Pouilles, et c'est de là que vient l'effet de strates rocheuses sur l'étiquette, réalisé à l'aide de trois types de papier dans trois tons de blanc. Cette superposition raffinée est en fait le résultat d'un long processus de recherche et a nécessité un équipement spécial. Ces étiquettes auto-adhésives à trois épaisseurs concentriques n'avaient jamais été faites auparavant dans le cadre d'une production automatisée, mais une fois le système mis au point, les coûts de production ont pu être abaissés, avec des étiquettes parfaitement identiques.

HENNESSY
XO EXCLUSIVE COLLECTION

Project Management: Patrick Marrot (Hennessy)
Brand Management: Clément Beloqui (Hennessy)
Design: Tom Dixon
Production: Virojanglor
Country: France
Category: Casks, cases, gift boxes, ice buckets

BRONZE PENTAWARD 2014

VEUVE CLICQUOT PONSARDIN
CLICQUOT SUITCASE

Design: Candido de Barros
Company: Servaire & Co
Country: France
Category: Casks, cases, gift boxes,
ice buckets, glorifiers

SILVER PENTAWARD 2015

MOËT & CHANDON
ROSÉ IMPÉRIAL

Design: François Takounseun, Gérald Galdini,
Aurélie Sidot, Gabriel Brouste
Company: Partisan du Sens
Country: France
Category: Casks, cases, gift boxes, ice buckets

SILVER PENTAWARD 2014

MOËT & CHANDON, MOËT IMPÉRIAL SO BUBBLY BATH

Design: Carré Basset
Creative Direction: Franck Basset
Art Direction: Dimitri Rastorgoueff
Production: Dapy/Do International
Company: Dapy/Do International
Country: France
Category: Casks, cases, gift boxes,
ice buckets, glorifiers

SILVER PENTAWARD 2015

Für den 250. Geburtstag von **Hennessy** wurde ein ganz besonderer Verschnitt aus 15 bis 35 Jahre altem Branntwein zusammengestellt, der dann in 250 handgefertigten 250-Liter-Fässern reifte. Dieser außergewöhnliche Cognac wurde dann in eine speziell designte Karaffe gefüllt und in eine Luxusgeschenkbox gelegt. Eine auffällige Assemblage veranschaulicht die Verbindung zwischen dem Brandwein und den Fässern, in denen er reifte. Besonders anschaulich wird der luxuriöse und moderne Appeal durch das Modell eines demontierten Cognacfasses demonstriert, dessen hochglanzpolierte Fassreifen die Farben der Flüssigkeit in einem subtilen Lichtspiel reflektieren.

Pour le 250ᵉ anniversaire de **Hennessy,** un mélange très spécial a été mis au point à partir d'eaux-de-vie de 15 à 35 ans d'âge, puis a terminé sa maturation dans 250 tonneaux faits à la main de 250 l chacun. Ce cognac exceptionnel a ensuite été doté d'une carafe conçue tout spécialement et présenté dans un coffret cadeau de luxe. Le magnifique présentoir a été pensé pour illustrer le lien entre le mélange et les tonneaux dans lesquels il a été fini, tout en exprimant son caractère luxueux et contemporain. L'effet a été obtenu avec la maquette d'un tonneau de cognac déconstruit, dont les cerceaux polis reflètent les couleurs du liquide dans un subtil jeu de lumière.

HENNESSY 250 COLLECTOR BLEND

Art Direction: Tanguy Kabouende
Creative Direction: Joseph Hascoët
Production: Jackel
Company: Atelier Casanova
Country: France
Category: Casks, cases, gift boxes,
ice buckets, glorifiers

GOLD PENTAWARD 2015

For **Hennessy**'s 250th anniversary a very
special blend was put together from eaux-de-vie
aged 15-35 years, then left to complete its aging
in 250 hand-crafted barrels of 66 gal (250 liters)
each. This exceptional cognac was then furnished
with a specially designed carafe and encased in a
de luxe gift box. The stunning display assemblage
was designed to illustrate the link between the
blend and the barrels in which it was finished,
while also demonstrating its luxury and contemporary appeal, and achieved this with the model
of a deconstructed cognac barrel whose highly
polished hoops reflect the colors of the liquid in
a subtle play of light.

PORTO FERREIRA
SOGRAPE VINHOS

Design: Diogo Gama Rocha
Company: Omdesign
Country: Portugal
Category: Casks, cases, gift boxes,
ice buckets, glorifiers

SILVER PENTAWARD 2016

In recent years, booming international travel has significantly increased the opportunities for sales of luxury goods, a sector in which champagne features prominently even though a bottle is a more difficult item to transport. **Veuve Clicquot Ponsardin** has long enjoyed an international reputation, and combining these ideas led to the development of a new luxury packaging which functions as a stylish and secure item of luggage. The carrying case is formed of two brushed aluminum shells with a soft, molded grey interior, snugly housing one 75cl bottle of Veuve Clicquot Yellow Label Brut: an elegant extension of packaging which also makes an impressive gift.

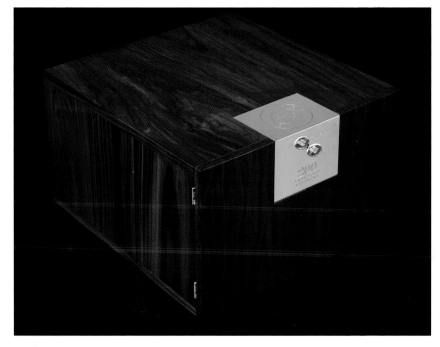

In den letzten Jahren steigerte der zunehmende internationale Reiseverkehr wesentlich die Möglichkeiten zum Erwerb von Luxusgütern. In dieser Sparte ist Champagner ein prominenter Artikel, auch wenn Flaschen nicht einfach zu transportieren sind. **Veuve Clicquot Ponsardin** genoss lange schon eine internationale Reputation. Die Kombination dieser Fakten führte zur Entwicklung einer neuen Luxusverpackung als stilvolles und sicheres Reisegepäck. Den Koffer bilden zwei gebürstete Aluschalen mit grauer, weicher Innenfütterung, in die sich eine 75-cl-Flasche Veuve Clicquot Yellow Label Brut kuschelig schmiegt. Diese elegante Erweiterung der Verpackung sorgt ebenfalls für ein eindrucksvolles Geschenk.

Ces dernières années, l'essor des voyages internationaux a causé une augmentation significative des opportunités de vente des articles de luxe, un secteur où le champagne occupe une bonne place même si une bouteille peut être difficile à transporter. **Veuve Clicquot Ponsardin** jouit d'une réputation internationale bien ancrée, et la combinaison de ces idées à conduit à la mise au point d'un nouvel emballage de luxe qui fait également office de bagage. La valise de transport est formée de deux coques en aluminium brossé avec un intérieur moulé gris où se niche une bouteille de 75 cl de Veuve Clicquot Brute Carte Jaune : un emballage élégant qui est aussi un cadeau mémorable.

CÎROC
ICE BUCKET

Design/Creative Direction: Denis Boudard
Photography: Studio Eric Jacquet
Company: QSLD Paris
Country: France
Category: Casks, cases, gift boxes, ice buckets

GOLD PENTAWARD 2011

KRUG CHAMPAGNE FLÂNERIE

Design: Gérald Gladini, François Takounseun,
Gabriel Brouste
Company: Partisan du Sens
Country: France
Category: Casks, cases, gift boxes, ice buckets
BRONZE PENTAWARD 2012

DOM RUINART

Design: Gérard Galdini, François Takounseun
Company: Partisan du Sens
Country: France
Category: Casks, coffrets, gift boxes
SILVER PENTAWARD 2010

BOMBAY SAPPHIRE

Design: Samantha Wilkes, Guillaume Furminger, Gary Nettleton,
Sabine Merfeld, James McAllister, Lucy Russell, Asiya Hasan Damen
Company: Webb deVlam
Country: UK
Category: Casks, cases, gift boxes, ice buckets

SILVER PENTAWARD 2013

Keeping **Bombay Sapphire**'s brand philosophy, "Infused with Imagination", central to the packaging design, the winner in the busy travel retail sector is the one that can grab the attention of travelers who are in a hurry and are confronted by a wealth of purchasing options. Technology offers much for design, and although electroluminescent ink is not new this was the first time it was successfully integrated into a packaging design. Electro begs to be picked up off the shelf, and when this happens it activates a hidden mechanical switch which sends a current through the pathways in sequence, creating a mesmerizing cascade for the eyes.

Im rührigen Reiseeinzelhandel gewinnt, wer die Aufmerksamkeit der Travelers erlangt, die in Eile und von den vielen Kaufmöglichkeiten überwältigt sind. So bleibt die Markenphilosophie von **Bombay Sapphire** „Infused with Imagination" Kern des Verpackungsdesigns. Technologie ermöglicht neue Wege in der Gestaltung: Obwohl elektroluminesizierende Druckfarbe nichts Neues ist, wurde sie hier zum ersten Mal erfolgreich ins Verpackungsdesign integriert. Electro drängt sich förmlich auf, vom Regal genommen zu werden: Dann schickt ein versteckter mechanischer Schalter Strom in einer bestimmten Folge durch die Leitung, was zu einer faszinierenden optischen Kaskade führt.

Le leader du duty free est celui capable d'attirer l'attention des voyageurs pressés et exposés à une quantité d'options. La technologie joue pour beaucoup dans le design, et même si l'encre électroluminescente n'est plus une nouveauté, elle l'a été à sa première utilisation pour un design d'emballage. Fidèle à sa philosophie « Infused with Imagination », la marque **Bombay Sapphire** a lancé Electro. Tout dans cet emballage invite à le choisir : un mécanisme caché s'active alors et envoie en séquence une lumière dans les sillons, offrant un hypnotique effet de cascade.

BALLANTINE'S 12 GIFT PACK

Design: Graeme Bridgeford (AirInnovation)
Head of Packaging Development: Kilmalid (Chivas Brothers)
Production: Virojanglor
Country: France
Category: Casks, cases, gift boxes, ice buckets

BRONZE PENTAWARD 2013

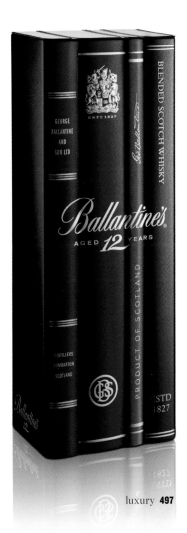

GREY GOOSE VODKA BY CHOPARD
Executive Creative Direction: Pierre Abel
Creative Direction: Vincent Fichet
Design: Marc Usmati
Company: Future Brand
Country: France
Category: Casks, cases, gift boxes, ice buckets
SILVER PENTAWARD 2011

DOM PERIGNON PULSAR BOX
Design: Dom Perignon
Production: Dapy/Do International
Country: France
Category: Casks, cases, gift boxes, ice buckets
SILVER PENTAWARD 2013

LOUIS XIII
RARE CASK

Design: Betc Design team
Company: Betc Design
Country: France
Category: Casks, coffrets, gift boxes

SILVER PENTAWARD 2010

The **Rare Cask** packaging is definitely considered a part of the product experience itself, during purchasing, drinking, and sharing. This laced-up, metallic-stitched exclusive packaging works like a safe. Lights appear when the two halves are slid apart like curtains, revealing the beautifully illuminated Baccarat-crystal carafe displayed in a jewellery case with a pattern-engraved mirror behind. The lily-flower quadrilobe pattern has been especially designed to be the Rare Cask's trademark. The central feature is to keep **Louis XIII** as the cognac's cultural reference, the height of luxury in drinking. It was essential for Louis XIII to indicate the sheer scarcity of Rare Cask by taking the iconic Louis XIII packaging and turning it into a piece of art. Each carafe in this collection limited to only 786 pieces is customised with its own engraved serial number to emphasise its uniqueness.

Bei **Rare Cask** gehört die Verpackung bei Erwerb und Genuss wesentlich zur Produkterfahrung dazu. Diese exklusive Umhüllung mit ihren Verzierungen aus Metall gleicht einem Tresor: Werden die beiden Hälften wie Vorhänge auseinander gezogen, erstrahlt die wunderschöne Karaffe aus Baccarat-Kristall im Licht und zeigt sich wie in einer Schmuckschatulle vor einem mit eingravierten Mustern geschmückten Spiegel. Das vierblättrige Lilienmuster ist speziell als Markenzeichen für Rare Cask gestaltet worden. Als zentrale Eigenschaft soll **Louis XIII** als kulturelle Referenz für Cognac und als höchste Luxusklasse beim Trinkgenuss bewahrt werden. Louis XIII verdeutlicht die außergewöhnliche Seltenheit von Rare Cask damit, dass die symbolträchtige Verpackung von Louis XIII in ein Kunstwerk verwandelt wird. Jede Karaffe dieser auf nur 786 Stücke begrenzten Kollektion trägt ihre eigene Seriennummer, was ihre Einzigartigkeit unterstreicht.

L'emballage de **Rare Cask** est sans conteste considéré comme faisant partie intégrante du produit, au moment de l'acheter, de le boire et de le partager. Cet emballage exclusif, lacé de mailles métalliques, fonctionne comme un coffrefort. Lorsque les deux moitiés s'écartent comme un rideau, les lumières qui s'allument révèlent une magnifique carafe en cristal de Baccarat présentée dans un écrin, adossée à un miroir gravé. Le motif de la fleur de lis a été dessiné tout spécialement pour devenir l'emblème du Rare Cask. L'intention est de conserver à **Louis XIII** sa place de cognac de référence, de summum du luxe dans la culture de l'alcool haut de gamme. Il était essentiel d'indiquer la rareté extrême du Rare Cask en faisant de l'emballage emblématique de Louis XIII une véritable œuvre d'art. Dans cette collection limitée à seulement 786 unités, chaque carafe porte un numéro de série gravé qui souligne son caractère unique.

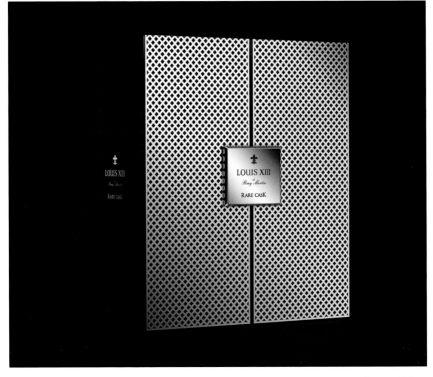

BISQUIT L'ORIGINE

Design: Benoît Maltier, Jean-Noël Dollet
Company: Bisquit
Country: France
Category: Casks, cases, gift boxes,
ice buckets, glorifiers

SILVER PENTAWARD 2016

Um die außergewöhnliche Geschichte von **Veuve Clicquot Ponsardin** und den Abenteuergeist, der die Marke umgibt, zu würdigen, hat man dieses markante Verpackungsdesign zum Werbethema ‚Clicquot Journey' entworfen, das dem Label zusätzlich Präsenz verleiht. Inspiration lieferten Verkehrsschilder. Die Metallverpackung in Pfeiloptik enthält eine 75-cl-Flasche Veuve Clicquot Yellow Label Brut und zeigt eindeutig, „wo es langgeht". Zum Sortiment gehören 29 globale Destinationen wie Tokio, Los Angeles, Rom oder Paris. Die Verkäufer können diese Sammlergeschenkkästen so für eigene Reiserouten nutzen, als Werbematerial oder Schaufensterdeko.

Ce concept spectaculaire a été conçu dans le cadre du thème « Voyage de Clicquot » pour rendre hommage à l'histoire exceptionnelle de **Veuve Clicquot Ponsardin** et à son esprit d'aventure et d'exploration du monde, ainsi que pour améliorer la visibilité de la marque. Le coffret en métal Arrow (flèche) s'inspire des panneaux de signalisation et contient une bouteille de 75 cl de Veuve Clicquot Brut Carte Jaune. La gamme comprend 29 destinations, de Tokyo à Los Angeles, Rome ou Paris, ce qui permet aux distributeurs de créer leur propre itinéraire, sous forme de matériel promotionnel ou de décoration de vitrine avec ces coffrets cadeau à collectionner.

VEUVE CLICQUOT PONSARDIN
CLICQUOT ARROW

Design: Candido De Barros, Sébastien Servaire
Graphics: Justine Dauchez
Glass: Erwann Pivert
Production: Virojanglor
Company: Servaire & Co, Virojanglor
Country: France
Category: Casks, cases, gift boxes,
ice buckets, glorifiers

GOLD PENTAWARD 2016

To pay tribute to the exceptional **Veuve Clicquot Ponsardin** story and its spirit of adventure throughout the world, as well as enhancing the visibility of the brand, this striking packaging design was conceived as part of the 'Clicquot Journey' theme. Drawing inspiration from the form of road signs, this Clicquot Arrow metal case contains one 75cl bottle of Veuve Clicquot Yellow Label Brut, and clearly "points the way". The range features 29 global destinations, from Tokyo to Los Angeles, Rome or Paris, thereby enabling vendors to create their own itinerary, in promotional material or as a window display by means of these collectable gift boxes.

VEUVE CLICQUOT
MR CLICQUOT

Art Direction: Sébastien Servaire,
Candido de Barros
Technical Development: Erwann Pivert
Photography: Veuve Clicquot Ponsardine,
R'Pure Studio
Company: Servaire & Co
Country: France
Category: Casks, cases, gift boxes, ice buckets

GOLD PENTAWARD 2012

The Mr Clicquot champagne-bottle stopper is one amongst a number of accessories created for the animation and events marking the invention of Veuve Clicquot. The global animation concept that goes by the name of **Mr Clicquot** is an entire universe with an offbeat narrative inspired by the dandy's stylish image and which perfectly expresses the brand's positioning. The creative intention was to imagine an essential but non-conformist accessory that would result in a new "chic" attitude: by fitting the bottle with a stopper shaped like an umbrella-handle, it could be carried on the arm, hung on a bar, in a tree, from the ceiling! Shops were also totally renewed by virtue of this original idea.

VEUVE CLICQUOT PONSARDINE

Design: Grapheine
Design: Julien Ceder (Veuve Clicquot)
Project Management: Mathilde Le Scornet (Veuve Clicquot)
Production: Virojanglor
Company: Virojanglor
Country: France
Category: Casks, cases, gift boxes, ice buckets

SILVER PENTAWARD 2012

Der Champagnerflaschenverschluss Mr Clicquot gehört zu einer Reihe von Accessoires, die für die Events zu Ehren der Erfindung von Veuve Clicquot geschaffen wurden. Das globale Animationskonzept firmiert unter dem Namen **Mr Clicquot**. Es bildet ein ganzes Universum mit einer ausgefallenen Geschichte, die vom stilvollen Image des Dandys inspiriert ist, und drückt hervorragend die Positionierung der Marke aus. Die kreative Intention war ein wesentliches, aber nicht-konformistisches Accessoire, das auf neuartige Weise „chic" sein sollte: Die Flasche mit ihrem Verschluss in Form eines Schirmgriffs kann am Arm getragen, an eine Theke oder einen Ast oder gar an die Decke gehängt werden! An den jeweiligen Verkaufsstellen entstanden durch diese originelle Idee völlig neue Möglichkeiten.

Le bouchon stoppeur de Veuve Clicquot fait partie d'une gamme d'accessoires créée pour les animations et événements qui célèbrent l'invention de la marque. Le concept d'animation global, baptisé **Mr Clicquot**, est tout un univers bâti autour d'un fil conducteur excentrique inspiré par l'image élégante du dandy, et exprime parfaitement le positionnement de la marque. L'intention créative était d'imaginer un accessoire essentiel mais anticonformiste qui donnerait naissance à une nouvelle attitude « chic » : un bouchon en forme de manche de parapluie monté sur la bouteille permet de la porter au bras, de l'accrocher à une barre, un arbre, ou même au plafond ! Cette idée originale a aussi complètement renouvelé les options sur le point de vente.

MOËT HENNESSY
VEUVE CLICQUOT CLICQ'UP ICE BUCKET

Design: Mathias Van De Walle
Production: MW Creative
Company: MW Creative
Country: UK
Category: Casks, cases, gift boxes, ice buckets

SILVER PENTAWARD 2012

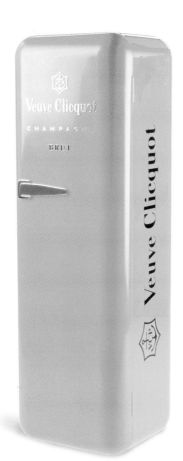

VEUVE CLICQUOT
Design: Denis Boudard (QSLD)
Development/Production: Dapy
Company: Dapy/Do International
Country: France
Category: Casks, coffrets, gift boxes

GOLD PENTAWARD 2010

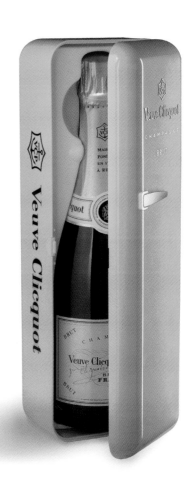

Die Verpackung von Champagner ist ein wesentlicher Faktor für Image und Erkennbarkeit der Marke. Hier baut das Design die Form des typischen Weinkühlers aus und schafft ein ästhetisches und doch funktionales Objekt. Um dem Pop-Spirit von Carte Jaune Brut treu zu bleiben, ließ man sich fürs Design durch das berühmte Kleid von Marilyn Monroe inspirieren. Die zylindrische Packung springt auf und wird zum Eiskühler. Gleichzeitig kleidet sie die symbolträchtige Flasche in eine attraktive, plissierte Hülle. Sie ist chic, wiederverwendbar und setzt durch vernünftige Kosten und einfache Materialien ein cleveres Lifestyle-Statement.

Les emballages de champagne sont déterminants pour l'image et l'identification de chaque marque. Ici, le design s'éloigne de la forme standard pour créer un objet esthétique et pratique à la fois. Fidèle à l'esprit pop du Brut Carte Jaune, il réinterprète une idée de mode en partant de la robe de Marilyn. L'emballage cylindrique se déploie et devient un seau à glace qui gaine la bouteille emblématique d'une superbe robe plissée. Le manchon est réutilisable, son coût de fabrication raisonnable et les matériaux simples : toute une leçon sur l'art de vivre !

VEUVE CLICQUOT
AMERICAN MAILBOX

Art Direction: Sébastien Servaire
Client: Chloé Stefani, Marco De Dionigi, Nicolas Remy (Veuve Clicquot)
Production: Virojanglor
Company: Servaire & Co
Country: France
Category: Casks, cases, gift boxes, ice buckets

SILVER PENTAWARD 2014

VEUVE CLICQUOT ICE BUCKET

Art Direction: Sébastien Servaire
Creative Direction: Candido Debarros
Graphic Design Direction: Justine Dauchez
Product Development Direction: Erwann Pivert
Account Direction: Amélie Anthome
Account Management: Emeline Piers
Photography: Arnaud Guffon
Company: Servaire & Co
Country: France
Category: Casks, cases, gift boxes, ice buckets

GOLD PENTAWARD 2014

Champagne packaging is a key factor in each brand's image and identification, and here the design extends beyond the form of the typical case to create an aesthetic object which also has functional use. In keeping faithful to the pop spirit of Carte Jaune brut, the design revisits a fashion idea by taking inspiration from the Marilyn dress. The cylindrical packaging pops out and becomes an ice bucket, at the same time clothing the emblematic bottle in an attractive, pleated dress. The sleeve is reusable and chic, with reasonable costs and simple materials—a smart lifestyle statement!

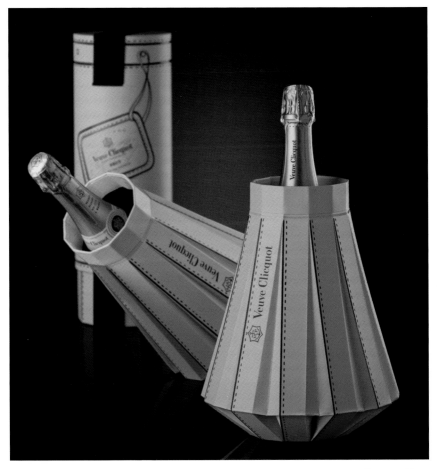

ZWYERCAVIAR
THE BLACK PEARL

Design: Roger Zwyer,
Alexander Zwyer, Roger Dejakum
Company: ZwyerCaviar
Country: Switzerland
Category: Gourmet food
GOLD PENTAWARD 2009

The Black Pearl is a design cooling-box for the world's first super-premium caviar which protects it from external conditions, cools it during transportation, and with its look presents it in a stylish manner. It's a reference to the black pearl of the Pacific Ocean, the rarest of all pearls. The Black Pearl is produced in Switzerland and Germany, and can carry optionally one or two caviar tins. The conventional caviar tins of the same brand are then placed in a secondary sphere, a pearl-like shaped package.

Black Pearl ist eine Designer-Kühlverpackung für den weltweit ersten Super-Premium-Kaviar. Der Kaviar wird dadurch vor äußeren Einwirkungen geschützt, beim Transport gekühlt und sehr elegant präsentiert. Diese Verpackung spielt auf die schwarze Perle aus dem Pazifik an, die seltenste aller Perlen. Black Pearl wird in Deutschland und der Schweiz produziert und kann optional eine oder zwei Kaviardosen enthalten. Die herkömmlichen Kaviardosen derselben Marke werden dann in eine zusätzliche Sphäre gesetzt – eine perlenförmige Verpackung.

La **Black Pearl** est une boîte réfrigérante pour le caviar le plus précieux au monde, qui le protège des conditions extérieures, le refroidit pendant le transport, et le présente avec style. C'est une référence à la perle noire de l'Océan Pacifique, la plus rare de toutes les perles. Elle est fabriquée en Suisse et en Allemagne, et peut contenir au choix une ou deux boîtes de caviar. Les boîtes de caviar classiques de la même marque sont placées dans un récipient sphérique secondaire en forme de poire.

HALLERTAU
HEROIC RANGE

Design: Ryan Henderson, Alicia Christie
(Degree Design), Cleve Cameron (Toot Group)
Illustration: Evan Purdie
Sculpture: Eden Small
Company: Degree Design
Country: New Zealand
Category: Gourmet food

SILVER PENTAWARD 2010

BLESSING CULTIVATED

Design: Jennifer Tsai, Janice Kao, Brenda Chang
Company: Proad Identity
Country: Taiwan
Category: Gourmet food
SILVER PENTAWARD 2009

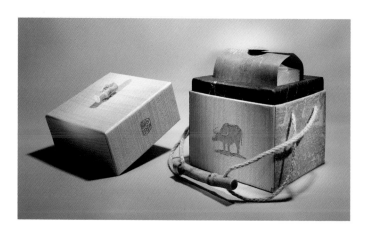

MIOGEE

Design: Kang Weijie
Company: 12 Degree Branding
Country: China
Category: Gourmet food
SILVER PENTAWARD 2013

TRIKALINOS
GREY MULLET BOTTARGA

Creative Direction: Minos Zarifopoulos
Photography: Stavros Kostakis
Company: Office Communication Consultants
Country: Greece
Category: Gourmet food
BRONZE PENTAWARD 2009

LINTAR OLIVE OIL

Design: Izvorka Juric
Company: Tridvajedan
Country: Hungary
Category: Gourmet food

GOLD PENTAWARD 2010

The brand and packaging design of **Lintar** olive oil are inspired by the shape of the funnel and pouring. The Maline font aims to express the oil pouring on the surface and creating the name. The visual identity of this product is both traditional and contemporary, which is particularly evident in the specific combination of colors and shapes. The dark-brown glass bottle is hand painted in a very light yellow-green tone and text elements are printed on the surface. The label, with basic information about the product, is attached to the bottle handle, and other information is printed on a cardboard box with a finger handle. The name Lintar derives from the Greek word for "funnel" and is the old name for the Kastela Gulf, the geographical origin of the oil.

Für das Design der Marke und der Verpackung von **Lintar** Olivenöl ließ man sich durch die Form eines Trichters und das Gießen des Öls inspirieren. Die Schriftart Maline soll vermitteln, wie das Öl auf eine Oberfläche gegossen wird und so der Name entsteht. Die visuelle Identität dieses Produkts ist gleichermaßen traditionell und modern, was besonders bei der speziellen Kombination aus Farben und Formen deutlich wird. Die dunkelbraune Glasflasche ist mit einer sehr hellen, gelb-grünen Tönung handbemalt, und die Textelemente werden auf die Oberfläche aufgedruckt. Ein Etikett mit wichtigen Informationen über das Produkt wird am Flaschengriff angebracht. Auf dem Flaschenkarton mit einem Loch zum Tragen finden sich weitere Infos zum Produkt. Der Name Lintar stammt vom griechischen Wort für „Trichter" ab und ist der alte Name für den Golf von Kaštela (Kroatien), dem geografischen Ursprung des Öls.

La marque et l'emballage de l'huile d'olive **Lintar** sont inspirés de la forme d'un entonnoir. La police de caractères Maline représente l'huile qui coule sur la surface, et dessine son nom. L'identité visuelle de ce produit est traditionnelle et contemporaine à la fois, ce qui est particulièrement évident dans la combinaison de couleurs et de formes. La bouteille en verre brun foncé est peinte à la main dans un vert-jaune très clair, et le texte est imprimé sur la surface. L'étiquette portant les informations de base sur le produit est attachée à l'anse de la bouteille, et les autres informations sont imprimées sur la boîte en carton, dotée d'une poignée étudiée pour y passer un doigt. Le nom Lintar vient du terme grec signifiant « entonnoir », et est l'ancien nom du golfe de Kastela, le lieu d'origine de cette huile.

LADOLEA

Graphic Design: Leandros Katsouris
Product Design: Spyros Kyzis
Company: Melissi
Country: Greece
Category: Gourmet food
SILVER PENTAWARD 2014

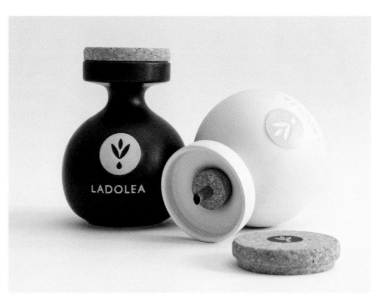

PIERRE HERMÉ
PACKAGING FOR 24 MACARONS

Design: Agnès Cambus, Manuel Bonnemazou
Company: Bonnemazou Cambus
Country: France
Category: Gourmet food

SILVER PENTAWARD 2010

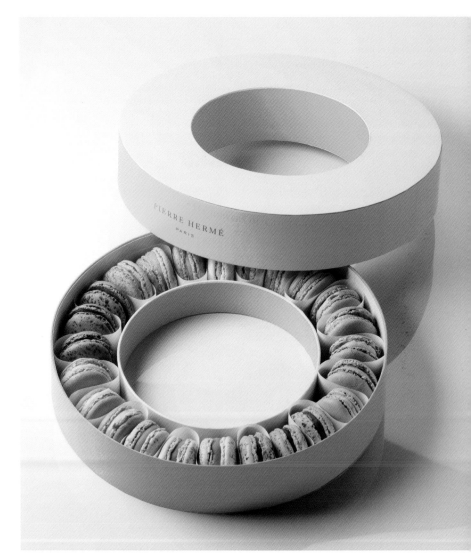

THE JME FOOD RANGE

Creative Direction: Shaun Bowen
Copywriting: Sylvie Saunders
Design: Sarah Pidgeon, Natalie Chung
Senior Digital Artwork: Henry Preston
Digital Artwork: Lucy Milne
Account Direction: Beth Marcall
Account Management: Erin Tucker
Realisation Management: Tracy Sutton
Company: Pearlfisher
Country: UK
Category: Gourmet food

SILVER PENTAWARD 2009

TRATA ON ICE BY KONVA

Creative Direction: Yiannis Charalambopoulos,
Alexis Nikou, Vagelis Liakos
Photography: Kostas Pappas
Company: Beetroot Design Group
Country: Greece
Category: Gourmet food

GOLD PENTAWARD 2011

The fish's tail is one of the main visual elements
used on this frozen seafood packaging series, both
for the logo and the structure of the packages
themselves. The black background and under-
stated typography were used in conjunction with
seafood illustrations to suggest delicatessens and
a quality product, whilst the window holes on the
designs match the part of the seafood contained
within and allow customers to see exactly what
they are buying.

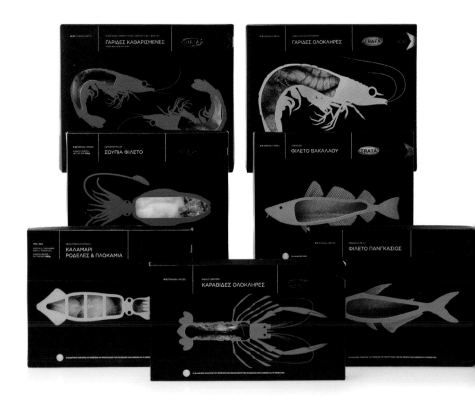

Der Fischschwanz ist eines der wichtigen visuellen Elemente, das bei dieser Verpackungsserie für Tiefkühlfisch sowohl für das Logo als auch die Struktur der Packung selbst eingesetzt wird. Zusammen mit dem schwarzen Hintergrund und der zurückhaltenden Typografie wurden Illustrationen von Meeresfrüchten genutzt, um Delikatesse und Qualitätsprodukte zu suggerieren. Die in die Packung gestanzten Öffnungen passen zu dem darin enthaltenen Meerestier, und der Kunde sieht sofort, was er kauft.

La queue de poisson ou de crustacé est l'un des principaux éléments visuels utilisés sur cette série de boîtes de fruits de mer congelés, que ce soit pour le logo ou pour la structure même des boîtes. Le fond noir et la typographie sobre sont complétés par des illustrations de fruits de mer afin de suggérer la saveur et la qualité du produit, tandis que les fenêtres découpées sur les dessins correspondent par leur forme à la partie de l'animal et permettent aux clients de voir ce qu'ils achètent.

KIMURA SUISAN FUNAZUSHI

Creative Direction: Masahiro Minami
Design: Shuji Hikawa
Company: Masahiro Minami Laboratory
Country: Japan
Category: Gourmet food

SILVER PENTAWARD 2011

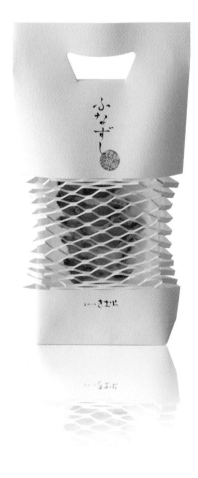

Design: Dimitris Koliadimas,
Dimitris Papazoglou
Company: Designers United
Country: Greece
Category: Gourmet food
GOLD PENTAWARD 2012

FIVE
Extra virgin
olive oil

5

FIVE
Extra virgin
olive oil

FIVE
Organic
extra virgin
olive oil

5

FIVE
Organic
extra virgin
olive oil

FIVE
Ultra premium
extra virgin
olive oil

5

FIVE
Ultra premium
extra virgin
olive oil

RICE CASTLE
Design: Jennifer Tsai
Company: Proad Identity
Country: Taiwan
Category: Gourmet food
BRONZE PENTAWARD 2010

ETESIAN GOLD
Creative Direction: Gregory Tsaknakis
Illustration: Ioanna Papaioannou
Company: Mousegraphics
Country: Greece
Category: Gourmet food
SILVER PENTAWARD 2012

GAEA OIL AND VINEGAR

Creative Direction: Greg Tsaknakis
Art Direction: Kostas Vlachakis,
Kostas Kaparos
Design: Kostas Kaparos
Company: Mousegraphics
Country: Greece
Category: Gourmet food
SILVER PENTAWARD 2015

Products made from Greek olives and grapes are popular with Chinese consumers, a fact which led to the development of this gift version of the **Gaea** brand. The set was designed so that each item was small and felt precious, like an offering, with the bottles made from opaque glass to add a sense of mystery. There were individual carton boxes for the oil and vinegar as well as a special twin-set version which contained both, in a high-quality case of the type often used for perfumes. The austere black and white palette, the simple outline shapes of the grape and olive (the bottles can also be set beside each other in a yin-yang kind of balance), and the clean use of typography complete the design.

Produkte aus griechischen Oliven und Trauben sind bei chinesischen Verbrauchern beliebt. Diese Tatsache sorgte für die Entwicklung einer Geschenkversion der Marke **Gaea**. Das Set wurde so gestaltet, dass jeder Artikel klein ist und sich kostbar anfühlt wie eine Opfergabe. Die Flaschen sind aus opakem Glas und lassen Geheimnisvolles ahnen. Öl und Essig sind jeweils in Extrakartons erhältlich, aber auch eine spezielle Zwillingsversion mit beiden in einem qualitativ hochwertigen Kasten der Art, wie er oft für Parfüms verwendet wird. Die strenge Schwarz-Weiß-Palette, die einfache Umrissform von Traube und Olive (beide Flaschen kann man in Yin-Yang-Balance auch nebeneinanderstellen) sowie die klare Typografie vervollständigen das Design.

Les produits faits à partir d'olives et de raisins grecs sont populaires auprès des consommateurs chinois, ce qui a conduit à cette version cadeau de la marque **Gaea**. Le coffret a été conçu de sorte que chaque article soit petit et précieux, comme une offrande, et les bouteilles en verre opaque ajoutent un sentiment de mystère. L'huile et le vinaigre ont des boîtes en carton individuelles, et une version twin-set spéciale contient les deux, dans un type de boîte souvent utilisé pour les parfums. La palette austère en noir et blanc, les silhouettes simples de raisin et d'olive (les bouteilles peuvent également être posées l'une à côté de l'autre pour un effet yin-yang) et la typographie épurée achèvent le concept.

MALEAS OLIVE OIL

Art Direction: Simos Saltiel
Design/Illustration: Elina Steletari
Company: Red Creative
Country: Greece
Category: Gourmet food

SILVER PENTAWARD 2014

LABEYRIE HAPPY CAVIAR

Design: Gazel Design, Véronique Kéchichian
Production: Dapy/Do International
Company: Dapy/Do International
Country: France
Category: Gourmet food

SILVER PENTAWARD 2015

LA MAISON NORDIQUE

Creative Direction: Jean-Sébastien Blanc
Project Management: Vincent Baranger
Design: Ségolène Huet
Company: 5.5 designstudio
Country: France
Category: Gourmet food
BRONZE PENTAWARD 2016

KAVIARI
EN-K DE CAVIAR

Design: Armand Delsol
Company: Vanille Design
Country: France
Category: Gourmet food
SILVER PENTAWARD 2012

NEUHAUS
LADY CHEFS

Design: Hugues Tomeo, Gaby Gentenaar
Company: Neuhaus
Country: Belgium
Category: Gourmet food

BRONZE PENTAWARD 2011

FORTNUM & MASON
CHIC NOVELTIES

Creative Direction, Brand Language: Holly Kielty
Creative Direction: Emma Follett
Design Direction: Chloe Templeman
Senior Design: Hayley Barrett
Copywriting: Caroline Slade
Design: Morgan Swain
Visualization: Francesca Forzoni
Client Direction: Rebecca Yorke
Client Management: Alice Goss
Illustration: Paul Desmond
Company: Design Bridge
Country: UK
Category: Gourmet food
GOLD PENTAWARD 2016

物事のはじまりは小さい

rerum principia parva sunt.

Omnium rerum principia parva sunt.

COMMEMORATIVE WHISKY

Creative Direction: Shizuko Ushijima
Art Direction: Akiko Furusho
Design: Shizuko Ushijima, Akiko Furusho
Company: Suntory
Country: Japan
Category: Limited editions, event creations

SILVER PENTAWARD 2016

This original whisky was created in tribute to Kaoru Kasai, the art director who won the "purple ribbon medal", one of Japan's most prestigious awards. The words of his favorite motto have been branded on to the cork, while the special whisky was aged in domestically grown white oak (mizunara) casks. The same wood is used in a mortised design for the case holding the bottle, which opens as two joined halves and is dyed purple where these pieces meet, in reference to the award and clearly showing the skilled craftsmanship involved. For use after the bottle has been opened a replacement cork is provided, as a simple extra hanging from the neck of the bottle, which also serves as a focal point for the design.

Dieser Whisky wurde ursprünglich als Tribut an den Artdirector Kaoru Kasai kreiert, der mit der Medaille am Purpurband geehrt wurde, einer der prestigeträchtigsten Auszeichnungen Japans. Die Worte seines Lieblingsmottos sind auf den Korken geprägt, und dieser spezielle Whisky reifte in Fässern aus heimischer Mizunara-Eiche (Weißeiche). Das gleiche Holz wurde für das miteinander verzapfte Design der Flaschenschatulle verwendet, die sich in zwei Hälften öffnet. Dort, wo sich beide Teile berühren, ist sie purpurn gefärbt: als Referenz auf die Auszeichnung und das handwerkliche Geschick. Nach dem ersten Öffnen nimmt man den Reservekorken, der einfach am Flaschenhals hängt und auch als Blickfang für das Design dient.

Ce whisky original a été créé en hommage à Kaoru Kasai, un directeur artistique qui a remporté la médaille à ruban pourpre, l'une des récompenses les plus prestigieuses au Japon. Les mots de sa devise préférée sont marqués au fer chaud sur le bouchon, et le whisky a vieilli dans des fûts en chêne blanc (mizunara) local. Le même bois est employé pour le coffret à mortaise qui abrite la bouteille. Il s'ouvre en deux moitiés et est teint en pourpre à l'endroit où ces parties se rejoignent, en référence à la médaille. C'est une magnifique pièce d'artisanat. Un bouchon supplémentaire est fourni, à utiliser une fois que la bouteille a été ouverte. Il est simplement accroché au col de la bouteille et fait office de point de mire.

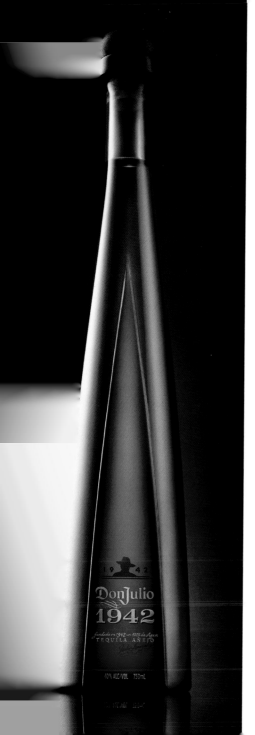

DIAGEO
TEQUILA DON JULIO 1942
Design Direction: Tosh Hall, JB Hartford
Executive Creative Direction: Richard Brandt
Client Management:
Pamela Mazzocco, Sam Gardner
Company: Landor Associates
Country: USA
Category: Limited editions,
limited series, event creations
GOLD PENTAWARD 2010

BACARDI
DEWAR'S LEGACY COLLECTION
Creative Direction: Glenn Tutssel
Design: Olly Rudd, Glenn Tutssel
Production Direction: Andrew Smith
Company: Brand Union
Country: UK
Category: Limited editions,
limited series, event creations
SILVER PENTAWARD 2014

Dewar's
LEGACY
COLLECTION
1893
BLENDED SCOTCH WHISKY
70cl No 0001/1000 40% Vol

D'ARENBERG THE SUPERS

Creative Direction: Anthony De Leo,
Scott Carslake
Design/Illustration: Kieran Wallis
Company: Voice
Country: Australia
Category: Limited editions, event creations
BRONZE PENTAWARD 2016

HAKUSHIKA

Design: Keiko Hirano
Company: Communication
Design Laboratory
Country: Japan
Category: Limited editions,
limited series, collectors' items
BRONZE PENTAWARD 2011

CARCHELO WINES
EXTENSIVE

Art Direction/Design: Eduardo del Fraile
Company: Eduardo del Fraile
Country: Spain
Category: Limited editions,
limited series, collectors' items

SILVER PENTAWARD 2011

SUNTORY STONES BAR
THE ROLLING STONES
50TH ANNIVERSARY WHISKY

Creative Direction: Tsuneki Maeda
Art Direction/Design: Satoshi Ito
Design: Kotobuki Seihan Printing Design Center
Company: Suntory Business Expert
Country: Japan
Category: Limited editions, limited series, event creations

SILVER PENTAWARD 2013

This whisky was produced by **Suntory** to commemorate the 50th anniversary of the world's best-known rock 'n' roll band, the Rolling Stones. Only malts distilled and barreled in 1971, 1972, 1981 and 1990—special years for the Stones—were used for the blend. The bottle features a low-relief molding of the band's instantly recognizable lips and tongue logo on the front, which really comes to life when viewed from an angle. This element recurs up the neck of the bottle, to the stately silver stopper, while the containing box, looking not unlike an amplifier, is lined with black leather to create a unified design that embodies the rock 'n' roll lifestyle synonymous with the Rolling Stones.

Dieser Whisky wurde von **Suntory** zur Feier des 50. Geburtstags der Rolling Stones produziert, der bekanntesten Rock-'n'-Roll-Band der Welt. Nur Malts, die 1971, 1972, 1981 und 1990 – besondere Jahre für die Stones – gebrannt und in Fässer gefüllt wurden, waren in diesem Blend erlaubt. Die Flasche zeigt auf der Vorderseite das berühmte Logo der Band. Die ausgestreckte Zunge mit ihren Lippen fällt sofort ins Auge und wird lebendig, wenn sie von der Seite betrachtet wird. Dieses Element erscheint auch am Flaschenhals und dem prächtigen silbernen Verschluss. Der Flaschenkasten ähnelt einem Verstärker und wurde mit schwarzem Leder ausgekleidet. Dieses einheitliche Design verkörpert den mit den Stones gleichgesetzten Rock-'n'-Roll-Lifestyle.

Ce whisky a été produit par **Suntory** pour commémorer le 50ᵉ anniversaire du groupe de rock and roll le plus connu au monde : les Rolling Stones. Seuls des malts distillés et mis en fûts en 1971, 1972, 1981 et 1990, années spéciales pour le groupe, ont été utilisés pour le mélange. Moulée en bas-relief à l'avant de la bouteille, la forme emblématique des lèvres et de la langue s'anime en fonction de l'angle de vue. Cet élément se retrouve en haut du goulot, sur le majestueux bouchon en argent. Semblable à un amplificateur, la boîte est tapissée de cuir noir pour donner un design propre au style rock and roll rimant avec Rolling Stones.

HARDY COGNAC
LE PRINTEMPS

Design: Bénédicte Hardy
Crystal-maker: Lalique
Company: Hardy Cognac
Country: France
Category: Limited editions,
limited series, event creations

GOLD PENTAWARD 2014

In order to mark itself out from other cognacs, **Hardy** commissioned crystal-maker Lalique to design something rather special for its latest carafe. "Le Printemps" (Spring) takes the form of a scent bottle with feminine lines, and a spectacular, sculpted stopper with subtle green tints reminiscent of some of the creations by René Lalique himself from the early 20th century. This limited-edition design is the first in a series of four outstanding carafes, all by Lalique, with the other seasonal varieties of "Eté", "Automne" and "Hiver" following at two-year intervals. The colors and designs are being kept a close secret.

Um sich von anderen Cognacsorten abzuheben, beauftragte **Hardy** den Kristallhersteller Lalique damit, als aktuelle Karaffe etwas ganz Besonderes zu designen. „Le Printemps" (Der Frühling) greift in seiner Flakonform feminine Linien auf. Der spektakuläre, skulpturale Verschluss in dezent grüner Färbung erinnert an Schöpfungen von René Lalique selbst aus dem Anfang des 20. Jahrhunderts. Dieses Design in Limited Edition gehört zu einer Serie mit vier auffälligen Karaffen, die alle von Lalique gestaltet und in den jahreszeitlichen Varianten „Eté", „Automne" und „Hiver" in zweijährigem Abstand folgen werden. Farben und Designs werden streng geheim gehalten.

Afin de se démarquer des autres cognacs, **Hardy** a commandé à la célèbre Maison Lalique le design d'un modèle spécial pour sa dernière carafe. « Le Printemps » prend la forme d'un flacon de parfum aux lignes féminines ; dans les tons verts, son bouchon sculpté des plus spectaculaires n'est pas sans rappeler certaines créations de René Lalique du début du XXᵉ siècle. Ce design en édition limitée est le premier d'une série de quatre carafes uniques lancées à 2 ans d'intervalle, toutes signées Lalique, et répondant aux noms des saisons « Eté », « Automne » et « Hiver ». Les couleurs et les designs sont un secret bien gardé.

GLENROTHES 40 YEAR OLD

Design: Bronwen Edwards, David Beard
Company: Brandhouse
Country: UK
Category: Limited editions,
limited series, event creations
BRONZE PENTAWARD 2013

John Walker & Sons Diamond Jubilee is a limited-edition whisky created as a tribute to HM Queen Elizabeth II's 60 years of enlightened leadership. The diamond-shaped decanter stands on six pillars representing each decade of the Queen's reign, and has 60 facets to reflect the diversity and dynamism of the Commonwealth, the radiance of the decanter reflecting Her Majesty as the royal guiding light. The decanter is accompanied by two hand-engraved crystal glasses and a hand-bound booklet chronicling the detailed craftsmanship, all housed within a custom oak cabinet. The bottle was made for presentation to the Queen, with just 60 replica versions produced for sale. Diamond Jubilee profits will go to fund the Queen's charity, QEST, which supports craft education.

JOHN WALKER & SONS DIAMOND JUBILEE

Creative Direction: Laurent Hainaut, Lorena Seminario (Force Majeure Design), Katy Holford (Cumbria Crystal)
Project Lead: Steve Wilson (Invigor8tion)
Crystal Cold Workshop: Yves Parisse (Baccarat)
Silversmith & Workshop Management: John Hunt (Hamilton & Inches)
Cabinet Design: Neil Stevenson
Bookbinding: Lara West
Calligraphy: Sally Magnum
Glass Hand-Engraving: Philip Lawson Johnston
Global Design Direction: Jeremy Lindley (Diageo)
Design: Marco Leone, Alex Boulware (Force Majeure Design)
Design Direction: Harry Chong (Force Majeure Design)
Production Management: Linda Tseng (Force Majeure Design)
Company: Force Majeure Design
Country: USA
Category: Limited editions, limited series, collectors' items

GOLD PENTAWARD 2012
SLEEVER INTERNATIONAL PRIZE

Dieser Limited-Edition-Whisky **John Walker & Sons** Diamond Jubilee erschien zu Ehren des 60. Thronjubiläums Ihrer Majestät Queen Elizabeth II. Die sechs Säulen, auf denen der diamantförmige Dekanter ruht, stehen für die sechs Dekaden der Regentschaft Ihrer Majestät. Mit seinen 60 Facetten verweist der Dekanter auf die Vielfalt und Dynamik des Commonwealth, und seine glanzvolle Ausstrahlung reflektiert die königliche Autorität Ihrer Majestät. Zum Dekanter gehören zwei handgravierte Kristallgläser und ein handgebundenes Büchlein, in dem detailliert das Kunsthandwerk seiner Herstellung beschrieben wird. All dies befindet sich in einem extra angefertigten Eichengehäuse. Die Flasche wurde hergestellt, um vor der Königin präsentiert zu werden. Im Handel sind davon nur 60 Kopien erhältlich. Die durch Diamond Jubilee erzielten Einnahmen gehen an QEST. Diese von der Queen geförderte Wohltätigkeitsorganisation setzt sich für die Ausbildung im Handwerk ein.

John Walker & Sons Diamond Jubilee est un whisky en édition limitée en hommage aux 60 ans de règne illustre de SM la reine Élisabeth II. La carafe en forme de diamant repose sur six piliers qui symbolisent chacune des décennies du règne, et se compose de 60 facettes pour refléter la diversité et le dynamisme du Commonwealth, tandis que son éclat représente la lumière de la reine, guide de la nation. Elle est accompagnée de deux verres en cristal gravés à la main et d'un livret relié à la main qui relate tout le processus de fabrication artisanal, le tout abrité dans un coffret sur mesure en chêne. La bouteille a été fabriquée pour être présentée à la reine, et seulement 60 répliques ont été mises en vente. Les bénéfices de Diamond Jubilee ont été reversés à l'organisation caritative de la reine, QEST, qui soutient la formation à l'artisanat.

HOUSE OF SILLAGE

Design: June Lee (House of Sillage)
Production: Dapy/Do International
Country: France
Category: Limited editions, limited series, event creations

SILVER PENTAWARD 2013

Inside the special, limited-edition cap of this perfume bottle a miniature snowglobe scene of New York City can be discovered, decorated with lights and clothed in a coat of snow. The polycarbonate globe protects the delicate zamak figurines and tree, each piece being hand polished and then wrapped in silver or gold ornament by metalliztion. The central Christmas tree is decorated with 72 Swarovski stones, each carefully positioned and placed by hand. When the cap is turned upside down the magic happens and the small city comes to life under a fresh fall of snow.

Im Verschluss dieser Parfümflasche in Limited Edition befindet sich eine besondere Miniatur von New York City als Schneekugel, mit Lichtern geschmückt und von Schnee bedeckt. Die Kuppel aus Polykarbonat schützt die filigranen Zamakfiguren und den Baum. Jedes Stück wurde von Hand poliert und durch Metallisierung in silbernes oder goldenes Ornament gehüllt. Den zentralen Weihnachtsbaum dekorieren 72 Swarovski-Steine, alle sorgfältig per Hand positioniert. Wird die Flasche umgedreht, geschieht das Wunder, und die winzige Stadt wird unter den fallenden Flocken lebendig.

Le bouchon de ce parfum en édition limitée est une boule à neige renfermant une miniature de la ville de New York, qui est décorée de lumières et recouverte d'un manteau de neige. Le globe en polycarbonate protège les fragiles figurines et l'arbre en zamak, chaque élément ayant été poli à la main et recouvert d'argent ou d'or par métallisation. Le grand sapin de Noël au milieu est décoré de 72 pierres Swarovski placées à la main. Quand le bouchon est retourné, la magie se produit et la petite ville prend vie sous la neige.

LANCÔME
BLACK CRYSTAL LIGHT EDITION

Design: Gérald Galdini, François Takounseun,
Aurélie Sidot, Emilie Etchelecou
Company: Partisan du Sens
Country: France
Category: Limited editions,
limited series, event creations

GOLD PENTAWARD 2013
SLEEVER INT. PRIZE

JEAN-PAUL GAULTIER "CLASSIQUE" X COLLECTION

Design: Stéphanie Turan
Company: Servaire & Co
Country: France
Category: Limited editions,
limited series, event creations

BRONZE PENTAWARD 2013

LE POÈTE

Design: Eriko Misawa
Company: Shiseido
Country: Japan
Category: Limited editions,
limited series, event creations,

SILVER PENTAWARD 2010

LE POÈTE

Design: Eriko Misawa
Company: Shiseido
Country: Japan
Category: Limited editions,
limited series, event creations
GOLD PENTAWARD 2009

KABUKI, LUXURY SPIRITS

Design: Series Nemo team
Company: Series Nemo
Country: Spain
Category: Packaging concept
GOLD PENTAWARD 2015

Kabuki is a design concept, a contemporary vision for ultra-luxury spirits that presents two different bottle designs, honoring Kabuki performers. Kabuki is considered the most experimental type of theater in Japan, and these two adventurous designs are defined by their precise edges, inspired more by architectural forms than usual glass-working. The front and back are completely flat and perpendicular to the horizontal surface, evoking a calm sense of luxury through pure minimal shapes. The bottle's opening has also been reconceived, using a longitudinal arrangement that changes the overall impression of the bottle and offers a whole new way of serving the contents.

Kabuki ist ein Designkonzept, eine zeitgemäße Vision ultraluxuriöser Spirituosen in zwei verschiedenen Flaschendesigns zu Ehren der Schauspieler des Kabuki, des experimentellsten Theaters Japans. Diese beiden abenteuerlustigen Designs definieren sich durch präzise Kanten, eher inspiriert von Architekturformen als von eigentlichen Glasarbeiten. Front und Rückseite sind völlig flach und lotrecht zur horizontalen Oberfläche, was durch die reinen minimalen Formen den Luxus widerspiegelt. Auch die Öffnung der Flasche wurde neu konzipiert. Dazu verwendete man ein längs laufendes Arrangement, das den Eindruck der Flasche insgesamt veränderte und eine völlig neue Weise ermöglicht, die Inhalte zu kredenzen.

Kabuki est un concept de design, une vision contemporaine pour les alcools de grand luxe, qui présente deux bouteilles rendant hommage aux acteurs de kabuki, le type de théâtre le plus expérimental au Japon. Ces deux bouteilles sont définies par leurs contours précis, davantage inspirés par les formes architecturales que les objets en verre classiques. Les faces avant et arrière complètement plates et perpendiculaires à la surface horizontale évoquent un sentiment de luxe tranquille et de minimalisme. L'ouverture de la bouteille a également été revue dans le sens longitudinal pour modifier l'impression d'ensemble et offrir une toute nouvelle façon de servir le contenu.

TOWA KISEKI
ARTE ORAFA FURUYA

Art Direction/Design: Anna Sakaguchi, Harumi Sasaki
Company: Anna Sakaguchi, Harumi Sasaki
Country: Japan
Category: Packaging concept
BRONZE PENTAWARD 2016

ORUKA

Design and Concept: Gonzalo Jaén
3D Visualization: Marco A. Silva
Company: Digital Fish
Country: Spain
Category: Packaging concept
SILVER PENTAWARD 2016

This conceptual design moves away from what is conventionally a bottle, both in appearance and innovation. The form conceals a dosing system of 12 individual shots, which works by rotating the glass ring. Looking at the dry gin version, the blue liquid allows the full chambers to be distinguished from the empty ones. Black tungsten, glass and stainless steel are used for this variety, while the aged rum features an ebony-wood cap and rose-gold finishing for the metal. The logo follows the general aesthetics and is brown for the rum and turquoise for the gin, although vodka could equally be bottled in the steel version and cognac or brandy in the gold. **Oruka** is the word for ring in Yoruba, the West African language.

Dieses konzeptionelle Design entfernt sich von konventionellen Flaschen – sowohl vom Äußeren her als auch durch seine Innovation. Die Form verbirgt ein Dosiersystem mit zwölf Einzelportionen, die durch Drehen des Glasrings geöffnet werden. Schaut man sich die Dry-Gin-Version an, lässt die blaue Flüssigkeit erkennen, welche Kammern noch gefüllt sind. Für diesen Artikel wurden schwarzer Wolfram, Glas und Edelstahl verwendet, der gereifte Rum weist einen Verschluss aus Ebenholz und eine Metalloberfläche aus Rotgold auf. Das Logo folgt der allgemeinen Ästhetik: Braun für den Rum, Türkis für den Gin, Wodka hingegen kann genauso in der Edelstahlversion abgefüllt werden und Cognac und Brandy in der goldenen. **Oruka** ist in der westafrikanischen Sprache Yoruba das Wort für Ring.

Cet emballage conceptuel innove en s'éloignant de l'idée traditionnelle de bouteille. Son système de dosage de 12 shots individuels fonctionne en faisant tourner l'anneau en verre. Dans la version dry gin, le liquide bleu permet de distinguer les compartiments remplis de ceux qui sont vides. La bouteille est en tungstène noir, en verre et en acier inoxydable, tandis que celle de vieux rhum est ornée d'un bouchon en ébène et d'une finition or rose. Le logo suit la même esthétique, marron pour le rhum et turquoise pour le gin. La version en acier pourrait tout aussi bien contenir de la vodka, et la version dorée du cognac ou du brandy. **Oruka** signifie bague en yoruba, une langue d'Afrique de l'Ouest.

FILON

Design: Andrei Nedea
Company: Insus
Country: Romania
Category: Packaging concept
BRONZE PENTAWARD 2015

BLACK BEACH ORGANICS

Design: Sara Jones
Company: Anthem Worldwide
Country: UK
Category: Packaging concept

BRONZE PENTAWARD 2012

OSM
TOP OF THE OSM

3D Creative Direction: Guozheng Jiang
3D Design: Huang Feng
Graphic Creative Direction: Chen Dandan
Graphic Design: Ji Qiurong
Business Direction: Jin Jing
Company: Nianxiang Design
Country: China
Category: Packaging concept

BRONZE PENTAWARD 2016

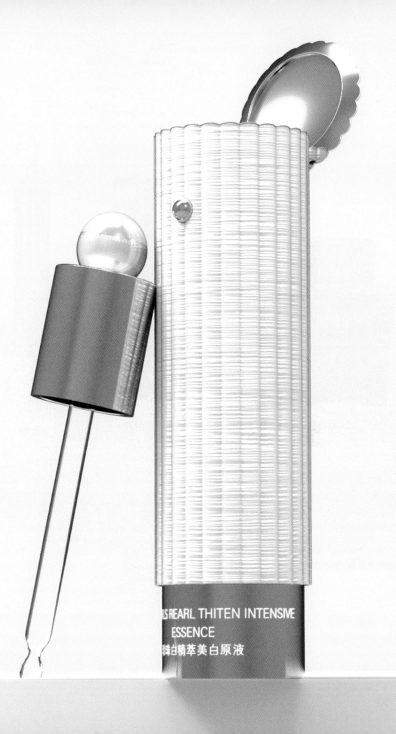

RS REARL THITEN INTENSIVE
ESSENCE
珠白精萃美白原液

HABIT

Design: Morey Reed Talmor (student)
School: Shenkar School of Engineering and Design
Country: Israel
Category: Packaging concept
SILVER PENTAWARD 2012

Habit is a company that specialises in drug rehabilitation and cessation products and believes in offering an exclusive and discreet service through its wide range of products. For the treatment of addictions ranging from nicotine to heroin, each product in the redesigned packaging line is housed in an individual black bottle or container to ensure rehabilitation with style. The project is equally a critique of the glamour and glitz associated with drug culture and at the same time a parody of the high-end luxury industry, while hoping still to be able to stand on its own as a product of beauty and design.

Die Firma **Habit** spezialisiert sich auf Hilfsmittel für Drogenentzug und Entwöhnung und setzt durch seine große Produktpalette darauf, eine diskrete und exklusive Dienstleistung zu erbringen. Die Behandlung von Abhängigkeiten reicht von Nikotin bis zu Heroin. Jedes Produkt aus der neu gestalteten Linie wird in einer individuellen schwarzen Flasche oder einem anderen Behälter verpackt, um eine stilvolle Rehabilitation zu gewährleisten. Das Projekt ist ebenso Kritik am Glanz und Glitter, der mit der Drogenkultur verknüpft wird, wie auch Parodie auf die Highend-Luxusindustrie – und außerdem hofft man, für sich allein als Produkt für Schönheit und Design stehen zu können.

Habit est une entreprise spécialisée dans le traitement de la toxicomanie et les produits de sevrage, proposant un service exclusif et discret à travers une vaste gamme de produits. Pour le traitement d'addictions allant de la nicotine à l'héroïne, chaque produit de la ligne remodelée est conditionné dans une bouteille ou un contenant noir individuel pour une réhabilitation tout en style. Ce projet est à la fois une critique du glamour associé à la culture de la drogue, et une parodie de l'industrie du luxe. Elle tente dans le même temps de s'imposer en tant qu'objet de design.

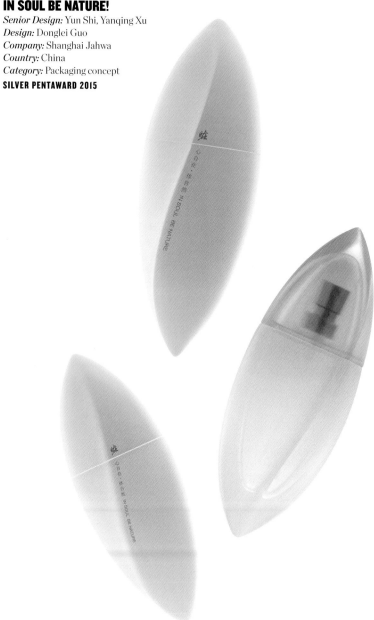

HERBORIST
IN SOUL BE NATURE!
Senior Design: Yun Shi, Yanqing Xu
Design: Donglei Guo
Company: Shanghai Jahwa
Country: China
Category: Packaging concept
SILVER PENTAWARD 2015

ZEN PERFUME

Design: Igor Mitin
Company: Good!
Country: Kazakhstan
Category: Packaging concept

SILVER PENTAWARD 2012

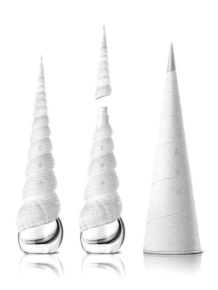

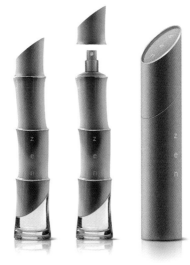

DAY & NIGHT

Art Direction/Design: Stepan Azaryan
Design: Lilit Arshakyan
Illustration: Anahit Margaryan
Company: Backbone Branding
Country: Armenia
Category: Packaging concept

GOLD PENTAWARD 2016

Creative Direction: Arman Auzhanov
CG Art: Maksim Shniak
Design: Alesia Hil
Copywriting: Lidia Dichkovskaya
Account Direction: Zhanna Kozyreva
Company: Armbrand/Arman Auzhanov
Country: Belarus
Category: Packaging concept
SILVER PENTAWARD 2015

Best of the category
Household maintenance, home improvement, decoration
Electronic, non-electronic, entertainment
Automobile products
Packaging brand identity programs

other
markets

Tobacco products
Pet products
Self-promotion
Packaging concept

FISHERMAN
RUBBER BOOTS

Design: Igor Mitin, Berik Yergaliyev,
Darina Baimukhanova, Rustam Gareyev,
Farhat Omirbaev, Andrey Serdyuk
Company: Good!
Country: Kazakhstan
Category: Best of the category
PLATINUM PENTAWARD 2012

Rubber boots are an underestimated product in
many respects—everyone is aware of their primary
function, protection from water, but as high-quality
specialised footwear for fishing the better brand
should make its advantages clear. Instead of using
a bland box with the manufacturer's logo, a packaging design was therefore developed depicting the
boot immersed in water and surrounded by poten-
tially harmful aquatic creatures. The packaging is
also intended to serve as a mini-stand and to promote the product in stores, distinguishing it dra-
matically from the competition since most such
boots are almost identical in appearance and are
typically located on the lower shelves in a dense
group, making it difficult for consumers to decide
on any particular brand.

Gummistiefel sind in mancherlei Hinsicht unterschätzte Gegenstände: Alle kennen ihre primäre Funktion, vor Wasser zu schützen. Aber wenn eine Marke für qualitativ hochwertiges Spezialschuhwerk zum Angeln besonders gut ist, sollte sie ihre Vorteile deutlich herausstellen. Anstatt nur das Logo des Herstellers auf einem langweiligen Karton zu zeigen, wurde darum ein Verpackungsdesign entwickelt, das den Stiefel in Wasser getaucht zeigt, umgeben von potenziell gefährlichen Wasserbewohnern. Der Packkarton fungiert wie eine Minibühne und bewirbt so das Produkt im Laden. Damit unterscheidet er sich dramatisch von der Konkurrenz, bei der alle Stiefel praktisch gleich aussehen und massenweise meist die unteren Regalreihen füllen. So können die Verbraucher sich kaum für eine bestimmte Marke entscheiden.

Les bottes en caoutchouc sont un produit sous-estimé à bien des égards. Tout le monde connaît leur fonction principale, protéger contre l'eau, mais les marques haut de gamme devraient mieux communiquer sur leurs avantages en tant que chaussures spécialisées pour la pêche. Au lieu d'utiliser une boîte sans imagination ornée du logo du fabricant, l'emballage montre donc un pied immergé dans l'eau et encerclé de créatures aquatiques potentiellement dangereuses. Il est également pensé pour servir de petit présentoir qui met le produit en valeur dans les magasins, en le démarquant spectaculairement de la concurrence puisque la majorité des bottes de ce genre sont habituellement toutes regroupées pêle-mêle sur les étagères du bas, ce qui n'aide pas les consommateurs à se décider pour une marque particulière.

PETROCOLL
SPATULA PUTTY

Design: Aris Pasouris
Company: Mousegraphics
Country: Greece
Category: Best of the category
PLATINUM PENTAWARD 2009

Mousegraphics in Athens created a surprising design for this range of **Petrocoll** cement bags that completely broke the mould in the field of construction. The agency's aim was to create a design for the product that would radically change the packaging compared to what all the competitors used, and thus get the brand much talked about. The design features elegant, non-provocative female figures, that does not resemble traditional cement bags, and therefore stands out both at the store and on construction sites.

Mousegraphics aus Athen überraschte mit seinem Design einer Reihe von **Petrocoll**-Zementsäcken, das im Bereich des Bauwesens völlig aus dem Rahmen fiel. Die Agentur wollte für das Produkt eine Gestaltung schaffen, die verglichen mit dem, was von der Konkurrenz bereits im Umlauf war, die Verpackung radikal verändert und so die Marke verstärkt ins Gespräch bringt. Die Gestaltung arbeitet mit eleganten, nicht-aufreizenden weiblichen Figuren. Es erinnert nicht an traditionelle Zementsäcke und hebt sich somit sowohl in den Verkaufsräumen als auch auf den Baustellen besonders hervor.

L'agence athénienne Mousegraphics a créé un design surprenant pour cette gamme de sacs de ciment **Petrocoll,** qui brise complètement le moule dans le secteur de la construction. Elle voulait créer un design qui transformerait complètement le packaging par rapport à ce que les concurrents utilisent, et ainsi faire parler de la marque. Les sacs sont illustrés de personnages féminins élégants, sans provocation, et ils ne ressemblent pas aux sacs de ciment traditionnels. Ils se démarquent donc sur le point de vente, mais aussi sur les chantiers.

SPARK

Design: Young Soo, Park Hyun Kyun,
Son Kwang Pil, Choi
Company: Aekyung Industrial
Country: South Korea
Category: Best of the category

PLATINUM PENTAWARD 2008

The **Spark** laundry detergent box speaks a universal language thanks to the creative washing-machine shape and there is no need for further explanation to the consumer. They can immediately recognize the type of product and its use and furthermore can see how much of it is left in the box, making repurchase easier. This package is also multi-use and can be filled again with a refill.

Der Karton für das Waschmittel **Spark** ist dank der kreativen Waschmaschinenform universell verständlich, und der Konsument braucht keine weiteren Erläuterungen. Er kann sofort den Typ des Produkts erkennen und wie es verwendet werden soll. Weil er auch immer sehen kann, wie voll die Box noch ist, wird der Nachkauf noch einfacher. Außerdem ist die Verpackung wiederverwendbar und kann aufgefüllt werden.

La boîte de lessive **Spark** parle une langue universelle grâce à sa forme créative de machine à laver, et le consommateur n'a pas de besoin d'autres explications. Il reconnaît immédiatement le type de produit et son utilisation. De plus, le hublot lui permet de voir le niveau de poudre qui reste dans la boîte, ce qui facilite le réachat. L'emballage est également réutilisable, et peut être rempli grâce à une recharge de lessive.

OUT_OF_ARK

Design: Joseph Poelzelbauer,
Simone Poelzelbauer
Company: Identis
Country: Germany
Category: Best of the category

PLATINUM PENTAWARD 2010

The Wild Bag Box is the packaging for
out_of_ark, a bag collection with three basic
models and 15 different motifs featuring animals
from five continents. The Crossover bags are
transported in the escape-proof Wild Bag Box—as
is fitting for wild bags. The Wild Bag Box is thus
intended to be more than just simple packaging,
as it becomes part of the story and affirms the
vitality of the products. The lively contents are
kept safe, but are still clearly visible through the
bars. The corrugated board, the basic material of
the packaging, is left in its natural state.

Die Taschenkollektion **out_of_ark** erscheint in drei Grundmodellen und mit 15 unterschiedlichen Motiven von Tieren aus fünf Kontinenten und wird in der Wild Bag Box verpackt. Die Crossover-Taschen werden in der ausbruchssicheren Wild Bag Box transportiert – für „wilde Taschen" sehr angemessen. Die Wild Bag Box ist somit mehr als bloße Verpackung, sie ergänzt die mit dem Produkt erzählten Geschichte und bekräftigt dessen Vitalität. Die „lebhaften" Inhalte werden sicher transportiert, sind aber durch die Stäbe immer noch gut sichtbar. Das Grundmaterial der Verpackung ist unbehandelte Wellpappe.

La Wild Bag Box est l'emballage de **out_of_ark**, une collection de sacs avec trois modèles de base et 15 motifs différents représentant des animaux des cinq continents. Les sacs Crossover sont transportés dans la cage de la Wild Bag Box, tout à fait approprié pour des sacs sauvages. La Wild Bag Box est donc plus qu'un simple emballage, car elle fait partie intégrante de l'histoire racontée au consommateur, et renforce la notion de produit vivant. Son contenu plein de vie est en sécurité, mais bien visible derrière les barreaux. Le carton ondulé, matériau de base dans l'emballage, est laissé à l'état brut.

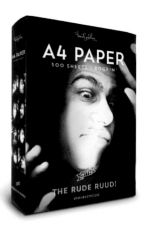
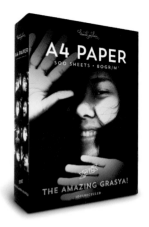
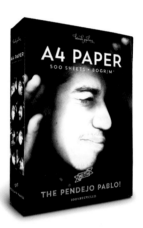
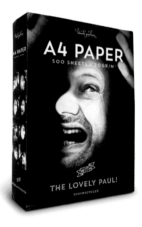

Jeder kennt Porträts von Leuten, die am Kopierer oder Scanner herumspielen. Diese simple Idee sorgt hier für ein tolles Design der Verpackung des Drucker-/Kopierpapiers dieser kleinen, unabhängigen spanischen Firma. Profimodels oder Fotografen waren hier nicht involviert, die „Agenturfamilie" kümmerte sich mit einem Scanner selbst darum! Die resultierenden Bilder wurden durch Zufallsprinzip ausgewählt, Käufer können unter neun verschiedenen Gesichtern wählen. Die nächste Porträtserie soll von den Kunden stammen, und zwar demnächst über einen Scanner-Wettbewerb auf Facebook.

Tout le monde a déjà vu les portraits que des personnes font pour s'amuser avec une photocopieuse ou un scanner. L'idée est simple et a donné lieu à un design réussi pour cette petite entreprise espagnole de papier à copier et à imprimer. Il n'a pas été utile de faire appel à un photographe et à des modèles professionnels : les collègues de l'agence et un scanner ont suffi. Les images obtenues sont utilisées de façon aléatoire et les clients ont le choix entre neuf visages. Par le biais d'un concours lancé sur Facebook, les propres clients ont été amenés à réaliser une nouvelle série de portraits.

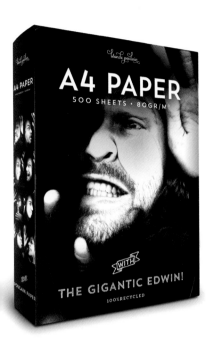
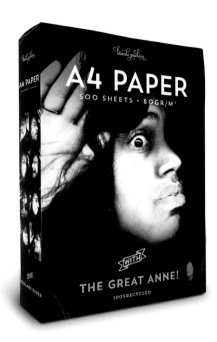

BLONDE POULAIN
A4 PAPER

Design: Paul Roeters, Pablo Nicolás Botía
Company: Studio Kluif
Country: Netherlands
Category: Best of the category
PLATINUM PENTAWARD 2014

Everybody recognizes the portraits people make when they're playing around with a copying machine or a scanner. It's a simple idea and made a great design for the packaging for this small independent Spanish company's copying/printing paper. No professional models or photographer were involved, just the "agency family" and a scanner! The resulting images are used randomly, and customers can choose from nine different faces. The next portrait series will be made by the customers themselves, through a Facebook-scanner contest in the near future.

INGRO

Creative Direction: Vladimir Fedoseev
Art Direction/Design: Arina Yushkevich
Design: Suzanna Belkina, Anna Lysenko
Company: Otvetdesign
Country: Russia
Category: Best of the category

PLATINUM PENTAWARD 2015

How to market low-priced Russian domestic pumping equipment? The target audience consists of sales managers from hardware stores where packaging isn't used, and summer visitors who buy pumps individually as they're needed. So, a series of clear-cut characters was developed for the boxes, every bit as alive as your next-door neighbors: a strong Russian woman, the mainstay of the house; a male couple who definitely cannot do without their dekaliter; a sharply dressed gangster who enjoys the dirty work but operates quietly and efficiently. Punning slogans describe the characters at the same time as the different equipment, thus turning soulless machines into stand-ups who'll never let you down.

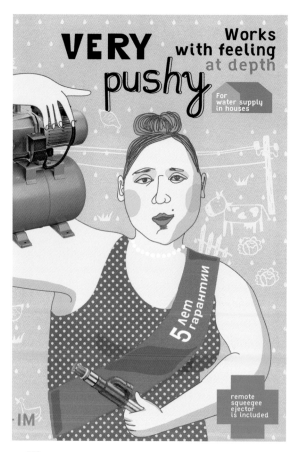

Wie kann man niedrigpreisige russische Haushaltspumpen vermarkten? Die Zielgruppe besteht aus Verkaufsmanagern von Eisenwarenläden, in denen keine Verpackungen genutzt werden, sowie Sommerbesuchern, die bei Bedarf Pumpen einzeln kaufen. Also wurden für die Kartons verschiedene eindeutige Charaktere entwickelt, jeweils so lebendig wie der Nachbar nebenan: eine starke russische Frau als „Säule" des Hauses, ein männliches Paar, das ohne seinen Dekaliter definitiv nicht klarkommt, oder ein schick gekleideter Gangster, der die Drecksarbeit genießt, aber gerne still und effektiv arbeitet. Slogans mit Wortspielen beschreiben die Charaktere und gleichzeitig auch die verschiedenen Gerätschaften. So werden seelenlose Maschinen zu einem Beistand, der einen nicht im Stich lässt.

Comment vendre des pompes domestiques russes bon marché? Le public cible se compose de directeurs commerciaux de magasins de bricolage où l'emballage n'est pas utilisé, et de visiteurs estivaux qui achètent des pompes selon leurs besoins. Une série de personnages très typés a été mise au point pour les boîtes, aussi vivants que vos voisins : une femme forte russe, le pilier de la maison ; un couple d'hommes qui ne peuvent pas se passer de leur décalitre ; un gangster sur son trente-et-un qui ne rechigne pas à se salir les mains. Des slogans avec des jeux de mots décrivent les personnages et l'équipement, transformant des machines sans âme en compagnons qui ne vous laisseront jamais tomber.

ARGOS
SIMPLE VALUE

Executive Brand Direction: Dave Roberts
Design Direction: Mark Wood
Design: Brinley Clark, Matthew Hill,
Wayne Peach
Copywriting: Mike Reed (Reed Words)
Client: Rob Quartermain
Account Direction: Andrew Webster
Company: The Partners
Country: UK
Category: Best of the category
PLATINUM PENTAWARDS 2016

Consisting of 140 basic household items, the
Argos Simple Value range offers solid quality at
low prices. It was this combination of simplicity
with value that led to the name, and the packaging
also reflects the fact that these products speak for
themselves. But simple need not mean dull, and
while the product descriptions communicate
the basic values there are unexpected twists that
lift the copy into something that engages more
personally with customers. Different artworks
have also been created for all these items, and
with several hundred thousand units produced
per year the simplicity of the print production
makes it easier for international suppliers to
contribute to the range.

Das „Simple Value"-Sortiment von **Argos** bietet solide Qualität zu niedrigen Preisen und enthält 140 elementare Haushaltsartikel. Diese Kombination aus Einfachheit und Wert war namensgebend. Außerdem spiegelt die Verpackung die Tatsache wider, dass diese Produkte für sich selbst sprechen. Aber einfach bedeutet nicht glanzlos. Während die Produktbeschreibungen die Grundwerte vermitteln, verwandeln ungeahnte Wendungen den Werbetext in etwas, das Kunden direkt anspricht. Für jeden Artikel wurden verschiedene Designs geschaffen, doch die Einfachheit der Druckproduktion erleichtert es internationalen Lieferanten, zu dem Sortiment der jährlich mehreren Hunderttausend produzierten Einheiten beizutragen.

La gamme Simple Value d'**Argos** se compose de 140 articles pour la maison qui sont d'une qualité fiable et bon marché. C'est cette combinaison de simplicité et de valeur ajoutée qui a inspiré son nom, et l'emballage laisse les produits parler d'eux-mêmes. Mais simplicité ne signifie pas ennui, et les descriptions des produits contiennent des surprises qui transforment le texte en un outil de communication avec les clients sur un plan plus personnel. Différentes illustrations ont également été créées pour tous ces articles, et plusieurs centaines de milliers d'unités étant produites chaque année, la simplicité de l'impression permet aux fournisseurs internationaux de respecter facilement l'effet de gamme.

TRUEGLOVE

Art Direction: Nadie Parshina
Copywriting: Svetlana Chugunova
Tattoo: Dmitry Hendrikson
Photography: Polina Tverdaya
Company: Ohmybrand
Country: Russia
Category: Household maintenance

GOLD PENTAWARD 2014

These household gloves, with their bold tattoo prints, different on each hand, will make you want to put them on right away. They create a playful mood, stylishly exaggerated by the special packaging, so that the less glamorous chores around the house will no longer be boring or monotonous: with a little imagination, perhaps you're at a fashion show or in front of a mass of photographers, in your beautiful shoes and fancy gloves. The pack design is made up like a magazine cover, with tips and gossipy headlines, but as well as being informative it also links up through the QR code to the manufacturer's site where other designs can be found.

Diese Haushaltshandschuhe mit ihren auffälligen Tattoos (für jede Hand anders) möchte man am liebsten sofort anziehen. Sie versetzen einen in eine spielerische Stimmung, stylish betont durch die besondere Verpackung. So bleiben die weniger glamourösen Haushaltspflichten nicht länger langweilig oder monoton: Mit ein wenig Fantasie versetzt man sich z.B. in eine Modeshow oder vor eine Gruppe Fotografen und trägt schöne Schuhe und schicke Handschuhe. Die Packung mit ihren Tipps und Klatsch-Überschriften ist wie die Titelseite eines Magazins gestaltet, doch auch informativ, da sie über den QR-Code zur Website des Herstellers verlinkt, wo man weitere Designs finden kann.

Ces gants de ménage imprimés de tatouages différents pour chaque main sont totalement irrésistibles. Ils donnent un ton ludique que l'emballage original vient encore renforcer, afin que les tâches domestiques même les moins « glamour » ne soient plus ennuyeuses et monotones. Avec un peu d'imagination, vous êtes sur un podium de mode ou face à une foule de photographes, dans vos superbes chaussures et vos gants sophistiqués. L'emballage est pensé comme une couverture de magazine, avec conseils et titres aguicheurs. En plus des informations qu'il apporte, il comporte un code QR lié au site du fabricant, où d'autres modèles sont disponibles.

BRAWNY

Design Direction:
David Turner, Bruce Duckworth
Creative Direction:
Sarah Moffat, Jamie McCathie
Lead Design: Brian Labus
Illustration: Tavis Coburn
Senior Direction: Samantha Brown
Account Direction: Wyeth Whiting
Senior Account Management:
D'Arcy Danaher
Production Artwork:
Craig Snelgrove, Jeff Enslen
Company: Turner Duckworth,
London & San Francisco
Country: UK, USA
Category: Household maintenance
SILVER PENTAWARD 2016

As a popular American brand, **Brawny** nevertheless found sales were declining across its range of paper towels, and a new and flexible packaging system was required that would embrace its heritage as well as recapture the attention of consumers. This meant communicating the product's toughness in a distinctive way and so reinventing the Brawny man, giving him back his confidence and identity as the strong and capable giant. The resulting character was inspired by comic-book heroes, and the illustrator also made use of scale and cropping to create a figure with both mysterious strength and reassuringly calm appeal. The new packaging has proved successful with consumers and on social media.

Obwohl **Brawny** in den USA eine beliebte Marke ist, stellte man fest, wie die Verkaufszahlen bei Papiertüchern zurückgingen. Ein neues und flexibles Verpackungssystem war nötig, um die Tradition der Marke aufzugreifen und die Aufmerksamkeit der Kunden wieder auf sich zu ziehen. Dazu kommunizierte man auf charakteristische Weise die Robustheit des Produkts und erfand den Brawny-Mann, dem das Selbstvertrauen und seine Identität als starker und kompetenter Riese anzusehen sind, neu. Die Figur wurde schließlich von Comichelden inspiriert. Der Illustrator setzt Maßstab und Anschnitt geschickt ein, um eine Figur zu schaffen, die eine geheimnisvolle Kraft und eine beruhigende, gelassene Ausstrahlung vereint. Die neue Verpackung war bei Verbrauchern und in den sozialen Medien sehr erfolgreich.

La populaire marque américaine **Brawny** voyait ses ventes décliner pour toute sa gamme de papier absorbant, et il lui fallait un nouveau système d'emballage flexible pour exprimer son héritage tout en reconquérant l'attention des consommateurs. Cela impliquait de communiquer la robustesse du produit avec originalité, et donc de réinventer l'homme Brawny, en lui restituant son assurance et son identité de géant fort et compétent. Le personnage résultant s'inspire des héros de bande dessinée, et grâce au cadrage et à l'échelle, l'illustrateur a pu une figure dotée d'une force mystérieuse et d'un charme calme et rassurant. Ce nouvel emballage a séduit les consommateurs et les réseaux sociaux.

UP
PLAYFUL LIFE

Creative Direction: Paul, Huang You-Sheng
Art Direction: Rose, Lee Yuan-Chun
Company: Tsukito Design
Country: Taiwan
Category: Household maintenance

SILVER PENTAWARD 2013

AM

Design: Johan Liden, Rinat Aruh, Rogerio Lionzo,
Erik Jarlsson, Boliang Chen
Company: Aruliden
Country: USA
Category: Household maintenance

SILVER PENTAWARD 2014

HAMPI PRODUCTS
NATURAL TABLEWARE

Creative Direction: Marcel Verhaaf
Project Coordination/Artwork: Jeroen Meijer
Managing Direction: Robert Kuiper
Client Services Direction: Sabine Louët Feisser
Photography: Nishikie fotografie
Company: Brandnew
Country: Netherlands
Category: Home improvement, decoration

GOLD PENTAWARD 2011

Hampi natural tableware is a range of disposable plates and bowls made sustainably from fallen palm leaves. At first they were sold directly to caterers but to sell them as a lifestyle choice to consumers repackaging became necessary, whether they were to be sold in department stores or in supermarkets. The design depicts the story of this special product by showing the transformation of the leaf into reusable natural plates. The sides and top of the packs show the beautiful patterns the leaves create, whilst the shapes used in the logo were a source of inspiration for the actual boxes.

Das natürliche Geschirr von **Hampi** ist ein Sortiment aus Einmaltellern und -schalen, umweltverträglich hergestellt aus abgefallenen Palmenblättern. Zuerst wurde das Produkt direkt an Gastronomen geliefert, aber um das Geschirr als Lifestyle-Artikel auch dem Endverbraucher verkaufen zu können, wurde eine neue Verpackung notwendig, sei es für Kaufhäuser oder Supermärkte. Das Design schildert die Herstellungsgeschichte dieses besonderen Produkts, indem es darstellt, wie sich das Blatt in wiederverwendbares natürliches Geschirr verwandelt. Seiten und Deckel des Kartons zeigen die schönen Muster der Blätter, während die Formen im Logo als Inspirationsquelle für die eigentlichen Kartons dienen.

La vaisselle naturelle **Hampi** est une gamme d'assiettes et de bols jetables issus de la production durable, fabriqués à partir de feuilles de palme tombées à terre. Au début elle était vendue directement aux traiteurs, mais pour la vendre aux consommateurs en grand magasin ou en supermarché il a fallu revoir l'emballage en la positionnant comme un choix de style de vie. La boîte illustre l'histoire de ce produit très spécial en montrant la feuille qui se transforme en assiettes naturelles réutilisables. Les côtés et le haut des paquets montrent les superbes motifs des feuilles, tandis que les formes utilisées dans le logo ont été une source d'inspiration pour la forme des boîtes.

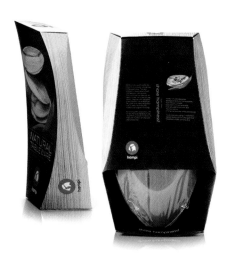

INTRATUIN

Design: Paul Roeters, Jeroen Hoedjes, Edwin Degenhart
Company: Studio Kluif
Country: Netherlands
Category: Home improvement, decoration

SILVER PENTAWARD 2014

ANOR

Design: Jennifer Tsai
Company: Proad Identity
Country: Taiwan
Category: Home improvement, decoration

GOLD PENTAWARD 2013

BOBBLE JUG

Creative Direction:
Stephanie Smiedt (Move Collective)
Associated Creative Direction:
Katie Eaton (Safari Sundays)
Art Direction: Craig Hench (Safari Sundays)
Design: Karim Rashid (Karim Rashid Inc.)
Account Direction: Jen Vest (Safari Sundays)
Company: Move Collective
Country: USA
Category: Home improvement, decoration
SILVER PENTAWARD 2012

For everyday household use, this smart reimagining of the water-filtering jug does away with the usual second reservoir, which drains slowly and typically needs to be filled several times, to deliver pure water in an instant. Holding more than its appearance would suggest (67oz/2l), the slim design also frees up space as the jug fits neatly into refrigerator doors. The **bobble** jug is free of BPA, phthalates and PVC and uses an activated carbon filter, which is super-effective at reducing the taint of chlorine commonly detected in tap-water. The filter is available in 6 vivid colours, visible through the packaging window, whilst the box's cut-out aligns with the jug's handle to make for easy carrying.

CERVERA
TABLE TOP STORIES

Creative Direction: Jacob Bergström; *Account Direction:* Maja Wetterberg
Senior Design: Johanna Karlsson; *Design:* Sara Modigh
Production Design: Kristofer Ekeblom; *Illustration:* Lina Ekstrand (Agent Molly)
Photography: Mattias Tiedermann (Agent Molly)
Company: Designkontoret Silver
Country: Sweden
Category: Home improvement

SILVER PENTAWARD 2015

Bei dieser pfiffigen Neuerfindung eines Wasserfilters für den Alltagsgebrauch im Haushalt wurde das zweite Reservoir abgeschafft. Früher musste es umständlich mehrmals befüllt werden und leerte sich nur langsam. Mittels neuem Filter erhält man sofort reines Wasser. Durch das schlanke Design nimmt die Karaffe mehr Wasser auf, als es den Anschein hat (bis zu 2 Liter), sie spart auch Platz, weil sie nun gut in die Kühlschranktür passt. Die Kanne **bobble** ist frei von BPA, Phthalaten und PVC. Sein Aktivkohlefilter reduziert höchst effizient das Chlor aus dem Haushaltswasser. Der Filter ist in sechs leuchtenden Farben erhältlich, die man durch ein Fenster im Karton sehen kann. Ein Ausschnitt im Karton macht es möglich, die Karaffe an ihrem Griff leicht zu transportieren.

Pour une utilisation quotidienne à la maison, cette réinvention astucieuse de la carafe filtrante abandonne le réservoir secondaire habituel, qui laisse passer l'eau lentement et qu'il faut remplir plusieurs fois, pour servir de l'eau pure en un instant. Elle contient plus qu'elle n'en a l'air (2 l), et sa ligne élancée lui permet de tenir dans les portes des réfrigérateurs. La carafe **bobble** ne contient ni BPA, ni phtalates ni PVC, et emploie un filtre au charbon actif, extrêmement efficace pour réduire les traces de chlore que l'on détecte souvent dans l'eau du robinet. Le filtre est disponible en 6 couleurs vives, visibles à travers la fenêtre de l'emballage, tandis que les découpes de la boîte s'alignent sur la poignée de la carafe pour faciliter le transport.

Die Sprachlernhilfe **Lingua Simplex** funktioniert wie ein Lernspiel und wird in einem auffälligen Karton angeboten. Ähnlich wie bei einem Memory-Spiel finden sich auf den Karten erklärende Symbole sowie Text, der den Mitspielern laut vorgelesen werden soll. Jede Spielepackung zeigt eine Person, die auf einem nationalen Stereotyp basiert. Wird die Packung geöffnet und der Deckel nach oben oder unten verschoben, erwachen die Illustrationen entsprechend der dargestellten Charakterzüge zum Leben. Um das Marketing zu testen, wurden die Spiele an Schulen und Sprachkursen in Unis verteilt – so erfolgreich, dass fünf weitere Sprachen ins Sortiment aufgenommen wurden.

Lingua Simplex est une méthode d'apprentissage linguistique présentée dans des emballages attrayants. Les jeux de paires incluent des cartes aux symboles pertinents, et d'autres avec des verbes qu'il faut lire à voix haute aux autres joueurs. Chaque boîte représente un personnage type d'un pays ; à son ouverture, le couvercle se déplace verticalement et les illustrations prennent vie en accord avec les attributs du personnage. Des tests promotionnels ont été réalisés en distribuant les jeux dans des écoles et dans des cours de langues en faculté. Le succès commercial remporté a motivé l'idée d'ajouter cinq autres langues.

LINGUA SIMPLEX PAIRS GAMES

Executive Creative Direction/
Design: Jonathan Sven Amelung
Editing: Alicia Maritza Amelung
Illustration: Angela Wittchen
Company: Amelung Design
Country: Germany
Category: Entertainment

GOLD PENTAWARD 2014

Lingua Simplex is a language-learning aid that works as an educational game presented in high-visibility boxes. The Pairs Games contain cards with explanatory symbols, and text cards concerning verbs to be read aloud to the other players. Each game pack represents a character based on a national stereotype and when the box is opened, and the lid moved up and down, the illustrations become partly animated in line with the character traits depicted. Promotional testing involved distributing the games in schools and on university language courses, while later market success has led to plans to add five further languages.

VAIN STHLM
ORIGINALS

Design: Identity Works team
Company: Identity Works
Country: Sweden
Category: Entertainment

SILVER PENTAWARD 2016

SONY
H.EAR

Art Direction: Tomoaki Takuma
Design: Kayoko Aoki
Company: Sony
Country: Japan
Category: Entertainment

GOLD PENTAWARD 2016

AUDIOVOX ACCESSORIES CORP. EARBUDEEZ

Creative Direction: David Jensen
Art Direction: Jerome Calleja
Design: Dean Kojima
Company: JDA, Inc. Retail Ready Design
Country: USA
Category: Electronic

GOLD PENTAWARD 2009

Audiovox Accessories' research indicated younger customers purchased ear buds for their personal music-players as fashion accessories. With this in mind, JDA, Inc. Retail Ready Design set out to create a package directed to attracting this youthful customer. Changing completely the norms for this category, they strove for fun, edgy, unique, full-of-personality packaging designs.

Die Recherchen von **Audiovox Accessories** legen nahe, dass junge Kunden Ohrhörer für ihre eigenen Musikabspielgeräte wie Modeaccessoires kaufen. Die Agentur JDA, Inc. Retail Ready Design berücksichtigte das und gestaltete eine Verpackung, die jugendliche Kunden direkt ansprechen sollte. Die Normen in dieser Kategorie wurden komplett verändert, und man legte die Verpackung in einer fröhlichen, auffälligen und unverwechselbaren Gestaltung mit ganz eigener Persönlichkeit an.

L'étude réalisée par **Audiovox Accessories** indiquait que les jeunes clients achetaient des écouteurs pour leur lecteur de musique personnel comme s'il s'agissait d'accessoires de mode. C'est avec cette idée à l'esprit que JDA, Inc. Retail Ready Design a cherché à créer un packaging conçu pour attirer ce profil de clients jeunes. L'agence a complètement bouleversé les normes dans cette catégorie et a parié sur des concepts drôles, tendance, uniques et pleins de personnalité.

PLUSMATE
EARPHONE SERIES

Creative Direction: Hyunjoo Choi
Design: Kayoung Lee
Company: Emart
Country: South Korea
Category: Entertainment
GOLD PENTAWARD 2013

Plusmate, a private-label brand owned by South Korea's Emart hypermarket chain, developed this earphone series to express the differences between the characteristic tones of various genres of music, such as jazz, classical, country or rock. Consumers can then choose the earphones best suited to their taste, with musicians playing stringed instruments being used to represent the four musical genres. The cable is wound up neatly and positioned on the pack to replace the strings of the different instruments, while the heads of the earphones become the eyes of the musicians, adding a humorous note to the overall design.

Plusmate ist eine Eigenmarke, der südkoreanischen Hypermarktkette Emart. Für sie wurde diese Kopfhörerserie entwickelt, um die Unterschiede zwischen den typischen Klängen der verschiedenen Musikgenres wie Jazz, Klassik, Country oder Rock auszudrücken. Die Käufer wählen jene Kopfhörer, die am besten zu ihrer Lieblingsmusik passen. Die Musiker darauf repräsentieren mit ihren Saiteninstrumenten die vier musikalischen Genres. Das Kabel wurde so auf die Verpackung gewickelt, dass daraus die Saiten der verschiedenen Instrumente entstehen, während die Ohrknöpfe zu den Augen der Musiker werden. Das verleiht dem Design insgesamt seine humorvolle Note.

Plusmate, marque maison de la chaîne de supermarchés Emart en Corée du Sud, a conçu cette gamme d'écouteurs pour illustrer les différences entre les genres musicaux, comme le jazz, la musique classique, le country ou le rock. Les consommateurs peuvent choisir les écouteurs adaptés à leur goût, avec des musiciens jouant des instruments à cordes et illustrant les quatre styles de musique. Le câble est savamment enroulé de façon à imiter les cordes des instruments, alors que les écouteurs forment les yeux des musiciens pour ajouter une note humoristique au design.

HAPPY PLUGS
CHARGE CABLES AND EARBUDS

Design: Andreas Vural
Company: Happy Plugs
Country: Sweden
Category: Entertainment

SILVER PENTAWARD 2014

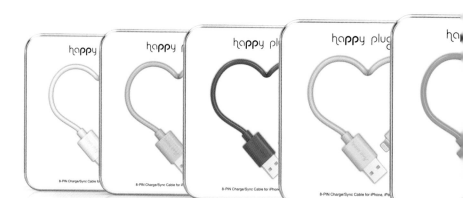

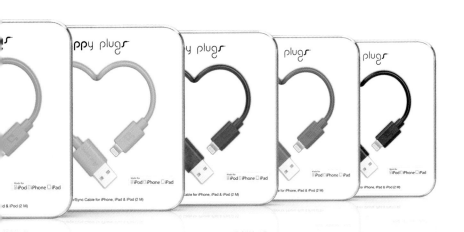

KEY
PLEASURE TOYS

Creative Direction: José García Eguiguren,
Mateo Flandoli
Company: Gworkshop Design
Country: Ecuador
Category: Entertainment

SILVER PENTAWARD 2013

Our little secret...

KEY
Presented by JOPEN

Pyxis Finger Massager
Playful and full of energy, this innovative finger massager is designed to explore.

Lay back and enjoy the ride...

KEY
Presented by JOPEN

Comet Wand
KEY's signature wand is just what you need for unparalleled pleasure.

Small package, big reward...

KEY
Presented by JOPEN

Charms Petite Massager
Cupid

Lift off in 3, 2, 1...

KEY
Presented by JOPEN

Io Mini Massager
Your key to pleasure that's

It's your lucky night...

KEY
Presented by JOPEN

Nyx Mini
Sleek,
could y

It's your lucky night...

KEY
Presented by JOPEN

Nyx Mini
Sleek, e
could y

It's your lucky night...

KEY
Presented by JOPEN

Nyx Mini
Sleek, e
could y

RAMPANT**RABBIT**®
The Ballsy One

Ann Summers

RAMPANT**RABBIT**®
The G Spot One

Ann Summers

RAMPANT**RABBIT**®
The Thrusting One

Ann Summers

RAMPANT**RABBIT**®
The Twisty One

Ann Summers

RAMPANT**RABBIT**®
The Responsive One

Ann Summers

RAMPANT**RABBIT**®
The Realistic One

Ann Summers

RAMPANT**RABBIT**®
The Intense One

Ann Summers

ANN SUMMERS RAMPANT RABBIT

Creative Direction: Adam Ellis
Design: Martyn Hayes, Digby Gall
Copy: Laura Forman
Account Direction: Caroline Dilloway
Company: Elmwood
Country: UK
Category: Entertainment

GOLD PENTAWARD 2012

The original **Rampant Rabbit** from Ann Summers was the first vibrator to offer simultaneous stimulation to vagina and clitoris. However, its success led to a flood of imitations and this meant there was an urgent need to relaunch the range and re-claim ownership of these classic sex toys, thereby making them all the more desirable. The revamp took in everything from structure to pack copy, with the initial R of the logo being turned upside-down to make it look like a rabbit's head. The styling of the letter recalls the neon signs of sex shops, while the "vibration lines" around it repeat the movement of the vibrator itself, in its newly styled premium box.

Der originale **Rampant Rabbit** von Ann Summers war der erste Vibrator, der gleichzeitig Vagina und Klitoris stimuliert. Durch seinen Erfolg diente er einer Flut von Nachahmern als Vorbild. Somit gab es großen Bedarf, dieses Produkt wieder auf den Markt zu bringen und die Eigentümerschaft an diesem klassischen Sex Toy erneut zu betonen. Gleichzeitig wird es so noch begehrenswerter. Bei der grundlegenden Überarbeitung der Gesamtgestaltung nahm man sich von der Struktur bis zu den Packungstexten alles im Einzelnen vor. Der Anfangsbuchstabe R wurde als Logo umgedreht, um wie ein Hasenkopf auszusehen. An der neu gestalteten Premiumbox spielt das Styling des Schriftzuges auf Sexshop-Neonschilder an, während die „Vibrationslinien" drumherum die Bewegungen des Vibrators aufgreifen.

Le **Rampant Rabbit** original d'Ann Summers a été le premier vibromasseur à permettre la stimulation simultanée du vagin et du clitoris. Mais son succès a mené à un déluge d'imitations, et il était urgent de relancer la gamme et de réaffirmer l'autorité de la marque sur ces sex toys classiques, en les rendant encore plus désirables. Tout a été revu, depuis la structure jusqu'au texte de l'emballage, et le R du logo a été renversé pour le faire ressembler à une tête de lapin. Son graphisme évoque les néons des sex shops, tandis que les vibrations suggérées autour de lui reprennent le mouvement du vibromasseur, à l'abri dans sa nouvelle boîte de luxe.

LOGITECH
ULTIMATE EARS

Creative Direction/Design: Suncica Lukic
Illustration: Suncica Lukic,
Slavimir Stojanovic, Cristina Bermudez
Company: Nonobject
Country: USA
Category: Entertainment

SILVER PENTAWARD 2016

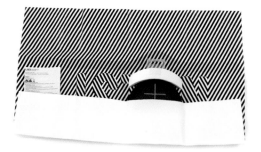

The **UE Roll** brings music to places where speakers can't be used and its packaging had to reflect this sense of adventure, while retaining the clean lines and polish of other UE products. Not confined to the usual cylindrical box, it is wrapped in a sheet of paper that clearly reveals its form, and has no small boxes for accessories or plastic sleeves for protection, just music ready to go. The inside of the paper is printed with a commissioned piece of art, different for each product color, and the result is a unique way of packaging in the consumer electronics category. It's also very cost-efficient and sustainable, and has received widespread praise for challenging established industry norms.

Die **UE Roll** bringt Musik dorthin, wo keine Lautsprecher verwendet werden können. Die Verpackung musste diese Abenteuerlust widerspiegeln, durfte dabei aber die klaren Linien und die Vollendung anderer UE-Produkte nicht unter den Tisch fallen lassen. Nicht auf die übliche Zylinderbox eingegrenzt, ist das Objekt in Papier gehüllt, das eindeutig seine Form erkennen lässt. Es hat keine kleinen Kartons für Accessoires und keine Schutzhülle – einfach Musik zum Loslegen. Die Innenseite des Papiers ist mit speziellen Designs bedruckt, für jede Produktfarbe eines. Als Ergebnis erhält man eine einmalige Verpackungsart in der Kategorie Verbraucherelektronik. Sie ist außerdem sehr kosteneffizient und nachhaltig. Etablierte Branchenstandards wurden hier auf den Prüfstand gestellt, was vielfaches Lob eingebracht hat.

L'**UE Roll** fait entrer la musique là où l'on ne peut pas utiliser de haut-parleurs, et son emballage devait exprimer cette idée d'aventure tout en conservant les lignes épurées et la finition soignée des autres produits d'UE. Libéré de l'habituelle boîte cylindrique, il est enveloppé d'une feuille de papier qui révèle sa forme, et aucune boîte à accessoires ou protection supplémentaire ne vient entraver l'expérience de la musique à emporter. À l'intérieur, le papier est imprimé d'une œuvre d'art différente pour chaque couleur. Le résultat est un emballage unique dans la catégorie de l'électronique grand public. Il est aussi très économique et durable, et a été acclamé pour être sorti des normes du secteur.

METALLICA
DEATH MAGNETIC DIGI CD

Creative Direction:
David Turner, Bruce Duckworth
Design Direction: Sarah Moffat
Design: Emily Charette, Marty O'Connor,
Jamie McCathie
Design Assistant: Brian Labus
Retouch: Peter Ruane, Craig Snelgrove
Photography: Anton Corbijn, Robert Daly,
Andy Grimshaw, Britt Hull, Gavin Hurrell,
Mike Kemp, Harper Reed, Tom Schierlitz,
Craig Snelgrove, David Turner,
Missouri State Highway Patrol
Artwork: Craig Snelgrove
Company: Turner Duckworth,
London & San Francisco
Country: UK/USA
Category: Entertainment
GOLD PENTAWARD 2009

Challenged with creating an engaging packaging piece for **Metallica**'s ninth studio album, **Death Magnetic**, Turner Duckworth offices in London and San Francisco developed an iconic, three-dimensional CD package using a conspicuous, sunken-grave image and an innovative, layered die cut. The end product shows dirt being sucked down towards a coffin, which lies low in a deepening pit. The classic Metallica logo was re-worked and a signature typographic style created. As well as this, a design kit including logos, imagery, and graphics was distributed to the band's record companies to use as promotional material around the world, ensuring this album was truly one of a kind.

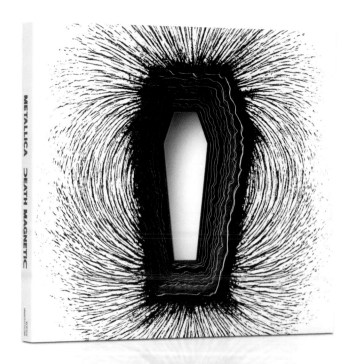

Als sie vor der Herausforderung standen, eine spannende Verpackung für das neunte **Metallica**-Studioalbum **Death Magnetic** zu schaffen, entwickelten die Büros von Turner Duckworth in London und San Francisco eine symbolträchtige, dreidimensionale CD-Hülle. Dafür bedienten sie sich des sehr auffälligen Bildes eines eingesunkenen Grabes und einer innovativen mehrschichtigen Stanzung. Das Endprodukt zeigt, wie Schmutz von einem Sarg angezogen wird, der in einer tiefen Grube liegt. Das klassische Metallica-Logo wurde überarbeitet und mit einer auffälligen Typographie umgesetzt. Obendrein wurde ein Design-Kit mit Logos, Bildern und Grafiken an die Plattenfirmen der Band weitergegeben, das als Promotion-Material weltweit eingesetzt werden sollte, um zu verdeutlichen, wie einzigartig dieses Album ist.

Confrontés au défi de créer une pochette originale pour le neuvième album studio de **Metallica**, intitulé **Death Magnetic**, les bureaux de Turner Duckworth de Londres et San Francisco ont imaginé une pochette de CD tridimensionnelle emblématique à l'aide d'une image de tombe creusée et d'une technique innovante de découpe par couches. Le produit final évoque la terre aspirée vers un cercueil qui repose tout au fond d'une tombe. L'agence a retravaillé le logo classique de Metallica et a créé un style typographique propre au groupe. Un kit de design comprenant les logos, les visuels et les graphismes a également été distribué aux maisons de disques du groupe à travers le monde afin qu'elles l'utilisent pour leurs supports promotionnels, et fassent ainsi de cet album un objet réellement exceptionnel.

PUMA
PING PONG PADDLE CASE

Design: Johan Liden, Tyler Askew
Company: Aruliden
Country: USA
Category: Entertainment

SILVER PENTAWARD 2009

SHURE
UNIDYNE SPECIAL EDITION
MICROPHONE

Creative Direction: John Ball
Design Direction: Angela Renac, Dylan Jones
Photography: Steve Simar
Copywriting: David Fried
Account Direction: Holly Houk
Company: MiresBall
Country: USA
Category: Entertainment

GOLD PENTAWARD 2015

This limited-edition version of the classic **Shure** Unidyne 55 microphone, using the original birdcage design, was issued to celebrate its 75th anniversary. An unmistakable piece of stage and recording equipment with a rich history, the Unidyne commemorative microphone was housed in suitably resonant packaging by printing up vintage ads and extracts from catalogs on the box. This presented the spirit of the Shure brand, with reference to archival Unidyne packaging and sales brochures, while a removable glossy sleeve documented the microphone's history in a series of detailed photographs.

Die Limited Edition des Mikrofonklassikers Unidyne 55 von **Shure** mit seinem originalen Vogelkäfigdesign wurde zum 75. Geburtstag produziert. Ein unverwechselbares Bühnen- und Aufnahmegerät mit reicher Vergangenheit. Die Packung für dieses Gedenkmikro von Unidyne mit seiner aufgedruckten altmodischen Werbung und den Katalogausschnitten verleiht den Kontext. So präsentiert sich der Geist der Marke Shure und verweist auf archivierte Verpackungs- und Verkaufsbroschüren von Unidyne. Die Fotoserie auf einem ablösbaren glänzenden Etikett dokumentiert die Geschichte des Mikrofons.

Cette édition limitée du classique microphone **Shure** Unidyne 55 reprend la structure en cage d'oiseau originale pour célébrer son 75ᵉ anniversaire. Équipement de scène et d'enregistrement emblématique fort d'une riche histoire, le microphone commémoratif est présenté dans une boîte tout aussi résonnante, imprimée de publicités rétro et d'extraits de catalogues, fidèle à l'esprit de la marque Shure, avec une référence à l'emballage et aux brochures commerciales du modèle d'origine. Un manchon brillant amovible documente l'histoire du micro avec une série de photographies détaillées.

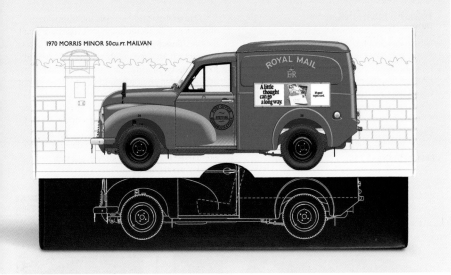

ROYAL MAIL

Creative Direction: Richard Scholey
Design: Harry Heptonstall, Mika Shephard
Illustration: Graeme Jenner
Company: The Chase
Country: UK
Category: Entertainment

SILVER PENTAWARD 2013

PHILIPS LIGHTING
HUE

Structural Packaging Design:
Flex/the Innovationlab
Communication Design: Iris Worldwide
Client: Philips Lighting
Company: Flex/the Innovationlab
Country: Netherlands
Category: Electronic & non-electronic

GOLD PENTAWARD 2013

This new personal wireless-lighting system allows people to create and control their home lighting from their personal smart device, changing colors or setting different shades of white according to choice. It can be used anywhere, and to create light settings based on favorite photos or by using expert light recipes or timers. The device of the color wheel attracts consumers and strongly conveys the possibilities of playful interactivity in a wordless manner, also adding value on an informative level—after opening the box, the reverse of the color wheel becomes a step-by-step installation guide.

Dieses neuartige funkgesteuerte Beleuchtungssystem erlaubt, dass Nutzer ihre Haushaltsbeleuchtung mit dem eigenen Smartphone bedienen und Farben beliebig ändern oder unterschiedliche Weißtöne einstellen. Es kann überall verwendet werden, es lassen sich Lieblingsfotos integrieren, Expertenlichtlösungen oder Timingfunktionen einsetzen. Das Farbrad des Systems spricht den Nutzer an. Es vermittelt eindrücklich die Möglichkeiten spielerischer Interaktivität ohne Worte und wertet somit auch die informative Ebene auf: Nach Öffnen der Verpackung wird die Rückseite des Farbrads zur schrittweisen Installationsanleitung.

Ce nouveau système d'éclairage sans fil pour la maison permet de contrôler l'illumination des pièces depuis un dispositif intelligent, de changer de couleur et de choisir différentes intensités de lumière blanche. Il peut être utilisé partout, permet de faire des réglages à partir de vos photos préférées et inclut des minuteries. La roue de couleurs est attrayante et illustre à elle seule les possibilités d'interactivité ludique. Elle a aussi une valeur informative : une fois la boîte ouverte, le dos de cette roue présente un guide détaillé d'installation.

CONTÉ À PARIS

Creative Direction:
David Turner, Bruce Duckworth
Design Direction: Jamie McCathie
Design: David Blakemore, Jamie McCathie
Photography: Craig Easton
Typography: Nick Cooke
Illustration: Geoffrey Appleton
Artwork: James Norris
Retouching: Peter Ruane
Company: Turner Duckworth,
London & San Francisco
Country: UK, USA
Category: Electronic & non-electronic

SILVER PENTAWARD 2013

Nicolas-Jacques Conté invented the graphite lead and the Carré pastel, which in 1795 led to the establishment of the **Conté à Paris** brand, specializing in sketching pencils and pastels. Instead of the usual uninspiring packaging, with sketches of still-lifes drawn using the contents of the particular set, these packs show scenes of Paris to inspire people to want to draw, tied to each set of colors. A set of black-only Conté pastilles features a black cat on a dark night walking on a Parisian cobbled street; a set of white shows the famous dome of Sacré Cœur cathedral: and the putty rubber sits in front of a Parisian rubbish cart. The logo is a redesign based on an old trademark Conté à Paris used in the 1800s.

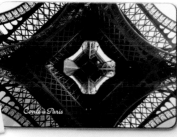

Nicolas-Jacques Conté erfand den modernen Graphitbleistift und die Carré-Pastellkreide. Das führte 1795 zur Gründung der Marke **Conté à Paris**, spezialisiert auf Zeichenbleistifte und Pastellkreiden. Man verzichtet auf die übliche, wenig inspirative Verpackung mit Stilllebenskizzen, wie man sie mit dem jeweiligen Inhalt zeichnen kann. Vielmehr zeigen diese Packungen je nach enthaltener Farbgruppe Pariser Momente, um Menschen zum Zeichnen zu inspirieren. Auf einer Packung mit schwarzer Zeichenkreide huscht eine schwarze Katze bei dunkler Nacht über Pariser Kopfsteinpflaster, die weiße Zeichenkreide krönt die berühmte Kuppel der Kathedrale Sacré Cœur, und das Radiergummi sitzt vor einem Pariser Kehrwagen. Das Logo wurde anhand eines alten, im 19. Jahrhundert von Conté à Paris verwendeten Warenzeichens neu designt.

Avec l'invention par Nicolas-Jacques Conté de la mine graphite et des pastels Carré, la marque **Conté à Paris** a vu le jour à Paris en 1795, se spécialisant en crayons et pastels. Au lieu de l'habituel emballage montrant des croquis de natures mortes faits avec le contenu du kit, ces boîtes présentent des images de Paris encourageant au dessin. Les scènes apparaissent dans plusieurs gammes de couleurs : un jeu de pastilles Conté noires représente un chat noir marchant la nuit dans une rue pavée parisienne, un jeu de blancs montre le célèbre dôme du Sacré Cœur, et une gomme mie de pain est placée devant un conteneur de poubelles de la ville. Le design du logo a été repensé à partir d'une ancienne marque Conté à Paris utilisée dans les années 1800.

SLICE

Design: Tom Crabtree,
Joshua Swanbeck, Eileen Lee
Company: Manual
Country: USA
Category: Non-electronic
GOLD PENTAWARD 2010

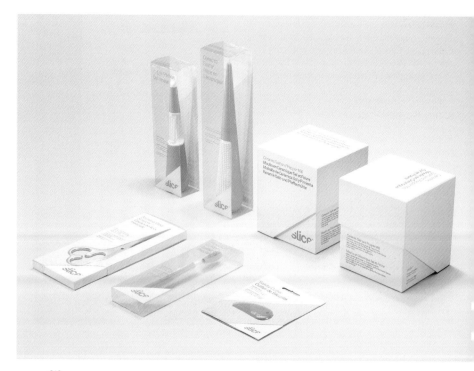

P AROUND

Design: Somchana Kangwarnjit,
Chidchanok Laohawattanakul,
Mathurada Bejrananda
Company: Prompt Design
Country: Thailand
Category: Non-electronic
BRONZE PENTAWARD 2011

MICHELIN
MOUNTAIN BIKE TYRES
Design: Sébastien Canu, Lorenzo Santangelo,
Florent Soissons, Claire Bourlange
Company: Japa
Country: France
Category: Automobile products
SILVER PENTAWARD 2010

PSA PEUGEOT CITROËN
STORE PACKAGING
Design: Pulp creative team
Company: Pulp
Country: France
Category: Automobile products
SILVER PENTAWARD 2011

KMC PINK LADY

Creative Direction: David Pan
Management Direction: Zoe Huang
Design: David Lin, Yihuey Lin, May Weng
Company: Gidea Group
Country: Taiwan
Category: Automobile products

GOLD PENTAWARD 2011

NOT FOR SALE

Creative Direction/Design: Tosh Hall
Design: Jessica Minn
Company: Hall
Country: USA
Category: Brand identity programs
SILVER PENTAWARD 2013

Not For Sale is a non-profit organization working to stop human trafficking, and to provide dignified work for women vulnerable to exploitation in Amsterdam and abroad—in Amsterdam alone, over 25,000 women work as prostitutes. With this series of products the aim was to create a story that was as powerful as the brand name and mission, to support the launch of Not For Sale Soup. In Amsterdam's red-light district, Not For Sale offers culinary training to people in need, helping them prepare soups that are sold to help women working in the brothels. Not For Sale transforms the exploited into the empowered, and with every jar of soup the women are promised a new future. This soup is Not for Sale. We are Not For Sale.

Die Non-Profit-Organisation **Not For Sale** setzt sich gegen Menschenhandel und Zwangsprostitution in Amsterdam und anderswo ein. Allein in Amsterdam arbeiten 25.000 Frauen als Prostituierte. Diese Produktserie setzt sich das Ziel, eine Story zu schaffen, die ebenso kraftvoll ist wie der Markenname und seine Mission, den Start der Not For Sale Soup. Im Rotlichtbezirk von Amsterdam bietet Not For Sale Kochkurse für Hilfsbedürftige an. Sie lernen Suppen zuzubereiten, deren Verkauf in Bordellen beschäftigten Frauen helfen soll. Not For Sale bringt ausgebeuteten Menschen ein Gefühl der Handlungsmacht zurück, und jeder Teller Suppe verspricht den Frauen eine neue Zukunft. Diese Suppe ist Not For Sale. Wir sind Not For Sale.

Not For Sale est une association à but non lucratif qui lutte contre la traite de personnes et pour offrir un travail digne aux femmes en risque d'exploitation à Amsterdam et dans le monde. Seulement à Amsterdam, plus de 25 000 femmes exercent la prostitution. Avec cette série de produits, l'objectif était d'inventer une histoire aussi puissante que le nom et la mission de l'association pour lancer Not For Sale Soup. Dans le quartier rouge d'Amsterdam, Not For Sale propose des formations culinaires aux personnes dans le besoin pour qu'elles préparent des soupes, lesquelles sont vendues pour aider les femmes travaillant dans les maisons closes. Not For Sale rend aux personnes exploitées leur autonomie et chaque pot de soupe donne à ces femmes l'espoir d'un avenir meilleur. Cette soupe est Not for Sale. Nous sommes Not For Sale.

COCA-COLA IDENTITY

Creative Direction:
David Turner, Bruce Duckworth
Design Direction: Sarah Moffat
Design: Jonathan Warner, Radu Ranga,
Josh Michels, Rebecca Williams, Chris Garvey
Company: Turner Duckworth,
London & San Francisco
Country: UK/USA
Category: Brand identity programmes
GOLD PENTAWARD 2009

Over the years, Coke's packaging had become covered in drips and bubbles, emulating the fizzy refreshment inside. As a generic approach, every other soft drink could also do the same. So **Coca-Cola** asked Turner Duckworth offices in London and San Francisco to create a visual identity system in line with Coke's "21st Century refreshment" strategy. They responded by removing extraneous elements to reveal that only Coke can have the Spencerian script and the ribbon design creating emotional resonance with the fewest possible elements.

Im Laufe der Zeit bekam die Verpackung von Coke immer mehr Tröpfchen und Bläschen, die die darin enthaltene sprudelnde Erfrischung nachahmen sollten. Doch einen solch allgemeinen Ansatz kann man auch bei jedem anderen Erfrischungsgetränk finden. Also beauftragte **Coca-Cola** die Büros von Turner Duckworth in London und San Francisco, ein System für die visuelle Identität zu schaffen, das zur Coke-Strategie einer „Erfrischung des 21. Jahrhunderts" passt. Turner Duckworth entfernten dafür überflüssige Elemente. So wurde deutlich, dass nur Coke mit dieser Kursivschrift, der Spencerian Script, und dem Ribbon Design, also den geringstmöglichen Elementen, für emotionale Resonanz sorgt.

Au cours des années, le packaging de Coca-Cola s'était couvert de gouttes et de bulles pour imiter la boisson pétillante qu'il contient. Comme les autres marques de soda pouvaient adopter la même démarche, **Coca-Cola** a demandé aux agences Turner Duckworth de Londres et San Francisco de créer un système d'identité visuelle cohérent avec la stratégie « boisson rafraîchissante du XXIᵉ siècle » de la marque. La réponse a été d'éliminer tous les éléments superflus pour révéler que seul Coca-Cola peut créer une résonance émotionnelle avec sa police Spencerian et son ruban, avec le moins d'éléments possible.

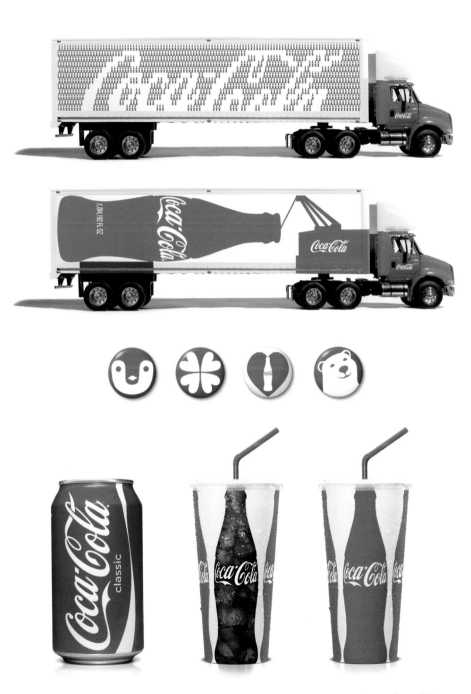

618

THE DELI GARAGE

Executive Creative Direction: Stefan Kolle
Creative Direction: Katrin Oeding
(Kolle Rebbe, Korefe)
Art Direction: Reginald Wagner
(Kolle Rebbe, Korefe)
Graphic Design: Jan Hartwig, Jan Simmerl,
Paul Svoboda, Santa Gustina
(Kolle Rebbe, Korefe)
Copywriting: Lorenz Ritter (Kolle Rebbe),
Till Grabsch, Katharina Trumbach,
Madelen Gwosdz (Kolle Rebbe, Korefe)
Production: Frank Witte
(Produktionsbüro Romey von Malottky),
Stephan Gerlach (Kolle Rebbe)
Company: Kolle Rebbe
Country: Germany
Category: Brand identity programmes
GOLD PENTAWARD 2010

COORS LIGHT

Executive Design Direction:
David Turner, Bruce Duckworth
Creative Direction: Mark Waters
Design Direction: David Thompson
Design: David Thompson, Matt Lurcock,
John Randall, Stuart Madden, Adam Cartwright
Production: James Norris, Will Rawlings
Visualization: Alex Poupard
Retouching: George Marshall, Peter Ruane
Account Management: Fay Bandoula, Kate Elkins
Company: Turner Duckworth, London & San Francisco
Country: UK, USA
Category: Packaging brand identity programs

GOLD PENTAWARD 2016

To combat ebbing sales in a changing market, **Coors Light** wanted to reach out to its occasional drinkers and younger, multi-cultural consumers. By reaffirming the beer's status as an American brand and an innovator in terms of its cold brewing, the Born in the Rockies redesign has a contemporary style and sets a template to build on in the 21st century, with its simple graphic for the mountains and redrawn logo being ideally suited for all media and consumer outlets. With extra visual elements also contributing, the identity system can be rolled out across packaging, tap handles, glassware and so on, with the outcome being a marked positive growth in sales.

Um gegen sinkende Verkaufszahlen in einem sich ändernden Markt zu kämpfen, will **Coors Light** Gelegenheitstrinker und jüngere Multikulti-konsumenten erreichen. Das Bier wird als amerikanische Marke rundenerneuert. Innovativ ist auch das Kaltbrauen. Das neue „Born in the Rockies"-Design setzt einen modernen Stil ein, auf dessen Grundstein man im 21. Jahrhundert bauen kann. Die einfache Berggrafik und das neu gezeichnete Logo passen ideal zu allen Medien und den Outlets für Verbraucher. Auch weitere visuelle Elemente helfen, die Identität über Verpackung, Zapfhähne, Gläser usw. einheitlich zu gestalten. Am Ende haben die Verkaufszahlen deutlich positiv angezogen.

Pour combattre le déclin des ventes sur un marché changeant, **Coors Light** voulait communiquer avec ses consommateurs occasionnels et son public jeune et multiculturel. En réaffirmant son statut de marque américaine et pionnière de la brasserie à froid, le nouveau design « Born in the Rockies » (Née dans les Rocheuses) adopte un style contemporain et donne le ton pour le XXIᵉ siècle, avec un graphisme simple pour les montagnes et un logo revu pour s'adapter à tous les médias et points de distribution. Ce système d'identité peut s'appliquer à tout l'emballage, aux manettes de tireuse, aux verres et pichets, etc. Il s'est traduit par une hausse des ventes.

AMERICAN RED CROSS VISUAL IDENTITY

Creative Direction: David Turner,
Bruce Duckworth, Sarah Moffat
Design: Britt Hull, Robert Williams
Lead Production: Craig Snelgrove
Photography: American Red Cross staff,
Turner Duckworth staff
Company: Turner Duckworth,
London & San Francisco
Country: UK, USA
Category: Brand identity programs
BRONZE PENTAWARD 2013

KOREAN MINISTRY OF CULTURE, SPORT AND TOURISM

Design: Paul Roeters, Jeroen Hoedjes
Company: Studio Kluif
Country: Netherlands
Category: Packaging brand identity programs

SILVER PENTAWARD 2016

COCO DE MER
PLEASURE COLLECTION

Creative Direction: Garrick Hamm
Design Direction: Fiona Curran
Design: Fiona Curran, Chris Ribet
Senior Account Direction: Emmanuelle Hilson
Company: Williams Murray Hamm
Country: UK
Category: Packaging brand identity programs

SILVER PENTAWARD 2016

Nell
PLEASURE SEED

Coco de Mer
LONDON

Catherine
PLEASURE BALLS

Coco de Mer
LONDON

Georgiana
PLEASURE WAND

Coco de Mer
LONDON

Radiant Bloom
ANAL LUBRICANT

Roseravished
MASSAGE OIL

Coco de Mer
LONDON

Coco de Mer
LONDON

Roseravished
MASSAGE OIL

TAHWA
BRUCE LEE

Design: TigerPan design team
Company: TigerPan Packaging Design Lab
Country: China
Category: Tobacco products

SILVER PENTAWARD 2014

GITANES
L'ESPRIT

Design: Gildas Boissier
Company: Enjoy Design
Country: France
Category: Tobacco products

GOLD PENTAWARD 2013

IVXX
PREMIUM QUALITY CANNABIS

Creative Direction: Carl Mazer
Design Direction: Teresa Diehl
Design: Sebastian Fraye, Miri Chan, Kimberley Bates,
Production Direction: Daryl Buhrman
Account Direction: Bill Larsen
Company: Anthem
Country: USA
Category: Tobacco products
BRONZE PENTAWARD 2015

BIC
FLICK MY BIC

Executive Creative Direction:
Sam J. Ciulla
Design Direction: Shelley Scheer,
Julie Wineski
Design: Krzysztof Tenenberg
Company: Ciulla Assoc.
Country: USA
Category: Tobacco products
SILVER PENTAWARD 2011

CAMACHO CIGARS
MASTER BUILT SERIES,
AMERICAN BARREL-AGED

Art Direction: Megan Reddish
Creative Direction: Michael Olsson,
Peter Smyth, Briana Lints
Executive Creative Direction:
Ben Applebaum
Account Management: John Simon,
Matt Snow, Amanda Torres
Copywriting: Steve Tredennick
Company: Colangelo
Country: USA
Category: Tobacco products
SILVER PENTAWARD 2016

PLUME & COMPAGNIE

Project Management: Hadrien Lecca
Design Direction: Marie-Pierre Fricou
Design: Marie Schockweiller
Company: Brand Union
Country: France
Category: Pet products

GOLD PENTAWARD 2014

WHISKAS
CATS PLAY HOUSE

Design: Guillermo Acevedo Beltran
Company: Vaya! Agency
Country: Colombia
Category: Pet products

BRONZE PENTAWARD 2013

AGRI RETAIL
BOERENBOND WELKOOP

Design: Tahir Idouri, Jobert van de Bovenkamp
Company: Millford
Country: Netherlands
Category: Pet products

SILVER PENTAWARD 2013

CAT LEADER

Creative Direction: Dimitris Gkazis
Design: Vicky Nitsopoulou
Copywriting: Nikos Paleologos
Company: Busybuilding
Country: Greece
Category: Pet products

SILVER PENTAWARD 2013

PETCUREAN
PET NUTRITION GO!

Creative Direction:
Matthew Clark, Roy White
Design: Matthew Clark
Copy: Pete Pallet, Jaimie Turkington,
Matthew Clark
Illustration: Liz Wurzinger (pet icons)
Photography: Go! Packaging
Pets: David Ellingsen
Production: Peel Plastics
Company: Subplot Design
Country: Canada
Category: Pet products

GOLD PENTAWARD 2012

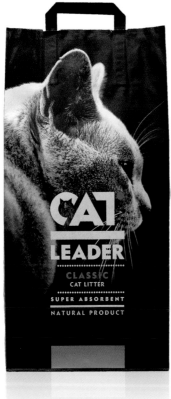
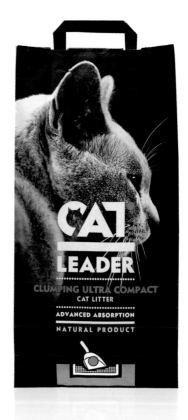

SAVOUR LIFE

Creative Direction: Ben Croft
Design: Evan Papageorgiou
Company: Channelzero
Country: Australia
Category: Pet products
SILVER PENTAWARD 2014

Damit die Packung für dieses neue Sortiment Hundefutter auch den meisterlichen Referenzen von **Vonziu Elite** gerecht wird und wirklich die Aufmerksamkeit des Verbrauchers bannt, setzte man den Vorfahren der Hunde in den Hauptfokus. Der Wolf in diesem klaren, ausgefeilten Design erhebt sich aus dem Schatten und blickt den Betrachter mit intensiven Augen an. Deren Farbcodierung weist auf die verschiedenen Varianten des Sortiments hin. Durch ein durchdachtes Montagesystem des dreifach laminierten Films der Tüten scheint silbernes Material in verschiedenen Stärken durch die weiße Farbe. Das sorgt mit dem Glanz der Grafik für fast 3-D-förmige Linsenbewegungen und ein glitzerndes Schillern – fast als wären die Augen lebendig.

Un loup ancestral a été placé au centre du concept afin que l'emballage de cette nouvelle gamme d'aliments pour chiens soit à la hauteur des performances de **Vonziu Elite** en championnats, ainsi que pour attirer l'attention des consommateurs. Sur le paquet épuré et sophistiqué, il émerge de l'ombre profonde et darde un regard pénétrant dont la couleur diffère selon les variantes de la gamme. Grâce à un système astucieux d'assemblage du film laminé en 3 couches des sacs, le matériau argenté brille à travers différentes épaisseurs d'encre blanche, afin que son éclat donne à l'image un mouvement lenticulaire presque tridimensionnel et donne l'impression que les yeux sont vivants.

VONZIU
ELITE PUPPY

Design: Mark Turner
Company: Kre8ive Partners
Country: UK
Category: Pet products
GOLD PENTAWARD 2016

To create a packaging design for this new range of dog food that lived up to the championship credentials of **Vonziu Elite** and would really catch the consumers' attention the ancestral wolf was used as the main point of focus. Emerging from the dark shadow of this clean, sophisticated design, the wolf stares out with penetrating eyes that are color-coded to distinguish each variety in the range. By means of a clever system of assembly for the 3-ply laminated film of the bags, silver material shines through different strengths of white tint so that the luster gives an almost 3D lenticular movement to the graphic and produces a shimmering irides-cence as if the eyes were alive.

STRANGER & STRANGER
ULTIMATE DECK

Creative Direction: Kevin Shaw
Design: Cosimo Surace, Ewa Oliver, Francesco Graziani
Company: Stranger & Stranger
Country: UK
Category: Self-promotion
GOLD PENTAWARD 2013

Every year Stranger & Stranger creates a limited-edition product to mark the festive season and celebrate success with the people who make it happen. Taking a decisive break from the customary Christmas bottle, on this occasion the agency elected to give out the **Ultimate Deck**, a pack of 54 picture cards from Dan and Dave. This departure commemorated the breaking-out from their comfort zone in 2012 to dabbling in fine foods, cosmetics and luxury luggage. For the first year, the agency also had a second limited batch produced, of just 100, and offered to the public for sale.

Jedes Jahr schaffen Stranger & Stranger als Sonderauflage ein Produkt, um die Feiertage am Jahresende zu betonen und mit jenen Menschen den Erfolg zu feiern, die ihn verdient haben. Man beschloss, sich deutlich von der üblichen Geschenkflasche zu Weihnachten abzusetzen: Die Agentur wählte für diese Gelegenheit das **Ultimate Deck**, ein Kartenspiel mit 54 Karten von Dan and Dave. Dieses Ausscheren feierte auch den Ausbruch von 2012 aus der Komfortzone: Seitdem versucht man sich in Feinkost, Kosmetik und luxuriösem Reisegepäck. Die Agentur hat in diesem Jahr auch zum ersten Mal eine zweite Auflage von insgesamt nur 100 Stück produzieren lassen, die in den öffentlichen Handel ging.

Chaque année, Stranger & Stranger sort un produit en édition limitée pour marquer le début des fêtes de fin d'année et célébrer les réussites avec les personnes y ayant contribué. Pour rompre avec la coutume de la typique bouteille pour Noël, l'agence a pour cette occasion choisi d'offrir **Ultimate Deck**, un jeu de 54 cartes illustrées par Dan et Dave. Ce choix est venu marquer la sortie de leur zone de confort en 2012 pour se lancer dans les produits gourmets, les cosmétiques et les bagages de luxe. Pour la première fois, l'agence a produit une seconde édition limitée de 100 unités seulement qu'elle a mises en vente.

DREAMCATCH

Creative Direction: Carole van Bekkum
Senior Creative Design: Léonie van Dorssen,
Rob van Berkel
Company: DreamCatch
Country: Netherlands
Category: Self-promotion

GOLD PENTAWARD 2015

STRANGER & STRANGER
EAU DE STRANGER

Design: Stranger & Stranger
Company: Stranger & Stranger
Country: UK
Category: Self-promotion

GOLD PENTAWARD 2016

Oft macht man sich wenig Gedanken bei Weihnachtsgeschenken. Doch bei diesem Give-away sollten die Kunden daran erinnert werden, dass die Agentur sich auf die Entwicklung von Verpackung für Weine und Spirituosen spezialisiert hat. Durch enge Zusammenarbeit mit Etikettenherstellern wurden die verfügbaren Techniken ausgenutzt. Variabler Datendruck führte zu verschiedenen Etiketten. Dazu band man die Gesichter von Team und Kunden ein und druckte jedes mit einer anderen Maskierung. Das Ergebnis: eine unmittelbar persönliche Verbindung zu den Kunden, die ihre eigenen Gesichter auf den Etiketten erkannten. Die jeweiligen Masken wurden mit verschiedenen Techniken gedruckt und daran verdeutlicht, welch kreative Ideen und Fähigkeiten Label and Litho bieten.

Pour ce concept, l'idée était de rappeler aux clients de l'agence sa spécialisation : les emballages pour vins et spiritueux. Le travail s'est réalisé en étroite collaboration avec les imprimeurs d'étiquettes afin de définir les techniques disponibles. Le résultat : une série d'étiquettes créées à l'aide de l'impression de données variables, ce qui permet d'utiliser les visages des membres de l'équipe et de clients avec un déguisement différent à chaque fois. La connexion s'établit immédiatement avec les acheteurs, qui peuvent reconnaître leur propre visage. Les déguisements sont imprimés à l'aide de différentes techniques pour mettre en valeur les capacités et la créativité de Label and Litho.

THE CREATIVE METHOD/
LABEL AND LITHO PRINTERS
XMAS LABEL

Design: Tony Ibbotson, Lee Nichol
Company: The Creative Method
Country: Australia
Category: Self-promotion
SILVER PENTAWARD 2016

If Christmas gifts are often given little thought the idea with these ones was to remind the agency's clients that they specialize in developing packaging for wine and spirit labels. Working closely with the label printers to establish what techniques were available led to a series of labels being created using variable data printing, which allowed the faces of staff and clients to be incorporated and printed each with a different disguise. The result was an immediate personal connection with the clients, who could see their own face on the labels, with the individual disguises being printed using different techniques to show off Label and Litho's capabilities and creative thinking.

DOGGIE DAZZLE
DOG GROOMING

Design: Mathilde Solanet (student)
School: CAD (College of Advertising & Design)
Country: Belgium
Category: Packaging concept

GOLD PENTAWARD 2012
BIC STUDENT PRIZE

MAGIC WIPES

Creative Direction: Kirill Konstantinov
Concept: Julia Turusheva
Design: Evgeny Morgalev
Company: Kian Branding Agency
Country: Russia
Category: Packaging concept
SILVER PENTAWARD 2012

Magic Wipes is a brand of paper napkins designed to be fun for children. Tissues that are sold in transparent plastic bags don't offer much scope for design, but the packaging for these wipes transforms our expectations in a simple way. Something very ordinary is turned into something amazing by the magician's top hat, and children can do tricks by pulling out a rabbit with white wipe ears. The packaging is made from recycled cardboard and has two rolls inside; when they are used up, the hat bottom can be easily removed and new rolls put in.

BOOLBOOL PACK

Design: Igor Palichev, Ramil Sharipov,
Dima Zeibert, Larisa Mamleeva
Company: Dark Design Group
Country: Russia
Category: Packaging concept

BRONZE PENTAWARD 2012

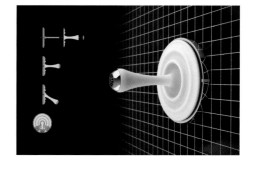

Magic Wipes ist eine Papierserviette, deren äußere Gestaltung Kindern Spaß machen soll. Wenn Papiertücher in transparenten Plastikhüllen verkauft werden, bietet das nur geringe Möglichkeiten fürs Design, aber die Verpackung dieser Serviette transformiert auf einfache Weise unsere Erwartungen. Etwas ganz Alltägliches verwandelt sich durch den Zauberzylinder in eine erstaunliche Sache. Die Kinder entdecken sich selbst als Zauberer, indem sie an weißen Serviettenohren ein Kaninchen hervorziehen. Die Verpackung besteht aus recyceltem Karton und enthält zwei Rollen Papier. Sind diese leer, öffnet man den Zylinderboden und tauscht sie aus.

Magic Wipes est une marque de lingettes en papier conçues pour les enfants. Les mouchoirs vendus dans des sachets en plastique transparent ne se prêtent guère à un design original, alors que l'emballage de ces lingettes déjoue nos attentes en toute simplicité. Le chapeau claque du magicien transforme un produit très ordinaire en jouet étonnant, et les enfants peuvent faire des tours en attrapant les oreilles de lapin que forment les lingettes. L'emballage est fabriqué en carton recyclé et contient deux rouleaux. Lorsqu'ils sont vides, il suffit d'ouvrir le fond du chapeau pour les remplacer.

ROTTEN' FRUIT

Design: Manon Fauvel (student)
Teacher: Jackie Stewart
School: ECV Paris
Country: France
Category: Packaging concept

SILVER PENTAWARD 2014

POILU

Design: Simon Laliberté (student)
Supervisor: Sylvain Allard
School: École de Design,
Université du Québec à Montréal (UQAM)
Country: Canada
Category: Packaging concept

GOLD PENTAWARD 2013
BIC STUDENT PRIZE

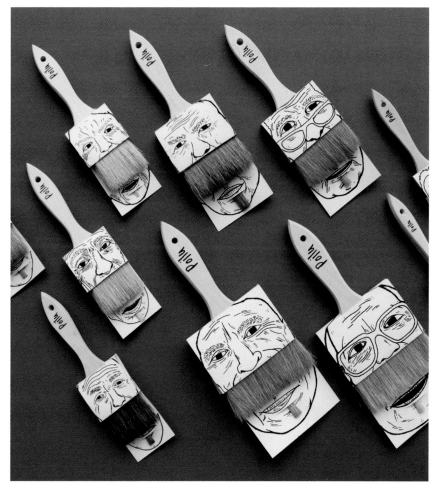

KINKY TOYS

Art Direction: Patrick De Grande; *Design:* Kobe De Keyzer
3D Artwork: Hendrik Colenbier
Company: Quatre Mains
Country: Belgium
Category: Packaging concept

SILVER PENTAWARD 2013

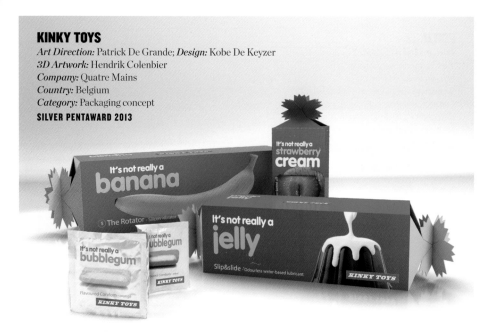

Even today, buying sex toys can still be a bit of a private activity. To avoid any sense of embarrassment this design builds on familiar comparisons between food and certain body parts, but in a playful way without being vulgar. The packaging looks like a special treat, with the bright colors and twisted ends combining sex and food like they were made for each other—see them as forbidden fruits, or an innocent but naughty snack. The "what" and "how" is covered on the reverse of the packaging, with the teasing image and "not really..." tagline left to do the work on the front. The inoffensive packaging is intended to appeal to the curious novice, as well as perhaps interesting non-specialized retailers and in turn reaching new consumers.

Auch heutzutage gehört der Kauf von Sexspielzeug eher zu den privaten Aktivitäten. Um jegliche Peinlichkeit zu vermeiden, spielt dieses Design auf die bekannten Vergleiche zwischen Essen und bestimmten Körperteilen an – aber spielerisch, ohne vulgär zu sein. Die Verpackung wirkt mit ihren leuchtenden Farben und den zusammengedrehten Enden wie ein besonderes Bonbon. Hier werden Sex und Lebensmittel kombiniert, als wären sie füreinander gemacht – man betrachte beide als verbotene Früchte oder als unschuldigen, aber unanständigen Snack. Das „Was" und „Wie" erscheint verdeckt auf der Packungsrückseite, um alles andere kümmern sich das verlockende Bild und der Slogan „Not really ..." der Vorderseite. Die unaufdringliche Verpackung spricht den neugierigen Neuling ebenso an wie vielleicht interessierte, nichtspezialisierte Einzelhändler, und so erreicht man wiederum neue Kunden.

CUTLERY
MR. KITCHEN SERIES

Creative Direction: Yoshio Kato
Art Direction: Yoshio Kato,
Mitsuharu Takehiro, Eijiro Kuniyoshi
Design: Naoki Mochizuki
Illustration: Bago Design
Company: Kotobuki Seihan Printing
Country: Japan
Category: Packaging concept
SILVER PENTAWARD 2016

Aujourd'hui encore, acheter des gadgets sexuels relève du domaine du privé. Pour éviter tout possible embarras, ce design repose sur des comparaisons courantes entre la nourriture et certaines parties du corps, d'une façon amusante et sans tomber dans le vulgaire. L'emballage fait penser à une collation, avec des couleurs vives et une forme de papillote. Il associe sexe et nourriture comme s'ils avaient été faits l'un pour l'autre, tels des fruits défendus ou un en-cas innocent mais osé. Le « quoi » et le « comment » figurent au dos de l'emballage, avec l'image taquine et le slogan « not really ... » à l'avant qui fait passer le message. L'emballage inoffensif a été conçu pour attirer le novice curieux, mais aussi intéresser les commerces non spécialisés cherchant à capter de nouveaux clients.

Die Rezepturen für diese gekühlten „Hunde-Fertiggerichte" könnten auch Herrchen und Frauchen schmecken und sie die Mahlzeiten mit ihren Haustieren teilen lassen. Schon vorgekocht wird dieses Sortiment aus der Packung heraus warm oder kalt serviert. Wie ein feines Essen ähnlen die Gerichte aus gesunden Zutaten mit verschiedenem Geschmack wohl dem, was bei Tisch übrig bleibt. Das Hausschuh-Design erinnert an etwas, in das zu beißen ein Hund kaum widerstehen kann. Die je nach Rezeptur verschieden gestaltete Verpackung setzt den Inhalt spielerisch-unterhaltsam um. Das Trockenfutter „Dog's Breakfast" ist in Pillow Packs verpackt, die einer zusammengerollten Zeitung ähnlen – einem weiteren beliebten Hunde-„Snack", der morgens durch den Briefschlitz fällt.

Cette gamme de repas réfrigérés pour chiens se base sur des recettes que leurs maîtres aimeraient partager avec eux. Précuisinés, ils peuvent être servis chauds ou froids, directement dans leur emballage-plateau. Dignes de restes d'un repas qui finiraient dans la gamelle du chien, les mélanges incluent des ingrédients sains et tout un éventail de saveurs. Le design de la pantoufle, avec laquelle tout chien aime jouer, est décliné dans plusieurs styles attrayants en accord avec les recettes. « Dog's Breakfast » est une gamme d'aliments secs présentés dans un emballage qui imite un journal roulé, autre objet que les chiens aiment attraper.

DOG'S DINNER

Design: Chris MacDonald,
Kelly Bennett, Moyra Casey
Company: Afterhours
Country: UK
Category: Packaging concept
GOLD PENTAWARD 2014

A range of chilled 'ready meals' for dogs based on recipes their owners might enjoy and share with their pets, precooked, so they can be served hot or cold in the tray. Healthy ingredients and a range of flavors are presented in a mashed-up mix, just like the leftovers from a meal: in fact, a bit of a 'dog's dinner'. The slipper design—something a dog can't resist getting its teeth into—comes in different styles to match the recipes in a playful, engaging way. The 'Dog's Breakfast' is a range of dried food packaged in 'rolled newspaper'-style pillow packs, another favorite 'snack' for dogs as it falls through the letterbox in the morning.

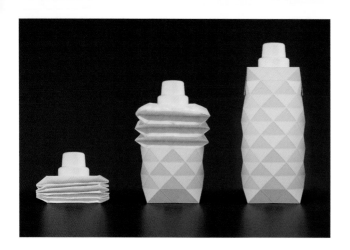

CLEANTEX
Design: Aliia Glimkhanova (student)
School: British Higher School of Art & Design (Moscow)
Country: Russia
Category: Packaging concept
BRONZE PENTAWARD 2016

AMBER
Design: Tanya Chursina (student)
School: British Higher School of Art & Design (Moscow)
Country: Russia
Category: Packaging concept
SILVER PENTAWARD 2016

DULUX
KIDS SPACE

Creative Direction: Paul Williams
Visualization: Stuart Witter
Company: Springetts Brand Design Consultants
Country: UK
Category: Packaging concept

GOLD PENTAWARD 2016

PENTAWARDS JURY

MICHAEL AIDAN
France
Danone Waters

Graduated in marketing from ESCP, Paris, in 1988. + Brand Manager at P&G and YSL international perfumes division. + Account & Marketing Director at Cato Gobe & Associates, New York. + Marketing Manager from 1993 to 2006, responsible for major brands at Pepsico (Lays, Pepsi-Cola, Tropicana). + VP Marketing at Danone Waters. + Lecturer in master's degree classes at ESCP-EAP and HE.

JACOB BERGSTRÖM
Sweden
Brand & Executive
Creative Director,
Designkontoret Silver

Graduated from Grafiskt Utbildningscenter and Berghs School of Communication in Graphic Communication, Marketing Communication and Strategic Marketing. + Started his career at SDR Reklambyrå in 1992 and since 2010 has been Brand & Creative Director at Silver, working for clients such as ICA, Cervera, Orkla Foods, Mondelēz, Actavis and OBH Nordica. + Jury member for Guldägget (Design), Cannes Young Lions (Design), Resumé Månadens Design, and the Pentawards.

OLEG BERIEV
Russia
Mildberry Brand
Building Solutions

Born in 1967, started his career in marketing in 1990. + His career spans being head of sales for an import/export company to being vice-president of marketing of one of the largest Russian companies. + Set up the Mildberry agency in 1999, the first Russian packaging-design agency and currently the leader on the Russian market with branches in Brussels, London, and Milan.

GÉRARD CARON
France
Chairman, Pentawards
International Jury

Regarded as the founder of marketing design in France and Europe. Set up Carré Noir in 1973 (today a member of the Publicis group). + Co-founder and former president of PDA (Pan-European Brand Design Association). + Author of many publications, organizer of conferences and seminars. + Designed the most complete website for design www.admirabledesign. com + Has created no fewer than 1,200 brand identities and 13,000 package designs.

MOYRA CASEY
United Kingdom
Creative Partner,
Afterhours

Graduated in 1997 from the Glasgow School of Art and started her career at Springetts (UK). + Specialized in brand identity and packaging. + Clients include: Twinings, AkzoNobel, P&G, Noble Foods and Mondelēz International. + Awards: 10 Pentawards including Platinum and Gold, several Fab Awards (including a Fabulous) and also Fresh, Dieline and Mobius awards (including a best in show).

STANLEY CHURCH
USA
Founder, Chief Creative Officer, Wallace Church

Graduate and former faculty member of Parsons School of Design. + Member of the Art Directors' Club, AIGA, Type Directors' Club, and Design Management Institute. + Judge in national and international design competitions. + Guest speaker at different organisations around the USA. + Winner of several Awards: at the Art Directors' Club, AIGA, ADLA, the Advertising Club of New York's ANDY, the CLIO Gold & Silver, and at Pentawards.

ASA COOK
United Kingdom
Creative Director
Design Bridge

A Creative Director at Design Bridge London, where he has worked since 2002, focusing primarily on branding and packaging. + Various design accolades include those won at the following competitions: the Scottish Design Awards, the New York Festivals, Communication Arts Awards, DBA Design Effectiveness Awards, the Design Week Awards and numerous Pentawards. + Asa is heavily involved in student education both for Design Bridge and D&AD, and in 2012 set and judged the D&AD student packaging brief. In 2013, he was a judge for the Design Week awards and was Chair of the packaging design jury in 2013.

MARK COWAN
Australia
Founder, Managing Director, Cowan

Started his career in the Safeway Head Office in Melbourne as a grocery buyer and special projects marketer. + This led to Mark becoming a keen judge of packaging communication and an excell predicting success rates of new launches. + In 1987, Mark launched Cowan, a consumer brand communications company. + Cowan is now the largest consumer brand design agency in Australia. + Offices in Melbourne, Sydney, London, Auckland, Shanghai, Beijing, and Ho Chi Minh City. + Clients include blue chip FMCG brands such as Coca-Cola, Arnotts, Yoplait, Heinz, Nestlé, and Uncle Toby.

ISABELLE DAHLBORG LIDSTRÖM
Sweden
Creative Director and Managing Partner, Nine

Graduated from Berghs School of Communication and Beckmans Designhögskola in Sweden. + More than 20 years' experience in the international design industry in NYC, Copenhagen and Stockholm. + A passion for solving business challenges by using structural and graphic design, form and function, paired with a deep understanding of the challenges of business and industry. + Awards include: Pentawards – Diamond: Best of Show and several Silver awards; Green Good Design Award, Red Dot Design Award, IF Award, the Water Innovation Awards, three times Bronze at Guldägget design awards, IDEA silver. + Clients include: Altia, Astra Tech, Tetra Pak, BillerudKorsnäs, Absolut, SCA and Carlsberg. + Member of the Berghs School of Communication Advisory Board since 2010 and the Design Committee of the Swedish Association of Communication Agencies. + Design juries: Eurobest, Guldägget, Core 77, Kolla and LIA.

RAF DE GEYTER

Belgium
Principal Design Manager,
P&G

Master's in Industrial Design, Artesis Hogeschool Antwerp. + Master's in Marketing Management, Vlerick Leuven Gent Management School, Ghent. + Joined Procter & Gamble in 1998, gaining 15 years' experience in leading package and product design for brands such as Ariel, Lenor, Dreft, Tide, Swiffer, and Mr. Clean. + Currently responsible for upstream design innovation programs in fabric care.

DAN DITTMAR

USA
Director of Brand Design,
BIC USA

BS Graphic Design, University of Maryland. + MS Organizational Leadership, Quinnipiac University. + Previous experience leading brand design and packaging identity for the Campbell Soup Company across multiple product categories. + Currently leading brand and packaging identity for all BIC branded categories (BIC Stationery, BIC Lighter and BIC Shaver portfolio segments). + Previous Presenter at Design Management Institute International Conference. + Presenter at Destination Design Management Conference AIGA Metro-North Speaker Panelist.

BRUCE DUCKWORTH

United Kingdom
Founding partner of
Turner Duckworth

Bruce established Turner Duckworth in 1992 with David Turner, specialising in brand identity and packaging. + Based in London, Bruce is jointly responsible with David Turner for the creative output of both studios for clients as varied as the Coca-Cola Company, Homebase, Shaklee, Johnson & Johnson and Metallica. + Over 200 international design awards including: Cannes Festival Inaugural Design Lions Grand Prix 2008, D&AD Silver Award, DBA Design Effectiveness Award, Clio Awards, Design Week Awards, LIAA, Pentawards, FAB Awards Agency of the Year 2008, Creativity Awards, EPICA, Graphis. + Judging stints: ADC New York's 87th Annual Design jury, D&AD Awards, Design Week Awards, LIAA Royal Society of Arts Student Design Awards, Pentawards 2009/2010. + Lectures/Speeches: numerous lectures at art colleges and universities/British Council, Design Council, International Institute of Research, The Design Show.

MARTIN GRIMER

United Kingdom
Global Creative Director,
Blue Marlin

Joined Blue Marlin as Global Creative Director in January 2006 after leaving his role as Creative Director at Coley Porter Bell. + Martin has 15 years' experience as a Creative Director, and an industry profile built around outstanding creative work with Unilever, Cadbury, Pernod Ricard, Kimberly-Clark, BAT, Nestlé, and GlaxoSmithKline. + He has numerous accolades under his belt, including a Clio Gold & Best of Show Award, a Design Week award, a DBA Design Effectiveness award, and a Pentaward. + Has also been nominated numerous times for a D&AD, and has been a member of many juries in recent years.

LAURENT HAINAUT

USA
President and Founder
of Force Majeure

A founding member and partner of Force Majeure, an international design house established in New York in 1998, with offices in New York City and Paris. + An industrial designer by training, the French-born Hainaut has almost 30 years' experience in visual strategy, brand identity, product design, packaging design, retail environments & experiences, consumer product innovation and global design management. + Clients include: Unilever, Diageo, PepsiCo, Danone Waters, L'Oréal, and many others.

DAYTON HENDERSON
USA
Senior Director, Global Design,
Kimberly-Clark Co.

Began his career as a graphic designer before joining Kimberly-Clark in 1984. + Held varied and progressive design leadership roles for the company while gaining experience across its brands and businesses. + Under the leadership of Lisa Hurwitz, the K-C design team is responsible for brand design strategies, resources, deployment and training to build K-C's Consumer and Professional businesses globally. + Awards include: a Diamond, Gold and Silver Pentawards.

ANDRÉ HINDERSSON
Sweden
Creative Director and
Co-founding Partner
of Silver in Stockholm

His design work embraces brand and company identities, services and packaging design for a wide range of clients ranging from iconic global brands such as Oriflame and H&M to local heavy-metal record labels. + He lives in Stockholm but has had a second home in London since his student years at CSM. + A specialist in cosmetic packaging for years, André always aims to bring out the personality of the product, often adding a humorous twist. + Holds an MA in Communication Design from Central Saint Martins college (CSM) in London and a BA from Grafiska Institutet at Stockholm University.

BRIAN HOUCK
USA
Director, Creative Services,
the Dial Corporation,
a Henkel Company

Bachelor of Fine Arts, Northern Arizona University. + Previous experience includes advertising for diverse companies in the Southwest and event design and staging for clients such as Norelco and Delta Airlines. + Has led the package design for Dial brands for 21 years

including Dial Soap, Right Guard Antiperspirant, Purex Detergents, Renuzit Air Fresheners and Soft Scrub Cleansers. + Winner of numerous industry awards in package design and printing.

SOMCHANA KANGWARNJIT
Thailand
Executive Creative Director,
Prompt Design

Graduated from King Mongkut's Institute of Technology Ladkrabang with a degree in Industrial Design. + Founded Prompt Design in 2009. + Clients include Nestlé, Pfizer, CP, Singha, Meiji, Lotte, Kimberly-Clark, Friesland Campina, Diageo and Berli Jucker. + Jury member for various design competitions and President of Thai Package Design Association (ThaiPDA). + Guest columnist for different publishers as well as professor at top universities. + Awards include: Platinum, Gold, Silver and Bronze Pentawards, Asian Young Designer of the Year from Designnet, the Dieline Awards, Red Dot Design Awards, Fab Awards, Spark Awards, Communicator Awards and ASIA Star Packaging Award.

YOSHIO KATO
Japan
Creative Director,
Suntory Beverage & Food

Graduated from Aichi Prefectural University of Fine Arts and Music (major in Design) in 1979. + Joined Suntory Design Department in 1979. + 1997: Creative Director and General Manager, Suntory's Design Department. + 2011: Senior Specialist and Creative Director, Suntory Design Department. + 1997: Vice-chairman of the Board, Japan Package Design Association. + 2014: President of the Japan Package Design Association; member of Japan Graphic Designers Association. + 2003–2014: Part-time lecturer at Tokyo-Art University of Fine Art and Music. + 1997–2014: Part-time lecturer at Aichi University of Fine Arts and Music. + 2008–2014: Part-time lecturer at Tama Art University Department of Graphics.

KYU-WOO KU
South Korea
Managing Director,
Aekyung Design Centre

Graduated from Dankook University in 1983.
+ Joined Aekyung Industrial Design Department
in 1991. + External positions: President of Korea
Package Design Association, Vice-president of
Korea Design Management Association. + Design
Organization Member of the Asian Games
Organizing Committee for 2014.

JEREMY LINDLEY
United Kingdom
Global Design Director,
Diageo

Responsible for design across Diageo's current
brands and new products worldwide, including
Johnnie Walker, Crown Royal, J&B, Windsor,
Buchanan's and Bushmills whiskies, Smirnoff,
Ciroc and Ketel One vodkas, Baileys, Captain
Morgan, Tanqueray and Guinness. + Prior to
joining Diageo he was Head of Design for Tesco
and spent his early career working as a design
consultant and university lecturer. + Graduated
with an Honours Degree in Design, he is also a
Fellow of the Royal Society of Arts and is active
in a number of design industry bodies.

ANNA LUKANINA
Russia
Executive Director and
Partner, Depot WPF

Vice-president at European Packaging Design
Association (EPDA) and representative of Global
Local Branding Alliance in Russia, with over ten
years' experience in marketing. + In 2002 joined
Depot WPF and since 2009 has been its managing
director. + In 2008 joined the executive committee
of EPDA, serving as its president in 2011–13. +
Winner of the 2014 Philip Kotler Marketing
Award in the Branding category and named
Russian Media Manager the same year. + Speaker
at the World Communication Forum in Davos
(Switzerland) and at Interpack (Germany).

+ Jury member of various marketing competitions
and festivals, including the Silver Mercury Festival
(representing the Globes Award in Russia), Dairy
Innovation Awards (UK), Golden Label Award
(Austria) and International Beer Award (USA).

SARAH MOFFAT
USA
Executive Creative Director,
Turner Duckworth

Born and raised in the north of England, she has
been with Turner Duckworth since graduating
from Kingston University with a degree in Graphic
Design. + Since then her time has been divided
between London and San Francisco over the last
18 years. + Responsible for the strategic and
creative output of the US studio, as well as the
constant exchange of ideas and design critiques
for the London studio. + Clients include: the
Coca-Cola Company, Mondelēz, Google, Visa,
Levi's and MillerCoors. Awards include: a Cannes
Lions Grand Prix, a Grammy, D&AD, Clio Hall of
Fame and several Pentawards.

YOJI NOBUTO
Japan
Art Director at Shiseido

Born in Tokyo in 1966. + Graduated from the
School of Art at Tokyo University in 1992. +
Started his career at Shiseido in 1992. + Worked
at Shiseido, New York, and is at present working
in Tokyo. + In charge of various design projects
chiefly for cosmetics. + Has won several awards:
Tokyo Art Directors' Club ADC Awards
2002/2004. + Gold Awards of Japan Package
Design Awards 2003/2005, Japan Grand Awards
of Package Design Awards 2005, Merit Awards
of New York Art Directors' Club Awards, D&AD
Awards, Excellent Awards of Japan Display
Design Awards, among others.

ELIE PAPIERNIK
France
Managing Partner & Creative
Director, Centdegrés

Graduated from the Ecole Nationale Supérieure de Création Industrielle, and co-founded the independent international design agency Centdegrés in 1988. + His working ethos can be described in the following phrases: Search for meaning and give it shape. + Talents working together create value in a broad sense. + The quest for accuracy, for the essential. + Working to create beautiful brands, but also to advance the world. + Think big, open, new. Believe.

ADRIAN PIERINI
Argentina
Founder and General Creative
Director, Pierini Partners

Graduated, with honours, as a graphic designer in 1992. + Pierini Partners develops branding and packaging designs for companies in Argentina, Brazil, Mexico, China, Japan, Colombia, Paraguay, and the UK. + Started his professional career in some of the most prestigious design studios in Argentina, the USA, and Mexico. + Teaches courses on such subjects as "Design and Brand Image", "Packaging Design", and "Introduction to Strategic Design" in a private university in Argentina, and gives a number of seminars on design in universities and institutions in Argentina, Bolivia, Chile, Colombia, Ecuador, Mexico, Peru, and Paraguay. + He has written various articles for specialised media and "Designers Go!" on applied methodology oriented to students and young professionals (Comm Tools Editorial, 2006).

CHRIS PLEWES
Canada
Vice-president and Creative
Director, Davis Design

Creative Director at Davis Design with over 30 years of branding and package design experience. + Having resided in Singapore and Toronto, he has extensive experience in global and regional brands.

+ With Davis he is active on large and small branding assignments in US, Canadian, European and Asian markets.

CHRISTOPHE PRADÈRE
France
CEO and Founder,
BETC Design Paris

Master's in design from Domus Academy in Milan in 1992. + Euro RSCG Design 1995–2000: responsible for the retail and corporate design divisions of clients such as Air France, Peugeot and also luxury brands such as Lancôme and Christofle. + Founded BETC Design in 2001. + Focus on global design and design management approaches in the creative industry markets for customers including: Orange, Air France, Peugeot, Louis Vuitton, Rémy Martin, Louis XIII, Chivas, Jean-Paul Gaultier, L'Oréal and Piper Heidsieck. + He develops his brand experience through a holistic approach combining social sciences, marketing and global creative strategy. + Lecturer posts: Parsons School for Design, IFM, ESSEC, École Nationale Supérieure des Arts Décoratifs and SKEMA Business School.

JONATHAN SANDS
United Kingdom
Chairman, Elmwood

Jonathan Sands led a management buyout of Elmwood in 1989, aged 27. + With offices in Asia, North America and Europe, Elmwood is an ideas-based branding business and Jonathan in particular always has the courage of his convictions. + Clients include: ASDA, BBC, Durex, The COI, Glasgow 2014, McCain, Royal Mail, Nestlé and Nike.

GRAHAM SHEARSBY
United Kingdom
Group Creative Director,
Design Bridge

Born in East London, Graham entered the creative world in 1979, straight from school. + Joined the John Blackburn Partnership as a studio junior and won a D&AD Yellow Pencil for Typography for Cockburn's Ports in 1985. + Joining Allied International Designers in 1986, he met his future partners in what would, later that year, become the fledgling Design Bridge. + Graham has spearheaded the company's creative growth and seen it acquire a wealth of international awards.

JAMIE STONE
Singapore
Global Head of Design/
Nutrition, GSK

A UK-born graduate of Northumbria University, Design for Industry Degree in 2001. + Worked as an in-house designer for P&G, before setting up Stone|Product Design, offering 3D and 2D design services to the multitude of P&G brand teams. Stone|Product Design merged into NewEdge in early 2008. + Partner and Head of Design for NewEdge, a UK/USA-based Design/Strategy/ Research agency with a focus on NDP pipelines for FMCG clients such as P&G, Kellogg's and Kraft. + Based in Singapore, with a seat on the Nutrition Leadership team, he is responsible for all creative strategy and output in 3D Structural Design, Technical Design, Branded Package Design, BTL and In-Store Activation for the full Nutrition & Digestive Health portfolios.

OLOF TEN HOORN
Australia
Design Director, The Key

Discovered his passion for Packaging Design in the course of an internship 20 years ago and has since worked for a long list of global brands, gaining much local experience in European, African and Asian markets. + Specializes in FMCG Packaging

and Branding, and as a Design Director and Creative Director he has won all varieties of Pentawards, including the coveted Diamond Pentaward in 2007.

JENNIFER TSAI
Taiwan
Managing and Creative
Director, Proad Identity

Taiwan's Top 10 for excellence and China Outstanding Woman. + Jury of iF Communication Design Award 2008, Red Dot Communication Design Award 2008. + Honoured for her work in branding design with 30 awards, including iF, red dot, Pentawards, and Good Design Awards. + In a fusion of Eastern and Western culture, she devoted herself to presenting the Eastern elements in Western design and to working on linking international alliances and associations, such as Global Design Source, Pan-European Brand Design Association, and Total Identity in Amsterdam.

GREGORY TSAKNAKIS
Greece
Creative Director and
Manager, Mousegraphics

Born in Thessaloniki in 1963, he studied Graphic Design at the Technological Institute in Athens and started Mousegraphics at almost the same time. + With some luck, attitude and, of course, great love for design, he started working on packaging design. + Mousegraphics today employs 11 people working on projects in all fields of visual branding. + Awards include: Pentawards, Epica Award, Red Dot Communication Design Award, German Design Award, the Dieline, European Design Award, Ermis Award, and the Greek Graphic Design & Illustration Award.

TAKESHI USUI
Japan
Deputy Director,
the Pola Museum of Art,
and the Pola Art Foundation

+ Graduated from Aichi Prefectural University of Fine Arts and Music (Major in Design) in 1979 and joined the advertising department of Pola Inc. + In 1985 moved to the Design Laboratories of Pola Chemical Industries, Inc., with responsibility for package design, container and package development together with direction of cosmetics, medicines and health foods as in-house designer. + Directed design and museum goods for the Pola Museum of Art before being appointed Creative Director and General Manager, Design Department in 2000 and then in 2005, Head of Design Laboratories of Pola Chemical Industries, Inc. + Since 2012, Deputy Director of the Pola Museum of Art, Pola Art Foundation. + Awards: Gold, Silver and Bronze Pentawards, Japan Packaging Competition Grand Prix, London International Awards Winner, the New York PDC Gold Prize, Red Dot Design Award, iF Design Award, New York Festivals Finalist, WorldStar Winner, Japan Package Design Association Gold Prize.

LARS WALLENTIN
Switzerland
Designer of training courses

Born in Sweden and resident of Switzerland. + Worked for 40 years at Nestlé in its design department. + International reference in design management. + Teaches and organises conferences all over the world. + Involved in thousands of international packaging projects at Nestlé. + Author of numerous articles and publications on communication by design. + Launched in 2010 the website devoted to packaging design: www.packagingsense.com

ROY WHITE
Canada
Co-Founder and Creative Partner, Subplot Design

Began his career at The Partners, and Carroll, Dempsey and Thirkell in London, before founding The Third Man, working with clients such as Virgin Records and the Royal Opera House. + Moved to Australia in the early 1990s and worked on Olympics-related branding projects, most notably the Olympic Village and Olympic Stadium identities. + In 1998 he moved to Canada, and formed Subplot in 2003, one of the country's most respected packaging design consultancies. + Commendations and awards include: Creative Review, AR 100, Society of Graphic Designers of Canada, Graphis, HOW, Graphics World, Australian Designers Association, Lotus Awards, New York Festivals, Applied Arts, Coupe Awards and Pentawards.

ADRIAN WHITEFOORD
United Kingdom
Pemberton & Whitefoord

Graduated with a 1st Class Honours Degree from Maidstone College of Art in 1983, then proceeded to complete a Postgraduate Degree at the Royal College of Art. + Agency experience includes: Conran Associates, The Partners and Lewis Moberly. + Formed Pemberton & Whitefoord (P&W) in 1987 with Simon Pemberton. + Clients include: Tesco, Nestlé, Colgate Palmolive, M&S, and Seicomart (Japan). + P&W were the only UK design consultancy commissioned to design own-brand packaging for Fresh & Easy (Tesco's first retail venture in the USA). + P&W have won over 60 international design and marketing awards.

YUAN ZONGLEI
China
Chief Designer, Shanghai Inoherb Cosmetics

Awarded Bachelor of Fine Arts, Shanghai Institute of Technology, and started his career at Shanghai Jahwa in 1992, in charge of various design projects, essentially for Packaging, Display Design and Interior Design. + Has worked since August 2015 at Shanghai Chicmax Cosmetics Company. + Winner of numerous industry awards in packaging design.

INDEX

Symbols

2yolk Branding & Design, *281*
5.5 designstudio, *207, 525*
12 Degree Branding, *513*

A

ADK, *34*
Aekyung Industrial, *565*
Afterhours, *363, 417, 651*
Akaoni Design, *108*
Alnoor Design, *435*
Amelung Design, *587*
Ampro Design Consultants, *215*
Anthem, *343, 550, 628*
ARD Design Switzerland, *316*
Armbrand, *557*
Aruliden, *85, 579, 603*
Atelier Casanova, *491*

B

BabyQ Shop, *375*
Baccarat, *538*
Backbone Branding, *80, 100, 227, 301, 556*
BAS, *328*
Beetroot Design Group, *257, 518*
Bek Tasarim, *74, 316*
Betc Design, *31, 75, 500*
Bex Brands, *101*
BIC USA, *392*
Big Dog Creative, *129*

Big Fish, *308*
Billy Blue College of Design, *227*
Bisquit, *502*
Blue Marlin Brand Design, *72*
Bob Studio, *158*
Bonnemazou Cambus, *516*
Bosin Design, *270, 305*
Brandever, *142, 276*
Brandhouse, *140, 180, 537*
Brandimage – Desgrippes & Laga, *433, 437, 471*
Brandnew, *306, 580*
Brand Society, *321*
Brand Union, *168, 197, 482, 530, 630*
Bravis International, *302*
British Higher School of Art & Design (Moscow), *333, 341, 342, 415, 417, 652*
Bullet, *64*
Busybuilding, *632*
Button Button, *185*

C

CAC 110 Creativity Advertising, *249*
CAD, *642*
Cadú Gomes Design, *218*
Calcco, *163*

Cameo Metal Products, *467*
Canaria, *400*
Carré Basset, *438*
Cartils, *90*
CBX, *241*
Centdegrés, *441*
Channelzero, *634*
Chaohong Fu HD Design, *110*
Chen, Alan, *125*
China (Shenzhen) Superman Valley Marketing, *175*
Ciulla Assoc., *629*
Cloud8, *386, 390, 391*
CMGRP Italia, *383*
The Coca-Cola Company, *38, 82, 188, 201*
Coca-Cola UK, *197*
Colangelo, *629*
Coley Porter Bell, *326, 426, 463*
Communication Design Laboratory, *455, 459, 532*
Container, *393*
Corretjé Comunicació Gràfica, *143*
Cosmos, *144*
Cowan Design, *134, 210, 240*
Crown Speciality Packaging, *320*
Cumbria Crystal, *538*
Curious Design, *121, 178*

D

Dapy/Do International, *208, 490, 499, 507, 524, 540*
Dark Design Group, *374, 645*
Davis, *262*
dBOD, *56, 199*
Degree Design, *511*
Delamata Design, *87*
del Fraile, Eduardo, *60, 157, 161, 260, 380, 533*
Dentsu Kyushu Inc., *431*
DeOfficina, *278*
Depot WPF, *162, 254, 257, 324*
Design Bridge, *75, 134, 136, 176, 179, 242, 527*
Design Bridge Amsterdam, *28, 289*
Designers Journey, *162*
Designers United, *520*
Designkontoret Silver, *372, 396, 585*
Designworks, *128*
Dessein, *364*
Devours Bacon, *271*
Deziro, *319*
Diadeis, *190*
Diageo, *538*
Digital Fish, *548*
Dipco, *399*
Dom Perignon, *499*
Dorian, *166*
Dragon Rouge, *420*
DreamCatch, *638*

Dreamglobe Branding Design, *76*
Dutch Design House, *137*

E

ECV Paris, *646*
Elmwood, *599*
Emart, *592*
Enjin, *264, 290*
Enjoy Design, *627*
Enprani, *389*
Enric Aguilera Asociados, *341*
Established, *45, 409, 442, 444, 453*
Etude, *348, 390, 398, 399*
Evian (Danone Group), *43, 75, 192, 193*

F

Family Business, *40*
Flex/the Innovationlab, *606*
Force Majeure Design, *469, 538*
Freyland, Heiko, *347*
Fritz Müller, *157*
Future Brand, *298, 383, 499*

G

Gidea Group, *613*
GK Graphics, *274*
Gloji, *78*
Good!, *555, 560*

Graeme Bridgeford, *497*
Grand Angle Design, *43*
Grenache Bottle Design, *68*
Gworkshop Design, *596*

H

Hall, *145, 615*
Hamilton & Inches, *538*
Hangzhou Dongyun Advertising Design, *250*
Hang Zhou Wahaha Group, *248*
Happy Plugs, *594*
Happytear, *50*
Hardy Cognac, *536*
Harry Allen Design, *380, 434*
Hatch Design, *146*
Here Design, *422*
Horse, *62*
House of Sillage, *540*

I

Identis, *566*
Identity Works, *588*
ID kommunikation, *256*
Imkm Design, *226*
Insight Creative, *124*
In Spirit Design, *79*
Insus, *549*
Invigor8tion, *538*
Iris Amsterdam, *56, 199*
Istratova, Alexandra, *228*

J

Japa, *612*
Jian Wei Miao, *485*
Jia Tian, *250*
J Inc., *264*
JJ Bertran Studio, *150*
Jones Knowles Ritchie, *47, 138, 187*

K

Kao Corporation, *384*
Karim Rashid Inc., *70, 85, 89, 96, 452, 464, 584*
Karloff, *171*
Karystios, Marios, *266*
Keiko Akatsuka & Associates, *361*
Kempertrautmann, *347*
Kenzo Parfums, *446*
Kian Branding Agency, *332, 644*
Kimberly-Clark, *33, 377, 378*
Kolle Rebbe, *205, 325, 619*
Korea Yakult, *258*
Kosé Corporation, *454*
Kotobuki Seihan Printing, *87, 649*
Kre8ive Partners, *635*
Kuroyanagi Jun, *173, 469*

L

L3 Branding Experience, *259*
LA+B, Love for Art and Business, *94, 123*
Laguna Made, *443*
Landor Associates, *181, 530*
Latona Marketing, *304, 357*
Lavernia & Cienfuegos, *204, 406, 408, 411, 429, 486*
L&C Design, *280*
Le Chocolat des Français, *290*
Left and Right Design, *484*
Linea, *465, 466*
Lin Shaobin Design, *112*
Logic Design, *287*
Loved, *347*

M

Maison Mumm, *479*
Manual, *610*
Maru, *123*
Masahiro Minami Laboratory, *251, 519*
Mayday, *182*
Melissi, *515*
Metaphase Design Group, *59*
Millford, *263, 631*
MiresBall, *604*
Miyake, Issey, *192*
Moberly, Lewis, *117*

Moruba, *130*
Mousegraphics,
*91, 92, 102, 267, 275,
283, 285, 307, 308,
320, 355, 359, 376,
521, 522, 562*
Move Collective, *584*
MW Creative, *506*

N
Neuhaus, *526*
Newby Teas, *117*
Nianxiang Design, *550*
Nice, *447*
Nine, *37, 414*
Nongshim
Communications, *286*
Nonobject, *600*
No Picnic, *37, 168, 482*
Nosigner, *233, 403*

O
Oenoforos, *165*
Office Communication
Consultants, *513*
Ohesono Design
Works, *252*
Ohmybrand, *222, 574*
O-I, *134*
Omdesign, *492*
Oracle Creativity
Agencies, *112*
Otvetdesign, *279, 570*

P
Packlab, *296*
Partisan du Sens, *424,
489, 495, 542*
Peace Graphics, *366,
367*
Pearlfisher, *98, 119,
120, 258, 312, 352,
371, 411, 470, 517*
Pemberton &
Whitefoord, *206,
234, 331*
PepsiCo Design &
Innovation, *86, 191*
Pergamen Trnava,
171, 480
Pesign Design, *239*
Pierini Partners, *196*
Pixelis, *201*
Platform, *97*
Pola, *122, 388, 401,
445, 456*
Proad Identity, *512,
521, 583*
Product Ventures, *385*
Prompt Design, *322,
368, 397, 611*
Proud Design, *115*
Pulp, *612*
Purpose-Built, *404*

Q
QSLD Paris, *494*
Quatre Mains, *321, 648*

R
R2H (UK), *66*
Rare Fruits Council, *176*
Red Creative, *523*
Remark Studio, *223,
224*
Rengo, *292*
Reverse Innovation, *164*
Ricard, *208*
Rice Creative, *293*
Rita Rivotti – Wine
Branding & Design,
155, 481
Rong Design, *247*

S
Sadowsky Berlin, *249,
382*
Safari Sundays, *199, 584*
Saga, *70*
Sakaguchi, Anna, *547*
Sasaki, Harumi, *547*
Sayuri Studio, *447*
Schmidt/Thurner/
von Keisenberg
Büro für visuelle
Gestaltung, *157*
Sedley Place, *471*
Selfridges, *197*
Sephora, *413*
Series Nemo, *73, 152,
168, 172, 546*
Servaire & Co, *448,
449, 451, 460, 488,
503, 504, 508, 509,
543*
Shanghai Jahwa, *554*

Shenkar School of
Engineering and
Design, *552*
Shenzhen Baixinglong
Creative Packaging,
181
Shenzhen Excel Brand
Design Consultant,
478
Shenzhen Excel
Package Design, *470,
475, 476, 477*
Shenzhen Lajiao
Design, *110*
Shenzhen Oracle
Creative Design, *111*
Shenzhen Thinkland,
125
Shenzhen Yuto
Packaging
Technology, *115*
Shigeno Araki
Design & Co., *303*
Shiseido, *365, 451, 452,
457, 461, 544, 545*
Sidel, *71, 219*
Sleever International,
31, 197, 317
Smith, Paul, *193*
SMR Creative, *217*
Sony, *589*
Spazio Di Paolo, *487*
Spread, *370*
Springetts Brand
Design Consultants,
*194, 236, 335, 336,
653*

Stranger & Stranger,
  148, 172, 175, 178, 202,
  472, 636, 639
Strømme Throndsen
  Design, 268, 280, 387
Studio Cuculic, 474
Studio H, 77
Studio Kluif, 315, 569,
  582, 623
Studio Sonda, 484
Subplot Design, 105,
  632
Suntory, 87, 88, 94, 103,
  191, 220, 221, 529
Suntory Business
  Expert, 99, 534
Supperstudio, 296
Svoe Mnenie, 141, 272

T

Tangram Design, 69, 85
Tether, 86
The Chase, 605
The Creative Method,
  213, 216, 265, 294, 641
The Grain, 217
The Partners, 572
The Taboo Group, 126
This Way Up, 116
TigerPan Packaging
  Design Lab, 114, 626
Toscara, 467
Toyo Seikan, 339, 340,
  416
Tridvajedan, 514
Truly Deeply, 299
Tsukito Design, 578
Turner Duckworth,
  38, 53, 55, 82, 132,
  161, 188, 189, 311,
  313, 576, 602, 608,
  616, 620, 622
Txaber, 225

U

Uniqlo, 412
Unique, 402
UQAM (Université du
  Québec à Montréal),
  647

V

Vanille Design, 525
Vaya! Agency, 630
Victor Branding Design
  Corp., 244
Viktor & Rolf, 31
Villéger Summers
  Design, 440
Virojanglor, 488, 497,
  503, 505, 508
Voice, 106, 108, 160,
  532

W

Wallace Church & Co.,
  211
War Design, 81
Webb deVlam, 496
White Studio, 483
Williams Murray
  Hamm, 394, 624
Win Win Branding, 284
Wolff Olins, 350
Woongjin Foods, 98

Y

Yellow Dress Retail, 293
Ypsilon Tasarim, 74, 316
Y&R New Zealand, 311
Yuhan-Kimberly, 385
Yurko Gutsulyak Studio,
  194

Z

ZwyerCaviar, 510

100 Interiors Around the World

100 Contemporary Houses

100 Contemporary Wood Buildings

Contemporary Concrete Buildings

Julius Shulman

Small Architecture

Green Architecture

Interiors Now!

Tree Houses

Cabins

Bauhaus

Bookworm's delight:
never bore, always excite!

TASCHEN
Bibliotheca Universalis

Case Study Houses

Modern Architecture A–Z

Frédéric Chaubin. CCCP

Decorative Art 50s

Decorative Art 60s

Decorative Art 70s

domus 1930s

domus 1940s

domus 1950s

domus 1960s

domus 1970s

Design of the
20th Century

Industrial Design A–Z

The Grand Tour

1000 Chairs

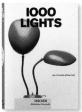

1000 Lights

Scandinavian Design

Living in Mexico

Living in Bali

Living in Morocco

Living in Japan

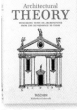

Architectural Theory

Piranesi.
Complete Etchings

The World
of Ornament

Racinet.
The Costume History

Fashion History

100 Contemporary
Fashion Designers

20th Century Fashion

Illustration Now!
Fashion

Funk & Soul Covers

Jazz Covers

Extraordinary
Records

Tiki Pop

100 Illustrators

Illustration Now!
Portraits

Logo Design.
Global Brands

Form meets function

The industrial designs that shape our lives

If you take even the slightest interest in the design of your toothbrush, the history behind your washing machine, or the evolution of the telephone, you'll take an even greater interest in this completely updated edition of *Industrial Design A–Z.* Tracing the evolution of industrial design from the Industrial Revolution to the present day, the book bursts with synergies of form and function that transform our daily experience. From cameras to kitchenware, Lego to Lamborghini, we meet the individual designers, the global businesses, and above all the genius products, that become integrated into even the smallest details of our lives.

"This invaluable bible will tell you all about the origin of the objects around you."

— *Elle Décoration*, Paris

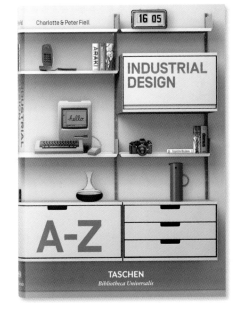

Industrial Design A-Z
Charlotte & Peter Fiell
616 pages
EDITIONS IN: ENGLISH / DEUTSCH / FRANÇAIS / ESPAÑOL / ITALIANO

2194

2195

2196

2198

2199

2200

2202

2203

2204

2206

2207

2208

Sure signs

Diverse logos from around the world

A good logo can glamorize just about anything. Now available in our popular *Bibliotheca Universalis* series, this sweeping compendium gathers diverse brand markers from around the world to explore the irrepressible power of graphic representation. Organized into chapters by theme, the catalog explores how text, image, and ideas distil into a logo across events, fashion, media, music, and retailers. Featuring work from both star names and lesser-known mavericks, this is an excellent reference for students and professionals in design and marketing, as well as for anyone interested in the visuals and philosophy behind brand identity.

"An excellent visual reference..."

— *Curve Magazine*, Sydney

Logo Design
Julius Wiedemann
664 pages
TRILINGUAL EDITION IN:
ENGLISH / DEUTSCH / FRANÇAIS

IMPRINT

© 2022 TASCHEN GmbH
Hohenzollernring 53, D–50672 Köln
www.taschen.com

English Translation
Isabel Varea Riley for Grapevine Publishing
Services, London
German Translation
Jürgen Dubau, Freiburg
French Translation
Aurélie Daniel and Valérie Lavoyer
for Delivering iBooks & Design, Barcelona

Printed in Bosnia-Herzegovina
ISBN 978-3-8365-5552-4